RADICAL FOOD GEOGRAPHIES

Food and Society

Series Editors: **Michael K. Goodman**, University of Reading and **David Goodman**, University of California, Santa Cruz

---

The Food and Society: New Directions series takes an interdisciplinary and integrative approach to food studies. Authors undertake critical assessments of key topics, controversies and thematic trends across all aspects of food systems and their diverse geographies in order to map out research agendas that bring cutting-edge perspectives to the study of food.

Find out more about the new and forthcoming titles in the series:

bristoluniversitypress.co.uk/
food-and-society

RADICAL FOOD GEOGRAPHIES

Power, Knowledge, and Resistance

Edited by
Colleen Hammelman, Charles Z. Levkoe,
and Kristin Reynolds

With a foreword by
M. Jahi Chappell

First published in Great Britain in 2024 by

Bristol University Press
University of Bristol
1–9 Old Park Hill
Bristol
BS2 8BB
UK
t: +44 (0)117 374 6645
e: bup-info@bristol.ac.uk

Details of international sales and distribution partners are available at bristoluniversitypress.co.uk

© Hammelman, Levkoe, Reynolds, 2024

British Library Cataloguing in Publication Data
A catalogue record for this book is available from the British Library

ISBN 978-1-5292-3341-4 hardcover
ISBN 978-1-5292-3343-8 ePub
ISBN 978-1-5292-3344-5 ePdf

The right of Colleen Hammelman, Charles Z. Levkoe, and Kristin Reynolds to be identified as editors of this work has been asserted by them in accordance with the Copyright, Designs and Patents Act 1988.

All rights reserved: no part of this publication may be reproduced, stored in a retrieval system, or transmitted in any form or by any means, electronic, mechanical, photocopying, recording, or otherwise without the prior permission of Bristol University Press.

Every reasonable effort has been made to obtain permission to reproduce copyrighted material. If, however, anyone knows of an oversight, please contact the publisher.

The statements and opinions contained within this publication are solely those of the editors and contributors and not of the University of Bristol or Bristol University Press. The University of Bristol and Bristol University Press disclaim responsibility for any injury to persons or property resulting from any material published in this publication.

Bristol University Press works to counter discrimination on grounds of gender, race, disability, age and sexuality.

Cover design: blu inc
Front cover image: 'Harvest Horizons' by Rosalía Torres-Weiner

We dedicate this book to those who have and continue to take physical and intellectual risks in the work towards more just and sustainable food systems throughout time and space.

Artist Statement

Charlotte, NC-based artist Rosalía Torres-Weiner is well known for her series of portraits of 'Dreamers', colourful murals, vibrant paintings, and social work. Coming from a place of privilege in art and culture, growing up in the Latin American capital of murals, Mexico City, and then moving to Los Angeles, also the alternative capital of street art in the US, Torres-Weiner found her calling. In the Americas, art has always been political; exemplified by the work of those socially committed Mexican artists post-1910 revolution (muralists and graphic artists in particular). Their work profoundly impacted the art of the US during the mid-20th century and beyond. That is the origin that guides Torres-Weiner and her own journey through the US (from the West coast to Charlotte, NC). Her cosmopolitan condition and exposure to multiple aesthetics has helped her to sink her Mexican heritage and tune her talent to use art as a tool to highlight the struggles of migrants and the necessity of art education for all.

That is how, for a decade, Torres-Weiner has increasingly focused on the stories of undocumented youth, the so-called 'Dreamers', creating portraits of many of them – 'She has developed arts programs specifically to help young people process the trauma that develops from extended periods of anxiety—and for many, the loss of one or both parents because of deportation. Torres-Weiner now calls herself an "ARTivist"' (Mint, 2022) – a contemporary synthesis of the long tradition of Latin American and Caribbean artists that now encompasses her role as an artist, muralist, and social activist.

> I created 'Harvest Horizons' to represent the stories, people and knowledge captured in *Radical Food Geographies*. It was important to me to show the diverse nature of the narratives collected, and to feature a richness of cultures, perspectives, and most importantly food. I was inspired by the work of so many people who are documented in these pages, but I especially connected with the women who were nurturers and caregivers. My art focuses on social justice and giving voice to those who are often unheard, and it is my hope that 'Harvest Horizons' lifts those voices.

Contents

List of Figures and Tables	ix
Notes on Contributors	xi
Acknowledgements	xviii
Foreword by M. Jahi Chappell	xix

Introduction   1
Kristin Reynolds, Charles Z. Levkoe, and Colleen Hammelman

1   Growing a Radical Food Geographies Praxis   17
Charles Z. Levkoe, Colleen Hammelman, and Kristin Reynolds

PART I Scale

2   Fostering Racial Justice via Values–Based Food Procurement   37
in the Good Food Buffalo Coalition
Jessica L. Gilbert-Overland

3   With Pots and Pens to Parliament: Understanding and   53
Responding to Crises through a Critical Feminist Lens
in Cape Town, South Africa
Sanelisiwe Nyaba, Caroline Peters, Jane Battersby, and Nicole Paganini

4   Radical Food Intersections: Pandemic Shocks, Gentrification   71
Mutation, Essential Labour, and the Evolution of Struggle
Joshua Sbicca and Alison Hope Alkon

5   Racialized Migrant Labour in Organic Agriculture in   86
Canada: Blind Spots and Barriers to Justice
Susanna Klassen

PART II   Spatial Imaginaries

6   Radical and Intersectional Food Systems in the Context of   105
Multiple Crises: The Case of *Ollas Comunes* in Chile
Francisco García González, Cristina Bonilla Araya,
Paula Neumann Novack, and Fernando Toro

7	Radical Legal Geographies of the Food Desert Spatial Imaginary *Erica Zurawski and Alanna K. Higgins*	120
8	Consuming Chinatown: Gentrifying through Taste and Design *Lynn Huynh*	136
9	Developing Black Urban Agrarianism *Brittany D. Jones*	154

PART III Human and More-than-Human Relations

10	Beyond 'Good Intentions': Fostering Meaningful Indigenous–Settler Relationships to Support Indigenous Food Sovereignty *Rosie Kerr, Charles Z. Levkoe, Larry McDermott, Jessica McLaughlin, Julie Price, Glenn Checkley, Alex Boulet, Erika Bockstael, Sarah Craig, and Amanda Froese*	171
11	Reshaping Collective Dreams for a Just Food Future through Research and Activism in Western Avadh, India *Sudha Nagavarapu, Surbala Vaish, Om Prakash, Kamal Kishore, Richa Singh, Richa Kumar, and Sangtin Kisan Mazdoor Sangathan (SKMS)*	187
12	Food-Making in the Sisterhoods of Bourj Albarajenah Refugee Camp: Towards Radical Food Geographies of Displacement *Yafa El Masri*	206
13	The Possibilities of Geopoetics for Growing Radical Food Geographies and Rooting Responsibilities on Indigenous Lands *Christine Añonuevo, Sarah de Leeuw, Katya Korol-O'Dwyer, and Monika Krzywania*	223
14	Radical Food Geographies Un/Settlings: The Weaponization of Food and its Discontents in Occupied Palestine and the Ch'orti' Maya East *Danya Nadar and Jennifer J. Casolo*	244
15	Epilogue *Colleen Hammelman, Kristin Reynolds, and Charles Z. Levkoe*	261

Index	266

List of Figures and Tables

A pdf containing all the colour images in their original form can be viewed at: https://bristoluniversitypress.co.uk/radical-food-geographies

Figures

0.1	Cover artwork designed by Rosalía Torres-Weiner	7
1.1	The three interconnected elements of a radical food geographies praxis	18
3.1	The personal is political: by unpacking the political reason for women's personal challenges, the community kitchens empowered women to become activists who championed women's causes (such as the 16 Days campaign) across Cape Town	55
3.2	The community kitchen of the Callas Foundation operates in a private home	56
3.3	Community kitchen volunteers came together in a three-day workshop to present their stories, celebrate successes, and envision the future of their kitchens as communal spaces	60
3.4	Analysis of the photovoice exercise through fishbowl discussions	60
8.1–8.2	A mainstay of Diho Square since the complex's construction, Welcome Food Center is an Asian grocery store that has undergone Diho Square's remodels	141
8.3	Bellaire Food Street	142
11.1	Map of India with the study region	188
11.2	Study region with nearby cities	189
11.3	A mixed crop field with barnyard and foxtail millet, pulses, and oilseeds	192
11.4	Focus Group Discussion	194
11.5	Poster comparing local fruits with expensive 'city' fruits	200
11.6	Saathis at the processing unit	201
12.1	Women preparing food together in Bourj Albarajneh Palestinian refugee camp during the Art on the Wall and Culture for All festival	207

| 12.2 | A photo I took of my mother's sisters, walking in Bourj Albarajenah alleyways, 2021 | 214 |

Tables

5.1	Total number of approved TFW positions in primary agriculture in comparison to number on organic certified farms, by province	92
8.1	All existing restaurants in Diho Square as of October 2020 (collected by author)	144
8.2	All existing restaurants in Bellaire Food Street as of October 2020 (collected by author)	145

Notes on Contributors

Alison Hope Alkon is Associate Teaching Professor of Community Studies and Sociology at University of California Santa Cruz. She thinks, writes and teaches about how processes of racial capitalism shape unequal environments, exposures, and opportunities with regard to food. She is currently co-editing *Nurturing Food Justice*, a forthcoming volume of food justice scholar-activism in the US.

Christine Añonuevo is the daughter of Filipino migrants deracinated from their ancestral islands and archipelagos. She is a PhD candidate in Human and Health Sciences at the University of Northern British Columbia. She lives with her Gitxsan-Wet'suwet'en partner and family, where they tend to bees, flowers, and vegetables.

Cristina Bonilla Araya is a geographer from Pontifical Catholic University of Valparaíso and holds a Masters in Environmental and Territorial Politics from the University of Buenos Aires, Argentina. She is an advisor to the Ministry of Housing and Urban Planning, Valparaíso and a member and founder of the Association of Feminist Geographers of Chile.

Jane Battersby is an urban geographer based at the University of Cape Town. Her work focuses on urban food security, food systems, and their governance in the African context. She works extensively with policy processes, from local to global, and works to increase agency at the community level.

Erika Bockstael is a social science researcher at Integral Ecology Group and the former Director of Indigenous Partnerships & Programs with Canadian Feed the Children.

Alex Boulet is a settler of Dutch and French ancestry who has worked in food justice all his life as a grower/harvester/researcher/grant writer. At the time of writing Alex worked as the co-lead of *Gaagige Zaagibigaa*.

Jennifer J. Casolo (PhD Geography, University of California at Berkeley) is a life-time activist and popular educator in Central America, a late blooming anti-colonial researcher and founding member of the Pluriversidad Maya Ch'orti' in Guatemala, researcher at the Institute of Development Policy at the University of Antwerp, and associate researcher at the Institute for Research and Development, Nitlapan University Centroamericana – Nicaragua (until the 2023 cancellation of the legal status of the latter by the Nicaraguan state).

M. Jahi Chappell is the Director of the Center for Regional Food Systems, Professor, and W.K. Kellogg Foundation Endowed Chair in Food, Society, and Sustainability in the Department of Community Sustainability at Michigan State University. He is the author of *Beginning to End Hunger* (2018) and co-author of *Agroecology Now! Transformations Towards More Just and Sustainable Food Systems.*

Glenn Checkley is from Biinjitiwaabik Zaaging Anishinaabek (Rocky Bay First Nation) and at the time of writing was the Director of Indigenous Partnerships & Programs with Canadian Feed the Children.

Sarah Craig is a member of the Algonquins of Pikwàkanagàn and at the time of writing was a project coordinator at Plenty Canada.

Sarah de Leeuw is a geographer, creative writer, and a Canada Research Chair (Humanities and Health Inequities) whose research, activism, and creative practices focus on anticolonial and feminist praxis. Sarah works in the Northern Medical Program with the University of British Columbia's Faculty of Medicine.

Yafa El Masri is both a refugee and a researcher. She is a Postdoctoral Research Associate in Human Geography at the University of Durham, UK. She is also the co-leader of Decolonizing Development Research Group at the DecolDev COST Action.

Amanda Froese is a team member at Northern Manitoba Food, Culture, and Community Collaborative.

Francisco García González is a PhD student in Development Planning at University College London. He holds an MSc in Environment and Sustainable Development from University College London and a bachelor's degree in Business from the University of Chile. His research interests are focused on socio-environmental justice, food sovereignty, urban resilience, and participatory action-research approaches.

NOTES ON CONTRIBUTORS

Jessica L. Gilbert-Overland is Assistant Professor in the Department of Geography and Sustainability Studies at SUNY Geneseo and is, at the time of writing, interim Campaign Director of the Good Food Buffalo Coalition. Her research is community-driven and is situated at the nexus of food systems and racial justice. To ensure that her work is guided by the priorities of those most impacted by food injustice, she participates in many of the initiatives and coalitions that are the focus of her scholarship, such as the Good Food Buffalo Coalition.

Colleen Hammelman is Associate Professor in the Department of Geography & Earth Sciences at the University of North Carolina at Charlotte. She is also the Director of the Charlotte Action Research Project (CHARP). Her community-engaged research and teaching focus on social justice concerns, particularly among migrant communities, in urban food systems across the Americas. She is author of *Growing Greener Cities: A Political Ecology Analysis of Urban Agriculture in the Americas.*

Alanna K. Higgins is Assistant Professor in Rural and Environmental Geography in the School of Geography at the University of Nottingham. Her work draws on her training as an interdisciplinary environmental social scientist, examining questions of food sovereignty and justice, legal geographies, and political ecologies.

Lynn Huynh is a writer, designer, and hospitality professional exploring food, race, and design in the city, particularly paying attention to the ways these landscapes shape Asian American identity/community. Based in Brooklyn, NY, and raised in Texas, her scholarship, creative practice, and aspirations are grounded in the idea that we must (and can) radically reimagine and rebuild a world made for us. She is an alum of Wing On Wo and Co's Bridging Futures programme, and is currently working on Chinatown Photo Album: a community-driven archival project preserving Manhattan Chinatown's cultural heritage in the face of gentrification.

Brittany D. Jones is a self-proclaimed 'scholactivist' who uses her research to inform food system development and policy in post-industrial cities. The daughter of Black community advocates, she looks to inspire activism for human rights through food. She obtained her PhD in Spatially Integrated Social Sciences at the University of Toledo from the Geography and Planning Department.

Roseann (Rosie) Kerr is a settler of mixed Scottish and Irish ancestry and a post-doctoral fellow in the Sustainable Food System's Lab at Lakehead University, with a doctorate in Education from Queen's University.

xiii

Kamal Kishore is a farmer-labourer, active with Sangtin Kisan Mazdoor Sangathan (SKMS), a farmer-labourer collective in central Uttar Pradesh, India since 2007. Along with organizing campaigns for constitutional entitlements and local concerns, he is a member of its farming and food team. In this role, he discusses food and nutrition, and promotes millet-based mixed cropping and healthy foods in the region.

Susanna Klassen is a postdoctoral researcher in the Department of Sociology at the University of Victoria on the traditional territory of the Ləkʷəŋən and WSÁNEĆ nations. Her scholarship examines the intersections of labour, food, and climate justice in agricultural systems. She is a settler of German Mennonite heritage.

Katya Korol-O'Dwyer recently completed her MSc in Interdisciplinary Studies at the University of Northern British Columbia, where her research examined health-related experiences of food sovereignty and Indigenous food sovereignty in northern BC. Katya's interests in food systems and health stem from her time working on organic farms in New Zealand.

Monika Krzywania is a PhD Candidate in Health Sciences at the University of Northern British Columbia. Born to Polish immigrants, she lives with her partner and two voracious children in North Bay, Ontario (Robinson Huron Treaty territory), where they grow fruits and vegetables in their small urban front yard.

Richa Kumar is Associate Professor of Sociology and STS at the Indian Institute of Technology, Delhi. She works at the intersection of agriculture, food, health, and the environment. She is a co-founder of the Network of Rural and Agrarian Studies, a group of scholars and activists working on agrarian issues in India.

Charles Z. Levkoe is the Canada Research Chair in Equitable and Sustainable Food Systems, a Member of the College of New Scholars, Artists, and Scientists of the Royal Society of Canada, and Professor in the Department of Health Sciences at Lakehead University. His community-engaged research uses a food systems lens to better understand the importance of, and connections between, social justice, ecological regeneration, regional economies, and active democratic engagement.

Larry McDermott is Algonquin from Shabot Obaadjiwan First Nation, and is the Executive Director of Plenty Canada. Larry was a humble student for many years of the late Algonquin Elder, Grandfather William Commanda.

NOTES ON CONTRIBUTORS

Jessica McLaughlin is a member of the Long Lake 58 First Nation and grew up in Nakina, Ontario. She is a founding member of the Indigenous Food Circle. At the time of writing, she was the co-lead of *Gaagige Zaagibigaa*.

Danya Nadar is a PhD candidate at the Institute of Development Policy (IOB) at the University of Antwerp, focusing on the racialized disruptions of Indigenous food systems. She has been politically involved during Egypt's revolution and working in solidarity in the quest for the liberation of Palestine.

Sudha Nagavarapu works with grassroots organizations in India to design and implement interventions in health care, livelihoods, food, and agriculture. She has co-conceptualized and coordinated community-driven, collaborative research on health systems, food cultures, and agrarian histories. She volunteers with various campaigns to counter hate and strengthen constitutional values.

Paula Neumann Novack is a geographer with a Masters in Geography from the Federal University of Pelotas, Brazil. She obtained a PhD in Geography from the Pontifical Catholic University of Chile with a period of study at the University of Leeds, UK. Currently, she conducts post-doctoral research at the São Paulo State University in Presidente Prudente, Brazil and is a Member of the Association of Feminist Geographers of Chile.

Sanelisiwe Nyaba is an artist, co-researcher, and food activist. She is Head of Communications at Food Agency Cape Town, a co-research-led organization doing research. She is pursuing her Masters at the University of Cape Town where she is exploring the intersection of food and motherhood using qualitative art methodology.

Nicole Paganini is Programme Lead at TMG Research, overseeing the Urban Food Future programme. With a background in social geography and a commitment to intersectional perspectives, she uses critical feminist methodology and art in her research. Her interests revolve around exploring food issues in cities from a social justice perspective.

Caroline Peters is an African feminist, human rights defender, and a recognized and award-winning activist against gender-based violence. She is Executive Director and founder of Callas Foundation, Coordinator of the Cape Flats Women's Movement, Human Rights Defenders Programme coordinator of Women's Legal Centre, and Provincial Coordinator for South African Women in Dialogue.

Om Prakash is a farmer-labourer and street theatre performer, and has been active in SKMS since 2007. An effective communicator and raconteur, he plays an important role in organizing and capacity-building, in Sangtin's cultural team and as a youth mentor. He has represented SKMS in state-level and national campaigns.

Julie Price is of mixed European ancestry and lives in Winnipeg with her family. She is a team member at Northern Manitoba Food, Culture, and Community Collaborative.

Kristin Reynolds is Associate Professor and Chair of Food Studies and Director of the Food and Social Justice Action Research Lab at The New School in New York City. She is also Associated Researcher at the European School of Political and Economic Sciences in Lille, France, and Affiliated Faculty at Yale Center for Environmental Justice. Her scholarship and activism centre on racial and economic equity in the global food system using critical participatory/action research approaches. She is co-author of *Beyond the Kale: Urban Agriculture and Social Justice Activism in New York City.*

Sangtin Kisan Mazdoor Sangathan (SKMS) is a collective of female and male farmer-labourers in western Avadh, Uttar Pradesh, India. SKMS *Saathis* are overwhelmingly Dalit, and are economically and socially marginalized. Together, they campaign for effective implementation of constitutional rights and entitlements, against discriminatory policies, and for gender and caste justice.

Joshua Sbicca is Associate Professor of Sociology and Director of the Prison Agriculture Lab at Colorado State University. He is the author of *Food Justice Now!: Deepening the Roots of Social Struggle* and a co-editor of *A Recipe for Gentrification: Food, Power, and Resistance in the City.*

Richa Singh is a founder-member of Sangtin, a grassroots organization in central Uttar Pradesh, India, as well as Sangtin Kisan Mazdoor Sangathan (SKMS). As a district coordinator for Mahila Samakhya, a women's organization, she organized pioneering campaigns on gender issues. Subsequently, she has worked on constitutional rights, livelihoods, youth empowerment and more, and is on the state and national committees of several rights-based networks.

Fernando Toro is a PhD student in Development Planning at University College London (UCL). He holds an MSc in Urban Development Planning from UCL. His research interests include financialization of the habitat, urban neoliberalism, urban poverty, and social movements. He has co-founded platforms to fight for the right to housing and the city.

Surbala Vaish is a founder-member of Sangtin and Sangtin Kisan Mazdoor Sangathan (SKMS). She spearheads Sangtin's interventions on issues such as livelihoods, constitutional entitlements, and health care, and is instrumental in the capacity-building of SKMS activists.

Erica Zurawski is a PhD candidate in Sociology at the University of California Santa Cruz, and a JD from the University of Wisconsin. Her research weaves together critical food studies, legal and human geographies, and urban studies to interrogate the varied mobilizations of the food desert concept.

Acknowledgements

This book was made possible by the many scholars and activists that have contributed to discussions about radical food geographies (RFG) praxis through workshops and sessions sponsored by the Geographies of Food and Agriculture Specialty Group (GFASG) at the American Association of Geographers' (AAG) annual meetings, the Food Justice Scholar-Activist/Activist-Scholar community of practice (FJSAAS), the Royal Geographical Society's Food Working Group, and the Canadian Association for Food Studies. This includes a 2019 pre-conference on RFG that preceded the AAG Annual Meetings in Washington, DC, that was co-organized by the co-editors with Xavier Brown, Rafter Ferguson, Garrett Graddy-Lovelace, Yuki Kato, Joshua Sbicca, Beverly Wheeler, and Annelise Ivy Straw. This book was also foregrounded in 2020 by a special journal issue on RFG that Colleen Hammelman, Charles Levkoe, and Kristin Reynolds guest-edited in *Human Geography*, and the insightful and inspiring articles in that issue. We are grateful for the continued engagement with these collaborators in thinking through world-making possibilities through RFG praxis. Further, we thank the Bristol University Press' (BUP) *Food and Society* Series editors Michael K. Goodman and David Goodman and external reviewers for their insightful and helpful feedback on early versions of this manuscript, along with Emily Watt and Anna Richardson at BUP for their work shepherding this book project from proposal to publication.

Charles would like to thank his family (especially Airin Stephens) for supporting his work on this project. Colleen expresses her deepest gratitude to her family (especially Bill Hammelman) for always being supportive of this work. Kristin thanks her family for consistently supporting her work within and beyond the academy.

Foreword

M. Jahi Chappell

The book you have before you represents a vibrant step forward towards more just, sustainable, diverse, and joyful food systems – in other words, further progress in the development of radical food geographies (RFG).

This exciting collection may elicit a sense of irony as it explores the theory and practice ... of action. One might be reminded of comedian-artist Martin Mull's comment, 'Writing about music is like dancing about architecture'. But just as his evocatively silly quip cheekily overlooks the richness of writing about music over the centuries, the book before you contains important and enriching multitudes about action for justice. Hammelman, Levkoe, and Reynolds have brought together a variety of voices, geographies, practices, and approaches to compose a hallmark effort of critical reflection. The collected pieces here do not simply move RFG forward as a field, but also advance its aims of engagement and confrontation of power and structures of oppression; action through academic, social movement, and civil society collaborations; and analyses making use of a broadly defined geographic lens. Further, as much as many contributions to this book are, in fact, writing about action, the authors and editors are no mere observers. The practitioners and scholar-activists/ activist-scholars behind these pieces are in most cases committed participants and co-conspirators for deep, radical, inclusive, and equitable change. In short: rest assured that they are not merely 'dancing about architecture' but are rather walking the walk. Though, with their appreciation of the necessity of joy and creativity in research and change, they also may at times be literally dancing the dance alongside the labourers, farmers, activists, and community leaders who create RFG through their expertise and lived realities of action.

It's also worth noting that this effort calls to mind similar advancements occurring elsewhere in geography, particularly the project of critical physical geography (CPG) (see, for example, Lave et al, 2018). CPG's core intellectual tenets include transdisciplinarity ('substantive interweaving of physical and social science'), reflexivity, and power and justice (Robertson et al in Lave et al, 2018: 232). Like RFG, CPG is 'concerned with what the world ought to be' (Lane et al in Lave et al, 2018: 25) and embraces reflection, self-critique, and the proactive inclusion of multiple ways of knowing. And, alongside these efforts by scholar-activists and activist-scholars in geography, many working within the 'meta-field' of political ecology have also voiced similar commitments, noting, in the words of Paul Robbins, that ecological systems are power-laden rather than politically inert, and that systems of power, influence, and inequality are 'tractable to challenge and reform. They can be fixed' (Robbins, 2019: 10).

In other words, the concepts and commitments of RFG appear to be in a growing zeitgeist. This itself represents an important step forward. While from a certain point of view, it may raise the question of 'if others have said similar things, why say them again?' But when we examine change processes, it is important to recognize that growing and unifying collective voices, coming to common realizations – amplifying a growing zeitgeist – *is* the point. While novelty is often an academic value, growing sympathy and synchrony are pragmatic requirements for growing change. For the radical to become the real; for critique and reflection to become embodied as the common-sense reasons we 'no longer do it that old way' – reiterating and growing recognition is part of power-building, community-building, dissemination, conversation, updating, and modification such that the radical is realized to be, in reality, the reasonable. And given the current state of things, from social inequality, continued hegemonies of White heteropatriarchy, climate change, settler colonialism, biodiversity loss, violent conflict, and structural violence – what some have described as 'polycrisis' – it is definitively unreasonable to *not* be radical.

Brazilian sociologist Ana Maria Doimo once observed that scholars will always lag behind social movements, because social movements create the new realities that scholars study (Doimo, 1995). As a scholar-activist who participated heavily in Brazil's social movements contesting dictatorship, inequality, and poverty, Doimo also walked the walk as a co-conspirator and co-creator of change. The editors and authors of this book are the inheritors of many long legacies such as that of Doimo and the 20th-century Brazilian scholar-activist Josué de Castro. They have poised this text as an invitation for even greater radical praxis in the pursuit of justice. It is certainly an invitation that I hope you will accept.

References

Doimo, A.M. (1995) *A Vez e a Voz do Popular: Movimentos sociais e participação política no Brasil pós-70*, Rio de Janeiro: Relume-Dumará/Associação Nacional de Pós-Graduação em Ciências Socias.

Lave, R., Biermann, C., and Lane, S.N. (2018) *The Palgrave Handbook of Critical Physical Geography*, Cham: Palgrave Macmillan.

Robbins, P. (2019) *Political Ecology: A Critical Introduction* (3rd edn), Oxford: Wiley-Blackwell.

Introduction

Kristin Reynolds, Charles Z. Levkoe, and Colleen Hammelman[1]

> The plague of universal hunger ... is a characteristic result of [a] debt: man's [*sic*] deficit in his enterprise of colonizing the world.
>
> Josué de Castro, 1952

Josué de Castro was a Brazilian geographer, physician, diplomat, and activist, whose writing on hunger, geography, and politics were forerunners to the concept of geopolitics and critical development studies. His book *Geografía da Fome* (1946) identified hunger as a consequence of social, rather than natural, structures. His most influential book *Geopolitica da Fome* (1951) set forth an understanding of hunger as a global political-economic phenomenon. Key themes in these works were a strident and explicit anti-Malthusianism. de Castro pinned the origins of hunger, neither to the deficits of 'poor' people worldwide nor to the quantitative limits of global food production, but to the expansion of the global capitalist economy. Prior to the establishment of critical development studies (for example, see Escobar, 2011), de Castro argued that 'underdevelopment' and hunger as a corporeal reality – rather than a disembodied one – was a result of colonialism, racism, and Western-dominated geopolitics (de Castro, 1952).

While these perspectives are fairly common today in most critical scholarship and activism, de Castro's righteous naming of geopolitical, colonial, and racist structures in the 1940s and 1950s as the underlying causes of hunger was a rare and courageous analytical pursuit, particularly writing from the context of the majority world.[2] Importantly, de Castro was not only a theoretician, despite the scholarly nature of his research and writing. Ferretti (2021) notes that de Castro's analysis was rooted in knowledge born of both scholarly pursuits and his upbringing in Recife, the focus area of his *Geografía da Fome* (1946) and 1970 novel *Of Men and Crabs*. Recife is a region in north-eastern Brazil where predominantly Indigenous and African-Brazilian people lived at that time, and often in economic poverty.

de Castro was of mixed Indigenous and European descent and was clear in his analyses that racism was among the driving factors of social inequity (Monbeig, 1948; Chappell, 2018; Ferretti, 2021).

de Castro influenced and was influenced by French scholars, and was involved in international policy, eventually serving as the head of the United Nations' (UN) Food and Agriculture Organization from 1952 to 1956 and as Brazil's Ambassador to the UN from 1963 to 1964 (New York Times, 1973; Ferretti, 2022). However, he was forced to leave Brazil in exile following the US-supported military coup in 1964 and spent the remainder of his life in France. There, he founded the Centre International pour le Développement (CID) and continued his research, teaching (at Université Paris VIII, then in the Vincennes section of central Paris, a historically leftist branch of the University of Paris system aligned with radical geographies scholarship of the time) and advocacy until his death in 1973 (Ferretti, 2021, 2022).

Despite his intellectual innovations and diplomatic charges, de Castro, his work, and its contributions to geography, geopolitics, and contemporary thinking about food insecurity remain under-recognized, particularly in the anglophone minority world (Ibarra García and Talledos Sánchez, 2020; cf Ferretti, 2021). The lack of recognition of de Castro's influence is not an isolated case, however. It is emblematic of the erasure of the knowledge of food systems and inequity born from the lived experiences of global majority peoples, communities, and regions of the world. In recent years, there has been a resurgence of interest in, and attention to, de Castro's work through written work, multimedia fora, and interdisciplinary seminars (see Da Fome à Fome: Diálogos com; Chappell, 2018; Ferretti, 2021, 2022). These and similar efforts to revive the important intellectual and activist work of scholar-activists who have experienced erasure are long-overdue steps towards a more complete understanding of the intersections between many forms of knowledge and experience, theory, place, and action for social justice.

While de Castro is indeed an under-recognized example inspiring our thinking about radical food geographies (RFG), we note similar inspiration from female scholars such as Chilean geographer Graciela Uribe Ortega who, in the 1960s, wrote her doctoral thesis on the spatialized and unequal economic effects of industrial development, and was known for her insistence that geography be politically useful (Vargas, 2018; Smith and Desbiens, 2000). At the moment of the 1973 US-supported military coup in Chile, Uribe Ortega, along with many leftist intellectuals, was taken prisoner by the military. With the aid of diplomatic intervention, she then exiled to Scandinavia for several years, eventually returning west to join the faculty at the Universidad Nacional Autónoma de México (Vargas, 2018; Smith and Desbiens, 2000). Uribe Ortega's is yet another story demonstrating the intertwining of radical geographic scholarship and politics in Latin America.

We find great inspiration in de Castro and Uribe Ortega's legacies as an entry point to this book, *Radical Food Geographies: Power, Knowledge, and Resistance*. We conceive of RFG praxis as having three interconnected elements: (1) theoretical engagement with power and structures of oppression both inside and outside the academy; (2) action through academic, social movement, and civil society collaborations; and (3) analysis through a broadly defined geographic lens (see Levkoe et al, Chapter 1 for a more detailed description of RFG; see also Hammelman et al, 2020). Principles of RFG are represented in many aspects of de Castro's work and life through his courageous theorizing, research, activism, and commitment to communication about the interrelated nature of hunger, geography, and systemic injustices. His efforts to understand and transform the power structures giving rise to hunger; his drive to eliminate hunger as a researcher, diplomat, and member of civil society, even in exile; and his geographic analyses elucidated the broader meaning of geography beyond academic work to encompass variegated spatial understandings of food systems, which is central to RFG praxis. Sharing de Castro's and Uribe Ortega's stories also serves to push back against the privileging of elite, anglophone, and minority world knowledges that contributes to the subordination of social, political, and scholarly spaces that embrace different ways of knowing and the people and communities that hold them. Resisting such privileging is something we have also attempted to do in this book.

We came to this book with the intention to explore the possibilities of RFG as a world-making project. World-making refers to the collective creation of the spaces we inhabit by making meaning through stories, ideas, traditions, and struggles. Beyond identifying and critically analysing the forces and activities that have caused so much social and environmental devastation, we present RFG as an opportunity to (re)imagine, (re)shape, and (re)structure the world as we know it. Based on the power and privilege we embody as White, settler scholars employed by post-secondary institutions in the minority world, we recognize the limits of our own knowledge and experiences. We are committed to feminist, anti-racist, and anti-colonial approaches in our scholarship and through our practice. Thus, we approach this RFG project as a relational journey to better understand how to think and work within spaces of collaborative co-creation and resistance. RFG is an always imperfect and evolving concept. Together with the contributors to this book, we offer RFG as an opportunity for theorizing, action, and analysis. We build on the foundations laid by de Castro, Uribe Ortega and the many other scholars and activists engaged in world-making efforts, particularly as it plays out in food systems in diverse spaces, regions, and timescales.

We also argue throughout this book that the ongoing crises of the current moment – the sacrificing of front-line food workers to achieve capitalist imperatives, the violence perpetrated against marginalized peoples and lands in the name of settler colonial objectives, the use of food as a weapon to control populations, implicit and explicit racism, and the climate crisis that continues to wipe away lives, livelihoods, and our more-than-human relations amid widespread political inaction – and their roots in systemic oppressions, demand action. We recognize that acting on this political imperative takes emotional and physical work and presents substantial risks for some. Pursuing solidarities necessarily involves crossing borders – across identities, knowledges, and environments – and contemplating what shared visions of social and environmental justice look and feel like. It also entails risk, sacrifice, and embracing vulnerability. It is these demands that drive us towards an RFG praxis.

Building an RFG praxis

In this book, we aim to critically reflect and expand on both the theory and practice of RFG. The seeds of RFG were first planted in 2018 when we were involved in co-organizing a collaborative workshop in Washington, DC, in advance of the 2019 annual meeting of the American Association of Geographers (AAG). The workshop, 'Radical Food Geographies: Connecting Knowledges, Cultivating Practices, (re)Imagining Governance', aimed to engage with questions about how geographers, social movements, and civil society organizations could work collaboratively and effectively to advance food justice and food sovereignty. Over 100 participants from academic and community-driven spaces participated in the workshop which included dynamic discussions that ultimately provided a basis for RFG. In 2020, we curated a special issue on the theme of RFG in the academic journal *Human Geography* to continue engaging with these evolving ideas. We also furthered these discussions through themed sessions at several academic conferences between 2020 and 2023. While these efforts were a valuable step towards reflecting on and developing RFG, we were cognizant of their limitations. For example, we recognized that the articles in *Human Geography* focused primarily on anglophone, minority world initiatives and literatures (though to an extent also francophone, hispanophone, and translated lusophone scholarly literature), and that our efforts did not go far enough in refuting Eurocentric[3] and anglophone epistemological dominance.

As a concept and practice, RFG brings attention to power, knowledge, and resistance to inequities in them, and draws key elements from radical geographies[4] and critical food systems[5] scholarship towards making food systems more just and sustainable. Critical to the RFG approach is a praxis that pushes food systems scholars and activists to pursue work that is simultaneously grounded in theorizing, action, and reflection related to the intersections of place and spatiality (see Levkoe et al, Chapter 1 for a more detailed overview of the scholarly foundations of RFG).

INTRODUCTION

We developed this book with the aim of continuing to critically analyse and explore the theory and practice of RFG, and to engage a broader diversity of scholars in terms of epistemology, geopolitical location of their work, and positionality. We seek to build upon and decentre Eurocentric and anglophone epistemologies about food systems and geography through the inclusion of knowledge, theorizing, and experiences of scholars and geographies that are too often under-represented in dominant food systems and geography scholarship. To this end, in inviting chapters for the book, we distributed the call for proposals beyond exclusively academic venues in an attempt to reach scholars beyond traditional channels of recruitment and outside dominant positionalities among scholars within North America. We provided multiple opportunities for contributors to collaboratively engage with each other, including interactive discussions, workshops, conference sessions, and a collaborative peer review process. We also worked to support some authors (at their request) to workshop chapters over a year-long process in preparing the book. Further, while some readers may expect a conventional and neatly standardized book format, we note that certain non-conformities appear throughout the volume and that this is a political decision on the part of the book's editors. The inclusion of differing language registers, poetry, words beyond English, terminologies, and writing styles, alongside more dominant forms of academic writing and manuscript organization, enhance the diversity present in the book and contribute to our efforts to decentre Eurocentric and anglophone communication and epistemologies.

Scholars across the globe have pointed out that the vulnerability and risks that arise from political actions and solidarity should not be overlooked, but should also not prevent the work from proceeding. Instead, the fractures that arise in world-making projects should be approached as generative for forming relationships and creating more just and sustainable worlds. In reflecting on what this book presents as 'radical', we strove to include authors and perspectives that work across such fractures. This includes both writers grounded primarily in activist spaces, academics pursuing more 'radical paths', and those who are situated between those identities. We also want to underscore that while academic writing can, at times, be considered antithetical to radicalism (see Levkoe et al, Chapter 1), for some, writing itself can be a radical (and sometimes dangerous) act. While some tenured professors enjoy a degree of academic freedom and job security that enables them to express their perspectives with relative impunity, this safety is not a universal scholarly privilege. Many scholars – including adjunct and non-tenure track faculty, scholars with marginalized identities (including racialized people, women, and gender non-conforming individuals, as recent high-profile cases in US academia exemplify),[6,7] and those working in geopolitical locations where critical expression can face harsh punishment – are scarcely granted such liberty. These diverse positionalities are present in this book and

5

are representative of the various ways we think about what is 'radical'. The book thus provides a curated collection that enriches and expands the RFG concept through diverse understandings of the geographies of food systems grounded in Latin America, on the African continent, in the Middle East, and in Asia, in addition to North America and Western Europe.

RFG explicitly emphasizes the nexus of theory and action towards building more just and sustainable food systems at diverse spatial and temporal scales. As such, this book reaches beyond a singular food system focus to engage with contemporary issues, all drawing on an RFG perspective. These include spatial and action-oriented dimensions of Black agrarianism, Indigenous knowledges, gendered dimensions of food systems, implications of the COVID-19 pandemic, community kitchens in politically contentious settings, gentrification, borderlands and immigration, and scholar-activism. The authors are diverse, geographically – representing both the majority and minority worlds – and in terms of positionality, including individuals at various stages in their academic careers, community-based activists with varied levels of experience, and diverse racial, ethnic, and gender identities.

In curating the book we also sought artwork for the cover that connected not only with the themes of RFG, but also with the ethos of the project. To that end, we invited Rosalia Torres-Weiner,[8] an artist and social activist based in Charlotte, NC, to design the cover art (see Figure 0.1). Rosalia draws on her Mexican heritage to highlight migrant struggles, including, most recently, those of undocumented youth in the US. She is well known for her mural arts and for her activism that brings to light unheard stories and her efforts to make art education available to young people in marginalized communities (see Rosalia's note inside the front cover for more information).

Looking to de Castro and the many additional radical geographies and critical food systems thinkers across the globe whose influence is felt but often ignored, we reiterate the importance of working beyond the borders of what may be most accessible or easier, to engage in a more collective change-oriented praxis. The chapters in this volume, along with the contemporary and historical radical geographies, critical food systems- and action-oriented scholarship on which they rely for their analysis, contribute to filling in gaps we have identified.

An overview of RFG: power, knowledge, and resistance

The core elements of RFG are integrated into each of the chapters and each deal with key geographic concepts. In Levkoe et al (Chapter 1), 'Growing a Radical Food Geographies Praxis', we discuss the historical and contemporary

Figure 0.1: Cover artwork designed by Rosalía Torres-Weiner.

tributaries to RFG and situate it as growing out of intersections between radical geographies and critical food systems scholarship, thought, and action, and grounded in feminist, anti-racist, and anti-colonial approaches. The rest of the book's chapters are organized into parts on Scale, Spatial Imaginaries, and Human and More-than-Human Relationships. Below, we provide an outline of the book through these parts as well as key themes that run across the parts. While the chapters are organized into parts for ease of navigating through the book, many of their arguments, ideas, and contributions to RFG praxis are interwoven. Chapters share examples of how power, knowledge, and resistance to inequities in them are changing food systems around the world in diverse ways. They also engage with actions seeking to shape these systems towards justice and sustainability.

Scale

Castree et al (2013) define scale in terms of measurement, analysis, and hierarchy. At this most basic definition, scale can refer to concrete measurements (of distance, temperature, resolution, and so on) and the level of analysis. Radical, critical, and feminist geographers have expanded this definition to interrogate the social production of scale in the service of capitalism (Delaney and Leitner, 1997; Brenner, 1998). For these scholars, scale is a historical product that is both socially and politically contested and has impact beyond a timeless, asocial container. Feminist scholars, in particular, have called for attending to the individual and bodily scale (Marston, 2000), while scholars in other fields (such as political ecology) have noted the interdependence of global and local scales. Food systems scholars have also pointed out the need for a multiscalar analysis of interconnected food systems that is rooted within radical geographies, emphasizing social and communal life, place-based interventions, and approaches to food scholarship that attend to intertwined social-historical structures producing injustices (Sonnino et al, 2016). Highlighting the linkages between movements, places, and people can make visible the structural production of injustices and enable partnerships to bolster resistance against such forces.

Bringing together radical geographies and critical food systems scholarship to consider scale highlights power relationships that produce and regulate the flows and fixities of people (migration, whether voluntary or forced), resources (environmental and capital), and ideas and culture (foodways) across varying distances, places, and time. RFG rejects the hierarchical nature of scalar analysis, instead arguing for the interrelationship of actors and actions across scales. We understand food systems as embedded in powerful (political, economic, patriarchal, colonial) systems that produce hunger, dispossession, and environmental degradation across multiple, interrelated scales. This approach identifies the ways food systems are produced and resisted across different scales (for example, international trade agreements and different governance structures) but experienced in local places (for example, the effects of such agreements and decision-making on farming and fishing communities). Importantly, writers in this book also engage with how knowledge is produced in different ways across different scales.

The interrelatedness of different scales is made clear by Gilbert-Overland's (Chapter 2) analysis of linkages between the local scale of the Good Food Buffalo Coalition in New York State, US, with broader processes of systemic oppression and discrimination, and Nyaba et al's (Chapter 3) identification of the embodied impacts of organizing community kitchens in a post-apartheid South Africa plagued by COVID-19 and patriarchal systems. Nyaba et al also share personal experiences from leading community kitchens during the pandemic to emphasize the embodied nature of such care work.

Other chapters demonstrate how local struggles are grounded in systemic processes. For example, Alkon and Sbicca (Chapter 4) examine how the financialization of real estate threatens housing and food systems, and erodes the ability of families and individuals to meet their basic needs in the US. They call attention to the interconnections between the financialization of housing real estate and food injustices that were highlighted during the pandemic and suggest that such crises make visible how ongoing systems of oppression mutate. Klassen (Chapter 5) similarly demonstrates how racial capitalism both undergirds exploitation of migrant workers in Canada's organic agriculture industry and prevents social movements from fully addressing this structural foundation of injustice. In doing so, she brings to light the labour injustices that continue to persist in organic farming operations in Canada. Finally, all chapters in this part (and throughout the book) call for cultivating solidarities at local and regional scales to resist the injustices perpetrated in many places in the global food system.

Spatial imaginaries

RFG calls attention to the role of place and place-based networks in not only constructing food systems and relationships with food, but also in resisting injustices in those systems (Smith, 2019; Gilbert and Williams, 2020; Reese, 2020). It utilizes ideas of spatial imaginaries to consider the production of space and place as well as different meanings and discursive constructions of such concepts. Spatial imaginaries (and similar terminology that some scholars have used either interchangeably in providing more specificity to the terms, such as sociospatial imaginaries, geographic imaginaries, or imaginary geographies; or in re-imagining geographies of dispossession) are understood as social representations of places and spaces (Said, 2003; McKittrick, 2011; Watkins, 2015). Some geographers focus on the discourses that produce such imaginaries (Radcliffe, 1996; Cornwell and Atia, 2012; Millington, 2013) while others are concerned with their performative and embodied natures that transcend language (Pilkey, 2013; Talburt and Matus, 2014; Ramírez, 2015). Spatial imaginaries transmit ideas, anxieties, and divisions. They are used by stakeholders to advocate for future actions or to differentiate places. Watkins (2015) argues that spatial imaginaries can be broken into three categories – places, idealized spaces, and spatial transformations – that produce particular places as unique yet enmeshed in social relations (across scales).

In this volume, García et al (Chapter 6) identify the limitations of policy approaches that discount the expertise of community kitchen leaders in Chile when the kitchens are imagined by policy makers as domestic and female spaces. Further, Zurawski and Higgins' (Chapter 7) examination of the legal geographies of the US food desert spatial imaginary demonstrates how collective ideas about spaces and places can have material effects. Huynh (Chapter 8) describes the changing spatial imaginaries of Houston, US's Chinatown/Asiatown as the neighbourhood is embraced by new Asian chain restaurants that privilege consumers seeking Instagram-ready experiences. She further demonstrates the embodied nature of knowledge production as she traces the changing aesthetics of Chinatown/Asiatown through her memories of traversing those streets with her grandfather. The remaking of spatial imaginaries through contesting dominant narratives is also illustrated by Jones' (Chapter 9) examination of the ways in which Black Urban Agrarianism practices are reimagining urban lots as spaces of autonomy and food sovereignty in Ohio, US.

Human and more-than-human relations

Finally, RFG examines space and place in qualitative ways that engage with (differential) relationships between people and their surroundings (an essential contribution of Black-, Latinx-, and Indigenous geographies). Such engagements with human and more-than-human relations centre socio-ecological relationships, equity, and scholar-activism/activist-scholarship as the foundation for knowledge formation and sharing (Reynolds et al, 2018; Reynolds et al, 2020). RFG makes use of the interconnectivity between places, movements, and people, and relationality between land and people. A geographical lens can also make visible the human–environment relationships that produce and are produced through food systems. In theorizing about the Anthropocene (or Capitalocene), assemblages, and more-than-human geographies, animals, plants, waterways, and natural resources are understood as active co-producers of knowledge and action (Dowling et al, 2017; Askins, 2018; Elton, 2019). And, in taking Eurocentrism to task, theorizing about ways in which the Anthropocene concept may perpetuate colonialist praxis, scholars emphasize that many Indigenous peoples throughout the world have always and continue to exist within a world view that is relational (Whyte, 2017; Simpson, 2020). In line with theorizing in radical geographies and food systems scholarship, relational approaches attend not only to structural processes but also to the formation of power relations (Holt-Giménez, 2017). This approach considers, for example, how relationships among people have produced inequality but can also be transformed to create more equitable food systems; and insists that action is grounded in relationships forged over time through recognition of shared and divergent expertise and objectives embedded in existing power structures. Importantly, recognizing these relationships calls for attending to how knowledge creation is bound up in uneven power dynamics. Contributors throughout this book, thus, seek to highlight the material impacts of power–knowledge relations and the importance of engaging with diverse ways of knowing (cf. Foucault, 1990). Several chapters in this volume highlight the importance of relationships in RFG and the ways in which food systems also provide powerful opportunities for reconnecting people with each other, the land, more-than-human relations, and diverse sources of knowledge production. Kerr et al (Chapter 10) reflect on ways that Indigenous–settler partnerships established through ethical space can challenge assumptions and lift up diverse ways of knowing in order to advance Indigenous food sovereignty in Canada. In doing so, they invite scholars into ethical space as they reflect on their experiences in Indigenous–settler partnerships that challenged assumptions and existing ways of knowing. Nagavarapu et al (Chapter 11) also share their co-production of research among grassroots activists, researcher-activists, and scholars associated with Sangtin Kisan Mazdoor Sangathan in Uttar Pradesh, India. They argue that such co-production is critical for understanding the food system transitions that are embedded in systemic injustices and pursuing change through mutually enriching relationships. These chapters make clear that approaching inequity, and resistance to it, enables understanding both of these as actions that are produced through social relations within multidimensional economic, political, and cultural processes.

Many of the chapters in this part centre the role of land in human and more-than-human relationships. These contributors examine how relationships with the land are made and remade by systems of settler colonialism and dispossession, and active resistance to those systems. In this theorizing, many rely on teachings from Indigenous scholars who disrupt binaries separating peoples and land, public and private spaces, humans and environment (Kamal et al, 2015; Whyte, 2016; Robidoux and Mason, 2017; Askins, 2018; Daigle, 2019). Centring land (and the very concept thereof) calls forth opportunities to resist oppressive forces through maintaining ancestral seeds and foodways, returning land to Indigenous groups, and passing down land-based knowledge through generations. For example, El Masri (Chapter 12) uses auto-ethnography to show how sisterhoods forged in food provisioning reconnect Palestinian refugees in Lebanon to the histories and relationships with lands from which they have been dispossessed. Añonuevo et al (Chapter 13), as they contend with power and knowledge, and the roles of settler-scholars working within Indigenous spaces, make clear that Indigenous food sovereignty movements are embedded in broader struggles for Indigenous territories in Canada. Further, Nadar and Casolo (Chapter 14) focus on land–food relations in and between people in occupied Palestine and Ch'orti' Maya East. They provide first-hand reflections of working alongside dispossessed peoples in Palestine and the Guatemala/ Honduras highlands, to argue that racialized processes of colonization and capitalism are served through the weaponization of food across borders and generations. For authors in this part (and others in the book, such as

Jones, Chapter 9), land dispossession is embedded in colonial and racist political economic systems, and those systems must be undone, in part, through returning land to peoples and peoples to land. They argue that food geographies constructed through the weaponization of food have advanced settler colonial projects on, about, or because of land.

Conclusion

We see this book as part of a broader project to grow RFG. It is a project that is necessarily incomplete and always imperfect. This is not the beginning, nor is it the end. This book is not intended to be comprehensive, but rather a continuing conversation. Inspired by action-oriented thinkers such as de Castro and Uribe Ortega, we hope to encourage dialogue about ways to productively advance theorizing and action on spatial injustices in food systems. As such, while we have certainly left out important interventions in this work, we do not seek to foreclose RFG based on the analyses and perspectives presented here. Instead, this book serves as an invitation to a shared project for even greater radical praxis in pursuit of justice and sustainability in food systems across spaces and places, as the following chapters demonstrate.

Notes

[1] Equal authorship.

[2] We use the terms 'majority world' and 'minority world' in place of problematic terms such as 'developing', 'Third World', and 'low-income' countries. This choice aims to subvert dominant economic-centric and White supremacist ideas of hierarchy in respect to how the world is and should be. The term 'minority world' refers, in part, to the small population of countries in North America and Europe, while gesturing to the uneven distribution of resources and wealth between and within nations, globally. Such intentional language choices that we have made throughout the chapter reflect our approach to radical food geographies praxis more broadly. However, given the contentious and shifting nature of terminology we did not require chapter authors to conform to particular language choices like this.

[3] Eurocentric is often understood in dominant discourse as a stand-in for Whiteness. In using this term, we also recognize that equating 'European' with 'White' is erroneous and problematic because it obscures the ethnic and racial diversity always and still present in Europe, as shown by Boni-Claverie (2015) and Hawthorne (2022), for example. A full discussion of these connections between discourse, politics, and social equity are beyond the scope of this book. Still, we include this note here, following Hawthorne (2022: xviii), in an effort to 'mark what is typically left unmarked' in terms of normalizing 'European' as White by eliding Eurocentrism with that geopolitical region's dominant culture.

[4] In this chapter, we use 'radical geography' in the singular to refer to the specific subfield in the academic discipline of geography. We utilize 'radical geographies' in the plural to encompass both that subfield and the plurality of knowledges, epistemologies, and actions that engage geographic and spatial thinking towards social and political change.

[5] We conceive of food systems broadly to include elements from agriculture, fishing, harvesting, processing, and distribution through to consumption, foodways, and waste,

along with the socio-ecological processes and actors that influence those systems (Tansey and Worsley, 1995). We refer to food systems in the plural as a recognition of the many ways in which individuals and groups engage with the diverse and embodied relationships that bring food to their plates.

[6] See, for example, events at Harvard and the University of North Carolina, as discussed in Gassam Assari (2024).

[7] We also recognize the many ways in which the protections provided by tenure are being eroded worldwide (Killian, 2023; Tampa Bay Times, 2023).

[8] More information about Rosalia's work is available at https://redcalacastudio.com/.

References

Askins, K. (2018) 'Feminist geographies and participatory action research: co-producing narratives with people and place', *Gender, Place & Culture*, 25(9): 1277–94.

Boni-Claverie, I. (2015) *Trop Noire pour être Française*, ARTE, Strasbourg, France.

Brenner, N. (1998) 'Between fixity and motion: accumulation, territorial organization and the historical geography of spatial scales', *Environment and Planning D: Society and Space*, 16: 459–81.

Castree, N., Kitchin, R., and Rogers, A. (2013) *A Dictionary of Human Geography*, Oxford: Oxford University Press.

Chappell, M.J. (2018) *Beginning to End Hunger: Food and the Environment in Belo Horizonte, Brazil, and Beyond*, Berkely: University of California Press.

Cornwell, G. and Atia, M. (2012) 'Imaginative geographies of Amazigh activism in Morocco', *Social and Cultural Geography*, 13(3): 255–74.

Da Fome à Fome: Diálogos com Josué de Castro (n.d.), Available from: http://geografiadafome.fsp.usp.br/ [Accessed 15 April 2023].

Daigle, M. (2019) 'Tracing the terrain of Indigenous food sovereignties', *Journal of Peasant Studies*, 46(2): 297–315. DOI: https://doi.org/10.1080/03066150.2017.1324423

de Castro, J. (1946) *Geografia da Fome. A Fome no Brasil*, Rio de Janeiro: O Cruzeiro.

de Castro, J. (1951) *Geopolitica da Fome*, Rio de Janeiro: Editora Casa do estudante do Brasil.

de Castro, J. (1952) *The Geography of Hunger* (7th edn), Boston, MA: Little, Brown.

de Castro (1970) *Of Men and Crabs*, New York: Vanguard Press.

Delaney, D. and Leitner, H. (1997) 'The political construction of scale', *Political Geography*, 16: 93–7.

Dowling, R., Lloyd, K., and Suchet-Pearson, S. (2017) 'Qualitative methods II: "More-than-human" methodologies and/in praxis', *Progress in Human Geography*, 41(6): 823–31.

Elton, S. (2019) 'Posthumanism invited to dinner: exploring the potential of a more-than-human perspective in food studies', *Gastronomica*, 19(2): 6–15.

Escobar, A. (2011) *Encountering Development: The Making and Unmaking of the Third World* (Vol. 1), Princeton: Princeton University Press.

Ferretti, F. (2021) 'A coffin for Malthusianism: Josué de Castro's subaltern geopolitics', *Geopolitics*, 26(2): 589–614.

Ferretti, F. (2022) 'Decentring the lettered city: exile, transnational networks, and Josué de Castro's Centre International pour le Développement (1964–1973)', *Antipode*, 54(2): 397–417.

Foucault, M. (1990) *The History of Sexuality: An Introduction*, New York: Vintage.

Gassam Assari, J. (2024) 'Claudine Gay Resigns From Harvard: Why Black Excellence Is Never Enough', *Forbes*, [online] 2 January, Available from: www-forbes-com.cdn.ampproject.org/c/s/www.forbes.com/sites/janicegassam/2024/01/02/claudine-gay-resigns-from-harvard-why-black-excellence-is-never-enough/amp/

Gilbert, J.L. and William, R.A. (2020) 'Pathways to reparations: land and healing through food justice', *Human Geography*, 13(3).

Hawthorne, C. (2022) *Contesting Race and Citizenship: Youth Politics in the Black Mediterranean*, Ithaca: Cornell University Press, p 324.

Holt-Giménez E. (2017) *A Foodie's Guide to Capitalism*, New York: New York University Press.

Ibarra García, M.V. and Talledos Sánchez, E. (2020) 'Pioneers of Latin American critical geography: Josué de Castro and Antonio Núñez Jiménez', in Schelhaas, B., Ferretti, F., Novaes, A.R., and di Friedberg, M.S. (eds) *Decolonising and Internationalising Geography: Essays in the History of Contested Science*, New York: Springer, pp 17–26.

Kamal, A.G., Linklater, R., Thompson, S., and Dipple, J. (2015) 'A recipe for change: reclamation of Indigenous food sovereignty in *O-Pipon-Na-Piwin* Cree Nation for decolonization, resource sharing, and cultural restoration', *Globalizations*, 12(4): 559–75. DOI: https://doi.org/10.1080/14747731.2015.1039761

Killian, J. (2023) 'Their academic freedom in jeopardy, university faculty in NC, other southern states want out', *NC Newsline*, [online] 13 September, Available from: https://ncnewsline.com/2023/09/13/their-academic-free dom-in-jeopardy-university-faculty-in-nc-other-southern-states-want-out/ [Accessed 20 December 2023].

Marston, S.A. (2000) 'The social construction of scale', *Progress in Human Geography*, 24(2): 219–42.

McKittrick, K. (2011) 'On plantations, prisons, and a Black sense of place', *Social & Cultural Geography*, 12(8): 947–63. DOI: 10.1080/14649365. 2011.624280

Millington, N. (2013) 'Post-industrial imaginaries: nature, representation and ruin in Detroit, Michigan', *International Journal of Urban and Regional Research*, 37(1): 279–96.

Monbeig, P. (1948) 'Au Brésil: la "géographie de la faim" de Josué de Castro', *Annales Histoire Sciences Sociales*, 3(4): 495–500. DOI: 10.3406/ahess.1948.2365

New York Times (1973) 'Dr. Josue de Castro, 65, Dead; Diplomat Aided Third World', *New York Times*, [online] 25 September, Available from: www.nytimes.com/1973/09/25/archives/dr-josue-de-castro-65-dead-diplomat-aided-third-world-social-origin.html [Accessed 25 April 2023].

Pilkey, B. (2013) 'LGBT homemaking in London, UK: the embodiment of mobile homemaking imaginaries', *Geographical Research*, 51(2): 159–65.

Radcliffe, S. (1996) 'Imaginative geographies, postcolonialism, and national identities: contemporary discourses of the nation in Ecuador', *Ecumene*, 3(1): 23–42.

Ramírez, M.M. (2015) 'The elusive inclusive: Black food geographies and racialized food spaces', *Antipode*, 47(3): 748–69. DOI: 10.1111/anti.12131

Reese, A. (2020) '"DC is mambo sauce": Black cultural production in a gentrifying city', *Human Geography*, 13(3): 253–62.

Reynolds, K., Block, D., and Bradley, K. (2018) 'Food justice scholar-activism and activist-scholarship: working beyond dichotomies to deepen social justice praxis', *ACME: An International E-Journal for Critical Geographies*, 17(4): 988–98.

Reynolds, K., Block, D.R., Hammelman, C., Jones, B.D., Gilbert, J.L., and Herrera, H. (2020) 'Envisioning radical food geographies: shared learning and praxis through the food justice scholar-activist/activist-scholar community of practice', *Human Geography*, 13(3): 277–92.

Robidoux, M.A. and Mason, C.W. (eds) (2017) *A Land Not Forgotten: Indigenous Food Security and Land-Based Practices in Northern Ontario*, Winnipeg: University of Manitoba Press.

Said, E. (2003) *Orientalism* (revised edn), London: Penguin Classics.

Simpson, M. (2020) 'The Anthropocene as colonial discourse', *Environment and Planning D: Society and Space*, 38(1): 53–71.

Smith, B.J. (2019) 'Food justice, intersectional agriculture, and the triple food movement', *Agriculture and Human Values*, 36(4): 825–35.

Smith, N. and Desbiens, C. (2000). 'An interview with Graciela Uribe Ortega', *Environment and Planning D: Society and Space*, 18(5): 545–56.

Sonnino, R., Marsden, T., and Moragues-Faus, A. (2016) 'Relationalities and convergences in food security narratives: towards a place-based approach', *Transactions of the Institute of British Geographers*, 41(4): 477–89.

Talburt, S. and Matus, C. (2014) 'Confusing the grid: spatiotemporalities, queer imaginaries, and movement', *Gender, Place, & Culture: A Journal of Feminist Geography*, 21(6): 785–801.

Tampa Bay Times (2023) 'Post-tenure review regulation for Florida university professors approved', *Tampa Bay Times*, [online] 29 March, Available from: www.tampabay.com/news/education/2023/03/29/tenure-florida-university-professor-desantis-board-of-governors/

Tansey, G. and Worsley, A. (1995) *The Food System*, New York: Earthscan.

Vargas, H.M. (2018) 'Graciela Uribe Ortega y la transición de la geografía Mexicana', *Terra Brasilis*, 10.

Watkins, J. (2015) 'Spatial imaginaries research in geography: synergies, tensions and new directions', *Geography Compass*, 9(9): 508–22.

Whyte, K. (2016) 'Indigenous food sovereignty, renewal and US settler colonialism', in Rawlinson, M. and Ward, C. (eds) *The Routledge Handbook of Food Ethics*, New York: Routledge, pp 353–65.

Whyte, K. (2017) 'Indigenous climate change studies: indigenizing futures, decolonizing the Anthropocene', *English Language Notes*, 55(1): 153–62.

1

Growing a Radical Food Geographies Praxis

Charles Z. Levkoe, Colleen Hammelman, and Kristin Reynolds[1]

As a concept and practice, radical food geographies (RFG) praxis brings together attention to power, knowledge, and resistance to the inequities that shape food systems around the world in diverse ways.[2] RFG draws key elements from radical geographies[3] and critical food systems[4] scholarship towards making food systems more just and sustainable. Critical to the RFG approach is a praxis that pushes food systems scholars and activists to pursue work that is simultaneously grounded in theorizing, action, and reflection related to the intersections of place and spatiality. Praxis refers to the dynamic interconnections between theory and practice, critical reflection, and the resulting actions (for example, see Freire, 1970; Gramsci, 1971; hooks, 1994). We conceive of RFG praxis as having three interconnected elements: (1) theoretical engagement with power and structures of oppression both inside and outside the academy; (2) action through academic, social movement, and civil society collaborations; and (3) analysis through a broadly defined geographic lens (see Figure 1.1). In this chapter, we provide an overview of the scholarly[5] foundations of RFG praxis.

Radical geographies foundations

Radical geographies have integrated and built upon different geographical contexts, theories, and activities worldwide. They identify, explain, and impact relations of power, oppression, and capitalist exploitation in particular places and across space. In North America, what has been formally referred to as radical geography (a subdiscipline in the academic field of geography) traces its roots to a rejection of the US status quo in the 1960s (contemporaneous with the US Civil Rights Movement, the Black Power

Figure 1.1: The three interconnected elements of a radical food geographies praxis.

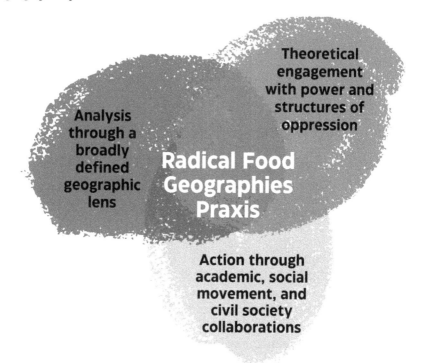

Source: Claire Stevens.

Movement, the Chicano Movement, the American Indian Movement, second-wave feminism, and opposition to the Vietnam War). The group of self-described 'radical geographers', grounded in Marxist and anarchist thinking, sought a restructuring of society. They were also challenging their discipline, one that was rooted in positivist and quantitative approaches that they insisted were unresponsive to societal crises and reproduced oppressive structures (Fuller and Kitchin, 2004).

The overarching position of these primarily anglophone and minority world-based individuals was that the field of geography needed to account for its complicity and contributions to the accumulation of power and capital. They emphasized the political and social construction of space and engaged with the empirical conditions of uneven development to produce philosophical considerations of justice and well-being (Brenner, 2009; Olson and Sayer, 2009; Smith, 2010). Importantly, radical geography scholarship of this era intervened in classical geographic thought to encourage sensitivity to differences and similarities that reinforced subordination and to make visible the struggles of marginalized groups. The emergence of radical geography scholarship in North America and Western Europe was also marked by the founding of *Antipode* in 1969, a scholarly journal established by students and faculty at Clark University in the US. The articles that comprised the journal's early editions connected to social justice and social movements, and argued for a deeper relationship between action for change and academic analysis (Peet, 2000).

However, despite disciplinary shifts that broadened its lens beyond quantitative sciences, Peake and Sheppard (2014) argue that the field of geography more broadly remained racially segregated and steeped in Eurocentrism, systemic racism, and patriarchy, and as a result, the dominant discipline of academic geography normalized Whiteness, colonialism, and Manifest Destiny (for example, see Mahtani, 2014; Heynen et al, 2018; Kobayashi, 2019). Feminist geographers continue to make visible the patriarchy within geography, and the challenges to pursuing geographic scholarship from marginalized social positions (Joshi et al, 2015; Mansfield et al, 2019). These patterns are evident in the many histories of radical geography that ignore the seminal role of women, Indigenous peoples, people of colour, and scholarship from the majority world in understanding spatial difference, often from either explicitly or implicitly counterhegemonic or subaltern perspectives. Further, debates have grappled with the elision of 'radical' and 'critical' geography as fields of scholarship, and observations that radical geography had lost its edge, with Castree (2000: 961) commenting, 'yesterday's untenured "radicals" are today's "critical" professors, fully integrated into the day-to-day structure of the tertiary sector'.

Beyond those more formally recognized as part of early radical geography traditions in North America and Western Europe, many others have engaged in spatial thinking and action towards social and political change, and more recent interventions have expanded the understanding of radical geography as a subfield (Antipode Editorial Collective et al, 2019). In our own readings, we have learned that in the midst of mid-20th century industrialization, geographers in several Latin American countries used spatial and quantitative analysis to uncover and understand uneven sociogeographic impacts of industrial development (see Introduction). Throughout the 1950s and onwards, radical and critical geographers in Latin America made important interventions, intertwined with political action. In the Introduction, we discussed Brazilian scholar and diplomat Josué de Castro and Chilean geographer Graciela Uribe Ortega, whose work and activism were critical to understandings of geography and food systems today. de Castro's life-long work against hunger and writings on hunger, geography, race, and politics were forerunners to the concept of geopolitics and critical development studies, even while living in exile. We also discussed both his under-recognition in the field of geography, and recent resurgence in interest in his work. de Castro's story exemplifies geography scholarship in this tradition (predating contemporary anglophone postcolonial scholarship) and calls attention to the colonizing forces of scholarship and global political economy (Herrera, 2019). Uribe Ortega's research on the spatial and unequal dynamics of industrial development alongside calls for making geography relevant demonstrated the ways in which radical geography and politics were intertwined in Latin America (Vargas, 2018; Smith and Desbiens, 2000). Feminist geographers in Latin America today continue to call attention to the injustices perpetrated in patriarchal society and differential power relationships in the production and reproduction of space (Vela-Almedia et al, 2020). While varying by country, female geographers' and feminist work in radical geographies in Latin America, too, have often been spearheaded by social movements and then, more timidly, taken up in academic spaces (Lan, 2016).

In Metropolitan (continental) France, subfields of critical and radical geography (also referred to in France as 'géographie sociale' or 'social geography') have roots in 1968 social and political upheavals, and in this way are similar to leftist political thinking and movements in (anglophone) North American and in Latin American traditions. And, the pattern of privileging White European scholarship and thinking in geography also extends to the francophone world including Metropolitan France but also the French Overseas Departments and Territories (in French referred to as DOM/TOM, and which are former French colonies on the African continent, and in Caribbean and South American regions), majority world nations in Sub-Saharan Africa (many of which were colonized in the 19th and 20th centuries by European nations), as well as other minority world countries (for example, Canada, Switzerland, and Belgium). Examples of radical geographies thinking in such contexts include arguments for a 'geography of marginality in Black Africa' (Courade, 1985), which would question how dominant systems use space to exclude certain groups and how these groups respond and take advantage of their territories to move beyond marginality.

Today, Black, Latinx, Indigenous, critical race, feminist, queer, and decolonial scholarship further expands radical geographies' understandings and analysis of diverse modes of oppression. This includes again calls for a greater recognition of, and accountability to, the discipline's colonial baggage and the need to be attentive to Indigenous perspectives that are using approaches that meaningfully promote reconciliation and resurgence (Johnson et al, 2007; Castleden et al, 2012; Frantz and Howitt, 2012; Smithers and Mandawe, 2017). Critical urban geography scholars, among others, contest the continuation of colonial thinking in studying global urban processes (that is, global cities, planetary urbanism, and imaginaries of modernity) solely from the lens of cities in the minority world (Roy, 2016; Robinson, 2022). Similar to previous arguments in this chapter, these scholars instead call for rethinking concepts like the urban and its spatial forms from the perspective and scholarship of the majority world. Further, scholars explicitly address Eurocentric and White supremacist conceptualizations of geographies. For example, Black geographies scholars in the US and Canada recognize and bring forth specific mapping practices and 'taken-for-granted' geographic knowledges to understand Black geographies and ways of expression, including poetics, food-nourishment maps, and music maps as part of this intellectual tradition (McKittrick, 2006, 2011; McKittrick and Woods, 2007). Indigenous geographies scholars have focused attention on the complicated and contested project of decolonizing geography in efforts towards 'unsettling geography within settler colonial contexts' (De Leeuw and Hunt, 2018: 3). While there is no single approach to this work, Daigle and Ramírez (2019: 78) argue that through 'embodied theories and praxes [*sic*] of liberation' decolonial geographies can be understood as 'constellations in formation, as embodied in the present, to envision radical spatial visions of the future'.

Critical food systems scholarship foundations

Critical food systems scholarship has evolved in parallel to food-related social movements and reflects changes in society more broadly. The interdisciplinary study of food systems can be traced to the mid-20th century and includes studies of power, foodways, gastronomy, and culinary history. Key examples include Frances Moore Lappé's (1971) argument for the need to attend to the environmental and political implications of a meat-based diet; Sidney Mintz's (1986) political economic analysis of how tastes and food identity evolved as a result of capitalist relations; and culinary historian and cookbook author Jessica B. Harris' ongoing examinations of links between foodways originating on the African continent and evolving foodways in the US (Harris, 1995; 2011). Food historians and anthropologists have also engaged with migrant foodways by considering a range of topics from public health restrictions on Mexican street food vendors on the US–Mexico border (Gabaccia and Pilcher, 2011) to the production of national cuisines through cookbooks (Appadurai, 1988).

Like radical geographies, critical food systems *thinking* predates the beginnings of a more formalized interdisciplinary field of scholarship (see Francis et al, 2003; Nestle and McIntosh, 2010; and Williams-Forson and Wilkerson, 2011 for foundational reviews). In the US, for example, enslaved Black chefs in the 18th century such as James Hemmings (Satterfield, 2021) or early 20th-century women writers on food and cooking, such as M.K. Fisher (Avakian and Haber, 2005), provided written accounts of food preparation that bridged scale and culture, under the weight of quite different degrees of oppression. In the 19th century, Booker T. Washington and George Washington Carver were Black innovators who used their education and knowledge to uplift Black farmers of their day, though with differing views on the best way to achieve racial equality (see White, 2018).

In contemporary settings, chefs, farmers, and authors provide parallel approaches for current and future generations. Examples in the US include chef and food justice activist Bryant Terry (2014; 2022) whose influential writing and cookbooks are reshaping thought on Black culinary foodways; author and restaurateur chef Sean Sherman (2017) whose work has made important steps to revitalize and expand awareness of Indigenous food systems; farmer, seed saver, plant breeder, and anthropologist Devon Peña (2017), whose work in Colorado and New Mexico pursues food sovereignty and environmental justice through preserving the practices and seeds of historic acequia agricultural communities; and farmer and food sovereignty activist and author Leah Penniman's (2018) leadership through agriculture and education supports a new generations of Afro-Indigenous farmers. These innovators, among many others, are a part of critical food systems scholarship that broadly informs our work and this book.

Today, theoretical underpinnings of radical geographies increasingly appear in the academic critical food systems scholarship, particularly with attention to uneven development, historical and global structures of oppression, and an emphasis on contributing to more just social and ecological systems (Guthman, 2004; Chappell and LaValle, 2011). Still, dominant discourse about critical food systems scholarship has tended to centre the anglophone, Eurocentric, minority world and White settler scholars, despite the actual diversity of thought that centres the political nature of inequity in food systems throughout the world. This work has often focused on the realities of colonialism/postcolonialism and the ecological damages caused by industrial agriculture. Some important examples include: Mahatma Gandhi's critique of Western science and its infusion into agriculture in India (Pathak et al, 2020); Martinican intellectual Aimé Césaire's linking of Western 'agricultural development' to the extension of colonialism (1939/ 1983); Japanese farmer and philosopher Masanobu Fukuoka's writings on the 'natural way of farming' in the context of ever-increasing agricultural industrialization (1975); Wangaari Maathai's work through her Green Belt Movement in Kenya to engage farmers in large-scale tree planting to confront the environmental degradation caused by forces including industrial agriculture (Maathai, 2003); and physicist and activist Vandana Shiva's work on ecofeminism, arguments connecting violence and the Green Revolution, and extensions to biopiracy (for example, Shiva, 1991).

Additionally, much of the critical food systems scholarship not only *studies* phenomena pertaining to agriculture, food, and on the ground social justice work, but also attempts to act in solidarity with it (Nestle and McIntosh, 2010). Important contemporary examples of this include the global grassroots movement for food sovereignty, which coalesced in 1993 and calls for the right to food and producer/harvester control of food-systems decision-making (Nyéléni, 2007). Academic scholars have played a role in supporting and participating in this movement (Patel, 2009; Wittman et al, 2010). The contemporary food justice movement, including its links to the longer-standing environmental justice movement begun and led by Black and Indigenous activists and scholars, has also inspired much critical food systems scholarship, in the US and Europe (Levkoe, 2006; Alkon and Agyeman, 2011; Hochedez and Le Gall, 2016; Reynolds, 2020).

A full review of critical food systems scholarship is beyond the scope of this chapter. However, we seek here to note as well some of the contemporary foundations that ground RFG praxis (as well as the chapters throughout this book). Specifically, contributors engage with critiques of capitalist processes in food systems, the embodied nature of experiencing and building food systems, and the importance of intersecting identities and interdependencies. One thread of critical food systems and geographic theorizing is rooted in Marxist and post-Marxist understandings of how capitalism requires the exploitation of new commodity frontiers that result in expansion and exploitation of agrarian life, colonization, and dispossession of land and people (Wittman, 2009; Carlisle, 2014, 2016; Edelman and Wolford, 2017). This includes attention to the devastating impacts of industrial agriculture and the corporate food regime that dispossesses multitudes from self-determination, property, and the means of production (Patel, 2012; Salvador and Bittman, 2020). Political ecologists have advanced this critical food scholarship through examining the metabolic circulation of socio-ecological flows in cities, politicizing sustainable food alternatives, making visible the historically situated co-production of nature and society, and bringing forth a more inclusive ontological reframing of food systems (Heynen, 2006; Agyeman and McEntee, 2014; Moragues-Faus and Marsden, 2017).

Critical food systems scholars have also emphasized the embodied nature of socio-ecological injustices (Slocum and Saldanha, 2013). These theorizations respond to intractable conditions of hunger and poverty in a world of plenty. Sen's (1981) early examinations of famine in India laid important foundations for contemporary examinations of the politics of hunger response as charity (Poppendieck, 1999; Fisher, 2017), in schools (Poppendieck, 2011), and examining the fundamental right to adequate food (Hammelman and Hayes-Conroy, 2015; Hayes-Conroy and Sweet, 2015). Further, Harper (2009, 2011) examines racialized representations of veganism, their manifestations in human bodies, and argues for building critical consciousness, through Black feminist thought, of the connections between interlocking systems of racialized and gender oppression as a commitment to health and liberation.

Further attention has been paid to intersecting identities and interdependencies that are produced in and through food systems

(Williams-Forson and Wilkerson, 2011). This includes increasing and renewed attention in dominant spaces to issues of patriarchy, White supremacy, settler colonialism, and other forms of oppression in food systems (for example, Probyn, 2003; Avakian and Haber, 2005; Williams-Forson, 2006; Harper, 2009; Joassart-Marcelli and Marcelli, 2018; Koch, 2019). For instance, colonial (and settler colonial) relationships construct and reconstruct oppressive structures and constrain the entitlements of colonized and Indigenous communities (Settee and Shukla, 2020). Black and Latinx geographies' engagements with food systems attend to the specific intersections of food, agriculture, and struggles for racial justice. This is evident in Ramírez's (2015) reimagining of Black farming as a site of power and transformation, Reese's (2019) analysis of geographies of self-reliance produced and relied upon by Black residents in Washington, DC (see also Garth and Reese, 2020), and in Peña et al's (2017) edited volume which traces the many ways Mexican-origin communities resist colonization through transforming food systems.

Action-oriented scholarship

Radical geographies scholarship in North America/Western Europe has called for moving beyond theorizing to engage directly with corollary social movements (Clark and Dear, 1978; Chouinard, 1994). This includes pointing to the political nature of research and the importance of grounding radical theory and practice in the fundamental necessities of survival that are threatened by material inequity, and to seek emancipatory alternatives (Chouinard, 1994; Heynen, 2006; Springer, 2014; Roy, 2016). In order to achieve these goals, it has been argued that radical geographers must recognize their humanity, differing privileges, and abilities to fight for social change (Heynen, 2006; Blomley, 2007). With recognition of the diverse ways that geography scholars experience relative comfort in academic settings, the evolution of radical geographic scholarship has often fallen short in terms of engagement with contemporary movements for political and social justice beyond (as well as within) the Ivory Tower (Castree, 2000).

As noted previously, much critical food systems scholarship provides useful examples of scholars engaged with social movements. For example, critical agrarianism is institutionalized in political action, non-governmental organizations, informal networks, and academia (McMichael, 2006, 2012, 2014; Patel, 2009; Bernstein, 2014; Edelman, 2014). Food systems scholars have also worked closely, and at times intertwined, with alternative food networks (AFNs) in North America. At the same time, while AFNs have made important strides in providing alternative modes of production and consumption and bringing visibility to problems in food systems, they have been critiqued as racially and economically exclusive, perpetuating neoliberal ideologies, and ignoring intersectional systems of oppression (for example, see Slocum, 2007; Guthman, 2008; Alkon and Mares, 2012). Food justice and food sovereignty activism and scholarship fill these gaps by calling attention to the interlocking structure of racism and social inequity, and emphasizing the self-determination and resilience of communities most negatively impacted by an unjust food system (Gottlieb and Joshi, 2010; Wittman et al, 2010; Alkon and Agyeman, 2011; Garth and Reese, 2020). Importantly, much of this scholarship has emerged from activist movements in both the majority and minority worlds. For example, the food sovereignty movement evolved from the collective work of global social movements and peasant farmers seeking to instil the right of peoples and nations to reclaim power and determine their means of self-reliance in the food system (Agarwal, 2014; LRAN, 2018).

Building on the work of these activists and scholars, we suggest that action-oriented critical food systems scholarship could have more impact through a deeper engagement with theories of power, oppression, and space while radical geographies scholarship could be more impactful through direct action. For example, using analytical frames that interrogate the uneven impacts of food access brings to light the systemic disinvestments in urban communities of colour that often stifle community-driven solutions to food inequities by imposing dominant conceptions of modern living, even as such strategies are rooted in resilience, as Reese (2019) demonstrates in her Washington, DC-based work. Such examples provide models for how food systems scholarship can problematize oppressive political economic systems and sociospatial arrangements that produce those inequities, leading to potentially more profound social change. Both radical geographies and critical food systems scholarship make clear that today's material conditions and injustices are predicated on historical structures. As a world-making project, RFG praxis recognizes and reflects on those bodies of scholarship and actions in order to build more just and sustainable futures.

Conclusion

In this chapter, we have provided an overview of RFG praxis as a concept and framework for food systems work. Considering its historical and contemporary tributaries, we have situated RFG praxis within the intersections of radical geographies and critical food systems scholarship, thought, and action, and grounded in feminist, anti-racist, and anti-colonial approaches. As a world-making project, RFG praxis is not static. To the contrary, we position RFG praxis as an imperfect, evolving concept that demands collaborative and sustained engagement, dialogue, and debate. We present RFG praxis here as an invitation for others to engage with the concept through an analysis of power, knowledge, and resistance along with the real-world actions that aim to build more equitable and sustainable food systems for all.

Acknowledgements

We thank Claire Stevens, Masters student in International Affairs at The New School, NY, for their work designing the RFG praxis image in this chapter, and Constance Smith, Masters student in Environmental Policy and Sustainability Management at The New School, NY, for their work copy-editing and formatting this chapter.

Notes

[1] Equal authorship.

[2] Parts of this chapter are adapted from Hammelman et al (2020).

[3] In this chapter, we use 'radical geography' in the singular to refer to the specific subfield in the academic discipline of geography. We utilize 'radical geographies' in the plural to encompass both that subfield and the plurality of knowledges, epistemologies, and actions that engage geographic and spatial thinking toward social and political change.

[4] We conceive of food systems broadly to include elements from agriculture, fishing, harvesting, processing, and distribution through to consumption, foodways, and waste, along with the socio-ecological processes and actors that influence those systems (Tansey and Worsley, 1995). We refer to food systems in the plural as a recognition of the many ways in which individuals and groups engage with the diverse and embodied relationships that bring food to their plates.

[5] By 'scholarly' we do not mean solely academic, but rather activities such as research, intensive study or reflection, and/or diverse forms of communication about observations made from the former, and so on (for a discussion, see Reynolds and Cohen, 2016; Reynolds et al, 2018).

References

Agarwal, B. (2014) 'Food sovereignty, food security and democratic choice: critical contradictions, difficult conciliations', *Journal of Peasant Studies*, 41(6): 1247–68. DOI: 10.1080/03066150.2013.876996

Agyeman, J. and McEntee, J. (2014) 'Moving the field of food justice forward through the lens of urban political ecology', *Geography Compass*, 8(3): 211–20. DOI: 10.1111/ gec3.12122

Alkon, A.H. and Agyeman, J. (eds) (2011) *Cultivating Food Justice: Race, Class, and Sustainability*, Cambridge, MA: MIT Press.

Alkon, A.H. and Mares, T.M. (2012) 'Food sovereignty in US food movements: radical visions and neoliberal constraints', *Agriculture and Human Values*, 29(3): 347–59. DOI: 10.1007/s10460-012-9356-z

Antipode Editorial Collective, Jazeel, T., Kent, A., McKittrick, K., Theodore, N., Chari, S., Chatterton, P., Gidwani, V., Heynen, N., Larner, W., Peck, J., Pickerill, J., Werner, M., and Wright, M.W. (2019) *Keywords in Radical Geography: Antipode at 50*, Hoboken: John Wiley & Sons.

Appadurai, A. (1988) 'How to make a national cuisine: cookbooks in contemporary India', *Comparative Studies in Society and History*, 30(1): 3–24. DOI: 10.1017/ S00104175000 15024

Avakian, A.V. and Haber, B. (2005) *From Betty Crocker to Feminist Food Studies: Critical Perspectives on Women and Food*, Liverpool: Liverpool University Press.

Bernstein, H. (2014) 'Food sovereignty via the "peasant way": a sceptical view', *Journal of Peasant Studies*, 41(6): 1031–63. DOI: 10.1080/ 03066150.2013.852082

Blomley, N. (2007) 'Critical geography: anger and hope', *Progress in Human Geography*, 31(1): 53–65. DOI: 10.1177/0309132507073535

Brenner, N. (2009) 'What is critical urban theory?', *City*, 13(2–3): 198–207. DOI: 10.1080/13604810902996466

Carlisle, L. (2014) 'Critical agrarianism', *Renewable Agriculture and Food Systems*, 29(2): 135–45. DOI: 10.1017/ S1742170512000427

Carlisle, L. (2016) 'Making heritage: the case of Black Beluga agriculture on the Northern great plains', *Annals of the American Association of Geographers*, 106(1): 130–44. DOI: 10.1080/ 00045608.2015.1086629

Castleden, H., Morgan V.S., and Lamb, C. (2012) '"I spent the first year drinking tea": exploring Canadian university researchers' perspectives on community-based participatory research involving Indigenous peoples', *The Canadian Geographer/Le Géographe Canadien*, 56(2): 160–79. DOI: 10.1111/ j.1541-0064.2012.00432.x

Castree, N. (2000) 'Professionalisation, activism, and the university: whither "critical geography"?', *Environment and Planning A: Economy and Space*, 32(6): 955–70. DOI: 10.1068/a3263

Césaire, A. (1939/1983) *Cahier d'un Retour au Pays Natal*, France: Presence Africaine.

Chappell, M.J. and LaValle, L.A. (2011) 'Food security and biodiversity: can we have both? An agroecological analysis', *Agriculture and Human Values*, 28: 3–26. DOI: 10.1007/s10460-009-9251-4

Chouinard, V. (1994) 'Reinventing radical geography: is all that's left right?', *Environment and Planning D: Society and Space*, 12(1): 2–6. DOI: 10.1068/ d120002

Clark, G.L. and Dear, M. (1978) 'The future of radical geography', *The Professional Geographer*, 30(4): 356–9. DOI: 10.1111/ j.0033-0124. 1978.00356.x

Courade, G. (1985) 'Jalons pour une géographie de la marginalité en Afrique noire', *Espace Géographique*, 14(2): 139–50. DOI: 10.3406/spgeo.1985.4017

Daigle, M. and Ramírez, M.M. (2019) 'Decolonial geographies', in Antipode Editorial Collective (eds) *Keywords in Radical Geography: Antipode at 50*, Hoboken: John Wiley & Sons, pp 78–84.

De Leeuw, S. and Hunt, S. (2018) 'Unsettling decolonizing geographies', *Geography Compass*, 12(7): e12376.

Edelman, M. (2014) 'Food sovereignty: forgotten genealogies and future regulatory challenges', *Journal of Peasant Studies*, 41(6): 959–78. DOI: 10.1080/03066150.2013.876998

Edelman, M. and Wolford, W. (2017) 'Introduction: critical agrarian studies in theory and practice: symposium: agrarianism in theory and practice', *Antipode*, 49(4): 959–76.

Fisher, A. (2017) *Big Hunger: The Unholy Alliance Between Corporate America and Anti-Hunger Groups*, Cambridge: MIT Press.

Francis, C., Lieblein, G., Gliessman, S., Breland, T.A., Creamer, N., Harwood, R., Salomonsson, L., Helenius, J., Rickerl, D., Salvador, R., and Wiedenhoeft, M. (2003) 'Agroecology: the ecology of food systems', *Journal of Sustainable Agriculture*, 22(3): 99–118.

Frantz, K. and Howitt, R. (2012) 'Geography for and with Indigenous peoples: Indigenous geographies as challenge and invitation', *GeoJournal*, 77(6): 727–31. DOI: 10.1007/s10708-010-9378-2

Freire, P. (1970) *Pedagogy of the Oppressed*, translated by M. Bergman Ramos, New York: Continuum.

Fukuoka, M. (1975) *The One-Straw Revolution*, Mapusa: Other India Press.

Fuller, D. and Kitchin, R. (2004) 'Radical theory/critical praxis: academic geography beyond the academy?', in D. Fuller and R. Kitchin (eds) *Radical Theory, Critical Praxis: Making a Difference Beyond the Academy?* Vernon: ACME e-book series, pp 1–20.

Gabaccia, D.R. and Pilcher, J.M. (2011) '"Chili queens" and checkered tablecloths: public dining cultures of Italians in New York City and Mexicans in San Antonio, Texas, 1870s–1940s', *Radical History Review*, 2011(110): 109–26. DOI: 10.1215/01636545-2010-028

Garth, H. and Reese, A.M. (eds) (2020) *Black Food Matters: Racial Justice in the Wake of Food Justice*, Minnesota: University of Minnesota Press.

Gottlieb, R. and Joshi, A. (2010) *Food Justice*, Massachusetts: MIT Press.

Gramsci, A. (1971) *Selections from the Prison Notebooks*, translated by Q. Hoare and G.N. Smith, London: Lawrence and Wishart.

Guthman, J. (2004) *Agrarian Dreams: The Paradox of Organic Farming in California*, Berkeley, CA: University of California Press.

Guthman, J. (2008) 'Neoliberalism and the making of food politics in California', *Geoforum*, 39(3): 1171–83. DOI: 10.1016/j.geoforum.2006.09.002

Hammelman, C. and Hayes-Conroy, A. (2015) 'Understanding cultural acceptability for urban food policy', *Journal of Planning Literature*, 30(1): 37–48. DOI: 10.1177/0885412214555433

Hammelman, C., Reynolds, K., and Levkoe, C.Z. (2020) 'Toward a radical food geography praxis: integrating theory, action, and geographic analysis in pursuit of more equitable and sustainable food systems', *Human Geography*, 13(3): 211–27. https://doi.org/10.1177/1942778620962034

Harper, A.B. (2009) *Sistah Vegan: Black Female Vegans Speak on Food, Identity, Health, and Society*, New York: Lantern Books.

Harper, A.B. (2011) 'Vegans of color, racialized embodiment, and problematics of the "exotic"', in A.H. Alkon and J. Ageyman (eds) *Cultivating Food Justice: Race, Class, and Sustainability*, Massachusets: MIT Press, pp 221–38.

Harris, J.B. (1995) *The Welcome Table: African-American Heritage Cooking*, New York: Simon & Schuster.

Harris, J.B. (2011) *High on the Hog: A Culinary Journey from Africa to America*, New York: Bloomsbury.

Hayes-Conroy, A. and Sweet, E.L. (2015) 'Whose adequacy? (Re) imagining food security with displaced women in Medellín, Colombia', *Agriculture and Human Values*, 32(3): 373–84. DOI: 10.1007/s10460-014-9546-y

Herrera, T. (2019) 'Radicalmente universal y diferencialista. POR Una geografía crítica desde América Latina', *Espiral, Revista De Geografías Y Ciencias Sociales*, 1(1): 45–58. DOI: 10.15381/espiral.v1i1.15845

Heynen, N. (2006) 'Justice of eating in the city: the political ecology of urban hunger', in N. Heynen, M. Kaika and E. Swyngedouw (eds) *The Nature of Cities : Urban Political Ecology and the Politics of Urban Metabolism*, New York: Routledge, pp 144–57.

Heynen, N., Aiello, D., Keegan, C., et al (2018) 'The enduring struggle for social justice and the city', *Annals of the American Association of Geographers*, 108(2): 301–16. DOI: 10.1080/24694452.2017.1419414

Hochedez, C. and Le Gall, J. (2016) 'Food justice and agriculture: Introduction', *Spatial Justice*, 9.

hooks, b. (1994) *Teaching to Transgress: Education as the Practice of Freedom*, London: Routledge.

Joassart-Marcelli, P. and Marcelli, E. (2018) 'Cooking at home: gender, class, race, and social reproduction', in P. Joassart-Marcelli (ed) *Food and Place: A Critical Exploration*, New York: Rowman & Littlefield.

Johnson, J.T., Cant, G., Howitt, R., et al (2007) 'Creating anticolonial geographies: embracing indigenous peoples? Knowledges and rights', *Geographical Research*, 45(2): 117–20. DOI: 10.1111/j.1745-5871.2007. 00441.x

Joshi, S., McCutcheon, P., and Sweet, E.L. (2015) 'Visceral geographies of Whiteness and invisible microaggressions', *ACME: An International E-Journal for Critical Geographies*, 14(1): 292–323.

Kobayashi, A. (2019) 'Issues of "race" and early radical geography: our invisible proponents', in *Spatial Histories of Radical Geography: North America and Beyond*, pp 37–58.

Koch, S.L. (2019) *Gender and Food: A Critical Look at the Food System*, New York: Rowman & Littlefield.

Lan, D. (2016) 'Los estudios de género en la geografía Argentina', in M.V. Ibarra García and I. Escamilla-H errera (eds) *Geografías Feministas De Diversas Latitudes: Orígenes, Desarrollo Y Temáticas Contemporáneas*, Mexico: UNAM, Instituto de Geografía, pp 55–70.

Lappé, F.M. (1971) *Diet for a Small Planet*, New York: Ballantine Books.

Levkoe, C.Z. (2006) 'Learning democracy through food justice movements', *Agriculture and Human Values*, 23(1): 89–98.

LRAN (2018) 'New challenges and strategies in the defense of land and territory' (LRAN Briefing Paper Series No. 4). Land research action network, focus on the Global South, Rede social de Justiça E Direitos Humanos, and La via Campesina, Available from: https://viacampesina.org/en/popular-agrarian-reform-the-new-call-for-agrarian-reform-in-the-21st-century/

Maathai, W. (2003) *The Green Belt Movement: Sharing the Approach and the Experience*, New York: Lantern Publishing.

Mahtani, M. (2014) 'Toxic geographies: absences in critical race thought and practice in social and cultural geography', *Social & Cultural Geography,* 15(4): 359–67. DOI: 10.1080/ 14649365.2014.888297

Mansfield, B., Lave, R., McSweeney, K., et al (2019) 'It's time to recognize how men's careers benefit from sexually harassing women in academia', *Human Geography*, 12(1): 82–7. DOI: 10.1177/194277861901200110

McKittrick, K. (2006) *Demonic Grounds: Black Women and the Cartographies of Struggle*, Minessota: University of Minnesota Press.

McKittrick, K. (2011) 'On plantations, prisons, and a Black sense of place', *Social & Cultural Geography*, 12(8): 947–63. DOI: 10.1080/ 14649365.2011.624280

McKittrick, K. and Woods C.A. (eds) (2007) *Black Geographies and the Politics of Place*, Toronto: Between the Lines.

McMichael, P. (2006) 'Reframing development: global peasant movements and the new agrarian question', *Canadian Journal of Development Studies/ Revue Canadienne d'études du développement*, 27(4): 471–83. DOI: 10.1080/ 02255189.2006.9669169

McMichael, P. (2012) 'Reframing development: global peasant movements and the new agrarian question', *Revista Nera*, 10(10): 57–71.

McMichael, P. (2014) 'Historicizing food sovereignty', *Journal of Peasant Studies*, 41(6): 933–57. DOI: 10. 1080/03066150.2013.876999

Mintz, S.W. (1986) *Sweetness and Power: The Place of Sugar in Modern History*, New York: Penguin.

Moragues-Faus, A. and Marsden, T. (2017) 'The political ecology of food: carving "spaces of possibility" in a new research agenda', *Journal of Rural Studies*, 55: 275–88. DOI: 10.1016/j.jrurstud.2017.08.016

Nestle, M. and McIntosh, W.A. (2010) 'Writing the food studies movement', *Food, Culture & Society*, 13(2): 159–79. DOI: 10.2752/175174410X12633934462999

Nyéléni 2007 International Steering Committee (2007) Nyéléni Forum for Food Sovereignty Synthesis Report, 2007, Available from: https://nyeleni.org/en/synthesis-report/ [Accessed 12 April 2024].

Olson, E. and Sayer, A. (2009) 'Radical geography and its critical standpoints: embracing the normative', *Antipode*, 41(1): 180–98. DOI: 10.1111/ j.1467-8330.2008.00661.x

Patel, R. (2009) 'Food sovereignty,' *Journal of Peasant Studies*, 36(3): 663–706. DOI: 10.1080/03066150903143079

Patel, R. (2012) *Stuffed and Starved: The Hidden Battle for the World Food System* (revised and updated edn), Brooklyn: Melville House.

Pathak, H., Suresh, P., and Mohapatra, T. (2020) *Mahatma Gandhi's Vision of Agriculture: Achievements of ICAR*, New Delhi: Indian Council of Agricultural Research.

Peake, L. and Sheppard, E. (2014) 'The emergence of radical/critical geography within North America,' *ACME: An International E-Journal for Critical Geographies*, 13(2): 305–27.

Peet, R. (2000) 'Celebrating thirty years of radical geography', *Environment and Planning A: Economy and Space*, 32(6): 951–53. DOI: 10.1068/a32202

Peña, D., Calvo, L., McFarland, P., et al (eds) (2017) *Mexican-Origin Foods, Foodways, and Social Movements: Decolonial Perspectives*, Fayetteville: University of Arkansas Press.

Penniman, L. (2018) *Farming while Black: Soul Fire Farm's Practical Guide to Liberation on the Land*, Chelsea Green Publishing.

Poppendieck, J. (1999) *Sweet Charity?: Emergency Food and the End of Entitlement*, Penguin.

Poppendieck, J. (2011) *Free for All: Fixing School Food in America*, Berkely: University of California Press.

Probyn, E. (2003) *Carnal Appetites: FoodSexIdentities*, London: Routledge.

Ramírez, M.M. (2015) 'The elusive inclusive: Black food geographies and racialized food spaces', *Antipode*, 47(3): 748–69. DOI: 10.1111/anti.12131

Reese, A.M. (2019) *Black Food Geographies: Race, Self-Reliance, and Food Access in Washington*, Chapel Hill: UNC Press Books.

Reynolds, K. (2020) 'Food, agriculture, and environmental justice: perspectives on scholarship and activism in the field', in *Environmental Justice*, London: Routledge, pp 176–92.

Reynolds, K. and Cohen, N. (2016) *Beyond the Kale: Urban Agriculture and Social Justice Activism in New York City*, Athens, GA: University of Georgia Press.

Reynolds, K., Block, D., and Bradley, K. (2018) 'Food justice scholar-activism and activist-scholarship: working beyond dichotomies to deepen social justice praxis', *ACME: An International E-Journal for Critical Geographies*, 17(4): 988–98.

Robinson, J. (2022) *Comparative Urbanism: Tactics for Global Urban Studies*, Oxford: Wiley.

Roy, A. (2016) 'What is urban about critical urban theory?', *Urban Geography*, 37(6): 810–23.

Salvador, R. and Bittman, M. (2020) 'Goodbye, U.S.D.A., Hello, Department of Food and Well-Being', *The New York Times*, [online] 13 December, Available from: www.nytimes.com/2020/12/03/opinion/usda-agriculture-secretary-biden.html [Accessed 12 April 2024].

Satterfield, S. (2021) 'Our Founding Chefs' (Episode 3, Season 1), *High on the Hog: How African American Cuisine Transformed America*, Netflix.

Sen, A. (1981) *Poverty and Famines: An Essay on Entitlement and Deprivation*, Oxford: Oxford University Press.

Settee, P. and Shukla, S. (2020) *Indigenous Food Systems: Concepts, Cases, and Conversations*, Toronto: Canadian Scholars' Press.

Sherman, S. (2017) *The Sioux Chef's Indigenous Kitchen*, Minnesota: University of Minnesota Press.

Shiva, V. (1991) *The Violence of the Green Revolution: Third World Agriculture, Ecology and Politics*, New York: Zed Books.

Slocum, R. (2007) 'Whiteness, space and alternative food practice', *Geoforum*, 38(3): 520–33.

Slocum, R. and Saldanha, A. (2013) *Geographies of Race and Food*, London: Ashgate.

Smith, N. (2010) *Uneven Development: Nature, Capital, and the Production of Space*, Athens, GA: University of Georgia Press.

Smith, N. and Desbiens, C. (2000) 'An interview with Graciela Uribe Ortega', *Environment and Planning D: Society and Space*, 18(5): 545–56.

Smithers, G.C. and Mandawe, E. (2017) 'Indigenous geographies: research as reconciliation', *International Indigenous Policy Journal*, 8(2): 1–19.

Springer, S. (2014) 'Why a radical geography must be anarchist', *Dialogues in Human Geography*, 4(3): 249–70.

Tansey, G. and Worsley, A. (1995) *The Food System*, New York: Earthscan.

Terry, B. (2014) *Afro-Vegan: Farm-Fresh African, Caribbean, and Southern Flavors Remixed [A Cookbook]*, Berkley: Ten Speed Press.

Terry, B. (ed) (2022) *Black Food: Stories, Art, and Recipes from Across the African Diaspora [A Cookbook]*, Berkley: Ten Speed Press.

Vargas H.M. (2018) 'Graciela Uribe Ortega y la transición de la geografía Mexicana', *Terra Brasilis*, 10: 1–21.

Vela-Almeida, D., Zaragocin, S., Bayón, M., et al (2020) 'Imaginando territorios plurales de vida: una lectura feminista de las resistencias en los movimientos socio-territoriales en el Ecuador', *Journal of Latin American Geography*, 19(2): 87–109.

White, M.M. (2018) *Freedom Farmers: Agricultural Resistance and the Black Freedom Movement*, Chapel Hill: University of North Carolina Press.

Williams-Forson, P. (2006) *Building Houses out of Chicken Legs: Black Women, Food, and Power*, Chapel Hill: University of North Carolina Press.

Williams-Forson, P. and Wilkerson, A. (2011) 'Intersectionality and food studies', *Food, Culture & Society*, 14(1): 7–28. DOI: 10.2752/175174411X12810842291119

Wittman, H. (2009) 'Reworking the metabolic rift: La Vía Campesina, agrarian citizenship, and food sovereignty', *Journal of Peasant Studies*, 36(4): 805–26. DOI: 10.1080/03066150 903353991

Wittman, H., Desmarais, A.A., and Wiebe, N. (2010) *Food Sovereignty: Reconnecting Food, Nature & Community*, Halifax: Fernwood Press.

PART I

Scale

2

Fostering Racial Justice via Values–Based Food Procurement in the Good Food Buffalo Coalition

Jessica L. Gilbert-Overland

On 14 May 2022, a white supremacist murdered ten people at a Tops Friendly Markets in a predominantly Black neighbourhood of Buffalo, NY. Residents mourned those killed and feared this massacre would inspire other racialized violence in their neighbourhoods. The immediate closure of Tops, the only supermarket in the area, added to this trauma and instantly rendered thousands – many of whom are food insecure and do not have personal transportation – without access to healthy food, toiletries, and other essentials (Stahl, 2022). While the (newly renovated) Tops soon reopened, enduring grief and fear prevent many residents from shopping there. The devastating impacts of the Tops massacre on the psychological and physical health of Buffalo's communities of colour are thus ongoing, exemplifying the enduring consequences of racialized violence on food (in)justice in the US today.

Buffalo, a post-industrial city with about 33 per cent of its more than 276,000 people identifying as Black, 12 per cent as Latino, and 45 per cent as white, is one of the most segregated cities in the US (Blatto, 2018; US Census Bureau, 2021). This segregation, together with decades of redlining and systemic disinvestment in Buffalo's communities of colour, created the preconditions enabling the racially motivated mass shooting at Tops: the only supermarket in the area, serving a predominantly Black population. In the immediate aftermath of the attack, discussions of segregation, food apartheid, and systemic disinvestment briefly inundated mainstream media and political conversations. Calls for food justice resounded and funding flooded local organizations. Yet much of this attention faded within months, leaving Buffalo communities still healing from this trauma.

I open this chapter with the 14 May Tops massacre for two reasons. First, I cannot write about food (in)justice in Buffalo without uplifting the beautiful souls murdered and acknowledging how this attack changed life for Buffalo residents. Second, we must counter mainstream discourses by recognizing the long history of food justice efforts in Buffalo; activists and community members have worked for decades to illuminate the issues so briefly highlighted by dominant narratives in this attack's aftermath. The Tops itself, opened in 2003, was a result of a decade of organizing by Buffalo residents who did not have access to a full-service supermarket (The Food Equity Scholars, 2022). Today, many continue this long legacy of food justice organizing in Buffalo.

The Good Food Buffalo Coalition (GFBC) exemplifies one such food justice initiative. Founded in 2018 – four years before the Tops massacre – the GFBC is a majority-people-of-colour-led coalition that unites over 30 member organizations under its mission to leverage public institutions' procurement power to shift their food supply chains to align with specific values, emphasizing racial justice. Perhaps the best-known examples of such values-based public institutional food procurement (VBP) are Farm to School programmes: school districts purchase locally produced food thereby improving nutrition and growing local economies. A second, increasingly popular example of VBP is the Good Food Purchasing Program (GFPP), which the GFBC engages as a tool to foster food justice in Buffalo. The GFPP advances five explicit values (animal welfare, environmental sustainability, local economies, nutrition, and a valued workforce) and three implicit principles (equity, transparency, and accountability) in food supply chains (The Center for Good Food Purchasing, n.d.; Farnsworth et al, 2018). An increasing number of coalitions across the US advocate for the GFPP because its trans-local approach offers exciting new pathways for addressing large-scale food systems issues while uplifting place-based contexts and priorities. Due to the growing popularity of the GFPP, it is important to critically examine its impact and how coalitions leverage the GFPP to build towards local priorities.

Many limitations characteristic of VBP programmes inhibit their ability to generate food systems change. These include restrictive policy environments, a reliance on market mechanisms, and their propensity to benefit large corporations to the detriment of small farmers and businesses (Guthman, 2007; Morgan and Sonnino, 2008). As a VBP programme, each of these limitations is present in the GFPP, as is the absence of racial justice – a GFBC priority – as an explicit GFPP value. These VBP limitations hamper the GFPP from achieving food justice goals. Why, then, does the GFBC continue to advocate for the GFPP, particularly as a tool to foster racial justice in Buffalo's food system?

In this chapter, I argue that centring racial justice provides the GFBC with a unique lens that deepens the coalition's understanding of systemic oppression and discrimination and advances their ability to navigate the limitations of the GFPP. I draw on social movement theory and literature exploring market mechanisms' potential to generate change to examine how coalitions engaging values-guided – rather than campaign-bound – advocacy expand the impact of VBP programmes. Delving into the opportunities and limitations of the GFPP, I explore how the GFBC's emphasis on racial justice expands the GFPP's ability to generate food systems change. Radical food geographies (RFG) praxis grounds this chapter, which Levkoe et al (Chapter 1) describe as: '1) Theoretical engagement with power and structures of oppression ... ; 2) Action through academic, social movement, and civil society collaborations; and 3) Analysis through a broadly defined geographic lens.' My exploration of systemic barriers inhibiting the GFPP from fostering racial justice and my multiscalar analysis of the role of local coalitions in this national social movement build on the first and third components of RFG and highlight the importance of critically examining scale in food justice movements.

I illustrate the second element of RFG praxis by synthesizing scholarship and activism in my methodology. I write from a privileged positionality as a white woman employed in academia. To hold myself accountable to those most impacted by racial injustice in and beyond Buffalo's food system, I actively participate in the GFBC, recently undertaking a leadership role as Campaign Director, through which I engage with, learn from, and advocate alongside local coalition members and state and national GFPP partners, coalitions, and networks. I am deeply committed to the coalition's work: coalition activities and priorities inform my research and my research helps to guide coalition advocacy.

The qualitative analysis herein stems from my role in the GFBC. The connections I have developed through this work facilitated 23 qualitative interviews with coalition members, members of other GFPP coalitions across the country, national GFPP partners, Black farmers, institutional partners, and food distribution company employees. My personal experiences, via participant observations, serve as a second data source to acknowledge the interplay between my research and coalition activities and to account for the many conversations and events that I have participated in that interviewees have not (England, 1994; Cahill, 2007; Mason, 2015). A calendar record of my interactions with the coalition and a weekly written account of my coalition-related activities from May 2020 through August 2021 document participant observations. Finally, I employ a content analysis of public-facing resources including websites and webinars to provide additional data needed for this study. A qualitative coding process of these data sources revealed the themes explored in the following analysis.

Leveraging public institutional food procurement

Public institutions such as school, hospitals, and jails spend billions on food each year (Smith et al, 2016). Because these funds are public tax dollars, many contend all food purchased should be produced and distributed in ways that uphold public values (Stefani et al, 2017; Richman et al, 2018). Others position VBP as a tool to shift food systems away from harmful dominant industrial practices towards practices that foster socio-ecological health and well-being (Morgan and Sonnino, 2008; Smith et al, 2016; Farnsworth et al, 2018). Yet, VBP remains a difficult and rarely used tool in the US (Morgan and Sonnino, 2008; Stefani et al, 2017). Federal and state laws restrict public institutions from procuring values-aligned food by mandating that they prioritize lowest price over other values to maintain economic competition. NY, for example, requires public institutions to award food contracts to the 'lowest responsible bidder' – essentially, the vendor offering the cheapest price. Such complex regulatory layers inhibit VBP programmes from enacting change (Guthman, 2007).

However, VBP limitations extend beyond procurement laws. By leveraging market mechanisms to enact change, VBP programmes problematically situate the power to generate food systems change with consumers (such as public institutions) (Fridell, 2007; Guthman, 2007). Participation is therefore voluntary and implementation efforts generally lack external accountability structures (Guthman, 2007). Thus, VBP programmes guarantee neither long-term viability nor positive impact (Murray et al, 2006; Fridell, 2007). Restrictive budgets further constrain the impact of VBP by inducing public institutions to procure large quantities of food at high economies of scale. Because values-aligned food is often more expensive, public institutional budgets inhibit their participation in VBP programmes (Morgan and Sonnino, 2008).

Finally, VBP risks benefiting large producers and corporations to the detriment of small producers and businesses (Guthman, 2007; Stefani et al, 2017). VBP programmes rely on certifications and third-party verification systems to ensure that food aligns with desired value(s). This creates numerous barriers to entry for small producers and businesses, who are less able than large producers and corporations to quickly pivot production and distribution methods and who lack resources to apply for many certifications (Guthman, 2007; Klooster, 2010; Richman et al, 2018). Certifications and third-party verification systems thereby render VBP programmes exclusionary (Farnsworth et al, 2018). Public institutions' need for high economies of scale further excludes small producers and businesses, who struggle to meet the large quantities and low price points set by institutional contracts (Murray et al, 2006). In sum, VBP's reliance on market mechanisms reproduces many of the barriers that these programmes seek to address and thus limits VBP's potential to enact food systems change.

However, despite the limitations of VBP, Guthman (2007: 474) writes that 'it might be folly to disregard the tools that have even a modicum of efficacy' and 'important to consider the spaces they open'. Linking social movements to VBP programmes creates such potential (Klooster, 2010). Social movements can hold public institutions accountable to their commitments by exposing discrepancies between institutional commitments and actions (Keck and Sikkink, 1998; Murray et al, 2006). Furthermore, social movements generally view the market critically and often integrate additional non-market-based approaches (Klooster, 2010). This is especially true of coalitions comprised of a range of actors advocating for specific values rather than adhering to pre-established structures of particular campaigns; such values-guided broad coalitions are better positioned to embrace the strengths of an advocacy approach while avoiding its weaknesses (Nicholls, 2009; Hess, 2018). Social movements thus offer pathways to overcome VBP limitations: by understanding both the possibilities and barriers of such programmes and (re)structuring campaigns to uphold their values, social movements can position VBP efforts within their broader goals, thereby pursuing strategies that simultaneously advance VBP programmes' potential while avoiding VBP weaknesses (Richman et al, 2018; Farnsworth et al, 2018). The following case study of the GFPP and the GFBC demonstrates the important role of values-guided broad coalitions in overcoming the limitations of VBP programmes.

The Good Food Purchasing Program

The Los Angeles Food Policy Council conceived the GFPP in 2012 to generate food systems-wide change in line with five values: animal welfare, environmental sustainability, local economies, nutrition, and a valued workforce, each implicitly grounded in equity, transparency, and accountability (Lo and Delwiche, 2016). The GFPP has since developed into a nationwide, trans-local programme in which coalitions around the country adapt the national model to meet place-based needs and priorities (Farnsworth et al, 2018). To date, over 20 local coalitions across the US have achieved 15 school, city, and county GFPP policies impacting 48 public institutions that collectively procure over $1 billion of food annually (Lappe, 2021).

According to interviewees, emphasizing local coalitions is one of the GFPP's greatest strengths. Local GFPP coalitions serve as liaisons between communities and public institutions, functioning as external enforcement mechanisms by holding public institutions accountable to local communities' needs and priorities, thereby tackling the voluntary nature of VBP. For example, the Washington, DC coalition successfully urged DC Public Schools to publicly share the current status of their food supply chain as related to the five GFPP values and to commit to implementing the GFPP. Equally important, local coalitions bring actors across the five GFPP values into close collaboration, often for the first time, thus providing a platform to learn about others' values and goals. Building local GFPP coalitions therefore helps seemingly disparate actors in food systems advocacy better understand one another, determine the overlaps between their priorities, and identify pathways for collaboration.

GFPP limitations

As a VBP programme, the GFPP's reliance on market mechanisms to generate food systems change limits its success. Interviewees acknowledged the GFPP does not transform underlying systems and structures that perpetuate broader injustices. Specifically, while the GFPP seeks to shift how public institutions purchase food, it neither transforms the institutions themselves nor addresses many populations' reliance on public institutions as a primary food source (such as incarcerated individuals or low-income students). One local coalition coordinator explained, "the GFPP is functioning within a structure of public institutions that are created to serve people who have fallen through the cracks because of racial injustice and food injustice, we're not really solving the issue of food sovereignty because we're working within that system". By operating within existing economic and institutional systems responsible for perpetuating injustices, the GFPP is positioned to make incremental changes within those systems rather than transforming food systems.

The GFPP's reliance on market mechanisms also risks reinforcing corporate control of food systems. Because public institutions often require large quantities of food to serve their constituencies, contracts are most often awarded to big corporations. One national partner summarised:

> 'GFPP rewards large corporations that already have the capacity and resources to turn on a dime and start sourcing along the five GFPP values ... if there aren't local businesses at the needed capacity to sell to large institutions, at the very least let's make sure those large corporations are aligned with the values.'

While interviewees observed that such shifts within corporate suppliers create interim benefits, they acknowledged that the GFPP risks prolonging corporate control of food systems unless pathways for integrating smaller food businesses and producers, such as breaking large contracts into smaller ones, are explicitly integrated into the programme.

Third, the GFPP lacks an explicit racial justice component. While equity implicitly underlies all five values, many local coalitions have observed that public institutions rarely achieve their equity goals because of the GFPP's voluntary nature. One local coalition coordinator explained:

> 'There's a recognition that racial equity should be sort of the foundation for all of those standards. But in reality ... for it to be included in everything, it's also optional for everything ... How do we ensure that GFPP truly creates racially equitable outcomes if it's not its own standard? Or ... how do we ensure ... there are racially equitable components that are mandatory?'

National partners and other local coalition members asked these questions, as well, recognizing that the current voluntary structure for incorporating equity into the GFPP is problematic because it does not require public institutions participating in the GFPP to integrate racially just procurement practices.[1]

Public institutions' need for high economies of scale further inhibits the GFPP's ability to address racial injustice. Because the vast majority of farmers and business owners of colour are small-scale, it is extremely difficult to integrate them into public institutional food procurement. One national partner explained:

> 'Ultimately, what [the GFPP] has resulted in is processes that don't work for small producers and producers of colour because they don't produce the quantities ... And so, just at a basic level, we know that there's just almost no avenue for producers of colour to enter [public institutions'] supply chains.'

However, many local GFPP coalitions persist in prioritizing racial justice, working both within and outside of the programme's boundaries to overcome these barriers. In doing so, these local coalitions are simultaneously developing a deeper understanding of systemic oppression and discrimination in food systems and gleaning critical insights into GFPP implementation more generally. The GFBC is an example of one such local coalition.

The Good Food Buffalo Coalition

Founded in 2018, the GFBC is comprised of over 30 member organizations that range across the five GFPP values, each contributing unique perspectives, goals, and priorities (Good Food Cities, n.d.). While no public institution in Buffalo has passed GFPP policy, doing so remains central to the GFBC's mission. However, the coalition pushes beyond the parameters of the national GFPP model by explicitly centring racial justice. Specifically, the GFBC vision statement reads in part: 'We envision a future where ... We undo racial disparities experienced by marginalized farmers and food businesses ... by ensuring equitable access to land and distribution of resources for all people of diverse racial and socio-economic backgrounds' (The Good Food Buffalo Coalition, 2020).

Racial justice has been a core GFBC value from the outset (Good Food Cities, n.d.). During its first year, the coalition hosted events such the 'Racial Equity in the Food System Timeline' for Buffalo's communities of colour and a Harvest Festival at Buffalo Public Schools featuring produce from a Black farmer (Good Food Cities, n.d.). Similar events hosted in subsequent years also centred racial justice, including a Farmers and Legislators Forum that highlighted regional Black farmers and a second Harvest Festival during which families participated in a grocery bag giveaway with fresh produce from two Black-owned farms and virtual cooking class led by a local chef and Black business owner (Good Food Cities, n.d.).

In 2020, the GFBC developed and unanimously adopted a mission, vision, and values, codifying the coalition's commitment to racial justice. This process of determining shared GFBC values, and centring the coalition's commitment to racial justice, helped unite the coalition by providing opportunities for the member organizations across the five GFPP values to understand how their priorities overlap and demonstrate their commitment to achieving them. Codifying racial justice as a coalition value therefore strengthened the GFBC by fostering trust between seemingly disparate member organizations and positioned the GFBC as a values-guided, rather than campaign-bound, coalition.

Identifying GFPP barriers to fostering racial justice

Advocating for racial justice has enabled the GFBC and other racial justice-oriented local coalitions, as values-guided coalitions, to understand and move beyond the limitations characteristic of the GFPP. Local coalitions prioritizing racial justice in GFPP advocacy, such as the GFBC and those in New York City (NYC) and Chicago, work to ensure that those most impacted by racial injustice lead GFPP discussions, thereby surfacing a layer of barriers – those inhibiting racially just GFPP implementation – that these coalitions would not otherwise have understood as deeply. Furthermore, the many similarities between the barriers experienced by farmers and business owners of colour and those faced by other small farmers and business owners enable these coalitions to translate these lessons to GFPP implementation generally. Efforts to overcome barriers to integrating farmers and business owners of colour into institutional food supply chains thus provide potential pathways for more effective GFPP implementation overall.

Barriers to racial justice: MWBE policies

Many procurement policies include minority- and women-owned businesses and enterprises (MWBE) certification as one exception to 'lowest responsible bidder' laws. In NY, all public food contracts over $25,000 must be reviewed for possible opportunities to procure from MWBEs. The GFBC and other local GFPP coalitions are thus exploring MWBE policies as one way to surmount barriers inhibiting racially just GFPP implementation. Yet, non-binding language such as 'possible opportunities' renders MWBE policies voluntary and public institutions rarely meet their MWBE procurement goals. As such, rather than facilitating entry for farmers and business owners of colour into institutional food supply chains, the GFBC and other local coalitions have learned that MWBE policies are extremely problematic.

MWBE policies create additional barriers to entry that further exclude farmers and business owners of colour from institutional markets. Obtaining MWBE certification is a difficult process requiring the applicant to provide proof of citizenship and gender, capital contributions, and business activity in NY, copies of their personal and business tax documents, additional business documents, and professional background information (NY Division of Minority and Women's Business Development, 2020). Interviewees explained that this complex and labour-intensive process deters many farmers and business owners of colour from applying for MWBE certification. This exception to the 'lowest responsible bidder' law thus does not foster racial justice in food systems because too few farmers and business owners of colour are MWBE-certified for it to have the desired impact.

Problematically, few institutions recognize the shortcomings of MWBE policies, thereby exacerbating MWBE's inability to address racial injustice. Some institutions use the voluntary nature of MWBE policies to justify inaction related to racial injustice. One NYC coalition member reflected that:

> 'It's very easy for them to push it off. I was just speaking with the heads of the Office of Food and Nutrition Services, and I was like, "So what's up with your MWBE contracts? What's been going on?" They're like, "Oh, you know, the pandemic. Oh, we're going to revisit the conversation at the start of the school year", ... And then come back to say, "Well, we have these goals, but they can't meet our scale."'

Additionally, many institutions equate incorporating MWBE vendors into their supply chains with enacting racial justice. Yet, because the MWBE certification process is so difficult, the vast majority of MWBE-certified businesses are owned by white women; therefore, even if an institution does reach its MWBE goals, it is still doing very little to foster racial justice. Finally, the $25,000 threshold over which institutions are expected to seek 'possible opportunities' to procure from MWBEs renders such contracts too large for many farmers and business owners of colour to meet.

Barriers to racial justice: infrastructure

Racial justice-oriented local GFPP coalitions identified a lack of infrastructure as a second barrier that inhibits integrating farmers and business owners of colour into institutional food supply chains. Interviewees noted that this particularly includes a lack of processing and distribution infrastructure. The majority of public institutions have very limited capacity to process food on-site and instead rely on pre-processed food items. Yet, most farmers and business owners of colour do not have access to processing facilities and primarily sell unprocessed food. A GFBC institutional partner further explained, "We have been trying for years to get ... any farmer to sell directly to the schools. We're giving the farmer more share of the dollar, but they don't handle distribution. So how do we get that product to 80-plus schools two to three times a week?" Because of these processing and distribution disconnects, public institutions typically purchase food from corporations and larger (white-owned) farms with access to this infrastructure rather than food sold by farmers and business owners of colour. By understanding such infrastructure barriers, the GFBC and other racial justice-oriented local GFPP coalitions have developed a more holistic analysis of how public institutional food procurement perpetuates systemic oppression and discrimination.

Barriers to racial justice: access to resources

Limited access to resources is a third barrier inhibiting the GFPP from addressing racial injustice in food systems because it contributes to the low number and small size of existing farmers and business owners of colour. In the words of one NYC coalition member, "when you have, according to the 2017 census, 139 Black farmers and 57,155 white farmers ... there's already a wall there". Resoundingly, members of racial justice-oriented local GFPP coalitions argued that insufficient access to resources such as land and capital continues to be the primary cause of the dearth of farmers and business owners of colour. Without these resources, farmers and business owners of colour cannot ensure the long-term sustainability of their operations or expand them, while people of colour seeking to become farmers or business owners are unable to access start-up land and capital.

Interviewees noted that farmers and business owners of colour require technical assistance to apply for programmes designed to support them in accessing needed resources, such as loans, grants, and trainings, and to submit bids for institutional contracts and understand procurement policies. Yet, many such technical assistance opportunities frequently present additional barriers: applying for them is too often labour intensive and complicated. In other words, many of these 'supports' exclude those who need these resources from accessing them. Local GFPP coalitions thus argue for increasing technical assistance for those applying to such programmes and for decreasing the time and labour required to apply for 'support' programmes and institutional contracts.

Lessons learned from identifying barriers to racial justice

The process of identifying policy, infrastructure, and resource barriers inhibiting the use of the GFPP as a lever to foster food justice has also helped local coalitions to glean critical insights regarding GFPP implementation more broadly. First, in striving for racially just GFPP implementation, coalitions have developed deep understandings of the policy environment grounding institutional procurement. One example is the GFBC's research into 'best value' procurement policy as a possible exception to NY's 'lowest responsible bidder' law (Cardoza, 2020). This research began as an effort to understand how to incorporate racial justice into institutional procurement without using MWBE policies but expanded to examine how it might apply to other values. Another example is the Chicago coalition's understanding of institutions' informal operating policies that constrain GFPP implementation, which developed as the coalition worked to break large contracts into smaller ones that farmers and business owners of colour could fulfil. One Chicago coalition member described: "We passed the uppercase 'P' policy, but it's all of these informal, unwritten policies and procedures ... that really require a larger paradigm shift in how we think about institutional food." These procurement policy lessons will support all efforts to advance GFPP campaigns, not only local coalitions focused on racial justice.

Second, many lessons learned about barriers inhibiting farmers and business owners of colour from integrating into institutional food supply chains apply to small farms and businesses in general. For example, while they may not be subjected to race-based oppression and discrimination, most small farms and businesses struggle to meet the quantities required by large institutional contracts, are impacted by a lack of infrastructure, and must undertake the labour of applying for contracts themselves. Similarly, lessons learned about MWBE certification, particularly its exclusionary nature and the complex certification process, apply to other third-party certifications that small farmers and businesses must attain to prove they are aligned with at least one of the five GFPP values. As such, many of the efforts to overcome these barriers, while they may be motivated by goals of advancing racial justice, will support a wider array of food systems actors.

Finally, advocating for racial justice has helped local GFPP coalitions understand how public institutional food procurement is couched within broader food systems issues, meaning that GFPP efforts must be combined with other approaches to achieve widespread food systems change. One national partner explained: "Procurement is one tool, but it is one of many, many tools. And it can help to uncover how much work is needed to be done … But it has to be in concert with a lot of other policy work, and fundamental shifts in our economy, in our democracy." By delving into the barriers inhibiting racially just GFPP implementation, local coalitions have unpacked many socio-ecological interconnections within food systems that perpetuate an array of injustices embedded within a long history of racism and colonialism. A member of the Chicago coalition situated the GFPP as an opportunity to "to invest in Black and Brown producers … that have been shut out of other markets historically or haven't been able to access credit or resources historically and currently because of systemic racism and interpersonal racism". Through such statements, those working to overcome the barriers inhibiting racially just GFPP implementation demonstrate that they recognize these barriers as local symptoms of broader issues and that enacting food systems change requires many other approaches in addition to the GFPP.

Racial justice-oriented local coalitions and their partners are applying these lessons to address the barriers inhibiting racially just GFPP implementation. For example, some public institutions such as Buffalo Public Schools are seeking to update their commissaries to include scratch cooking facilities that would augment their ability to process food in-house. Many institutions are breaking large contracts into smaller ones that small farms and businesses, particularly those owned by people of colour, can more easily fill. Local coalitions are also addressing broader policy constraints inhibiting racially just GFPP implementation. For example, the GFBC and the NYC GFPP coalition are collaborating to amend NY's 'lowest responsible bidder' law. This Good Food NY Bill centres racial justice by enabling public institutions to purchase from 'socially disadvantaged farmers', which has a pre-established legal definition and requires verbal commitment rather than formal certification, thereby removing some barriers often presented by third-party certifications. Embracing such multiscalar approaches to overcome implementation barriers within institutions and broader policies enables these coalitions to simultaneously address local manifestations and structural drivers of racial injustice in food procurement.

Advancing racial justice through values–based procurement

By highlighting the deadly impacts of segregation and disinvestment in communities of colour, the 14 May massacre at the Buffalo Tops supermarket demonstrated the critical need to address systemic oppression and discrimination within and beyond food systems. Although mainstream narratives only briefly spotlighted food justice initiatives in Buffalo in the wake of this tragedy, the city has a long legacy of efforts to address impacts of racialized violence on food (in)justice. By centring racial justice in its GFPP advocacy, the GFBC builds upon this legacy and exemplifies how organizations unite to address both local symptoms and broader causes of racial injustice in food systems. GFPP implementation is thus a tool the GFBC employs to foster food justice.

Such a values–guided, rather than campaign-bound, multiscalar advocacy approach enables the GFBC to embrace the strengths of the GFPP while avoiding its limitations. Engaging with the GFPP through a racial justice lens advances the GFBC's ability to identify barriers to integrating farmers and business owners of colour into GFPP implementation. Many of these lessons apply to small producers and businesses generally, thereby helping the GFBC to navigate the limitations of the GFPP more broadly, as well. The GFBC is thus simultaneously developing a deeper understanding of broader systemic oppression and discrimination in food systems and gleaning critical insights into local GFPP implementation. In other words, the GFBC's racial justice GFPP advocacy supports Guthman's (2007) argument for engaging with VBP programmes as tools with 'a modicum of efficacy' because, when linked with social movements, they open unintended spaces for food systems change.

This chapter confirms the value of employing RFG in food justice analyses. First, a theoretical engagement with power and structures of oppression highlights how combining local and statewide advocacy enables the GFBC to simultaneously address local manifestations and structural underpinnings inhibiting farmers and business owners of colour from integrating into VBP programmes. Second, a geographic lens reveals the benefits of situating such a multiscalar approach in place and place-based networks through local GFPP coalitions: by grounding their advocacy in the priorities of those most impacted by racial injustice in Buffalo's food system, the GFBC has learned how to navigate the barriers to racially just GFPP implementation and GFPP limitations generally. In doing so, the GFBC has developed a deeper understanding of structural drivers of racial injustice undergirding local food system issues. Finally, utilizing academic and social movement collaborations in knowledge production has advanced the GFBC's efforts to centre the priorities of those most impacted by racial injustice in food systems by generating a continuous interplay between academic research and food justice activism, with each routinely informing the other. Employing RFG in this chapter thus highlights core strategies for social movements working to advance racial justice through VBP: embrace a multiscalar approach while grounding advocacy in place and place-based networks and ensure that those most impacted by injustices in public institutional food procurement guide knowledge-production processes.

Acknowledgements
I am deeply grateful to the community partners who guided me in this work and shared their knowledge and experiences with me. This research is only possible with your support. Thank you, too, to Charles Levkoe, Colleen Hammelman, and Kristin Reynolds, for all of your feedback and support throughout this writing process.

Note
[1] This research utilizes the 2017 GFPP Standards, which are currently being updated to make racial justice more explicit.

References
Blatto, A. (2018) 'A City Divided: A Brief History of Segregation in Buffalo', *Partnership for the Public Good*, [online] 7 May 2018], Available from: https://ppgbuffalo.org/buffalo-commons/library/resource:a-city-divided-a-brief-history-of-segregation-in-buffalo-1/ [Accessed 28 February 2023].

Cahill, C. (2007) 'The personal is political: developing new subjectivities through participatory action research', *Gender, Place and Culture,* 14(3): 267–92.

Cardoza, E. (2020) 'Another voice: food buying program would benefit Buffalo schools', *Buffalo News*, [online] 5 October, Available from: https://bit.ly/3HDewdv [Accessed 14 December 2022].

England, K.V.L. (1994) 'Getting personal: reflexivity, positionality, and feminist research', *The Professional Geographer*, 46(1): 80–9.

Farnsworth, L.D., Delwiche, A., and McKinney, C. (2018) 'The Good Food Purchasing Program: a policy tool for promoting supply chain transparency and food system change', in S.E. Thottathil and A. Goger (eds) *Institutions as Conscious Food Consumers: Leveraging Purchasing Power to Drive Systems Change*, San Diego, CA: Academic Press, pp 103–26.

Fridell, G. (2007) 'Fair-trade coffee and commodity fetishism: the limits of market-driven social justice', *Historical Materialism*, 15(4): 79–104.

Good Food Cities (n.d.) 'Buffalo', *Good Food Cities*, [online] Available from: https://goodfoodcities.org/portfolio/buffalo/?portfolioCats=32 [Accessed 14 December 2022].

Guthman, J. (2007) 'The Polanyian way? Voluntary food labels as neoliberal governance', *Antipode*, 39(3): 456–78.

Hess, D.J. (2018) 'Energy democracy and social movements: a multi-coalition perspective on the politics of sustainability transitions', *Energy Research & Social Science*, 40: 177–89.

Keck, M.E. and Sikkink, K. (1998) *Activists Beyond Borders: Advocacy Networks in International Politics*, Ithaca, NY: Cornell University Press.

Klooster, D. (2010) 'Standardizing sustainable development? The Forest Stewardship Council's plantation policy review process as neoliberal environmental governance', *Geoforum*, 41(1): 117–29.

Lappe, A. (2021) 'Transforming the way public institutions purchase food', *Good Food Cities: Buffalo*, [online] 23 January, Available from: https://goodfoodpurchasing.org/program-overview/ [Accessed 14 December 2022].

Lo, J. and Delwiche, A. (2016) 'The good food purchasing policy: a tool to intertwine worker justice with a sustainable food system', *Journal of Agriculture, Food Systems, and Community Development*, 6(2): 1–10.

Mason, K. (2015) 'Participatory action research: coproduction, governance and care', *Geography Compass*, 9(9): 497–507.

Morgan, K. and Sonnino, R. (2008) *The School Food Revolution: Public Food and The Challenge of Sustainable Development*, London: Routledge.

Murray, D.L., Raynolds, L.T., and Taylor, P.L. (2006) 'The future of fair trade coffee: dilemmas facing Latin America's small-scale producers', *Development in Practice,* 16(2): 179–92.

Nicholls, W. (2009) 'Place, networks, space: theorising the geographies of social movements', *Transactions of the Institute of British Geographers*, 34(1): 78–93.

NY Division of Minority and Women's Business Development (2020) 'MWBE Certification Checklist', *NY Division of Minority and Women's Business Development*, [online], Available from: https://esd.ny.gov/sites/default/files/MWBECertificationChecklist-Dec2020.pdf [Accessed 14 December 2022].

Richman, N.J., Allison, P.H., and Leighton, H.R. (2018) 'Farm to institution New England: mobilizing the power of a region's institutions to transform a region's food system', in S.E. Thottathil and A. Goger (eds) *Institutions as Conscious Food Consumers: Leveraging Purchasing Power to Drive Systems Change*, San Diego, CA: Academic Press, pp 103–26.

Smith, J., Andersson, G., Gourlay, R., Karner, S., Mikkelsen, B.E., Sonnino, R., and Barling, D. (2016) 'Balancing competing policy demands: the case of sustainable public sector food procurement', *Journal of Cleaner Production*, 112(1): 249–56.

Stahl, J. (2022) 'What We Get Wrong About Food Insecurity in Places Like Buffalo's East Side', *Slate*, [online] 19 May, Available from: bit.ly/3VZRcem [Accessed 14 December 2022].

Stefani, G., Tiberti, M., Lombardi, G.V., Cei, L., and Sacchi, G. (2017) 'Public food procurement: a systematic literature review', *International Journal on Food System Dynamics*, 8(4): 270–83.

The Center for Good Food Purchasing (n.d.) 'The Program', *The Center for Good Food Purchasing*, [online], Available from: https://goodfoodpurchasing.org/program-overview/ [Accessed 14 December 2022].

The Food Equity Scholars, U.B. Food Lab (2022) 'Op-ed: East Buffalo Needs Community-Driven Structural Investments, Not Fly-In, Fly-Out Charity', *Civil Eats*, [online] 24 May, Available from: https://bit.ly/3j5wuv5 [Accessed 14 December 2022].

The Good Food Buffalo Coalition (2020) 'Our Coalition At-A-Glance', *The Good Food Buffalo Coalition*, [online], Available from: http://bit.ly/gfbc_at-a-glance [Accessed 14 December 2022].

US Census Bureau (2021) 'Quick Facts: Buffalo city, New York', *US Census Bureau*, [online], Available from: www.census.gov/quickfacts/buffalocitynewyork [Accessed 14 December 2022].

3

With Pots and Pens to Parliament: Understanding and Responding to Crises through a Critical Feminist Lens in Cape Town, South Africa

Sanelisiwe Nyaba, Caroline Peters, Jane Battersby, and Nicole Paganini

For decades, South Africa has been battered by crises and its people, tired and bruised, are raising their fists in resistance. The country continues to wrestle with the impact of decades of institutionalized racism, sexism, exclusion, structural violence, and other factors that undermine human development and social cohesion. The COVID-19 pandemic and lockdowns were associated with a spike in gender-based violence (GBV) and femicide. Power, patriarchy, and a lack of participation in decision-making processes and structures remain the most significant obstacles to the realization of food security. Here, hunger is a driver of social unrest and violence. It is a slow violence that eats away at the fibres of Cape Town's social fabric. In a national multiwave study to document the impact of lockdowns, 47 per cent of the respondents indicated not having money to purchase food in April 2020 and, of those living in urban spaces, shack dwellers in informal or marginalized areas were most vulnerable (Spaull et al, 2020; Van der Berg, 2021). In early 2020, the state temporarily closed informal trade and, with it, the main food sources for vast swathes of the population. People lost their jobs and their access to cash to purchase what little food there was. Urban farmers were banned from travelling to their gardens (Buthelezi et al, 2020). Yet, women played a major role in spearheading change and re-establishing hope. Their networks braided together to set up makeshift kitchens in private spaces where hot food was served daily, conversations bloomed, the shame of hunger began to dissolve, and dreams bigger than just bowls of soup took shape.

This chapter shares the perspectives of four of the women (co-authors of this chapter) who established networks of women running community kitchens during the pandemic. We use the term 'community kitchen' in this chapter as an overall description for local structures such as soup kitchens or communal feeding schemes that provide free meals in their immediate neighbourhoods. The kitchens we write about are situated across the low-income areas of the Cape Flats area of Cape Town, a city that maintains the blueprint of its apartheid history within its spatial framework, infrastructure, and political ecology; it is a city of contrasts, inequality, and a deeply contested food system.

All the community kitchens involved in this research are run by women of colour, most of whom have experienced food insecurity and many of whom have experienced or been exposed to GBV. These women were raised in the context of a racist, sexist post-apartheid South Africa, were burdened with intergenerational poverty, and continue to speak and act from a place of lacking. For them, sharing a slice of bread with a sibling for dinner is not unusual, yet we fed thousands during the pandemic and created safer spaces offering sisterhood and support. Their community kitchens were of paramount importance to their communities during the COVID-19 crisis and continue to provide unique insights into very particular places where food injustice is challenged through feminist activism and community-centred research aiming at destigmatizing hunger. Despite the heaviness of this work, we continue to emerge through the thick of crises at home and in their communities to serve those in need, often grappling with the lack of boundaries between their roles as community members feeding their families and kitchen managers feeding their communities. These challenges evoke the feminist perspective that 'the personal is political' and call upon resistance and reorganization in times of social injustice and crisis (see Figure 3.1).

The authors of this chapter have collaborated in community-led research on food security since 2020 (Paganini and Weigelt, 2023). Two authors form part of the community kitchen network; two authors steered the research with the co-researchers. We ground our writings in a critical feminist research framework in the context of power, oppression, and patriarchal capitalism, while remaining cognizant of power relationships among ourselves as a dual-heritage research team. This chapter provides a snapshot of a five-year research project led by TMG Research, a Nairobi and Berlin-based thinktank that cooperates with Food Agency Cape Town (FACT).

In this chapter, we build on the three key principles of radical food geographies (RFG) presented by Levkoe et al (Chapter 1) and Hammelman et al (2020). In the first section, we respond to RFG's call to action on historical and structural challenges and how those relate to power by

Figure 3.1: The personal is political: by unpacking the political reason for women's personal challenges, the community kitchens empowered women to become activists who championed women's causes (such as the 16 Days campaign) across Cape Town.

Source: Nyaba, 2022.

presenting our community kitchen case study from low-income areas in Cape Town where food insecurity continues to threaten communities oppressed by historic marginalization and power dynamics within current food systems. In the second section, we address RFG's call for action by highlighting the methodological process that led to this chapter. Then, we present two short stories that were written as part of a participatory process and speak to the importance of space and place in food justice processes. Throughout we demonstrate how feeding people at an individual scale is conditioned by systems of marginalization and disempowerment yet also contributes to broader impacts at the scale of food justice movements and anti-violence campaigns.

Community kitchens in Cape Town and the social capital of networks during crises

The community kitchens of Cape Town are as diverse as the neighbourhoods they serve. Community kitchens operate in neighbourhoods of different socio-economic and ethnic backgrounds and are often connected to mosques or churches, schools or early childhood development centres, community centres, and private homes. Often, these kitchens are run by volunteers (mainly women) and receive food donations through faith-based organizations, philanthropic organizations, the private sector, or governmental social development support (see Figure 3.2). The donations

Figure 3.2: The community kitchen of the Callas Foundation operates in a private home.

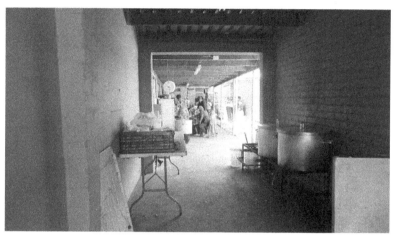

Source: Nyaba, 2022.

are sourced mainly via Cape Town's food retail market or, occasionally, large- or medium-scale farmers from the Philippi Horticulture Area, a vegetable production site in the peri-urban Cape Flats (Paganini et al, 2021b).

The economic landscape in Cape Town is characterized by a high-skill, formal economy, with 75 per cent of grocery trade dominated by large supermarket chains and an increasing presence of fast-food establishments in low-income neighbourhoods. This economic structure intersects with a concerning issue as household food insecurity is prevalent, reaching 55 per cent citywide and potentially soaring to 80 per cent in specific areas such as the Cape Flats. Notably, residents in these low-income regions heavily rely on social grants for food security, creating a paradox where nutritional compromises are made in the face of hunger (Paganini and Weigelt, 2023). Our research zoomed in on the community kitchen networks in the Cape Flat area of Cape Town: a peri-urban, low-income, high-density area shaped by apartheid and post-apartheid spatial policies that created and perpetuated segregation based on race and economic status. This urban geography reinforces social, economic, and political marginalization and creates conditions of social isolation in many communities. The state has not adequately addressed these challenges and has failed to act on food insecurity. The fragility of current systems leave those who live along the fault lines or at the intersections of vulnerabilities destitute (for example, women during the pandemic) (Bam and Humphreys, 2022; Groenmeyer, 2022). Even though the root cause of hunger in these areas clearly rests in segregation, marginalization, disempowerment, and lack of state intervention, food insecurity is understood by the communities we work with as their personal failures to attain liveable wages and budget sensibly. Their sense of shame around poverty and hunger spurred soup kitchen patrons to walk to distant kitchens to avoid their neighbours' stares (Paganini et al, 2021a) and erupted as a dominant theme in women's written reflections on their participation in community kitchens.

Yet, by unpacking hunger and its root causes in the Cape Flats' urban geography, community kitchen volunteers and patrons began shedding their sense of shame over intergenerational poverty and hunger and replacing it with a shared sense of resistance, hope, and change through social cohesion. Community kitchens can play a multifunctional role and enhance social cohesion among those who run them. Herein, in this sense of sisterhood, lies an opportunity for destigmatizing and reimagining community kitchens, replacing the conventional view of community kitchens as feeding schemes for the destitute.

Through women's work in networking, resourcing, and repairing, their community kitchens became places of learning, communication, sharing, healing, and recreation, and where the social challenges of our cities, our histories, and our future are explored through food. A look beyond the horizon to Latin America provides examples of how this vision may come into reality. There, soup kitchens are communal centres where community and solidarity come to the fore (see also, García et al, Chapter 6). Often these kitchens are embedded in municipal structures and supported by women's networks (Kogan, 1998; Immiink, 2001; Hartley, 2020). As Gennari and Tornaghi (2020: 86) suggest, 'The reasons for implementing community kitchens—and making food production and consumption a collective responsibility today still have characteristics in common with the past experiences but also depend on the new needs of contemporary cities in times of austerity, overcrowded cities, climate and environmental crisis'.

Mixing critical feminism and radical food geographies

Our research in community kitchens was conducted from a feminist research philosophy and methodology. Feminist research punctuates questions of power, not only in terms of gender, but also class, race, sexuality, ethnicity, geographical location, and disability (Andrews, Smith, and Morena, 2019). An intersectional analysis of inequality and social injustice helps to understand how interlocking forms of oppression and privilege are experienced and reproduced daily and supported by broader structural inequalities and systems (Davis and Hattery, 2018; Kiguwa, 2019). It requires a move away from 'single truth' objectivity towards understanding knowledge as situated and embodied (Haraway, 1988), affording new value to experiential knowledge and feelings. This includes a focus on researchers' reflexivity on their role and positionality, including making explicit the power complexities inherent in the research process (Kiguwa, 2019; Paganini et al, 2021b). RFG integrates radical geography with critical food system research by providing theoretical and activist contributions (Levkoe et al, Chapter 1; Hammelman et al, 2020). Reynolds, Block, and Bradley (2018) reflect on this growing body of work, in which activist-scholars collaborate with community-led organizations to include different voices into theory while acknowledging the difficulties behind these approaches – namely, power relations among author teams, lack of time to build trust, and the structural challenges of academic conventions in acknowledging different styles of writing and articulating. This is also a question that concerns us and poses challenges such as converting differing narrative styles into scientific text, without losing the character of multiple voices through editing.

Donna Andrew and Desiree Lewis' (2017) work significantly shaped our research approach. They encourage feminist and participatory approaches in food research to unpack root causes of hunger and women's daily struggles while drawing attention to the perceptions, voices, and feelings of marginalized groups. The visceral lived experience of hunger, which has been the lifelong reality of many of the women who actively contribute to the research project, is this research's thematic entry point. Thus, the concept of having voice has been a cornerstone for our work as well as the work of our partners including the FACT network, a community-based research network of community activists who often do not see themselves represented in research or discourse. Through integrative methodologies agreed upon by all co-researchers, our research moves beyond the purely analytical and into the emotive and embodied experiences of the research collaborators. For example, story writing retreats support the women who run voluntary community kitchens in finding the headspace we require to engage in deeper reflection on their daily practices. At the same time, these stories served as data and provided unique and profoundly personal perspectives into daily challenges around food.

As a co-research team, we were tasked with re-writing knowledge in explicitly decolonized ways. As a collective, we actively sought to remove the power imbalance between researchers and the researched and to employ the recommendations of a FACT co-research study that exposed the relationship between researchers who extract data from communities and, with it, community members' agency over what happens to it (Paganini et al, 2021a). While this is a messy undertaking, it would be naïve to claim the absence of power differences between community members affiliated with partner organizations and researchers affiliated with the project, between people of colour and White colleagues, and between students and supervisors. The trust-building process that underpinned the project was politically motivated and sought to address social inequality. Therefore, this project began and will end with the standpoints and experiences of the women running the community kitchens who shape the research agenda, methodology, analysis, interpretation of data, and dissemination. Our critical feminist approach through the co-research methodology challenges how knowledge is produced and whose knowledge holds power in the context of academia. Research must be informed by the insights of the communities where the research takes place to allow communities to bring their voices to the research processes and global discourse on food security and RFG.

What is cooking: methods for exploring community kitchens

As the pandemic dragged on, short-term government relief funds, civil society donations, and corporate donations dwindled. This starved kitchens of necessary supplies, suffocating the sustainability of community kitchens, perpetuating hunger, and removing communities' newfound platforms for support, hope, solidarity, and encouragement. While some kitchens were forced to close, some community kitchen staff dug even deeper into their networks to continue to provide essential nourishment, shelter, and spaces where neighbours could feel 'human again' (Battersby et al, 2022). Yet, mirroring experiences in the health care sector, little attention was paid to those kitchen workers who put in long stretches of work – sometimes without pay, while struggling to take care of their own families. A three-day retreat, organized by the authors (see Figure 3.3), provided 25 female kitchen heads with space to breathe, vent, reflect, dream, rethink, and co-design community kitchens as multifaceted hubs addressing their communities' diverse needs through food (Paganini et al, 2021a).

As part of the research process, we conducted 20 kitchen exchange visits and accumulated photovoice data. Photovoice is a qualitative method that allows researchers to gain insights into people's lived experiences (Milne and Muir, 2019). Twenty women leading community kitchens took photos during their exchange visits, which allowed them to reflect on their day-to-day work in the kitchens. A joint co-analysis of the photos was a decisive step; through conversation, expression, and description of everyday life, the photographs turned the ordinary into research content. Community kitchen heads and the authors of this chapter were invited to a gallery walk to leave comments about their observations, co-analyse, and identify key themes from the photographs. We discussed these in a fishbowl session where each kitchen leader shared what we observed and learned from other kitchens and how this learning applied to their own kitchens (Figure 3.4). This gave co-researchers a bird's eye view of community kitchens in Cape Town beyond their own community, the structures that drive them apart, the burdens we face, the exhaustion that plagues us, and the network of

Figure 3.3: Community kitchen volunteers came together in a three-day workshop to present their stories, celebrate successes, and envision the future of their kitchens as communal spaces.

Source: Nyaba, 2022.

Figure 3.4: Analysis of the photovoice exercise through fishbowl discussions.

Source: Nyaba, 2022.

like-intentioned women who model how to surmount these challenges. By sharing and sorting stories, co-researchers contextualized and interpreted their photovoice to produce short texts. Two of these pieces are presented in the following section.

Interconnectivity of food

Community kitchen leaders saw food as more than something served on plates. It was their entry point to responding to intersecting crises in communities. The conversations during the retreat highlighted the rich menu of services shared alongside food, from responding to domestic violence, nutrition and growing organic food, childcare or after-school care, to urging gang members to desist from gang violence. The value derived from community kitchens transcends the immediate need for food, offering critical community spaces for seeking and building connection, exchanging, and solidarity; querying norms; spearheading transformation; and giving voice to advocates for food system change. Community kitchens foster social values and (re)build communities' broken social fabric and the women who run them serve as trusted community advisors in the absence of government services. The kitchen heads described how the everyday practice of preparing and serving food had allowed them to identify and assist vulnerable individuals relationally, with dignity.

However, a dominating narrative during the retreat and photovoice exercise was to acknowledge the exhaustion, the dwindling resources, and the ongoing problem of donor conditionalities that undermined the women's vision of creating spaces of dignity. The women co-researchers also noted the lack of conversation about hunger during the COVID-19 pandemic. Through the year-long community research process, women who run community kitchens led discussions about taking food security out of the sole possession of public health statistics and recognized the intersectionality of compounding issues. In previous research, we argued that employing feminist approaches to food security research can unearth the root causes of broken systems and power struggles and amplify marginalized voices normally excluded in mainstream food security research approaches (Paganini et al, 2021b).

Serving stories alongside soup

In this section, we share the writing of two co-researchers from community kitchens. Their lived experiences speak powerfully to RFG by underscoring the importance of network building and allyship in food justice activism. These examples rely on the direct voice of community kitchen leaders to illustrate the importance of participatory processes and reflections and to show the interconnections between food, care work, and other social movements. The first example is one co-author's reflection on the vulnerability of kitchen heads and the multiple stresses and shame experienced by Cape Flats' women in the wake of systemic violence. The second example highlights a persistent theme that continuously surfaced during the retreat, in photovoice, and during writing workshops: violence against women, its causes, and how food insecurity among perpetuators amplifies it. The text below is a call to activism written by a Black, female gender advocate who mainstreams gender awareness and activism within community kitchens.

A process reflection: safer spaces, emotions, and building political voices through food

As a young activist, I had looked to the older women who run community kitchens in reverence, eager to join them in their brave food security activism. Yet, when we converged at the retreat, there were tears as each divulged her anger, stress, guilt, exhaustion, and physical pain. I was struck by the below piece of writing by a community member working at FACT who analysed the systemic violence that emerged during her struggles running a community kitchen.

> 'It was hammered into us, from my mother, from my community; it was echoed by everyone: your hunger must not be written on your face. Your poverty must never show. My mother raised us to know that if you don't have something, you must accept that situation until the next paycheque. Having to go next door to ask for something for the kitchen table shows your poverty; you only ask close relatives or go to bed hungry. Poor people were teased. My mother was working for a family and brought food leftovers home from work; you get teased for that, because you cannot afford your own. They call it eating the scraps from the White person's dinner table. The secrecy around our hunger came from the indignity of running out of food; it is shame. When it comes to shame, if you are transparent, people laugh at you. They gossip about you; they don't help you. So, most people don't want to be exposed and keep hiding their situation.' (quote collected during the photovoice documentation)

I was surprised to find something within these courageous leaders that I thought dwelled only within me, as a young Black woman: shame. Though they carry ample experience and expertise to transform local and global responses to food insecurity, they are not immune to the cycle of violence deeply embedded in Cape Town's historical context. Shame is deeply embodied here and haunts each of us. Through our community kitchen work, we had been drawn into community and opened ourselves to vulnerability; thus, I chose to reciprocate by sharing with them a poem I wrote titled 'Shame'. I could barely lift my eyes to look at the faces of

CRISES THROUGH A CRITICAL FEMINIST LENS

the women as I read it, but there was the need to recognize our shared burdens and find solidarity and space for discussions and planning as a collective community.

Shame
Feeling ashamed
of my body
with its breasts that part ways
violently
when I lay on my back,
that one breast goes and lays on one side
the other breast goes and lays on the other
I am ashamed
of the gleaming marks on
my bronze skin
You can see how far my
stomach must have stretched when it carried the baby
I was ashamed then
I am ashamed now
I was ashamed even
when I was too
young to be ashamed
or understand shame
So shame is a taunting little thing
that grows in size and likeness
and changes with you
When your thighs take the shape
of a curve
its muscles growing stronger to
withstand what weight you carry
shame has its own muscles
It grows taller with you
a second shadow that
does not disappear even when the sun
disappears from the sky
You carry your baby on your back
and somewhere your shame is attached
Perhaps a heavier load
perhaps it is why you tire so
quickly on your way to the taxi rank
I am not ashamed to admit
that I have nursed this shame
and fed it as I fed my growing child

> I have groomed shame, because
> letting go is a shame on its own

My poem is about no longer being beautiful and no longer conforming to an ideal. It's the same with hunger. We are either too thin from starvation or made overweight by the sugary fast foods that we can afford. In the same way we hide our bodies in shame, we hide our feelings. Rather than answering "How are you?" with "I am well", we have become adept at answering with, "I am surviving". We hide our shame about not being satiated behind platitudes, clothes, and our own belief that tomorrow will be better.

Silence kills: reclaiming DALLA

Challenges in the Cape Flats may seem overwhelming, but in coming together with other women who volunteer at community kitchens, we have found strength to keep going and form the community kitchen network which we call 'With pens and pots to parliament'. By exploring the kitchen work, we have discovered kindness, warmth, belonging, purpose, support, resilience, and solidarity. We have recognized the power of people, social relationships, and networks as most of our kitchens survived only through social networks and sharing. Our networking has allowed us to become part of something bigger than ourselves and inspired others to do the same. In solidarity, women can advocate for their needs using a unified voice.

Violence against women – physical, psychological, sexual, economic, and socio-cultural – is a conspicuous and widespread violation of human rights in South Africa. This violence pervades the political, economic, and social structures of society and is driven by strongly patriarchal social norms and complex and intersectional power inequalities, including gender, race, class, and sexuality. The relationship between gender inequality and GBV is well established: gender inequality legitimates violence and is further established by the use of such violence. The possibility of intervening in this relationship, however, presents a far more complex challenge.

Unbelievably, after 28 years of democracy, South African women are regularly confronted with systemic sexual harassment and violence. The government has failed to enforce laws and policies intended to safeguard women's rights. Even the police often fail to provide adequate protection. Instead of enjoying the fruits of democratic freedom, women constantly live in fear of rape, harassment, discrimination, and murder.

We argue that gender discrimination and violation of women's human rights should have punishable consequences and effective enforcement. Men, women, and people of the LGBTQ2SIA+ community[1] in South Africa are impacted by violence in multiple and intersecting ways. South Africa's rape rate, as a particular form of GBV, is one of the highest in the world

(UNODC South Africa, 2002). GBV as a product of many factors related to first and foremost hunger, HIV/AIDS, cultural negative practices and attitudes, gender stereotypes and inequalities, and extreme poverty continues to be a critical human rights and development issue for South Africa. "And how does this manifest in our work on food? We move! We DALLA!!"

Our community kitchen work's expansion has brought us together to reclaim 'dalla'. Dalla is a word used by gang members in Cape Town to encourage each other to immediate, intimidating, violent action that sends passers-by fleeing. As victims of gang violence for years, women and children are reclaiming the word as an act of resistance and have initiated the DALLA campaign with the Callas Foundation. The campaign gives a (female) voice to the demand to dismantle patriarchal society/systems and GBV in Cape Town. The campaign sees women coming together to educate and heal each other, protect their vulnerable, enforce the law, and mobilize resources in the form of expertise, knowledge, food, and violence prevention.

Today, we see women in the Cape Flats, Cape Town's low-income area, advocating using the hashtag #Patrickmustfall.[2] Patrick is the name chosen to symbolize patriarchy in South Africa. Patriarchy manifests in the violence against women and the violent environment of our cities. It is a physical manifestation in our food system and unpacks which food is available to whom. Healthy food is only affordable to the rich. If families have to cut corners, women step back to offer the meal to the son, husband, or other male family member. Patriarchy in food systems is oblivious to women's unpaid or underpaid care work in farming, grocery shopping, cooking, serving, and cleaning. Therefore, food activism is naturally rooted in feminism because, as bell hooks says, 'the work of feminism does not end with the fight for equality of opportunity within the existing patriarchal structure. We must understand that challenging and dismantling is at the core of contemporary feminist struggle' (2013: 5).

The feminist campaign, DALLA, pairs 'Patrick' with 'DALLA'. This is a campaign developed by the kitchen network. The women of DALLA reclaim the word and espouse it with a new meaning:

Deliberate: We are deliberate in our actions, thinking, and behaviours. We are determined to change the effects of GBV in our communities.

Action: We are committed to educating and creating awareness workshops and expert training on GBV. We involve all stakeholders.

Leading: We lead by example. We will not stop until we reach as many women and children from all corners and walks of life as possible.

Liberation: 'I am no longer accepting the things I cannot change; I am changing the things I cannot accept.' Angela Davis

Awareness: There is power in awareness – Knowledge is power! WOMANDLA[3,4]

The importance of claiming voice and space and seeking healing and destigmatization resonate within both of these stories. The stories show how food can be considered as political as it is not only a means to fill individual bellies, but to determine and be determined by the broader culture of communities and cities. If there is not enough food, shame prevents people from taking part in political processes and community work. Insufficient food supply and access also means an increase of violence, which manifests in the brutally high rates of GBV in South African cities and communities.

Concluding thoughts

This chapter had two focal areas – the first was the experience and vision of the community kitchens as they emerged in the wake of the COVID crisis. The second was the centring of co-researchers' voices within the research process. We, as a research team of academics, community-based researchers, and activists, believe that the story told here and the way it has been told make two valuable contributions to RFG.

The first contribution is to research orientation. The approach presented here builds on RFG by showing an example of how more accessible methods such as photovoice and story writing enables new perspectives to emerge through art in research. This re-writing of stories is grounded in African oral traditions and challenges conventional research methods. Central to this project was the insistence that leaders in the community kitchens must play a central role in the research process. The project involved participatory research processes in which co-researchers were not only active participants in the analysis of findings and legitimized the work of academic researchers but were also involved in every phase of the research process. The co-researchers worked with the academics to develop the community kitchen network to guide the research questions, develop the methods, conduct fieldwork and analysis, and write up findings. In an era of reporting against 'pathways to impact', what is being created here is emergent and shaped as much by community needs as by funder log-frames.

The work presented here represents an attempt to centre research processes locally as a critical feminist endeavour. In the context of RFG, critical feminism is important because it has helped to uncover the ways that gender, race, class, and other social categories intersect and shape knowledge production. It allowed the researchers to question the assumptions and biases that are often taken for granted in traditional research methods and to highlight the perspectives and experiences of marginalized groups. By doing so, critical feminism helped to create more nuanced and inclusive research practices that better reflected the diverse experiences and perspectives of the people being studied.

The second contribution is the way this research frames food. The work re-emphasizes the power of food as a lens through which to understand deep, systemic challenges. The power of the kitchens is their recognition that they are not just providing food to individuals as a bundle of nutrients, but that through the challenges of procuring, cooking, and distributing food, and through careful reflection on how recipients engage with the kitchens, the kitchen heads along with co-researchers from FACT gained new insights into the interlinked, systemic challenges of post-apartheid South Africa. Within this research, the food itself and the practice of feeding enabled new ways of seeing the connections across individual and systemic scales, between past and present injustices, and between social, economic, and political struggles. Furthermore, the work of the kitchens revealed the way food provided novel entry points to intervene in systemic challenges. The preparation and distribution of food provided kitchen heads with opportunities to identify particularly vulnerable individuals and households and intervene in ways that respected the dignity of participants. The kitchen network allowed for the sharing of food as a means to not just meet needs of other kitchens, but also to build solidarity. For example, kitchen heads have subsequently held shared training meetings on GBV. This work demonstrated the potential of everyday food practices as a means to understand complex social problems and as a shared background for mobilization.

Finally, the work presented in this chapter seeks to disrupt an outdated binary that has been constructed in African research, which is replicated in African food research. This binary reduces dynamic and diverse African food landscapes and their many ingredients, techniques, and stories that bind historically disconnected locations to a narrative of deficiency, framed by developmentalists' concepts of poverty, hunger, survival, and food insecurity (Critical African Studies, 2022). The work presented here recognizes that culture, politics, and identity are forged in the crucible of poverty, hunger, survival, and food insecurity, and that at the same time these developmental challenges cannot be addressed without addressing culture, politics, and identity.

Acknowledgements

The authors would like to thank all the women who participated in the kitchen research since we started in 2021. We want to thank all partner organizations; namely, FACT, Callas Foundation, Ubuntu Rural, Heinrich Boell Foundation Cape Town, African Centre for Cities at the University of Cape Town, and TMG Research. The Urban Food Future Programme is funded BMZ (Bundesministerium für Wirtschaftliche Zusammenarbeit und Entwicklung). We want to express our gratitude to Carmen Aspinall for editing this chapter and to Inviolata Lusweti for supporting us with background research.

Notes

[1] This acronym, and its many variations, is constantly being updated as awareness evolves. We use the acronym used by African authors at the African Book Festival in Berlin, where selected stories from our research were presented. The acronym stands for Lesbian, Gay, Bisexual, Transgender, Queer, 2 Spirit, Intersex, Asexual, and more.

[2] In South Africa it has been become common to frame social and economic struggles with the hashtag 'mustfall' in the wake of the 2015 #RhodesMustFall as statements of alignment to common movements towards decolonial actions.

[3] Womandla combines the word woman with the isiXhosa word *Amandla*, which means power and is a rallying call for resistance.

[4] Parts of this story were previously published in a blog post: https://tmg-thinktank.com/blog/with-pots-and-pens-to-parliament-understanding-and-responding-to-crises

References

Andrews, D. and Lewis, D. (2017) *Decolonising Food Systems and Sowing Seeds of Resistance*, African Centre for Biodiversity, Cape Town.

Andrews, D., Smith, K. and Morena, M.A. (2019) 'Enraged: women and nature', *Women's Power in Food Struggles*, (11): 10.

Bam, J. and Humphreys, R. (2022) 'Decolonising the representation of indigenous women in the Cape during COVID-19', in J. Bam-Hutchison and B. Muthein (eds) *Rethinking Africa: Indigenous Women Re-interpret Southern Africa's Pasts*, Critical Food Studies Opinion Brief Series, Cape Town, Jacanda, pp 103–20.

Battersby, J., Ben-Zeev, K., Buthelezi, N., Fabricci, I., Fakazi, M.T., Kiragu-Wissler, S., Magazi, Y., Njoroge, P., Nyaba., H., Nyaba, S., Nyambura, M.W., Owade, A., Paganini, N., Peters, C., Peuker, W., Silwana, P., Sango, E. and Weru, J. (2022). What's cooking? Adding critical feminist research to the pot – Community kitchens, school feeding programmes, and savings schemes in Cape Town, Nairobi, and Ouagadougou. TMG Research, 10.13140/RG.2.2.17302.63040

Buthelezi, N., Lemke, S., Karriem, A., Paganini, N., Stöber, S. and Swanby, H. (2020) 'Invisible urban farmers and a next season of hunger – participatory co-research during lockdown in Cape Town, South Africa', 10.13140/RG.2.2.34845.54247/1

Critical African Studies (2022) 'The meanings of food', https://think.taylorandfrancis.com/special_issues/critical-african-studies/?utm_source=TFO&utm_medium=cms&utm_campaign=JPG15743&fbclid=IwAR3Jr28foptz52u53EpY06X3NFQw_tdKw7NbSnPHQuHVEgz-SY0RIEnxbvM [Accessed 31 March 2023].

Davis, S.N. and Hattery, A. (2018) 'Teaching feminist research methods: a comment and an evaluation', *Journal of Feminist Scholarship*, 15(15). https://doi.org/10.23860/jfs.2018.15.05

Gennari, C. and Tornaghi, C. (2020) 'The transformative potential of community kitchens for an agroecological urbanism: preliminary insights and a research agenda', *Proceedings of the 9th International Conference of the AESOP Sustainable Food Planning Group*, p 12.

Groenmeyer, S. (2022) 'Pandemics past and present, valuing the increased and invisible workload of indigenous women', in J. Bam-Hutchison and B. Muthein (eds) *Rethinking Africa: Indigenous Women Re-interpret Southern Africa's Pasts*, Jacanda, pp 129–46.

Hammelman, C., Reynolds, K., and Levkoe, C.Z. (2020) 'Guest editor's introduction. Building a radical food geography praxis', *Human Geography* 13(3): 207–10. https://doig.org/10.1177.1943778620963465

Haraway, D. (1988) 'Situated knowledges: the science question in feminism and the privilege of partial perspective', *Feminist Studies*, 14(3): 575–99. https://doi.org/10.2307/3178066

Hartley, P. (2020) 'Lima's community-organised soup kitchens are a lifeline during COVID-19', *International Institute for Environment and Development*, [online], Available from: www.iied.org/limas-community-organised-soup-kitchens-are-lifeline-during-covid-19 [Accessed 20 May 2023].

hooks, b. (2013) 'Dig deep: beyond lean in', *The Feminist Wire*, [online], Available from: https://thefeministwire.com/2013/10/17973/ [Accessed 20 May 2023].

Immink, M.D.C. (2001) 'People's community kitchens in Peru: women's activism pro urban food security', *Ecology of Food and Nutrition*, 40(6). www.tandfonline.com/doi/abs/10.1080/03670244.2001.9991678

Kiguwa, P. (2019) 'Feminist approaches: an exploration of women's gendered experiences', in S. Laher, A. Fynn, and S. Kramer (eds) *Transforming Research Methods in the Social Sciences: Case Studies from South Africa*, South Africa: Wits University Press. https://doi.org/10.18772/22019032750

Kogan, L. (1998) 'Soup kitchens, women and social policy: studies from Peru', *Development in Practice*, 8(4): 471–8.

Milne, E.J. and Muir, R. (2019) 'Photovoice: a critical introduction', in L. Pauwels and D. Mannay (eds) *The Handbook of Visual Research Methods*, SAGE Publications, pp 282–96.

Paganini, N. and Weigelt, J. (2023) 'Pathways to transform urban food systems. Progressively realising the right to food through a strengthened informal sector in Cape Town and Nairobi', TMG Research Working Paper, http://doi.org/10.13140/RG.2.2.23410.17602/1

Paganini, N., Ben-Zeev, K., Bokolo, K., Buthelezi, N., Nyaba, S., and Swanby, H. (2021a) 'Dialing up critical feminist research as lockdown dialed us down: how a pandemic sparked community food dialogs in Cape Town, South Africa', *Frontiers in Sustainable Food Systems*, 5: 750331. https://doi.org/10.3389/fsufs.2021.750331

Paganini, N., Adams, H., Bokolo, K. Buthelezi, N., Hansmann, J., Isaacs, W. Kweza, N., Mewes, A. Nyaba, H., Qamata, V., Reich, V., Reigl, M., Sander, L., and Swanby, H. (2021b) 'A food justice perspective of food security in the Cape Flats and St. Helena Bay during the COVID-19 pandemic', *SLE Publication Series S285*, https://doi.org/10.18452/22877

Reynolds, K., Block, D., and Bradley, K. (2018) 'Food justice scholar-activism and activist-scholarship: working beyond dichotomies to deepen social justice praxis', *ACME: An International E-Journal for Critical Geographies*, 17(4): 988–98.

Spaull, N.B., Ardington C., Bassier, I., Bhorat, H., Bridgman, G., Brophy, T., Budlender, J., Burher, Ro., Burher, Ru., Carel, D., Casale, D., Christian, C., Daniels, R., Ingle, K., Jain, R., Kerr, A., Köhler, T., Makaluza, N., Maughan-Brown, B., Mpeta, B., Nkonki, L., Nwosu, C.O., Oyenubi, A., Patel, L., Posel, D., Ranchhod, V., Rensburg, R., Rogan, M., Rossouw, L., Skinner, C., Smith, A., van der Berg, S., van Schalkwyk, C., Wills, G., Zizzamia, R., and Zuze, L. (2020) 'Overview and findings: NIDS-CRAM synthesis report wave 1', Available from: https://cramsurvey.org/wp-con-tent/uploads/2020/07/Spaull-et-al.-NIDS-CRAM-Wave-1-Synthesis-Report-Overview-and-Findings-1.pdf

UNODC South Africa (2002) 'UNODC – Press Release—UNIS/NAR/746', United Nations: Office on Drugs and Crime, Available from: www.unodc.org/unodc/en/press/releases/press_release_2002-04-15_1.html

Van der Berg, S., Patel, L., and Brigman, G. (2021) 'Hunger in South Africa during 2020: results from NIDS-CRAM wave 3', Available from: https://cramsurvey.org/wp-content/uploads/2021/02/10.- Van-der-Berg-S.-Patel-L.-Bridgman-G.-2021-Hunger-in-South-Africa-during-2020-Resultsfrom-Wave-3-of-NIDS-CRAM-1.pdf [Accessed 8 April 2021].

4

Radical Food Intersections: Pandemic Shocks, Gentrification Mutation, Essential Labour, and the Evolution of Struggle

Joshua Sbicca and Alison Hope Alkon

When COVID-19 shut down most aspects of public life, the American public soon realized that many institutions society relies on for basic survival were vulnerable. Already structured in ways that harm marginalized groups, systems of food provisioning and shelter were sent into further shock. Food chain workers were deemed 'essential' and had to prepare, serve, sell, and deliver food to the masses of people needing to eat, often at great risk to their own health and safety. Non-essential workers and the newly unemployed were forced to stay home regardless of whether their living quarters were safe, and crowded living and working conditions meant increased potential exposure to the virus. Long, socially distanced modern-day breadlines became iconic images, symbolizing both dire hunger and inadequate state responses. All these conditions operated through pre-existing forms of racial capitalism, meaning the ways that economic development and underdevelopment are inherently racialized (Robinson, 2000). Black, Indigenous, and other people of colour disproportionately faced heightened risk as essential workers, experienced greater hunger, lived in more crowded conditions, and were again threatened by displacement. In sum, the prior vulnerability to premature death (Gilmore, 2007) was only amplified by the virus' spread.

However, not everyone had the same experience. Workers with greater occupational flexibility and without care responsibilities could work virtually from home, and images of homemade meals and sourdough bread were even more common on social media than they had been previously. Elite workers could also relocate to more desirable places outside the initial urban surge of COVID cases and benefit from the amenities and safety of smaller, more idyllic towns, often buying property at record-low mortgage rates. All the while the stock market reached astronomical heights and the portfolios of the well-to-do expanded. White and wealthy individuals and communities certainly benefited from this real estate and broader economic boom. But individual household gains pale when compared with the financialized interests, including hedge funds, pension funds, and tech companies, who were the period's greatest economic beneficiaries. During the COVID-19 pandemic, these institutions accelerated their real-estate investments, creating extraordinary wealth alongside crises of housing affordability and homelessness (Badger and Bui, 2022). Profits accumulated not only at the scale of the individual household or even neighbourhood, but became more concentrated within transnational corporations, in turn affecting people across the globe. It was at this scale that the life chances of poor communities, Indigenous communities, and communities of colour, including their ability to access adequate food and shelter, were structured.

This chapter uses a radical food geographies (RFG) praxis framework to examine the links between food, labour, and housing before and in the wake of the COVID-19 pandemic (see Levkoe et al, Chapter 1). We first reflect on previous approaches that use food as a lens to understand racialized and classed processes of gentrification and displacement. We use this discussion to suggest that new shocks, like a pandemic, reveal the pressing need to trace how ongoing systems of oppression mutate, producing new and altered intersections for radical food interventions. The multiscalar nature of the connections between housing and food requires both a structural account of how these basic needs are constituted through different systems of oppression and the place-based and lived conditions marginalized people encounter. Attention to these patterns and particularities reveals the interstitial spaces where individuals, communities, social movements, and institutions undertake diverse actions to reimagine and reconstitute our relationships to food, labour, and housing.

In this context, we argue that the mutual aid we witnessed during the pandemic, and the organizing work that has occurred since, may offer opportunities to remake the social fabric, including basic food and housing needs and support for essential workers, in radical ways that push back against the logic of racial capitalism. In this case, RFG requires emphasizing the paramount importance of land and the ways that the financialization of real estate brings ongoing threats of enclosure and expulsion, and the effects of these processes on access to adequate food, dignified work, and safe shelter. Our contribution therefore pushes for a form of scholar-activism committed to understanding the many systems that intersect with food systems – in this case, financial and housing systems as well as shifting labour dynamics – and pursuing grassroots alliances that foreground and expand the multiple ways we meet our basic needs. In concluding our chapter, we turn to the valiant, if temporary, successes won by various social movements during the pandemic, and offer a set of principles through which social movements can shift in this direction.

Food and gentrification before the pandemic

In the past three decades, city officials, planners, and non-profit organizations around the world have turned to green urban planning to improve healthy living conditions and limit resource consumption in the face of climate change (Garcia-Lamarca et al, 2021; Angelo, 2021). The non-profit Global Green (n.d.) describes the promise of green urbanism as a 'conversation between Rachel Carson and Jane Jacobs, [where cities are] planned, designed, and governed to increase natural capital, resilience, social equity, and human connection to nature'. Green urbanism can include urban parks, the restoration of rivers and waterfronts, improved public transit, and walk and bike-ability improvements. It also incorporates local food systems, health food stores, promoting farm-to-table restaurants, farmers markets, and community gardens (Anguelovski, 2015; Alkon et al, 2020).

Initially, urban greening initiatives were placed largely in affluent, white parts of cities while working-class, historically redlined communities of colour are zoned for industrial and other toxic land uses (Agyeman et al, 2003; Agyeman, 2005). But more recently, proponents of green urbanism have recognized a rent gap between current and potential future returns (Smith, 2010) and targeted marginalized neighbourhoods for development. This creates what is called green or eco-gentrification, increasing property values and displacing long-term residents (Dooling, 2009; Checker, 2011; Gould and Lewis, 2016). Thus, far from a post-political, unquestioned good, urban greening aids in land dispossession, gentrification, displacement, and widening inequalities (Safransky, 2014; Garcia-Lamarca et al, 2021).

Given the overwhelming interest in local and organic food over the same time period, it is no surprise that urban food systems have played an important role in green urbanism (Alkon and Cadji, 2020). The early 2000s saw explosive growth in farmers markets, community gardens, and urban farms. In many cases, young, white countercultural types were drawn to long-divested neighbourhoods for available land, a vibrant community of like-minded folks, and an excitement to share their passions for sustainable agriculture with communities that had been excluded from the food movement (Guthman, 2008; Alkon, 2012). Many succeeded in garnering support from cities by way of funding and access to public lands, enrolling the state in the project of food justice. Simultaneously, long-term community members, many of whom had been gardening in these cities for decades, began to position local food movements as a means to address the racial, economic, and health disparities that had devastated their neighbourhoods, and to build vibrant, alternative ways of being and seeing (Reese, 2019; Myers, 2022). But despite their shared devotion to local food, relationships between newer and long-term residents were often rocky due to uneven access to foundation resources and city support, which structured interpersonal and organizational relationships (Kato, 2013; Reynolds and Cohen, 2016; Kolavalli, 2023). Indeed, many of the initial activists who began such projects, got paid for their work, and called on cities to fund them were early wave gentrifiers (McClintock, 2018).

A wealth of scholarship criticizes US food movements as inadequate to achieve broad, transformative goals (Harrison, 2011; Minkoff-Zern, 2014; Lo and Koenig, 2017; Sbicca, 2018; Sbicca and Reese, 2022). The largely unacknowledged racial and class privilege held by the movement's most prominent activists and organizations prevents them from seeing that individual, market-based alternatives cannot possibly address the harms wrought by racial capitalism on historically marginalized communities (see Alkon and Guthman, 2017 for a summary). When looked at through the lens of green urbanism, it becomes clear that food movements and spaces can also *actively* do harm, reproducing food, housing, and labour inequalities. Our co-edited volume *A Recipe for Gentrification* demonstrated how upscale food spaces became a means for neighbourhood boosters to brand potentially gentrifying areas as hip, creative, and ripe for investment, a development strategy that led to the dispossession and displacement of long-rooted communities (Alkon et al, 2020; see also Ramírez, 2015; Reese, 2019; Joassart-Marcelli, 2021; Kolavalli, 2023; Huynh, Chapter 8). Developers and boosters imbued food spaces with cultural capital that translated into economic capital in the form of rising land values, drawing in new, largely white investors and residents and changing the occupational opportunity and demographic make-up of a neighbourhood.

Food and gentrification today

Today, food remains a lure for many cities' 'hottest' neighbourhoods. But land values are rising in places that have experienced food-focused gentrification, and in those that have not. Homeowners have amassed more than $6 trillion in wealth between 2020 and 2022, an astounding sum that omits the equity garnered through rental properties (Badger and Bui, 2022). According to the National Real Estate Association, in 2018, the median sales price of a single US family home rose in 99 per cent of the 183 markets it measures (Hyman, 2022). The median growth rate was 16 per cent, which equated to a $50,300 increase in home equity. US metropolitan areas with the highest rates of growth included cities commonly thought of as gentrifying, such as Austin

(33.5 per cent growth), Phoenix (25.8 per cent), and Boise (31.5 per cent), which has been growing so rapidly that National Public Radio called it 'the next Portland'. But cities like Naples and Ocala in Florida, largely unfamiliar to gentrification scholars, were also on the list of markets with the highest increases in home values. Even historically working-class cities have seen significant gains. Cleveland increased 23.7 per cent in 2022, and nearly 115 per cent from 2017 to 2022. Buffalo increased 12.4 per cent in 2022. Flint Michigan increased 29.2 per cent (Hyman, 2022). Real-estate blogs such as Movoto continue to emphasize food in these locations, but a description of Flint's Coney Dogs and barbeque scene makes a different cultural statement than the food-oriented eco-gentrification we observed previously (Sartorelli, 2014). And as property values rise in nearly all residential areas, working-class long-term residents who once read changing foodscapes as a signifier of coming rent increases have fewer affordable places to go.

Ethnoracial disparities continue to characterize the housing market. Black homeownership rates have changed little since the 1960s and Black homes are valued less on average than white homes (Perry, 2021). During the pandemic, communities of colour, who were disproportionately burdened by the disease, had higher rates of missed mortgage payments and were less likely to take advantage of low interest rates to refinance (Gerardi et al, 2021). While forbearance programmes greatly helped lower-income borrowers and borrowers of colour, once these ended, these groups were more likely to fall into delinquency and default compared with their wealthier and white peers (An et al, 2022). This pushes them into a rental market in which average rents across the US have increased 8.85 per cent *per year* since 1980 (iPropertyManagement, 2022), far outpacing growth in wages, which have been nearly stagnant for the bottom 90 per cent of workers (Schmidt et al, 2018). The cost of rental housing is the most significant factor in creating homelessness, with far more explanatory power than drug abuse, mental illness, or even poverty (Aldern and Colburn, 2022). Increasing rent also amplifies food insecurity, as households delay food purchases to prioritize rent (Ashbrook, 2023). Taken together, this means that Black, Indigenous, and Latinx workers are more likely to be severely rent burdened, food insecure, displaced by gentrification, and, in the worst cases, to experience homelessness (Kirkland, 2008; Hwang and Ding, 2020; US Department of Housing and Urban Development, 2022). Indeed, many unsheltered homeless individuals remain in the city, or even the neighbourhood, where they were formerly housed (Coalition for the Homeless, n.d.; Fagan, 2020). This is true in neighbourhoods with foodscape changes that contribute to gentrification, and in those without.

Economists point to low housing supply as the primary cause of escalating housing prices, augmented by many buyers' desires for more space during the pandemic. But there is significant evidence that corporations and other financial institutions such as hedge funds are buying up large amounts of housing, especially in lower-income neighbourhoods, and that this demand for profits rather than homes may be giving the market an additional lift (Goodman et al, 2023). Most notably, the real-estate listing company Zillow bought approximately 7,000 homes, chosen by algorithm, before closing their iBuying division and flipping the homes to other institutional investors such as BlackRock (Ballentine and Wells, 2021). In a prescient report, UN Special Rapporteur Lelia Farha (2017) refers to this as the financialization of housing. *The Washington Post* reported that investors bought nearly one in seven homes in American Metropolitan Areas in 2021, purchases that were disproportionately in Black neighbourhoods in the South and Rust Belt (Schaul and O'Connell, 2022).

Dispossession is clearly happening, and displacement is an ever-more-likely outcome (Hwang and Ding, 2020). But these rapid housing price gains push us to question whether gentrification is currently driving the housing market in the same way it once was, with or without its connection to food. The vibrant effects on the development of city spaces and urban life that are so linked to gentrification in the popular imagination may be wholly absent or amplified by this financialization of housing. Will food businesses have any incentive to follow these new buyers if the buyers themselves are not inhabiting their new purchases? How will the rising exchange value of urban land affect its use value? And who can and cannot use it?

We argue here that waning use of food as an urban development strategy may offer opportunities for activists to relink food and housing in radical ways that foreground basic needs, lived experiences, and labour. The pandemic has seen growing attention to the ways that communities must and do take care of basic needs, especially in relation to public health. Next, we turn to some of the successes movements achieved during the pandemic and speculate on how these successes might animate a broad and ongoing movement to ensure an inclusive right to the city.

Radical possibilities going forward

The pandemic made visible the essential relationships between food, housing, labour, and health. In doing so, it laid bare the structural inequalities in our food, labour, and housing systems. Once it became clear that without sustenance and shelter the human impact from the pandemic would be devastating, people organized and intervened at many scales, however imperfect and impermanent. As activist-scholars who have been working with and writing about food justice movements for nearly two decades, we want to use our institutional privilege to reflect on various strategies. Here, we consider place-based mutual aid and institutionally targeted political organizing. Based on this discussion we then ask what new kinds of RFG futures can be imagined because the pandemic occurred, focusing on a set of principles for praxis.

Place-based mutual aid

Almost immediately, mutual aid networks emerged to address basic needs in their communities. This 'resurgence of reciprocity' (Springer, 2020: 112) sprouted from many pre-existing social movement spaces. Anarchist free schools, the legacy of the Black Panther Party's Free Breakfast for Schoolchildren Program, Food Not Bombs chapters, social justice-inspired religious communities, Black Lives Matter networks, and more went to work to meet neighbours' needs. In Colorado, a group of librarians assembled meal kits for the elderly and children. In the months before personal protective equipment was widely available, San Francisco's Auntie Sewing Squad made hand-sewn masks for essential workers and Indigenous communities across the country. And in New York City, the Service Workers Coalition raised money for weekly stipends to distribute to newly unemployed restaurant workers (Tolentino, 2020). In a public conference call co-hosted with prison abolitionist Mariame Kaba, Representative Alexandria Ocasio-Cortez described these efforts as a way to "build a different world, even if it's just on our building floor, even if it's just in our neighborhood, even if it's just on our block" (Tolentino, 2020). The multiscalar understanding that underlies this vision – that worlds can be made and remade on the block – is noteworthy here.

Central to mutual aid work was a renewed discursive and material focus on an ethic of care. Much of the work that mutual aid groups do is care work, arranging childcare, checking on the elderly, raising money for rental assistance, and providing food. This was one thread through which care became essential during the pandemic. Moreover, participating in mutual aid networks created new bonds of care across social differences. Describing the affective power of mutual aid, Reese and Johnson (2022: 32) write that 'by being active participants in alternative economies, feelings of mutuality and solidarity can emerge and evolve through practice into a deeper sense of collective responsibility to land and to each other'. In doing so, they tie this work to bell hooks' (2001: 164) writings on mutuality and love, which she describes as capable of generating 'the experience of knowing we always belong'.

And yet, to realize the radical possibilities inherent in mutual aid, including the valorization of care work, we must be mindful of the ways that this work is both labour and feminized. Throughout the pandemic, women were disproportionately likely to care for children and elders, often while navigating or sacrificing their own careers (Power, 2020). Academic and popular writers empathized with women's new, sometimes seemingly impossible (though certainly class-differentiated) burdens (Matthewman and Huppatz, 2020; Grose, 2021; Mannon, 2020). Mutual aid work may add to this. While it has not been studied systematically, one researcher found that 80 per cent of those working as part of a Polish mutual aid network called Visible Hand were women (Łapniewska, 2022), and our own anecdotal observations confirm that mutual aid work in the US is also feminized. Mutual aid and its attendant ethic of care can help us to value care work, but we should still ask whether and how this can be done in a way that values – and valorizes – women's unpaid labour.

The radical possibility of mutual aid networks during the pandemic rested in their ability to ensure people were first immediately fed and housed, and then to link the reason that mutual aid became necessary to the inherent violence of the state and exploitations of racial capitalism (Spade, 2020). In Kaba's words, these networks worked "to address real material needs [in order to] build the relationships that are needed to push back on the state" (cited in Tolentino, 2020). Mutual aid networks joined with other political networks to advocate for government financial support, increases in food aid, and eviction and mortgage moratoriums, among other policies that had seemed unfathomable in less dire times. Moving forward, the radicalizing work of mutual aid networks will rest mainly in their contributions to broader demands for institutional change. It is only through these demands that we can avoid the depoliticization and non-profitization of mutual aid (Tolentino, 2020; Reese and Johnson, 2022), and radically restructure systems of food, labour, and housing to foreground the needs, abilities, and visions of those most harmed by the current arrangement.

Institutionally targeted political organizing

In ways not seen for decades, COVID-19 amplified and re-energized the struggles of workers who had already made significant though piecemeal gains in their fights for safer workplaces and better pay and benefits. The food sector has been particularly prominent on this front given its designation as an 'essential' form of work and its leadership in recent struggles for increased wages in the 21st century (Lo and Koenig, 2017). Food chain workers have long been poorly treated and held little power. But in the years since the lockdowns they have continued to organize. From Starbucks and Nabisco, McDonalds and Wendys, to Kroger and King Soopers, workers are striking, and in many cases winning better workplace conditions, respect, and remuneration. In the context of RFG, it is important to acknowledge that these are not only labour movements but also food movements, and that labour represents an essential and growing political front for RFG praxis.

Moreover, these victories come in the context of escalating food and housing prices, and are grounded in the knowledge that increased wages and improved working conditions can, most essentially, help workers meet the immediate demands of shelter and sustenance. Moreover, like mutual aid, unionization struggles push individual workers to see their conditions as tied to broader structural inequalities. Organizing demonstrates both the essential conflict between worker well-being and capitalist profit, as well as the power of collective action to meaningfully improve lives. Such an analysis has the potential to enrol striking workers beyond their individual campaigns into broader, more transformative struggles to leverage the power of the state against capital.

Homes, workplaces, and neighbourhoods became frontline sites for mutual aid, care work, and restructuring labour. So did policy spaces. The pandemic showed how the US government was largely unprepared to deal with the public health crisis on its hands, and it was only after it began to respond to actions of individuals and communities at smaller scales that the most pressing food and housing needs were addressed. Although only temporarily, Unemployment Insurance, Economic Impact Payments, and increases to Supplemental Nutrition Assistance Program benefits and the Child Tax Credit eased poverty and hunger levels. Eviction moratoriums and rental assistance kept more people in their homes longer than they would have otherwise. During the pandemic, the government provided a thicker social safety net in a way that had not been seen since the advent of the New Deal. But clearly, it could have done more. Demand at food banks remained escalated, stimulus payments were meagre compared with other industrialized countries, and unemployment and housing assistance waned while the effects of the pandemic persisted. Ethnoracial inequalities remain and government aid was insufficient to address the ways they were exacerbated by the pandemic. Clearly the state must be pushed to do more if lasting change is to become a reality. In one promising example, Democrats recently introduced Senate and House bills that would prevent hedge fund ownership of single-family homes, though this is unlikely to pass in a divided congress (Kaysen, 2023).

Social movements are one of the few forces capable of substantially shifting culture and institutions. Much like the labour movement helped to shift our understanding of class and essential work, the Movement for Black Lives upended many Americans' views on race and racism, policing, and the carceral state. Large widespread demonstrations and organizing pushed many institutions – including food and housing movement organizations – to more clearly address racial disparities, an essential ingredient to ensuring a right to the city for all. But social movements are not just reserved for the left. White supremacist, far-right nationalist, and anti-abortion movements have successfully made inroads into the state in the form of the Trump presidency and overturn of *Roe v. Wade*, the Supreme Court precedent protecting access to abortion. This too was amplified by the pandemic. There is a struggle to leverage the state for various ends, and the potential for advancing food and housing justice rests on the ability to mobilize at broader scales.

Principles for praxis

RFG requires both theoretical engagement with systems of power and action through academic, social movement, and civil society collaborations (Introduction to this volume). Without being overly prescriptive, we argue that the previous analysis should give rise to a praxis that embodies several basic principles. First, operate with grounded processes that centre the experiences and needs of those most impacted by food, labour, and housing inequities (Reese, 2019). This is especially important for groups that have traditionally worked in more privileged communities, or even those with mixed memberships, constituencies, or staff (Sbicca, 2018; Alkon and Cadji, 2020). Second, identify internal and external resources, both those in possession and those needed, to carry on a protracted struggle at various scales (Myers, 2022). Next, decide who are the people or political processes capable of making key decisions that would restructure some aspect of the food, labour, and housing systems. Perhaps working with a broader coalition, choose an appropriate target to change, leverage, or gain concessions (Harrison, 2011; Lo and Koenig, 2017). This might be a local, state, or national policy maker, a corporation, or an institution such as a local school system (Reynolds and Cohen, 2016).

In the course of taking action on these principles for praxis it is important to stay politically educated, individually, with allies, and community members, about the connections between food, labour, and housing and why structural solutions are necessary. Without a consistent and vigilant eye towards transformation, it may become easy to slip back into merely providing alternatives or services. Communicating this radical analysis, and ensuring that movement practices can comprise a theoretically informed praxis, can help build and maintain strong relationships with community members, through, for example, events, teach-ins or door-to-door campaigns, and/or inspire the creative use of social media, memes, wit, and humour to reach broader publics.

Taken together, these principles for praxis can inform the kind of place-based mutual aid and institutionally targeted political organizing capable of linking up with broader movement-building efforts. These principles moreover encourage a bold rethinking and reworking of how to recruit and retain a diverse and confrontational political bloc that is capable of enacting long-term change. The path is bound to be messy, and new conditions will inevitably require making adjustments, but if the COVID-19 pandemic has taught us anything it is that institutional transformations are both possible and necessary to ensure a society where everyone's needs are met.

In sum, COVID-19 exposed, amplified, and shifted the intersecting inequities in food systems, labour, and housing, which as a result set in motion new intersectional social movement dynamics rooted in the daily basic need for shelter and sustenance. Herein lie myriad potentials to enliven RFG, from mutual aid to community organizing and mass protest to policy work. At each scale, food and social justice movements are speaking back to each other in complex ways to offer analyses of racial capitalism and its deleterious effects on everyday lives, as well as radical visions of a society transformed to not only meet basic needs but also inspire new dreams and to value the care and labour necessary to flourish.

References

Agyeman, J. (2005) *Sustainable Communities and the Challenge of Environmental Justice*, New York: New York University Press.

Agyeman, J., Bullard, R.D., and Evans, B. (eds) (2003) *Just Sustainabilities: Development in an Unequal World*, Cambridge: MIT Press.

Aldern, C.P. and Colburn, G. (2022) *Homelessness Is a Housing Problem*, Berkeley, CA: University of California Press.

Alkon, A.H. (2012) *Black, White, and Green: Farmers Markets, Race, and the Green Economy*, Athens, GA: University of Georgia Press.

Alkon, A.H. and Guthman, J. (eds) (2017) *The New Food Activism: Opposition, Cooperation, and Collective Action*, Berkeley, CA: University of California Press.

Alkon, A.H. and Cadji, J. (2020) 'Sowing seeds of displacement: food justice and gentrification in Oakland, CA', *International Journal of Urban and Regional Research*, 44(1): 108–23.

Alkon, A.H, Kato, Y., and Sbicca, J. (eds) (2020) *A Recipe for Gentrification: Food, Power, and Resistance in the City*, New York: New York University Press.

An, X., Cordell, L. Geng, L., and Lee, K. (2022) 'Inequality in the time of COVID-19: evidence from mortgage delinquency and forbearance', Working Papers Research Department: Federal Reserve Bank of Philadelphia.

Angelo, H. (2021) *How Green Became Good: Urbanized Nature and the Making of Cities and Citizens*, Chicago, IL: University of Chicago Press.

Anguelovski, I. (2015) 'Healthy food stores, greenlining and food gentrification: contesting new forms of privilege, displacement and locally unwanted land uses in racially mixed neighborhoods', *International Journal of Urban and Regional Research,* 39(6): 1209–30.

Ashbrook, A. (2023) 'Food Insecurity and Housing Instability are Inextricably Linked', *Food Research and Action Center*, [online], Available from: https://frac.org/blog/food-insecurity-and-housing-instability-are-inextricably-linked#_ednref2 [Accessed 12 June 2023].

Badger, E. and Bui, Q. (2022) 'The Extraordinary Wealth Created by the Pandemic Housing Market', *New York Times*, [online], Available from: www.nytimes.com/2022/05/01/upshot/pandemic-housing-market-wealth.html [Accessed 12 June 2023].

Ballentine, C. and Wells, C. (2021) '"Don't Buy Zillow Homes": A Tale of Failure, Mistrust and Hot Housing Markets', *Bloomberg*, [online], Available from: www.bloomberg.com/news/articles/2021-11-03/why-is-zillow-sell ing-7000-homes-tale-of-failure-mistrust-hot-housing-market [Accessed 12 June 2023].

Checker, M. (2011) 'Wiped out by the 'greenwave': environmental gentrification and the paradoxical politics of urban sustainability', *City & Society*, 23(2): 210–29.

Coalition for the Homeless (n.d.) 'Myths and Facts', [online], Available from: www.coalitionforthehomeless.org/myths-and-facts [Accessed 12 June 2023].

Dooling, S. (2009) 'Ecological gentrification: research agenda exploring justice in the city', *International Journal of Urban and Regional Research*, 33(3): 621–39.

Fagan, K. (2020) 'The real pandemic is homelessness': those on Bay Area's streets share stories of fear, hope and survival', *SF Chronicle*, [online], Available from: www.sfchronicle.com/bayarea/article/Pure-survival-mode-15364213.php [Accessed 12 June 2023].

Farha, L. (2017) *Report of the Special Rapporteur on adequate housing as a component of the right to an adequate standard of living, and on the right to non-discrimination in this context*, United Nations.

Garcia-Lamarca, M., Anguelovski, I., Cole, H., Connolly, J., Argüelles, L., Baró, F., Loveless, S., Perez del Pulgar Frowein, C., and Shokry, G. (2021) 'Urban green boosterism and city affordability: for whom is the "branded" green city?', *Urban Studies*, 58(1): 90–112.

Gerardi, K., Lambie-Hanson, L., and Willen, P. (2021) 'Racial differences in mortgage refinancing, distress, and housing wealth accumulation during COVID-19', *Federal Reserve Bank of Boston*.

Gilmore, R.W. (2007) *Golden Gulag: Prisons, Surplus, Crisis, and Opposition in Globalizing California*, Berkeley, CA: University of California Press.

Global Green (n.d.) www.globalgreen.org

Goodman, L, A Zinn, K Reynolds and O Noble. 2023. A Profile of Institutional Investor-Owned Single-Family Rental Properties. *Urban Institute*. Available from https://www.urban.org/sites/default/files/2023-08/A%20Profile%20of%20Institutional%20Investor%E2%80%93Ow ned%20Single-Family%20Rental%20Properties.pdf [Accessed 12 June 2023].

Gould, K.A. and Lewis, T.L. (2016) *Green Gentrification: Urban Sustainability and the Struggle for Environmental Justice*, New York: Routledge.

Grose, J. (2021) 'The Primal Scream: America's Mothers are in Crisis. Is Anybody Listening to Them?', *New York Times*, [online], Available from: www.nytimes.com/2021/02/04/parenting/working-moms-men tal-health-coronavirus.html

Guthman, J. (2008) 'Bringing good food to others: investigating the subjects of alternative food practice', *Cultural Geographies*, 15(4): 431–47.

Harrison, J.L. (2011) *Pesticide Drift and the Pursuit of Environmental Justice*, Cambridge, MA: MIT Press.

hooks, b. (2001) *All About Love: New Visions*, New York: Perennial.

Hwang, J. and Ding, L. (2020) 'Unequal displacement: gentrification, racial stratification, and residential destinations in Philadelphia', *American Journal of Sociology*, 126(2): 354–406.

Hyman, M. (2022) 'Single-Family Home Prices Show Double-Digit Increase in 70% of 185 Metro Areas in 2022 Q1', *National Association of Realtors*, [online], Available from: www.nar.realtor/blogs/economists-outlook/single-family-home-prices-show-double-digit-increase-in-70-of-185-metro-areas-in-2022-q1 [Accessed 12 June 2023].

iProperty Management (2022) 'Average Rent by Year', *iProperty Management*, [online], Available from: https://ipropertymanagement.com/research/average-rent-by-year#:~:text=As%20of%202020%2C%20monthly%20rent,an%20annual%20rate%20of%204.17%25 [Accessed 12 June 2023].

Joassart-Marcelli, P. (2021) *The $16 Taco: Contested Geographies of Food, Ethnicity, and Gentrification*, Seattle, WA: University of Washington Press.

Kato, Y. (2013) 'Not just the price of food: challenges of an urban agriculture organization in engaging local residents', *Sociological Inquiry*, 83(3): 369–91.

Kaysen, R. (2023) 'New Legislation Proposes to Take Wall Street Out of the Housing Market', *NY Times*, [online], Available from: www.nytimes.com/2023/12/06/realestate/wall-street-housing-market.html [Accessed 12 June 2023].

Kirkland, E. (2008) 'What's race got to do with it? Looking for the racial dimensions of gentrification', *Western Journal of Black Studies*, 32(2): 18–30.

Kolavalli, C. (2023) *Well-Intentioned Whiteness: Green Urban Development and Black Resistance in Kansas City*, Athens, GA: University of Georgia Press.

Mannon, S.E. (2020) 'The new normal? Work, family, and higher education under COVID-19', *Journal of the Motherhood Initiative for Research and Community Involvement*, 12(1): 229–46.

McClintock, N. (2018) 'Cultivating (a) sustainability capital: urban agriculture, ecogentrification, and the uneven valorization of social reproduction', *Annals of the American Association of Geographers*, 108(2): 579–90.

Łapniewska, Z. (2022) 'Solidarity and mutual aid: women organizing the "visible hand" urban commons', *Gender, Work & Organization*, 29(5): 1405–27.

Lo, J. and Koenig, B. (2017) 'Food workers and consumers organizing together for food justice', in A.H. Alkon and J. Guthman (eds) *The New Food Activism: Opposition, Cooperation, and Collective Action*, Berkeley, CA: University of California Press, pp 133–56.

Matthewman, S. and Huppatz, K. (2020) 'A sociology of Covid-19', *Journal of Sociology*, 56(4): 675–83.

Minkoff-Zern, L.A. (2014) 'Challenging the agrarian imaginary: farmworker-led food movements and the potential for farm labor justice', *Human Geography*, 7(1): 85–101.

Myers, J.S. (2022) *Growing Gardens, Building Power: Food Justice and Urban Agriculture in Brooklyn*, New Brunswick: Rutgers University Press.

Perry, A.M. (2021) 'How racial disparities in home prices reveal widespread discrimination', *Brookings Institute*, [online], Available from: www.brookings.edu/testimonies/how-racial-disparities-in-home-prices-reveal-widespread-discrimination/ [Accessed 12 June 2023].

Power, K. (2020) 'The COVID-19 pandemic has increased the care burden of women and families', *Sustainability: Science, Practice and Policy*, 16(1): 67–73.

Ramírez, M.M. (2015) 'The elusive inclusive: Black food geographies and racialized food spaces', *Antipode*, 47(3): 748–69.

Reese, A.M. (2019) *Black Food Geographies: Race, Self-Reliance, and Food Access in Washington, DC*, Chapel Hill, NC: University of North Carolina Press.

Reese, A.M. and Johnson, S.A. (2022) 'We all we got: urban Black ecologies of care and mutual aid', *Environment and Society*, 13: 27–42.

Reese, A.M. and Sbicca, J. (2022) 'Food and carcerality: from confinement to abolition', *Food and Foodways*, 30(1–2): 1–15.

Robinson, C. (2000) *Black Marxism: The Making of the Black Radical Tradition*. Chapel Hill, NC: University of North Carolina Press

Reynolds, K. and Cohen, N. (2016) *Beyond the Kale: Urban Agriculture and Social Justice Activism in New York City*, Athens, GA: University of Georgia Press.

Safransky, S. (2014) 'Greening the urban frontier: race, property, and resettlement in Detroit', *Geoforum*, 56(3): 237–48.

Sartorelli, K. (2014) '29 things you need to know about Flint before you move there', *Movoto*, [online], Available from: www.movoto.com/guide/flint-mi/moving-to-flint/ [Accessed 12 April 2023].

Sbicca, J. (2018) *Food Justice Now!: Deepening the Roots of Social Struggle*, Minneapolis, MN: University of Minnesota Press.

Schaul, K. and O'Connell, J. (2022) 'Investors bought a record share of homes in 2021', *Washington Post*, [online], Available from: www.washingtonpost.com/business/interactive/2022/housing-market-investors [Accessed 12 June 2023].

Schmitt, J., Gould, E., and Bivens, J. (2018) 'America's slow-motion wage crisis: four decades of slow and unequal growth', *Economic Policy Institute*, [online], Available from: www.epi.org/publication/americas-slow-motion-wage-crisis-four-decades-of-slow-and-unequal-growth-2/ [Accessed 12 June 2023].

Smith, N. (2010) *Uneven Development: Nature, Capital, and the Production of Space* (3rd edn), Athens, GA: University of Georgia Press.

Spade, D. (2020) *Mutual Aid: Building Solidarity During This Crisis (and the Next)*, New York: Verso Books.

Springer, S. (2020) 'Caring geographies: the COVID-19 interregnum and a return to mutual aid', *Dialogues in Human Geography*, 10(2): 112–15.

Tolentino, J. (2020) 'What Mutual Aid Can Do During a Pandemic', *The New Yorker*, [online], Available from: www.newyorker.com/magazine/2020/05/18/what-mutual-aid-can-do-during-a-pandemic [Accessed 12 June 2023].

US Census (2021) *Rental Housing Finance Survey*, [online], Available from: www.census.gov/programs-surveys/rhfs.html [Accessed 12 June 2023].

US Department of Housing and Urban Development (2022) 'The 2021 Annual Homeless Assessment Report (AHAR) to Congress', Washington, D.C.

5

Racialized Migrant Labour in Organic Agriculture in Canada: Blind Spots and Barriers to Justice

Susanna Klassen

Organic agriculture represents a long-standing social movement to create an alternative to ecologically and socially exploitative farming. When it emerged in the 1940s, organic principles were focused on soil health and nutrient recycling (Heckman, 2006). However, as the movement gained momentum in the 60s and 70s, anti-corporate sentiment and human health concerns began to take a more prominent role (Obach, 2015).

Today, it is clear that not all organic certified agriculture offers a viable alternative to the dominant industrialized food system. While many actors in the organic sector still work to maintain its values-based commitments, growth, market mainstreaming, and corporate cooptation in the sector has undoubtedly complicated the picture (Jaffee and Howard, 2010). Incisive critiques from scholars – including from radical geography and critical food studies – have shown that as organic agriculture entered state regulatory regimes and carved out its own markets, the interests of profit and capital accumulation have, in many cases, eroded its ethical foundations (Sutherland, 2013; Guthman, 2014). Critiques of regenerative and organic agriculture have also drawn attention to its foundations in Indigenous agricultural practices and knowledge, often without acknowledgement (Heim, 2020). Moreover, there is a growing body of scholarship that demonstrates that organic farms do not necessarily offer better working conditions than their non-organic counterparts, as low incomes, musculoskeletal injuries, un(der)paid internships, and otherwise poor-quality jobs are all inequities that persist on organic farms (Harrison and Getz, 2015; Weiler, Otero and Wittman, 2016; Soper, 2019).

Yet, adherents to international principles of 'health', 'ecology', 'fairness', and 'care' – articulated and promoted by the International Federation of Organic Agriculture Movements (IFOAM) – continue to reject the view that organic agriculture is beyond saving (IFOAM, 2020a). In particular, the principle of fairness has become the focus of increasing discussions within the sector (Kröger and Schäfer, 2014), in part because it has no commensurate requirements in regulated organic standards (Klassen et al, 2023). In other words, despite the organic movement's explicit focus on fairness, it has yet to address the unjust nature of labour in an official way.

This chapter builds on previous research conducted by myself and collaborators about the organic movement's efforts to integrate fairness into organic agriculture in Canada (Klassen, Fuerza Migrante, and Wittman, 2022). Both the IFOAM and the Canadian organic standards define fairness as being 'characterized by equity, respect, justice and stewardship of the shared world, both among people and in their relations to other living beings', and specifies that 'those involved in organic agriculture should conduct human relationships in a manner that ensures fairness at all levels and to all parties', inclusive of workers (IFOAM, 2020b). That research (Klassen, Fuerza Migrante, and Wittman, 2022) set out to examine the strategies to advance fairness being proposed by organic movement[1] actors alongside the demands and approaches espoused by migrant justice groups in Canada.

The previous research project also sought to disrupt the typical inequitable relationship between academics and activists in practice through collaboration and co-authorship with a migrant worker collective – Fuerza Migrante. Instead of duplicating extractive research relationships where activists are treated as anonymous subjects, and whose work is extracted and decontextualized to be treated as 'data', we sought to share power, resources, and voice with Fuerza Migrante, and to use this project as an opportunity to further their work. From that research, we found that the organic movement's efforts showed promise to counteract the erasure of racialized migrant workers' experiences in organic farming, but that their efforts were limited by their focus on national standards, limited engagement with structural racism, and a lack of concrete action to improve worker representation in governance of the sector.

Here, I build on insights from this previous work by bringing together quantitative insights on migrant labour in organic agriculture in Canada, and analysis of qualitative data using the theoretical tool of racial capitalism. This chapter responds to queries from community partners seeking to better understand the extent of migrant labour on organic farms,[2] and asks the following questions: What are the patterns of employment of migrant workers on organic farms? And, how does racial capitalism inform our understanding of efforts to address unjust migrant labour in organic agriculture? I aim to embody a radical food geographies (RFG) praxis, which is characterized by a focus on structural power imbalances, an emphasis on space and place in food work, and actual engagement with food systems problems through reflexive praxis (Hammelman, Reynolds, and Levkoe, 2020; Levkoe et al, Chapter 1). I accomplish this by: (1) drawing from theories of racial capitalism to illuminate critique of the present and advance more just food futures; (2) building on participatory efforts to advance fairness and migrant justice in organic institutions; and (3) contributing geographic analysis that empirically explores the extent of migrant labour in the organic sector. I find that organic agriculture uses migrant labour at a similar rate to non-organic agriculture, and that individualist narratives are contributing to blind spots and barriers to meaningful collective action that could effectively challenge racial capitalism in the sector and beyond.

Racial capitalism and agriculture

With its origins in Cedric Robinson's (1983) *Black Marxism: The Making of the Black Radical Tradition*, theories and histories of racial capitalism tell an important truth: racialization is a defining logic of capitalism. In this foundational work, Robinson not only makes visible the contributions of international Black solidarity movements to shaping modern society, but also wields an important critique of Marxism in that it ignored the racial foundations of capitalism. He traces the way that racializing logics were used in feudal Europe to subjugate 'ethnic' groups as inferior, and thus exploitable. In doing so, he offered a rebuttal to theorists who treat capitalism as a departure from feudalism, and rather, asserts that racializing logics both predate and are foundational to capitalism.

Theories of racial capitalism continue to remind us that capitalism is – and has always been – racialized (Kelley, 2017; Gilmore, 2020). Jenkins and Leroy define racial capitalism as 'the process by which the key dynamics of capitalism –accumulation/dispossession, credit/debt, production/surplus, capitalist/worker, developed/underdeveloped, contract/coercion, and others – become articulated through race' (Jenkins and Leroy, 2021: 3). Fundamentally, Ruth Wilson Gilmore (2020) has succinctly explained that 'capitalism requires inequality, and racism enshrines it'.

Gilmore also refers to racial capitalism as being 'a mode of production developed in agriculture' (2017: 225). It should come as no surprise, then, that the agriculture sector specifically, and the food system more broadly, is rife with opportunities to bring into view the racial organization of these dynamics. Indeed, contemporary society's dominant relationship to land is defined by racial capitalism. In both the US and Canada, the majority of landowners and farmers are White settlers (Statistics Canada, 2011; Horst and Marion, 2019), whereas food production in both countries is largely reliant on the labour of Black and Brown workers, most of whom experience a form of unfreedom due to either their undocumented status (more common in the US) or their participation in state-sponsored managed temporary migration programmes (Weiler, Sexsmith, and Minkoff-Zern, 2020; Walia, 2021). The current agricultural model is rooted in plantation economics which relied on slavery and the dispossession of Indigenous land, and is built on exploitation of others (Manjapra, 2018; Rogaly, 2021). Racial capitalism reminds us that racialization has always been used to justify who those 'others' were, and that the 'interlocking workings of human worth, race, and space ... continue to organize contemporary geographic arrangements' (McKittrick, 2013: 6).

Temporary foreign worker programmes and migrant organizing in Canada

Canada's Temporary Foreign Worker Program (TFWP) is emblematic of racial capitalism at work. Walia writes: 'migrant workers provide liberal capitalist interests with cheapened labor without altering the racial social order through permanent immigration' (Walia, 2021: 133). Indeed, the managed migration programmes – where migrant workers from majority-world countries are temporarily permitted to enter Canada under specific visa arrangements in order to perform work that Canadians are unwilling to perform – are heralded internationally as a success *because* they do not lead to permanent immigration (Preibisch, 2012). In doing so, they effectively curb workers' access to rights and benefits despite their contributions to Canadian society. Unlike domestic workers with citizenship or residency, Temporary Foreign Workers (TFWs) are tied to a single employer as a condition of their status. Employers can choose not to renew their workers' contracts if they are unhappy with their performance, or even have them deported (Preibisch, 2010), resulting in many workers enduring conditions they might otherwise reject. This is why workers and scholar-activists alike have characterized the conditions faced by migrant workers as 'unfree', 'modern-day apartheid', and 'modern-day slavery' (Sharma, 2006; Cohen, 2019; Walia, 2021). These structural conditions underlie the material and corporeal realities experienced by farmworkers, which include poor housing, unsafe working conditions, barriers to accessing healthcare, abuse, and even preventable death (McLaughlin, Hennebry, and Haines, 2014; Strauss and McGrath, 2017; Weiler and Caxaj, 2022).

The first iteration of a migration programme for agricultural workers began in 1966 with the Seasonal Agricultural Worker Program (SAWP), based on an agreement between the Canadian and Jamaican governments. Today, SAWP workers come from participating Caribbean countries and Mexico for up to eight months of the year (Government of Canada, 2022b). The SAWP is now one stream of several under the larger umbrella of the TFWP, which includes the Agriculture Stream, where agricultural workers come from any country for up to two years (Government of Canada, 2022a).

State policy in Canada has worked to make racialized migrant labour more accessible to agriculture and food industries to benefit capital accumulation (Preibisch, 2012). Both the number and proportion of migrant agricultural workers have increased in recent years, representing 21 per cent of all workers in crop production in 2017, up from 9 per cent in 2005 (Zhang, Ostrovsky, and Arsenault, 2021). Nearly half of all agricultural workers who come to Canada via the TFWP are from Mexico, followed by Guatemala and Jamaica (Zhang, Ostrovsky, and Arsenault, 2021). All workers come from global-majority countries (Statistics Canada, 2021a), and nearly all are likely to be racialized as Black or Brown, resulting in a racialized global labour supply to perform work that domestic workers are unwilling to do (Preibisch and Binford, 2007; Hennebry, 2012). Further, workers' 'decisions' to migrate (and Canada's selection of sending countries) are driven by dire socio-economic conditions, often the result of neoliberal trade policy and structural adjustment programmes and violence (Otero, 2011; Minkoff-Zern, 2014).

In the face of widespread acceptance and justification of the TFWP, migrants and their allies fight for justice. Organizations such as Justice for Migrant Workers, Fuerza Migrante, Migrant Rights Network, and many others support migrants in their struggles for justice in a variety of ways, including mutual aid, worker education, government advocacy, and support with legal action or labour complaints. These organizations not only fill gaps left by government programmes, but also address the harm inflicted on workers and their communities as a result of the design of the TFWP. Because of the ways their work transcends legal strategies (for example, through direct action) and advocates for system-level change in a way that reflects the political economy of the food system (for example, by targeting labour practices at the top of the supply chain), migrant organizations have many lessons to offer the broader labour movement (Dias-Abey, 2018).

While this chapter focuses on the agriculture sector, migrant organizers and scholars alike have cautioned against the segmentation of workers by migration stream or sector (Hussan, 2021; Minkoff-Zern and Mares, forthcoming), as it obscures the common forces that oppress workers and stifles their collective power. As such, this examination of migrant labour in the organic sector is not intended to lose sight of these broader patterns and common struggles, but rather, to further elucidate why the organic sector is no exception to them.

I draw from multiple sources of data for the analysis presented in this chapter. First, I draw from national data from 2021 on migrant worker employment and organic farms to analyse the extent of migrant labour on organic farms in Canada. Second, I draw from semi-structured interviews and participant observation conducted as part of a participatory action research (PAR) project (2019–21) in collaboration with a certified organic association and a migrant rights collective (Klassen, Fuerza Migrante, and

Wittman, 2022). This chapter builds on and extends this work through new analysis informed by the lens of racial capitalism and RFG.

Migrant labour in organic agriculture

Until recently, little was known about the extent to which organic farms employed migrant workers in Canada. This question was raised several times by participants in this research – including those in positions of leadership in organic-sector organizations – seeking to better understand the current state of fairness in the sector. This question was also raised by migrant justice groups in personal communication and interviews. Their experiences dispel the myth that organic certification guarantees better conditions for farmworkers, as exemplified by the death of two farmworkers in an accident on an Ontario organic farm (Keung, 2010), instances of abuse and neglect on a British Columbia (BC) blueberry farm with organic production (Woodward, 2019), as well as research from other contexts suggesting broadly similar conditions and contexts of employment (Cross et al, 2008; Medland, 2016; Soper, 2019).

In order to estimate the number of migrant workers employed on organic farms, I drew from two sources of publicly available data: (1) the list of employers approved to hire TFWs based on positive Labour Market Impact Assessments (LMIA) and the number of positions per operation (Employment and Social Development Canada, 2021); and (2) the directories of certified organic farms from accredited certification bodies under the Canada Organic Regime (Government of Canada, 2023). While the number of positions approved for TFWs does not equate to the number of workers who come to Canada, many scholars rely on these LMIA data since more detailed data on the number of agricultural workers who arrive in Canada are limited. Both sources of data were based on the 2021 calendar year.

A total of 65,774 positions for migrant workers were approved for primary agriculture in 2021. This is similar to official statistics on the number of TFWs in agriculture (Statistics Canada, 2022). By cross-referencing the list of employers and organic operations, I estimate that at least 4,381 of these TFW positions were for organic operations, representing a total of 7 per cent of all approved positions for primary agriculture in Canada. Because organic farms represent only 3.2 per cent of all farms in Canada (Statistics Canada, 2021b), and because the estimate of TFW positions is likely to be an underestimate due to data limitations, this analysis suggests that organic farms hire migrant workers at a *higher* rate than other farms in Canada.

Regional patterns show some variation in the extent of migrant labour, but the use of TFWs by province follows a similar pattern in organic agriculture as it does the rest of agriculture (Table 5.1). The number of TFW positions on organic farms was highest in Ontario and Quebec, with 41 per cent and

Table 5.1: Total number of approved TFW positions in primary agriculture in comparison to number on organic certified farms, by province (no TFW positions were approved in any of the territories in 2021 according to Statistics Canada).

Province	Number of positions – all farms[3]	% of Canadian total	Number of positions – organic farms[4]	% of positions on organic farms
British Columbia	12,167	18	293	7
Alberta	2,093	3	65	1
Saskatchewan	472	1	8	0
Manitoba	650	1	38	1
Ontario	25,201	38	1,778	41
Quebec	22,554	34	2,044	47
New Brunswick	371	1	7	0
Nova Scotia	1,875	3	37	1
Prince Edward Island	364	1	111	3
Newfoundland and Labrador	27	0	0	0
Canada	65,774	100	4,381	100

47 per cent of the total approved positions for organic farms in Canada, respectively. Though somewhat smaller proportions, TFW positions for all farms were also concentrated in Ontario and Quebec, together accounting for 72 per cent of positions in Canada. The data for BC suggest a relatively lower reliance of organic farming on migrant labour when compared with other farms in the province, with 18 per cent of total approved positions for TFWs, but only 7 per cent of positions on organic farms.

While the concentration of TFW positions in BC, Ontario, and Quebec can be partially explained by their relatively large numbers of farms, it is also likely due to the concentration of tree fruit, berry, vegetable, and greenhouse production in these provinces. For these labour-intensive industries, the cheap, dependable, and flexible labour provided by the TFWP enables farmers to maximize profit and capital accumulation. Farm size likely also plays a role. While many small farms have labour-intensive operations, there are barriers for small farmers to participate in the TFWP, which may result in the programme being more heavily utilized by mid-size farms. This is supported by the relative under-reliance of BC farms on migrant labour, as the average size of farms is significantly smaller than other provinces (Klassen, 2022). Finally, the suitability of work for the TFWP is also likely a factor, as TFWs must be paid an hourly wage, limiting migrant labour in industries that utilize the piece-rate wage structure to incentivize hyper-efficient harvesting (for example, for blueberry agricuture in BC, which is dependent on immigrant labour for harvesting – Preibisch and Otero, 2014).

While it is tempting to make conclusions about organic farms' reliance on migrant labour relative to other farms in the same province, differences in the indsutry make-up of these sectors would have important impacts on these results, limiting conclusions from this coarse-grained analysis. Further research using more detailed data sources is needed to better examine the complex factors that lead to variation in labour-related dynamics by farm size, industry type, and organic status (Klassen, 2022).

Individualism blocking collective action

The use of migrant labour does not necessarily constitute unfair treatment of workers, nor are the findings presented above an indictment of organic farmers for utilizing this source of labour. However, knowing that the organic sector in Canada is similarly reliant on the TFWP and that these programmes exhibit conditions of structural inequity, disempowerment, and curbed access to rights and benefits, I now turn to examining the efforts by the organic movement to address unfairness in labour relations.

While the discussions, propositions, and ongoing work by organic movement actors captured in Klassen et al (2022) showed important potential for change, no formal progress towards justice for workers is discernible in the sector. Part of this is due to the long timeline for changing national oganic standards – the main focus of many organic community actors. However, there are other, and possibly more important, avenues for change, including organizational processes and possibilities for advocacy and solidarity (see Klassen et al, 2022 for a discussion of these). What is preventing meaningful change towards fairness?

Interviews and participant observation revealed that some actors view the problem of unfair labour as one of individual 'bad apple' employers, as opposed to constructed conditions of inequity, precarity, and unfreedom. When one participant, who is also an employer of migrant workers, was asked about whether they think organic employers provide better jobs than conventional ones, they responded:

'I think maybe the smaller ones are ... and even in those they're not all good operators and fair operators. I think some of the larger ones, my experience is that they are less than fair ... I guess the best way to say it is it cuts across all dynamics. Big, small. If they are a bad operator, they are a bad operator, they will exploit people. They get away with it!' (Participant 10, 21 October 2020)

While this employer does mention more widespread trends of exploitation that "cut across all dynamics" including the size of farms, they also perpetuate the view that the problems are caused by individual employers who are inherently "bad operators". As Weiler and colleagues (2016) explain, this moral economy framing – which relies on the individual's moral fibre (or blames a lack thereof) for mitigating exploitative working conditions – problematically obscures the systemic patterns that result in the marginalization of workers, regardless of the scale of farming operation. What we can add to this from a racial capitalism perspective is that such structural patterns are not an unfortunate by-product, but a necessary precondition for capital accumulation by others, including employers.

However, there are also instances of organic employers and community members who are drawing attention to the structural nature of issues with the TFWP and echoing migrant organizations' concerns. Jennifer Pfenning – a family owner at Pfenning's Organic Farm and President of the National Farmers Union – has been a public advocate for migrant justice within and beyond the organic sector, drawing attention to inadequate housing, limited rights, and unfree conditions as the rule rather than the exception for migrant farmworkers in Canada (for example, Pfenning, 2016). Pfenning has advocated for changes to the TWFP through food movement gatherings and in public media (for example, National Farmers' Union, 2020), including seeking permanent residency status for all migrants on arrival (#StatusForAll) – the uniting demand of migrant justice groups across Canada (Migrant Rights Network, 2020).

While advocacy efforts by individual farms are important, they belie more widespread inaction by the broader organic sector and its many constituent organizations to address labour and fairness more fully (for example, through formal statements, actions, or policies). Indeed, there was a general sense from participants in this research that even the group working to advance fairness in the sector doesn't have a clear sense of where to begin to address unjust labour relations. This lack of vision of a clear alternative was expressed by one participant who actively supports enforceable labour standards as part of organic certification:

> 'The point of a standard is to take a principle and turn it into something that you can actually do on the ground. And that's where I think we all just get very confused, and sit there going "I don't know how to approach this" … labour has always been a bit of a conundrum … this is what happens … we all get to this point: "yeah, it's really important!".' (Participant 3, 16 January 2020)

There is also some danger of individual efforts being held up as indicative of sector-wide change. Indeed, when asked about whether they could envision the organic sector collectively organizing around structural changes to the TFWP, one participant responded by recognizing individual "champions" for their work, effectively misinterpreting the question as one of good will at the scale of individuals, rather than coordinated efforts at the organizational or collective scale.

Interestingly, all participants responded positively when asked whether they could envision the organic sector taking a stand to support migrant workers' calls for structural changes to the TFWP, such as #StatusForAll. Despite the modicum of support for this central demand from workers, participants usually returned to discussing the barriers to changing the organic standards, with a focus on the inability to pay higher wages, and concerns of duplicating existing labour laws.

Theories of racial capitalism can shed light on the apparent constraints experienced by the organic movement to envision the sector using its platform to advocate in solidarity with migrant workers. Melamed reminds us of how racial capitalism imposes a 'forgetting of interconnections, of viable relations, and of performances of collectivity that might nurture greater social wholeness, but are deactivated for capital accumulation and state management' (Melamed, 2015: 79). As such, racial capitalism helps us appreciate the challenges that face the organic movement in terms of the performance of collectivity that migrant justice demands. Evidence from participants shows that there is will for such changes, but also blind spots that result from a lack of vision and capacity for enacting it.

Conclusion

I have framed the structural injustice of the TWFP in Canada as emblematic of racial capitalism and described the extent of employment of racialized migrant workers on organic farms using new analysis of quantitative data. This analysis further demonstrates the 'myth' of organic alterity in terms of labour relations, as it suggests similar or even higher employment of TFWs among organic farms in comparison with non-organic farms. Further, this chapter illuminates some of the blind spots and barriers that may prevent progress towards justice in organic agriculture by analysing the logics used by organic movement actors to justify their inaction on labour relations in their sector. Taken together, these analyses serve as yet another reminder that organic agriculture – even with its reified values-based principles – is still subject to the pervasive forces of racial capitalism.

There is an opportunity for RFG praxis to advance equitable ways of acknowledging activist, community, and organizational contributions, as discussed at the beginning of this chapter. Organic movement members that participated in this research recognized that action towards fairness is needed if the sector wishes to continue to offer a true alternative to the dominant form of agriculture. If moral imperatives align with market ones in a way that enables the sector to take action in solidarity with migrants – by formally joining the rallying calls for #StatusForAll, giving voice and power to workers in their governance, and advocating for other structural improvements to the TFWP – organic agriculture may have a role to play in advancing alternative labour relations. Activists (whether within or outside the organic community) should not lose sight of the broader landscape of migrant justice approaches that coalesce migrant power, rather than limiting their efforts to regulatory changes within organic agriculture. Fundamentally, if the organic movement seeks to challenge the racial inequities of labour relations in their sector, they will also need to address its racial capitalist foundations.

Acknowledgements

I am grateful to all participants from the organic and migrant justice movements who shared their experiences. Special thanks to Fuerza Migrante who were partners in the earlier work on which this chapter builds. Thanks also to Dr Sean Kearney for coding support for the quantitative analysis.

Notes

[1] I define the organic movement as the assemblage of farmers, inspectors, and organic association members who organize and advance the values-based commitments of organic farming both within and outside the market-based organic sector.

[2] While this research does respond to interests and questions of Fuerza Migrante, and previous research was co-authored with them, co-authorship for this chapter was not possible.

[3] The number of positions on all farms is based on data from Employment and Social Development Canada (2021).

[4] The number of positions on organic farms is based on original analysis by the author as outlined on page 91.

References

Cohen, A. (2019) '"Slavery hasn't ended, it has just become modernized": border imperialism and the lived realities of migrant farmworkers in British Columbia, Canada', *ACME*, 18(1): 130–48.

Cross, P. et al (2008) 'Comparative assessment of migrant farm worker health in conventional and organic horticultural systems in the United Kingdom', *Science of the Total Environment*, 391(1): 55–65. Available from: https://doi.org/10.1016/j.scitotenv.2007.10.048

Dias-Abey, M. (2018) 'Justice on our fields: can "Alt-Labor" organizations improve migrant farm workers' conditions?', *Harvard Civil Rights-Civil Liberties Law Review*, 53: 46.

Employment and Social Development Canada (2021) *Temporary Foreign Worker Program (TFWP): Positive Labour Market Impact Assessment (LMIA) Employers List – Open Government Portal, Government of Canada*. Available from: https://open.canada.ca/data/en/dataset/90fed587-1364-4f33-a9ee-208181dc0b97 [Accessed 11 April 2023].

Gilmore, R.W. (2017) 'Abolition geography and the problem of innocence', in G.T. Johnson and A. Lubin (eds) *Futures of Black Radicalism*, London and New York: Verso.

Gilmore, R.W. (2020) 'Geographies of Racial Capitalism with Ruth Wilson Gilmore'. Available from: https://antipodeonline.org/geographies-of-racial-capitalism/ [Accessed 16 December 2022].

Government of Canada (2022a) *Hire a temporary foreign worker through the Agricultural Stream – Overview*. Available from: www.canada.ca/en/employment-social-development/services/foreign-workers/agricultural/agricultural.html [Accessed 31 August 2022].

Government of Canada (2022b) *Hire a temporary worker through the Seasonal Agricultural Worker Program – Overview*. Available from: www.canada.ca/en/employment-social-development/services/foreign-workers/agricultural/seasonal-agricultural.html [Accessed 31 August 2022].

Government of Canada (2023) *List of certification bodies under the Canada Organic Regime, Canadian Food Inspection Agency*. Available from: https://inspection.canada.ca/organic-products/certification-bodies/list-of-certification-bodies/eng/1327861534754/1327861629954 [Accessed 7 April 2023].

Guthman, J. (2014) *Agrarian Dreams: The Paradox of Organic Farming in California* (2nd edn), Berkeley, CA: University of California Press.

Hammelman, C., Reynolds, K., and Levkoe, C.Z. (2020) 'Toward a radical food geography praxis: integrating theory, action, and geographic analysis in pursuit of more equitable and sustainable food systems', *Human Geography*, 13(3): 211–27. Available from: https://doi.org/10.1177/1942778620962034

Harrison, J.L. and Getz, C. (2015) 'Farm size and job quality: mixed-methods studies of hired farm work in California and Wisconsin', *Agriculture and Human Values*, 32: 1–18. Available from: https://doi.org/10.1007/s10460-014-9575-6

Heckman, J. (2006) 'A history of organic farming: transitions from Sir Albert Howard's War in the Soil to USDA National Organic Program', *Renewable Agriculture and Food Systems*, 21(3): 143–50. Available from: https://doi.org/10.1079/RAF2005126

Heim, T. (2020) 'The Indigenous origins of regenerative agriculture', *National Farmers Union*, [online] 12 October. Available from: https://nfu.org/2020/10/12/the-indigenous-origins-of-regenerative-agriculture/ [Accessed 6 July 2021].

Hennebry, J. (2012) *Permanently Temporary? Agricultural Migrant Workers and Their Integration in Canada, IRPP Study 26*, Montreal: Institute for Research on Public Policy.

Horst, M. and Marion, A. (2019) 'Racial, ethnic and gender inequities in farmland ownership and farming in the U.S.', *Agriculture and Human Values*, 36(1): 1–16. Available from: https://doi.org/10.1007/s10460-018-9883-3

Hussan, S. (2021) 'What is a migrant? And is she a revolutionary?', *Briarpatch*, [online] 3 May. Available from: https://briarpatchmagazine.com/artic les/view/what-is-a-migrant-and-is-she-a-revolutionary [Accessed 25 February 2022].

IFOAM (2020a) *The Four Principles of Organic Agriculture*. Available from: https://ifoam.bio/why-organic/shaping-agriculture/four-principles-orga nic [Accessed 3 June 2020].

IFOAM (2020b) *The Principle of Fairness*. Available from: https://ifoam.bio/ why-organic/principles-organic-agriculture/principle-fairness [Accessed 9 December 2020].

Jaffee, D. and Howard, P.H. (2010) 'Corporate cooptation of organic and fair trade standards', *Agriculture and Human Values*, 27(4): 387–99. Available from: https://doi.org/10.1007/s10460-009-9231-8

Jenkins, D. and Leroy, J. (eds) (2021) *Histories of Racial Capitalism*, New York: Columbia University Press.

Kelley, R.D.G. (2017) 'What Did Cedric Robinson Mean by Racial Capitalism?', *Boston Review*, [online] 12 January. Available from: https:// bostonreview.net/articles/robin-d-g-kelley-introduction-race-capitalism- justice/ [Accessed 26 November 2021].

Keung, N. (2010) 'Inquest sought into migrant farm worker deaths', *thestar. com*, [online]. Available from: www.thestar.com/news/investigations/2010/ 09/22/inquest_sought_into_migrant_farm_worker_deaths.html [Accessed 8 July 2021].

Klassen, S. (2022) 'Chapter 3: Different from the rest? Comparing socio- economic and ecological management of certified organic to non-organic crop farms in Canada', in *Just in Principle?: Assessing the Contributions of Organic Farming to Socio-Ecological Sustainability in Canadian Agriculture*, Vancouver, BC: University of British Columbia. Available from: https:// doi.org/10.14288/1.0421368

Klassen, S., Fuerza Migrante, and Wittman, H. (2022) 'Sharing the struggle for fairness: exploring possibilities for solidarity & just labour in organic agriculture', *Canadian Food Studies/La Revue canadienne des études sur l'alimentation*, 9(2): 147–79. Available from: https://doi.org/10.15353/ cfs-rcea.v9i2.536

Klassen, S. et al (2023) 'Beyond equivalency: comparing governance and sustainability of three North American organic standards', *Agroecology and Sustainable Food Systems*, 47(10): 1607–33. Available from: https://doi.org/ 10.1080/21683565.2023.2254717

Kröger, M. and Schäfer, M. (2014) 'Between ideals and reality: development and implementation of fairness standards in the organic food sector', *Journal of Agricultural and Environmental Ethics*, 27(1): 43–63. Available from: https:// doi.org/10.1007/s10806-013-9444-0

Manjapra, K. (2018) 'Plantation dispossessions: the global travel of agricultural racial capitalism', in S. Beckert and C. Desan (eds) *American Capitalism: New Histories*, New York: Columbia University Press, p 448.

McKittrick, K. (2013) 'Plantation futures', *Small Axe: A Caribbean Journal of Criticism*, 17(3): 1–15. Available from: https://doi.org/10.1215/07990 537-2378892

McLaughlin, J., Hennebry, J., and Haines, T. (2014) 'Paper versus practice: occupational health and safety protections and realities for temporary foreign agricultural workers in Ontario', *Perspectives interdisciplinaires sur le travail et la santé*, 16(2). Available from: https://doi.org/10.4000/pistes.3844

Medland, L. (2016) 'Working for social sustainability: insights from a Spanish organic production enclave', *Agroecology and Sustainable Food Systems*, 40(10): 1133–56. Available from: https://doi.org/10.1080/21683 565.2016.1224213

Melamed, J. (2015) 'Racial capitalism', *Critical Ethnic Studies*, 1(1): 11.

Migrant Rights Network (2020) *Status for All – for a Just Recovery from COVID-19*. Available from: https://migrantrights.ca/statusforall/ [Accessed 22 May 2020].

Minkoff-Zern, L.-A. (2014) 'Hunger amidst plenty: farmworker food insecurity and coping strategies in California', *Local Environment*, 19(2): 204–19. Available from: https://doi.org/10.1080/13549839.2012.729568

Minkoff-Zern, L.-A. and Mares, T. (forthcoming) *Will Work for Food: Labor Across the Food Chain*, Oakland, CA: University of California Press.

National Farmers' Union (2020) *Jenn Pfenning – Conventional Presenters*. Available from: www.nfu.ca/conf-speaker/jenn-pfenning/ [Accessed 7 September 2022].

Obach, B.K. (2015) *Organic Struggle: The Movement for Sustainable Agriculture in the United States*, Cambridge, MA; London, England: MIT Press.

Otero, G. (2011) 'Neoliberal globalization, NAFTA, and migration: Mexico's loss of food and labor sovereignty', *Journal of Poverty*, 15(4): 384–402. Available from: https://doi.org/10.1080/10875549.2011.614514729568

Pfenning, J. (2016) 'Canada's Seasonal Agricultural Worker Program Employs Migrant Workers', *Edible Toronto*, [online]. Available from: https:// edibletoronto.ediblecommunities.com/food-thought/canadas-seaso nal-agricultural-worker-program-employs-migrant-workers [Accessed 4 September 2022].

Preibisch, K. (2010) 'Pick-your-own labor: migrant workers and flexibility in Canadian agriculture', *International Migration Review*, 44(2): 404–41. Available from: www.jstor.org/stable/25740855

Preibisch, K. (2012) 'Migrant workers and changing work-place regimes in contemporary agricultural production in Canada', *International Journal of Sociology of Agriculture and Food*, 19(1): 62–82.

Preibisch, K. and Binford, L. (2007) 'Interrogating racialized global labour supply: an exploration of the racial/national replacement of foreign agricultural workers in Canada', *Canadian Review of Sociology/Revue canadienne de sociologie*, 44(1): 5–36. Available from: https://doi.org/10.1111/j.1755-618X.2007.tb01146.x

Preibisch, K. and Otero, G. (2014) 'Does citizenship status matter in Canadian agriculture? Workplace health and safety for migrant and immigrant laborers', *Rural Sociology*, 79(2): 174–99. Available from: https://doi.org/10.1111/ruso.12043

Robinson, C.J. (1983) *Black Marxism: The Making of the Black Radical Tradition*, Chapel Hill, NC: University of North Carolina Press.

Rogaly, B. (2021) 'Commentary: agricultural racial capitalism and rural migrant workers', *Journal of Rural Studies*, 88: 527–31. Available from: https://doi.org/10.1016/j.jrurstud.2021.07.006

Sharma, N. (2006) *Home Economics: Nationalism and the Making of Migrant Workers in Canada*, Toronto: University of Toronto Press.

Soper, R. (2019) 'How wage structure and crop size negatively impact farmworker livelihoods in monocrop organic production: interviews with strawberry harvesters in California', *Agriculture and Human Values*, 37: 325–36. Available from: https://doi.org/10.1007/s10460-019-09989-0

Statistics Canada (2011) *Highlights and analysis – 2011 census of agriculture.* Available from: www.statcan.gc.ca/en/ca2011/ha [Accessed 7 September 2022].

Statistics Canada (2021a) *Foreign workers in the Canadian agriculture industry.* Available from: www150.statcan.gc.ca/n1/pub/36-28-0001/2021004/article/00002-eng.htm [Accessed 7 September 2022].

Statistics Canada (2021b) *Organic products, Census of Agriculture, 2021.* Available from: https://doi.org/10.25318/3210036301-eng [Accessed 29 December 2023].

Statistics Canada (2022) *Table: 32-10-0218-01: Temporary foreign workers in the agriculture and agri-food sectors, by industry.* Available from: www150.statcan.gc.ca/t1/tbl1/en/tv.action?pid=3210021801 [Accessed 7 April 2023].

Strauss, K. and McGrath, S. (2017) 'Temporary migration, precarious employment and unfree labour relations: exploring the "continuum of exploitation" in Canada's Temporary Foreign Worker Program', *Geoforum*, 78: 199–208. Available from: https://doi.org/10.1016/j.geoforum.2016.01.008

Sutherland, L. (2013) 'Can organic farmers be "good farmers"? Adding the "taste of necessity" to the conventionalization debate', *Agriculture and Human Values*, 30: 429–41. Available from: https://doi.org/10.1007/s10460-013-9424-z

Walia, H. (2021) *Border & Rule: Global Migration, Capitalism, and the Rise of Racist Nationalism*, Chicago, IL: Haymarket Books.

Weiler, A.M. and Caxaj, C.S. (2022) 'For migrant farm workers, housing is not just a determinant of health, but a determinant of death', *The Conversation*, [online]. Available from: http://theconversation.com/for-migrant-farm-workers-housing-is-not-just-a-determinant-of-health-but-a-determinant-of-death-186043 [Accessed 31 August 2022].

Weiler, A.M., Otero, G., and Wittman, H. (2016) 'Rock stars and bad apples: moral economies of alternative food networks and precarious farm work regimes', *Antipode*, 48(4): 1–23. Available from: https://doi.org/10.1111/anti.12221

Weiler, A.M., Sexsmith, K., and Minkoff-Zern, L.-A. (2020) 'Parallel precarity: a comparison of U.S. and Canadian agricultural guest worker programs', *International Journal of Sociology of Agriculture and Food*, 26(2): 143–63.

Woodward, P. (2019) 'Guatemalan workers allege poor conditions at Aquilini berry farm', *CBC News*, *CBC*, [online]. Available from: www.cbc.ca/news/canada/british-columbia/aquilini-farm-workers-allege-poor-con ditions-1.5152875 [Accessed 29 December 2023].

Zhang, Y., Ostrovsky, Y., and Arsenault, A. (2021) 'Foreign workers in the Canadian agriculture industry', Ottawa, ON: Statistics Canada. Available from: www150.statcan.gc.ca/n1/pub/36-28-0001/2021004/article/00002-eng.htm [Accessed 9 August 2021].

PART II

Spatial Imaginaries

6

Radical and Intersectional Food Systems in the Context of Multiple Crises: The Case of *Ollas Comunes* in Chile

Francisco García González, Cristina Bonilla Araya,
Paula Neumann Novack, and Fernando Toro

In 2020, Chile,[1] like many countries across the globe, experienced a series of interrelated problems that affected the entire society. Besides the already known effects of climate change (Fernández et al, 2023), an unprecedented global pandemic resulted in high levels of inequality (Gozzi et al, 2021), escalating the already damaged situation of political-institutional representation after the October 2019 social revolt (Arias-Loyola, 2021). These crises mainly affected the most marginalized and vulnerable socio-economic groups, also manifesting the crisis of neoliberal capitalism. It was in this context, *ollas comunes* (communal kitchens) arose as a self-managed, solidarity-based, and collective response from multiple affected territories and communities. *Ollas comunes* are made up of self-organized groups of people providing free meals to their communities. It not only represents a local response to critical socio-economic circumstances, but also constitutes a political act of resistance and protest (Apablaza, 2021). These cooperative actions reveal several lessons and pathways towards food justice and sovereignty.

Ollas comunes have a long history in Latin American cities. In Chile, the rise of the *olla común* dates from approximately the 1930s, after the Great Depression, which directly affected the ability of people to access food due to the economic crisis (Gallardo, 1985). Led mainly by women in the 1980s, *ollas comunes* emerged in greater numbers in response to the deep economic crisis and weak state policy under the Pinochet military dictatorship which produced extreme poverty across the country (Hardy, 1986). With the return to democracy in the 1990s and greater economic prosperity, most *ollas comunes* disappeared, while a few became formalized as organizations providing food services for public schools (Richer, 2000).

In 2019, citizen discontent triggered by profound socio-economic inequalities of the prevailing neoliberal model led to social revolt throughout Chile. Several collaborative actions were developed, including *ollas comunes* (Fina et al, 2022). However, due to the 2020 COVID-19 pandemic and related deep health and economic crises, *ollas comunes* expanded massively in several Chilean cities in order to combat food insecurity among the most vulnerable parts of the population. Like the 1980s, women's leadership in *ollas comunes* might be seen as connected to their role of caring for families, communities, and their neighbourhoods (Geógrafas Chile et al, 2021). This is part of a revival of the collective gender memory of resistance practices in times of crisis (Hiner et al, 2022).

Building on a radical food geographies (RFG) approach (see Levkoe et al, Chapter 1), we embrace the idea of a new relational knowledge that challenges official, normative, and patriarchal statements as an interdisciplinary form of collaboration and mutual learning hand-in-hand with social movements, and with a situated practice, extending the role of sociocultural dimension and place.

As authors, we situate ourselves within socio-environmental justice, a gender perspective, and caring, to understand the praxis of the *olla común* through examples located in vulnerable neighbourhoods of Santiago,[2] Chile. To do this, we integrate the justice dimensions of distribution, recognition, and participation elaborated by Schlosberg (2009). In addition, we employ a gender perspective in our analysis focusing on public, community, and private spaces, and the *olla común* as a practice of self and community care (Jirón, 2020).

Building on RFG, this chapter reviews literature about *ollas comunes* in recent years and analyses how they represent spaces from which to move towards radical and emancipatory practices through solidarity-based, horizontal, and counter-hegemonic work. Qualitative data were collected through interviews with three *ollas comunes*' leaders in the city of Santiago, each located in a different district corresponding to Cerro Navia, Lo Prado, and San Joaquín in 2022.[3] With previous experience in community participation roles, these leaders were recruited based on their *ollas* continuing beyond the COVID-19 pandemic. Our research is aimed to understand *ollas comunes*' social composition, the role of gender, and their scope and functioning of socio-environmental justice (via distribution, recognition, and participation dimensions). We conclude by highlighting the ways in which RFG strengthens the socio-environmental justice lens with a gender perspective as a key element.

Three dimensions of socio-environmental justice

There has been a long debate on discourses and narratives of food systems related to the corporate food regime, food security, food justice, and food sovereignty. Some scholars have analysed food discourses from a political standpoint, regarding how they interact in times of crisis (see Holt-Giménez and Shattuck, 2011). In this chapter, we embrace the notion of food justice as 'the right of communities everywhere to produce, process, distribute, access, and eat good food regardless of race, class, gender, ethnicity, citizenship, ability, religion, or community' (IATP, 2012: 1). We also use a socio-environmental justice lens informed by Schlosberg (2009) because it provides an inclusive and comprehensive notion of justice in three dimensions: distribution, recognition, and participation.

First, the distributive dimension indicates a more equitable distribution among communities of both the benefits and drawbacks of economic and environmental issues. Food infrastructure plays a vital role in accessing local, fresh, and healthy food, yet marginalized neighbourhoods usually have fewer food supply places than wealthier areas, increasing food insecurity of vulnerable groups (Alkon, 2017). Alkon et al (2013) indicate that this may be due to the lack of incentives for food markets to establish in peripheral territories, along with stigma related to poverty and racism. Consequently, the link between the neighbourhood and urban scale plays a fundamental role.

Second, recognition has a political–cultural dimension that implies ensuring legitimate spaces for all people, especially those that have been historically marginalized. The right to food is a fundamental part of the cultural identity of food systems, which are becoming increasingly globalized, with diets consisting of highly processed foods instead of locally relevant options (Shiva, 2016). Indeed, this decline in the diversity of local food systems has significant implications for food security, health, and the environment (Shillington, 2013). This recognition advances intersectional notions that consider sociocultural diversity and specific practices, such as small-scale farmers (Feenstra, 2002) or of those who make *ollas comunes* possible as a practice of care.

Third, participation focuses on justice as political participation and decision-making for all people. This dimension places people at the centre of decision-making about their community's food circuit, from production to consumption (Shillington, 2013). However, decision-making is dominated by the corporate food regime and its profit-driven logics (Shiva, 2016), limiting political space and parity in food decision-making. This is evident when agribusinesses genetically modify crops, control seeds, and use market pesticides to increase their efficiency, without considering local communities and the needs and desires of small-scale farmers (Schlosberg, 2009).

The gender perspective and caring cities

The resurgence of *ollas comunes* is a form of spatial expression mediated by gender (Hiner et al, 2022). A gender perspective highlights how men, women, and non-binary people play important roles in the creation and potential transformation of urban spaces. In the case of *ollas comunes*, the dominant role of women in the domestic space with caring tasks also gains importance both in public spaces and in the leadership of community organizations that were impacted by the pandemic.

Cities represent spaces of power, capital accumulation, and material manifestations of patriarchy, where their design and planning are not neutral (Rico and Segovia, 2017; Col Lectiu Punt 6, 2019) and determine who belongs where and who is excluded (McDowell, 2000). According to Kern (2021), cities have historically been built with the needs and experiences of men in mind, often leading to the exclusion of women and other marginalized groups. In line with this, the division of labour in cities defines gender roles along two dimensions: the productive, which refers to public spaces, production, paid work, independence, and power, more associated with the figure of the masculine; and the reproductive, private, domestic, dependent, caregiver and limited power spaces, more associated with the role of the feminine (Col Lectiu Punt 6, 2019). Recognizing these dimensions, women are seen as active agents in the construction of urban space (ECLAC, 2000).

Within *ollas comunes*, the disproportionate role of women with care tasks (unpaid work) in the domestic space also gains importance in public spaces, crossing the threshold of public and community space, and representing a response to the emergency in a state that did not apply comprehensive measures to care for its citizens, especially those in a more precarious situation. The lack of food was a critical situation, which is why 'collaborative forms of support that use social networks to organize *ollas comunes* and collection centres' occurred in some parts of the country (Jirón, 2020: 78). The organizations behind the *ollas comunes* began to respond with care in the face of an uncaring state. Hence, it was necessary to work towards caring cities. This notion entails planning cities that can accommodate everyday life's responsibilities, facilitate the care and promotion of people's autonomy, and allow reconciling the different spheres of the private and public life of men, women, and non-binary people (Rico and Segovia, 2017).

Finally, the intersection of a gender perspective, RFG, and socio-environmental justice is a pathway towards food sovereignty where people can control their food systems according to their needs and ecological resources.

Ollas Comunes as distribution, recognition, and participation

This section explores how the three dimensions of socio-environmental justice are expressed in *ollas comunes*. First, the food distribution mechanisms are identified and described through multiple scales. Second, the dimensions of recognition and identity are described and analysed through an intersectional perspective, including gender, racial, migrant, and socio-economic components. Third, we describe and analyse formal and informal participation mechanisms.

Distribution: between circuits and formal and informal interlinkages

The COVID-19 pandemic affected the provision and distribution of food within cities. Specifically, lower-income populations experienced several difficulties in accessing sufficient, culturally appropriate, and healthy food (Rodríguez Osiac, 2020). In the urban periphery of Santiago, where residents with lower incomes more likely reside, people saw their purchasing power limited by the rise in food prices. This situation was exacerbated by the sanitary restrictions[4] imposed by the government, which limited the regular operation of *ferias libres* (open farmers' markets).

The Chilean government established a series of food-focused measures during the COVID-19 pandemic. On the one hand, the *Alimentos para Chile* (Food for Chile) programme delivered food parcels to homes affected by the crisis. These foods, however, were only delivered on limited occasions to help cope with the emergency and studies indicate that the food included in those parcels did not cover the minimum nutritional standard (INTA, 2020). On the other hand, *tu feria a la casa* (your farmers market to your home) was an initiative that connected *ferias libres* to food banks, who then distributed food recovered from the *ferias* to vulnerable sectors. Additionally, different municipalities across the country delivered gift cards to buy food in local stores, thus promoting economic reactivation. One interviewee commented: "The delivery of the food gift cards was more to support local businesses than help the functioning of the *olla común*. For example, the gift card could not be used at wholesale stores." However, none of these measures addressed the magnitude of the food crisis affecting the most vulnerable populations.

Beyond the institutional sphere, *ollas comunes* emerged as a self-managed response throughout the country. Formal and informal food distribution circuits began at the neighbourhood scale. While some *ollas comunes* still obtained part of their food basket from formal markets, multiple solidarity-based forms arose within a solidarity economy, understood as one that fosters social and systemic transformations, emphasizing issues of redistributive justice and alternatives to capitalism, as well as participatory democracy driven by active citizenship (Utting, 2015). For instance, collecting food through donations from neighbours, purchases in traditional markets, *ferias libres*, and local stores, bakeries, and butcher shops, created a system of alternatives for how food was obtained. Other distribution mechanisms included donations via social networks and solidarity raffles.[5] These resources, whether money or food, were managed through informal circuits.

Ollas comunes were not legally formalized but depended on other community-based organizations. This allowed them to access specific supports such as the Municipality's food bank and food donations from non-governmental organizations. This raises the value about the interaction between formal and informal circuits. In particular, those circuits interact in this first stage of collecting resources that allowed an *olla común* to cook food for communities built on mutual exchange.

An important aspect of distribution circuits was the role of a central node from which food was distributed. According to the information collected, a few *ollas comunes* functioned in open spaces where people were encouraged either to bring their cutlery or just take meals from a particular dining table to avoid direct contact between neighbours. In most cases, *ollas comunes* chose to pack lunches and distribute them to those most in need, generally walking for hours around the neighbourhood with a supermarket trolley. One interviewee described this: "Although we initially started delivering by car, due to the high cost of petrol, we switched to a supermarket trolley instead, walking from house to house. It takes us an hour on average to distribute all the lunches."

With this measure, while *ollas comunes* protected the population from possible spread of the virus, they also ensured that food reached those most in need, including the elderly and children. Consequently, the nature of the crisis also defined the distribution nodes and the role of the central node, where food was concentrated and prepared.

Ollas comunes not only acted as a central place from which food was distributed, but also developed other expressions that went beyond food. *Ollas comunes* were social spaces for connection and care among neighbours and with the environment. For instance, on some occasions, *ollas comunes* functioned as collection centres that distributed clothes and medicines (Vértice Urbano, 2021), nappies for children, and even wheelchairs and beds. This was highlighted by an *olla común* leader: "The *olla común* was transformed into a place of care, solidarity and empathy. For example, social support activities were put in place, visiting the sick, even collecting diapers and wheelchairs for neighbours."

In this way, the *olla común* was established as a social space that not only cooked food, but also generated a circular solidarity economy that included nodes and connections between diverse actors. This is also reflected in the management of waste for recycling, such as cardboard boxes. Part of the organic waste was also used for home composting bins, which have enabled small urban community gardens that supply medicinal herbs and other products, expanding the impact produced by *ollas comunes* in their local environment as well as the city.[6] This was described by an interviewee: "We had small community gardens in the neighbourhood. We started using compost bins. Also, seniors maintained the community gardens every day."

Recognition: feeding from identity and intersectionality

The people of Chile hold a variety of food identities across the territory, influenced by local cultures (Berdegué and Rojas, 2014), Indigenous people (Parraguez-Vergara et al, 2018), and, in recent years, by immigrant Latin American people (Imilan, 2015). However, the food available to the majority of citizens is strongly influenced by agribusiness, which undermines the region's food cultures and diversity (Cid Aguayo, 2011).

Despite the efforts to raise awareness and change consumption patterns through labelling laws (Schubert and Ávalos, 2020), Chileans consume the most ultra-processed foods in Latin America (Jensen, 2021). As a result, the most vulnerable populations do not have the mechanisms to efficiently replace ultra-processed food with fresh and healthy alternatives (Schubert and Ávalos, 2020). Within this context, this subsection discusses both the cultural recognition and the intersectional component of *ollas comunes*.

Ollas comunes are built on the knowledge and local dynamics of the territory. This means that *ollas comunes'* leaders plan their work of collecting, cooking, and distributing food, understanding the multiple identities of the community, including intersectionality in socio-economics, migratory status, gender, and reduced mobility, among other characteristics (Vértice Urbano, 2021). Although food preparation is based mainly on the recovery of the country's traditional recipes (Daniels et al, 2021), culinary elements of immigrant groups are also considered. One interviewee explained: "Two Peruvian people also participated in cooking in our *olla común*. For example, when we had chickens, they used their traditional recipes with seasonings, vinegar, and *chimichurri*." This practice of 'cooking together' shows how the multicultural landscape influences new tastes and recipes within *ollas comunes*. Yet, some voices continue to be under-represented, such as immigrants who have cultural or language barriers (Martínez Damia et al, 2021).

From a gender perspective, women play a predominant role in the organization and leadership of *ollas comunes*. Considering its voluntary and unpaid nature, this type of work reveals the disparity in community care roles, also understood as a representation of female home care responsibilities extended to the public space (Vértice Urbano, 2021). This not only highlights the role of women in the exercise of the *olla común*, but it also makes visible several inequalities that require further analysis. For instance, women in precarious economic conditions, and some of them migrants, had greater exposure to the COVID-19 virus. Furthermore, women also dealt with mobility restrictions within the territories, which diminished the delivery of food to families most in need. Since *ollas comunes* are not formalized organizations, they did not have the necessary permits for free transit during pandemic lockdowns. This led to one community leader being arrested by the police while she was delivering food. She explained: "Once, I was arrested by police for not having transit permits during the pandemic, even though they knew that we were distributing food to those most vulnerable. I was detained for five hours."

This is just one illustration of governmental control, characterized in some cases by violence and police persecution against *ollas comunes*, affecting their functioning (Diario Uchile, 2020). Likewise, generating a feeling of insecurity and uncertainty within the communities, when care, security, and protection were most needed. The latter affects the notion of recognition in multiple dimensions, not only prohibiting social organizations to face the multiple crises, but also prosecuting those who tried to help, mainly women and migrant communities.

Participation: between self-management and institutionality

In urban centres, social movements have emerged to feed the population in times of crisis by developing community gardens, as well as operating *ollas comunes*. At the neighbourhood level, these types of community organizations represent a local strategy to combat the control of food under an economic logic and, at the same time, take hold of a political opportunity to reappropriate public spaces by its inhabitants.

However, *ollas comunes* are not only a space for emancipation through which residents' voices emerge independently and collectively, but they are also spaces that show the lack of participation in decision-making in political instances; for example, in local government committees. In this regard, it can be said that the decision-making of *ollas comunes* is structured horizontally among all community actors in those activities related to the collection of food, the way of cooking and packaging the meals, and the cooperative distribution of food to the most vulnerable. One interviewee acknowledged: "Decisions were made together. For example, depending on what food was available to cook, we organized ourselves to collect what was missing with neighbours. They were always very committed."

Although *ollas comunes* are all different in terms of diversity of local realities and needs, in all cases, the community leaders fulfilled the role of obtaining food in times of scarcity by looking for creative solutions such as donations, buying food in large quantities at lower prices, and cooking recipes with the available products. These strategies are described by one of the leaders of an *olla común*: "At one point in the pandemic I opened a Twitter account without really knowing what it was about, aiming to spread the work of the *olla común* and raise donations. It worked quite well to increase help via social media." To some extent, this form of self-management meant control over the territorial food system, where the coordination and cooperation of different actors added to the emerging community leadership of *ollas comunes* and played a crucial role in advancing food sovereignty.

At the same time, when emergency actions were implemented to cope with the food crisis, the government did not consider the voice or the participation of *ollas comunes'* leaders. In fact, the state dismissed its role as caretaker, also demonstrating their disconnection with the food needs of the most vulnerable populations. In this vein, we identified three shortcomings in community participation: First, there was a lack of coordination and delay in the delivery of food boxes from JUNAEB,[7] a government agency that ensures the nutrition of students from public schools who could not attend classes due to pandemic health restrictions. One interviewee acknowledged: "The *olla común* emerged when the state left its feeding role during the pandemic. For example, the benefits of the JUNAEB took a long time to arrive. Especially children and adolescents who did not have their daily meals."

Second, the state's presence in the territory was not only charity-oriented, but also late and insufficient. There was no shared diagnosis and the role of local governments was weak. Furthermore, there was limited implementation of pertinent and comprehensive measures in the most vulnerable urban areas. Ironically, the few times that politicians visited such areas were for electoral campaigning. This was highlighted by an interviewee: "We only had one meeting with the mayor via zoom before the electoral campaign and nothing else. Besides that, cleaning items and detergents arrived once from the Municipality."

Third, the government created an expert public-private group for decision-making on food policies, particularly in developing a pandemic food security plan, without including *ollas comunes*, who really understood the territorial needs. Nevertheless, *ollas comunes* generally do not have legal recognition, and a network of *ollas comunes* to serve as a representative is still in development. Overall, if they had the space to participate in political decision-making spaces, there would still be a lack of representativeness and formalization to influence public food policy.

Ollas Comunes as RFG that feeds research and action

This chapter has explored *ollas comunes* in Chile through the lens of socio-environmental justice, whose pillars are distribution, recognition, and participation (Schlosberg, 2009). This lens helps to understand the work of *ollas comunes* as part of building more just and sustainable food systems. Moreover, the socio-environmental justice lens is significantly enhanced by engaging with RFG. By doing so, we considered the role of place, space, and the sociocultural and economic variables that encompass them. This implies the construction of an analytical lens that assumes local impact from interconnections with other scales and flows of people, resources, materials, products, and resources. We also considered the study of a local case situated in a specific period of multiple crises, in a particular territory impacted by historical legacies of neoliberal capitalism, and that promoted mutual learning process and action with leaders of *ollas comunes*.

Drawing on our study of the *olla común* movement from a gender perspective, and after verifying how the three justice dimensions were discussed, we highlighted the way that the socio-environmental justice lens is enhanced by RFG. As an application of RFG, we noted that geographic space and alternative food networks help to understand distributional realities. The idea of distribution considered as formal, informal, and interscalar circuit flows, allowed us to observe the value generation processes behind *ollas comunes*. Not only from an economic and institutional point of view, as it is usually defined, but also, as a distribution in terms of care and solidarity, represented primarily by women. Likewise, food distribution networks developed characteristics that go beyond the material, achieving interconnections with other needs and reaching new actors, often mobilized by solidarity. These are not only observed in the case of *ollas comunes* in itself but also transcend these specific practices towards the entire urban space, generating and promoting new tools, dynamics, and activities, as seen in the emergence of community gardens.

Also, recognition is evident, especially considering the food practices that underpin sociocultural structures. In line with RFG, assuming a situated and historical reality has shown that recognition also includes notions beyond the local dynamics of the territory and its history. For instance, the experience of migrant populations in some neighbourhoods where *ollas comunes* operated enriched and contributed new culturally sensitive food practices. This new multicultural landscape requires further investigation.

This chapter invites us to question traditional understandings of participation as the ability to influence decision-making and further examine how one participates, where one participates, and who participates. The *olla común* is a self-management strategy built on solidarity, collective care, and a practice defined as horizontal, which often questions whether the word 'participation' is unnecessary in these contexts. To question the idea of 'participation' within *ollas comunes* is a fundamental theoretical and practical step to validate parallel alternatives to the institutional logic of food systems.

Furthermore, it is also interesting to reflect on the ideas of scale and sociospatial imaginaries. *Ollas comunes* were quite effective in increasing distribution, recognition, and representation at the local neighbourhood level, but did not achieve the same results at the district level, where their efforts were not adequately supported and recognized, and their leaders were generally excluded from participation in decision-making. This kind of 'scaling-up' remains a challenge for grassroots initiatives. In the same way, much of this under-recognition and under-representation by the state can be linked to the fact that *ollas comunes* are generally imagined as female and domestic spaces.

In essence, beyond the idea of socio-environmental justice, we believe it is also important to highlight that the notion of RFG must be understood as a constant exercise of questioning the production of concepts, and working alongside communities and social movements. Assuming this position requires a permanent critical effort that transcends the mere academic exercise, transforming our own daily actions, building collective, solidarity-based networks, and contributing to public policies that take care of all inhabitants.

Acknowledgements

We are especially grateful for the generous support provided by the leaders of *ollas comunes* interviewed for the development of this chapter. If you want to be part of this network and support the work of *ollas comunes*, you can write to comunolla2020@gmail.com and formalize your contribution in food, money for food, or other. This chapter was based partly on the literature review of a Master's dissertation in Sustainable Development and Environment at DPU-UCL, and a subsequent working paper.

Notes

[1] Qualified as a neoliberal experiment in the 1980s, Chile is currently recognized as a highly centralized, privatized, liberalized, and unequal country (Vásquez et al, 2017), despite its relatively high gross domestic product per capita.

[2] Santiago is home to more than 6.5 million people. While it concentrates all political and economic power, it is also a highly segregated and unequal city (Garretón, 2017).

[3] The three districts are located in the urban area of the Santiago Metropolitan Region. Cerro Navia and Lo Prado are located in the north-western area and present poverty indicators above the regional average, while San Joaquín, situated in the city's southern area, presents poverty indicators that are similar to the regional average (Agostini, 2010).

[4] Sanitary restrictions in Chile were divided into four phases that vary based on the level of COVID-19 cases. Among the most restrictive measures include quarantine, which requires people to stay at home except for essential activities such as purchasing food or getting medical care. Moreover, non-essential businesses were closed, and social gatherings were restricted.

[5] Solidarity raffles aimed to collect resources collectively to support a social cause by offering numbers to buy and eventually win gifts or prizes among the participants.

[6] Despite the potential that community gardens have for the transition towards food sovereignty, their production is still insufficient for the daily meals required to feed all people.

[7] The National Board of School Aid and Scholarships (JUNAEB) is an agency of the Chilean state, dependent on the Ministry of Education. Among its objectives are the school system's management and distribution of food.

References

Agostini, C. (2010) 'Pobreza, Desigualdad y Segregación en la Región Metropolitana', *Repositorio Universidad Alberto Hurtado*, [online] n.d., Available from: https://repositorio.uahurtado.cl/bitstream/handle/11242/6693/inv242.pdf [Accessed 27 April 2023].

Alkon, A.H. (2017) 'Food justice: An environmental justice approach to food and agriculture', in Ryan Holifield, Jayajit Chakraborty and Gordon Walker (eds) *The Routledge Handbook of Environmental Justice*, Milton Park, Abingdon, Oxon; New York, NY: Routledge, pp 412–24.

Alkon, A.H., Block, D., Moore, K., Gillis, C., DiNuccio, N., and Chavez, N. (2013) 'Foodways of the urban poor', *Geoforum*, 48: 126–35.

Apablaza, M. (2021) 'The resurgence of "Ollas Comunes" in Chile: solidarity in times of pandemic', *Danish Development Research Network*, [online] 1 April, Available from: https://ddrn.dk/7091/ [Accessed 29 November 2022].

Arias-Loyola, M. (2021) 'Evade neoliberalism's turnstiles! Lessons from the Chilean Estallido Social', *Environment and Planning A: Economy and Space*, 53(4): 599–606.

Berdegué, J. and Rojas, F. (2014) 'La agricultura familiar en Chile', *Serie Documento de Trabajo*, (152): 1–42.

Cid Aguayo, B. (2011) 'Agroecología y agricultura orgánica en Chile: entre convencionalización y ciudadanía ambiental', *Agroalimentaria*, 17(32): 15–27.

Col lectiu Punt 6 (2019) 'Urbanismo Feminista por una transformación radical de los espacios de vida', Barcelona: Editorial Virus.

Daniels, B., Lataste, C., Bustamante, E., Sandoval, S., Basfi-fer, K., and Cáceres, P. (2021) 'Contribución de las organizaciones sociales "ollas comunes" a la alimentación de la población chilena en tiempos de pandemia por COVID-19', *Revista Chilena de Nutrición*, 48(5): 707–16.

Diario Uchile (2020) 'Denuncian "detenciones arbitrarias" y "represión" en olla común de Villa Francia', *Diario Uchile*, [online] 13 March, Available from: https://radio.uchile.cl/2021/03/13/denuncian-detencio nes-arbitrarias-y-represion-en-olla-comun-de-villa-francia/ [Accessed 1 September 2022].

ECLAC (2000) 'Ciudad y Relaciones de Género. Octava Conferencia Regional sobre la Mujer de América Latina y el Caribe, Lima Perú', [online] n.d., Available from: https://repositorio.cepal.org/bitstream/handle/11362/43116/ciudad_relaciones_genero.pdf?sequence=1 [Accessed 29 November 2022].

Feenstra, G. (2002) 'Creating space for sustainable food systems: lessons from the field', *Agriculture and Human Values*, 19(2): 99–106.

Fernández, F.J., Vásquez-Lavín, F., Ponce, R.D., Garreaud, R., Hernández, F., Link, O., Zambrano, F., and Hanemann, M. (2023) 'The economics impacts of long-run droughts: challenges, gaps, and way forward', *Journal of Environmental Management*, 344(118726): 118726.

Fina, D.D., Lamadrid, S., Figueroa Vidal, F., and Loaiza Cárdenas, C. (2022) 'De la revuelta al encierro: organización, resistencia y solidaridad feminista en Chile en tiempos de pandemia', *Polis (Santiago)*, 21(61): 154–80.

Gallardo, B. (1985) 'El Redescubrimiento del Caracter Social del Problema del Hambre: Las Ollas Comunes', Documento de Trabajo 247, *Flacso Chile*, [online] n.d., Available from: https://flacsochile.org/biblioteca/pub/memo ria/1985/000931.pdf [Accessed 30 January 2023].

Garretón, M. (2017) 'City profile: actually existing neoliberalism in Greater Santiago', *Cities*, 65: 32–50.

Geógrafas Chile, La Olla de Chile, and Universidad Alberto Hurtado (2021) 'Las ollas comunes en pandemia: estrategias locales ante la crisis del hambre', *UAH*, [online] 27 April, Available from: http://geografia.uahurtado.cl/las-ollas-comunes-en-pandemia-estrategias-locales-ante-la-crisis-del-ham bre/ [Accessed 29 November 2022].

Gozzi, N., Tizzoni, M., Chinazzi, M., Ferres, L., Vespignani, A., and Perra, N. (2021) 'Estimating the effect of social inequalities on the mitigation of COVID-19 across communities in Santiago de Chile', *Nature Communications*, 12(1): 2429.

Hardy, C. (1986) 'Hambre + Dignidad = Ollas comunes'. Santiago: Academia de Humanismo Cristiano.

Hiner, H., Peña Saavedra, A., and Castillo Delgado, A. (2022) 'Gender, pobladoras and ollas comunes in Chile: re-activating memory and history in order to survive the coronacrisis', *Gender & History*, 34(3): 708–26.

Holt-Giménez, E. and Shattuck, A. (2011) 'Food crises, food regimes and food movements: rumblings of reform or tides of transformation?', *Journal of Peasant Studies*, 38(1): 109–44.

IATP (2012) 'Principles of food justice', *IATP*, [online] n.d., Available from: www.iatp.org/documents/draft-principles-of-food-justice [Accessed 1 September 2021].

Imilan, W. (2015) 'Performing national identity through Peruvian food migration in Santiago de Chile', *Fennia-International Journal of Geography*, 193(2): 227–41.

INTA (2020) '¿Cómo optimizar la caja de alimentos otorgada por el Gobierno?', *INTA*, [online] 28 May, Available from: https://inta.cl/como-optimizar-la-caja-de-alimentos-otorgada-por-el-gobierno/ [Accessed 29 November 2022].

Jensen, M. (2021) 'Transformación de los sistemas alimentarios en Chile', *Estudios Internacionales*, 53(199): 61–90.

Jirón, P. (2020) 'De ciudades que producen a ciudades que cuidan. Los territorios como ejes para abordar la pandemia y la crisis social', *Revista Anales*, Séptima Serie, pp 71–83.

Kern, L. (2021) 'Feminist city: claiming space in a man-made world', New York: Verso Books.

Martínez Damia, S., Marzana, D., Alfieri, S., Pozzi, M., Marta, E., and Martinez, M. L. (2021) 'Psychological and structural barriers to immigrant community participation: the experience of Peruvians in Santiago de Chile', *American Journal of Community Psychology*, 67(3–4): 456–69.

McDowell, L. (2000) 'Género, identidad y lugar: un estudio de las geografías feministas', (Vol. 60), Valencia: Universitat de València.

Parraguez-Vergara, E., Contreras, B., Clavijo, N., Villegas, V., Paucar, N., and Ther, F. (2018) 'Does indigenous and campesino traditional agriculture have anything to contribute to food sovereignty in Latin America? Evidence from Chile, Peru, Ecuador, Colombia, Guatemala and Mexico', *International Journal of Agricultural Sustainability*, 16(4–5): 326–41.

Richer, M. (2000) 'Comendores populares, ollas comunes y cocinas colectivas: de iniciativas comunitarias de sobrevivencia a empresas de la Economía Solidaria'. *Fermentum*, 10(28): 231–53.

Rico, M. and Segovia, O. (2017) '¿Quién cuida en la ciudad?', *CEPAL*, [online] n.d., Available from: https://oiss.org/wp-content/uploads/2020/06/S1700617_es.pdf [Accessed 22 November 2022].

Rodríguez Osiac, L. (2020) 'Evitemos la inseguridad alimentaria en tiempos de COVID-19 en Chile', *Revista Chilena de Nutrición*, 47(3): 347–9.

Schlosberg, D. (2009) 'Defining environmental justice: theories, movements, and nature', Oxford: Oxford University Press.

Schubert, M.N. and Ávalos, D.E. (2020) 'Sistemas alimentarios globales y ley de etiquetado de alimentos en Chile', *Revista do Desenvolvimento Regional*, 25(2): 527–44.

Shillington, L.J. (2013) 'Right to food, right to the city: household urban agriculture, and socionatural metabolism in Managua, Nicaragua', *Geoforum*, 44: 103–11.

Shiva, V. (2016) 'Stolen harvest: the hijacking of the global food supply', Lexington, KY: University Press of Kentucky.

Utting, P. (2015) *Social and Solidarity Economy: Beyond the Fringe*, London: Zed Books and UNRISD.

Vásquez, A., Lukas, M., Salgado, M., and Mayorga, J. (2017) 'Urban environmental (in) justice in Latin America: the case of Chile', in R. Holifield, J. Chakraborty, and G. Walker (eds) *The Routledge Handbook of Environmental Justice*, London: pp 556–66.

Vértice Urbano (2021) 'El rol de las mujeres en las iniciativas solidarias y de ayuda en contextos de crisis de COVID-19: composición y características de organizaciones de la sociedad civil que entregan respuesta humanitaria', *ONU Mujeres*, [online] n.d., Available from: https://lac.unwomen.org/es/digiteca/publicaciones/2021/05/el-rol-de-las-mujeres-en-las-iniciativas-solidarias-y-de-ayuda-en-contexto-de-crisis-de-covid-19 [Accessed 22 November 2022].

7

Radical Legal Geographies of the Food Desert Spatial Imaginary

Erica Zurawski and Alanna K. Higgins

Sitting at the intersection of food systems scholarship and radical geographies, a radical food geographies (RFG) praxis tackles questions of power and assemblies of oppression to work towards direct action for social change (Levkoe et al, Chapter 1; Hammelman et al, 2020). This praxis involves drawing attention to places for action, struggle, and remaking our world. In this chapter, we aim to expand RFG through attention to the co-constitutive role law and geography play in maintaining and reproducing food system inequities. In examining the role that US legal institutions and policy have in the reproduction of these inequities, we argue that if food justice is a spatial concern (Reynolds et al, 2020), then RFG must also attend to the very spatial *and* legal strategies used to address food justice. We critically examine the construction and material consequences of what we call the food desert spatial imaginary. We invoke the term spatial imaginary to mean 'socially constructed ways of thinking – or schema – about the value, use, and access to places and spaces that authorize, affirm, and validate material practices and policies' (Jenkins, 2021: 116). This critical approach to the spatialization of the 'food desert concept' draws attention to the construction of this imaginary and how it influences the *material* reality of individuals and communities. Along with other authors in this section, our chapter foregrounds the relationship between the social representations of place and space, their dissemination, and tangible impacts to food systems.

Our analysis builds on critical food scholarship and activist pushback against the food desert concept, its construction, and its use. Community activists and food justice scholars have denounced the 'desert' metaphor as creating images of desolation and emptiness while naturalizing oppressions. This obscures community life and practices such as mutual aid and self-subsistence, while also ignoring that these inequalities and certain geographic areas have been deliberately created through racial capitalism and the policies that uphold it (Robeson, 2019; Mishan, 2021; Nargi, 2021; Cook, n.d.). Scholarship also notes how dominant mobilizations of the food desert concept reproduce colonial and racist pathologizations of communities and individuals (Guthman, 2014; Shannon, 2014; Reese, 2019). This results in certain areas, communities, and groups treated as abnormal or unhealthy without consideration of different experiences, bodies, and cultures. Following this, policies and programmes become focused on 'fixing' food deserts through top-down and aid-based solutions rather than systemic change attending to communities' needs (Short et al, 2007; Guthman, 2008a, 2008b; Taylor and Ard, 2015).

Despite these critiques, the concept continues to underline how food access is thought about, discussed, and acted upon within the US, even going so far as to underpin much of the policy and programming towards healthy food access. We argue that within the concept's dominance lies what we call a food desert spatial imaginary which spatializes the concept as a driver of major US legislation and policy. Far from a mere discursive or imaginative matter, this food desert spatial imaginary ignores the broader social, political, and economic structures affecting both food and its access. This in turn creates a specific institutional knowledge of food inequity which does not reflect the material realities of many communities across the US.

To examine this phenomenon, we bring critical legal geographies to RFG which allows us to examine how the construction and implementation of certain understandings of food access influence the material outcomes of federal policy. This highlights the ways that specific spatial imaginaries transmit ideas and divide policy towards a fixed 'solution'. Specifically, this chapter investigates a policy which draws from and relies upon the food desert spatial imaginary – the Healthy Food Financing Initiative (HFFI). The HFFI was first introduced in 2010 by the Obama Administration as part of former First Lady Michelle Obama's 'Let's Move' campaign. Authorized in the 2014 Farm Bill and reauthorized in the 2018 Farm Bill, the HFFI is held within the Rural Development wing of the United States Department of Agriculture (USDA) and currently administered by the Reinvestment Fund. As a public-private partnership it aims to address health, employment numbers and quality, and community development in the name of an 'equitable' food system (USDA Rural Development, 2021). The HFFI is a national, federally funded programme that lures food retailers into so-called 'food deserts' through community development financing and food business grants.

Investigating the construction and implementation of the HFFI, we conducted a legislative archaeology of US 'food desert' policy by gathering policy briefs, Congressional records and hearings, legislative and administrative reports, public remarks, and Presidential proclamations, along with agency funding and grant reports from the USDA, Reinvestment Fund, Community Development Financial Institutions Fund (CDFI), and other HFFI-related institutions. Through this archaeology, we articulate the food desert spatial imaginary within the HFFI as a monolith that forecloses and excludes other understandings of food access while structuring material interventions that do little to enact food justice. Applying a radical (legal) food geographies framework, we argue that the food desert concept is best understood as a spatial imaginary, with its particular understanding and representation of space, that is legitimized through US legal institutions and their interventions in the very places demarcated as 'food deserts'. Utilizing legal geographies allows us to draw attention to the institutions that (re)produce this representational practice. Specifically, we show how the food desert spatial imaginary is legally and spatially constituted through the USDA's food desert mapping and the resulting policy recommendations. Highlighting its construction and implementation, we argue that the food desert spatial imaginary not only (re)produces food injustice but also, in becoming the prevailing logic of food access discussions and policies, it precludes other understandings of food inequity.

Bringing legal geographies to radical food geographies

Legal geographies emerged to examine and confront representations of law and space that naturalize and reproduce exploitation, oppression, and injustice. This framework is used to examine how law *and* space relationally impact justice and injustice, viewing law as a social, cultural, and political project which produces spaces (Delaney, 2001; Delaney, 2016). It investigates the co-constitutive relationship between law and space, how 'law makes space' and 'space makes law' (Delaney, 2015: 97). Legal geographies' analysis of the mutually constitutive role that law *and* space have in naturalizing oppression and the resulting constricting alternative visions of justice aids in the wider struggle for progressive social change (Blomley and Bakan, 1992). This means investigating and naming the constellation of practices and institutions that reproduce and entrench dominant representations (Delaney, 2016).

In bringing together legal geographies and RFG, we draw attention to a new way to investigate these relationships – through spatial imaginaries. We follow Josh Watkins' (2015) definition of 'spatial imaginaries' as a transcendent concept that encompasses the diversity of theorist- and disciplinary-specific terms. A reference to spatial imaginaries therefore includes: imaginary geographies (Said, 1979); geographic imaginaries (Silvey and Rankin, 2011); environmental imaginaries (Davis, 2011); and spatial consciousnesses or geographical imaginations (Harvey, 2006). As collectively shared ideas, stories, mental maps, beliefs, and perceptions about spaces and places, spatial imaginaries are arenas that reproduce and change social relations (Driver, 2005; Martin and Simon, 2008; Watkins, 2015; Jenkins, 2021). Spatial imaginaries are more than discursive, passive representations. Rather, they 'transcend language as embodied performances by people in the material world' (Watkins, 2015: 509). Simply put, spatial imaginaries *manifest materially* by reconfiguring and producing space, drawing on arguments about the past of a place in order to prescribe what the future should be (Martin and Simon, 2008). Therefore, spatial imaginaries 'provide meaning to, enable, and legitimize certain material practices by (re)producing and changing perceptions about places' (Jenkins, 2021: 116). Drawing on legal geographies allows us to show how spatial imaginaries rationalize material practices, reinforce both the imaginary itself and its outcomes, and how they can naturalize injustices through the exclusion, constriction, and even silencing of alternative visions and action (Jenkins, 2021).

While they appear naturalized, factual, or cemented, spatial imaginaries are debatable, contestable, and thus a terrain of struggle (Said, 1979; Gregory, 1994). Attention to dominant spatial imaginaries and the 'alternative' imaginaries they overshadow is necessary, for spatial conflicts are not just physical but also conceptual (Soja, 2010). Therefore, we highlight the food desert spatial imaginary as one of these terrains of struggle. We use this framing to show the manifestation of spatial imaginaries in material projects such as the HFFI, along with its efforts to silence and 'other' more radical spatial imaginaries such as food apartheid.

As a refusal of the food desert concept, the term 'food apartheid' has been used by communities and activists as a demand to stay attentive 'to the root causes of inequity on the basis of race, class, and geography' (Washington, n.d.). Food apartheid thus attends to the very pitfalls of the food desert concept, holding on to how food inequitable landscapes result from uneven economic development *and* systemic anti-Blackness (Reese, 2019; Jones, Chapter 9). Therefore, Cooper (2022) argues it 'is a much more accurate representation of the structural racialized inequities perpetuated through our current system' (para. 3). This conceptualization draws attention to the multitudinous ways that inequitable food landscapes are (re)produced, such as land access, systemic racism and discrimination, and distribution of resources. We see food apartheid as another spatial imaginary – one grounded in the collectively shared experience and lived realities of the communities affected by racial capitalism's impacts on the food system (see also Sbicca and Alkon, Chapter 4, and Klassen, Chapter 5 for additional examples of the ways racial capitalism influences the food system). Unlike the food desert imaginary, which spatially binds and dehistoricizes the problem of food access, food apartheid brings in the temporal, social, political, and historical elements which have shaped – and continue to shape – inequalities within the food system. Perhaps most importantly, the food apartheid spatial imaginary incorporates a third dimension – community experiences – to the analysis of food systems and access.

As we aim to show, the struggle for food justice must include examinations of concepts, semantics, rhetorical choices, and spatial imaginaries used to justify food law and policy. We expand RFG to envision food justice strategies as also spatial and imaginative, while simultaneously rooted in material reality and experiences of food inequity. In the context of this chapter, we utilize legal geographies and RFG to examine the construction of the food desert spatial imaginary, demonstrating its material impact in communities and on food landscapes, and articulating how it excludes and silences other imaginaries such as food apartheid.

Constructing the food desert spatial imaginary

In the US, the food desert concept gained swift popularity among policy makers, organizers, and local developers in the early 2000s (Wolf-Powers, 2017; Rosenberg and Cohen, 2018). Its first appearance into US law was in the Food, Conservation, and Energy Act of 2008 which directed the USDA to conduct a one-year study on food deserts. The reports that followed and the USDA's 'Food Desert Locator Map' created a working definition that quantified and mapped food deserts (Ploeg et al, 2009, 2010; USDA ERS, 2020). Prior to these studies, a 'food desert' generally referred to areas that lack easy access to affordable and healthy food, such as fruits, vegetables, whole grains, milk, and other foods (Holzman, 2010). However, the explicit quantitative methods and metrics utilized by the USDA ERS redefined and spatialized a food desert to mean 'low-income census tracts with a substantial number or share of residents with low levels of access to retail outlets selling healthy and affordable foods' (USDA ERS, 2011).

As a legal institution, the USDA fostered this definitional transition, wherein the concept became a spatial imaginary that *solely* measures access through distance to a 'healthy-food retailer' (Dutko et al, 2012; Wolf-Powers, 2017: 417). This new *spatialized* 'food desert'[1] became infused with imaginaries about inequitable food landscapes, specifically constructing food access as geographic. This spatialization is taken for granted as a logical construction within government agencies, and helped lead to increased enthusiasm for addressing food deserts through regulations, policy, and programmes from the mid-2000s onwards (Block and Subramanian, 2015; Dimitri et al, 2015). It is in this instance that the food desert concept becomes a spatial imaginary, and through US legal institutions, regulations, policies, and programmes that the imaginary is concretized and materialized.

The food desert spatial imaginary remains dominant, underpinning much of the policy and programming towards healthy food access in the US despite its critiques. This pushback details how the concept and resultant policy is 'stigmatizing, inaccurate, and insufficient to characterise entrenched structural inequities' (De Master and Daniels, 2019: 241). Food desert policy both actively and passively (re)creates inequality through the inattention to structural forces and the complexity of food systems and access (Widener, 2018). In fact, critical geographers have recently argued that the reliance on geospatial analysis and focus on discrete areas 'can limit the resulting research by obscuring social processes and root causes' (Shannon et al, 2021: 1418). This type of analysis 'privilege[s] geographic solutions, as well as incorporate[s] whitened understandings of access to food' (Howerton and Trauger, 2017: 740) and results in recommendations and policy concentrated on individual circumstances and behaviours. Additionally, this reliance on mapping and spatial data when combined with Whitened cultural histories of alternative food (Guthman, 2008b) explains access through a limited lens that fails to see how racialized environments are subjected to uneven economic development *and* its attendant pathologization and stigmatization (Block, Scribner, and DeSalvo, 2004; Shannon, 2014; White, 2018; Reese, 2019). This stigma includes the 'alternative' and 'local' food movements' pathologization of fat, non-White bodies and eating habits, and failure to attend to the structural forces affecting their communities, the socio-biological processes which (re)produce the constructions of 'race', and the fat hatred underlying assumptions about health (Guthman, 2013, 2014; Mercedes, 2020, 2021).

From these critiques and refusals, we see the rising use of the term 'food apartheid'. The term pays comprehensive attention to the complex and intersecting socio-historical-political processes that undergird food injustice, foregrounding how those processes are unevenly experienced by communities of colour. Yet despite demands from the Movement for Black Lives, community activists, and critical food studies scholars, the concept has yet to fully replace the food desert concept in media, popular discourse, even scholarly work and in policy (Washington in Brones, 2018; Reese, 2019; O'Neil-White, 2020). We argue that this is the food desert spatial imaginary at work, as its dominance in practice excludes, constricts, and silences alternative spatial imaginaries such as food apartheid.

The food desert spatial imaginary in the Healthy Food Financing Initiative

While most proposed legislation directly addressing food deserts have died due to inaction, the HFFI remains a prolific programme both in its funding and influence of subsequent food policy initiatives. We focus specifically on the history and legacy of the HFFI to demonstrate the material impact of the food desert spatial imaginary.

The Obama Administration announced the HFFI in 2010 with a pledge for $400 million to 'boost public health by eliminating urban and rural food deserts within seven years' (Holzman, 2010: A156). It drew from Pennsylvania's Fresh Food Financing Initiative model (FFFI), which launched in 2004, and was 'designed to attract supermarket and grocery stores to underserved urban and rural communities' through the financing of loans and grants through CDFIs[2] and national fund managers (Holzman, 2010; Reinvestment Fund, n.d.). The ancillary benefit of the FFFI was 'to improve access to healthy foods in underserved areas, to create and preserve quality jobs, and to revitalize low-income communities by providing loans and grants to healthy food retailers and enterprises' (Reinvestment Fund, n.d.). In turn, the HFFI was coined as the federal government's first coordinated effort to specifically confront the challenge of food deserts by removing financial barriers for supermarkets to operate in certain areas and by stimulating investment of private capital into low-wealth communities through these retail markets (Capital Impact Partners, 2018). Weaving together the USDA's spatialization of the food desert with the FFFI model functioned to couple the spatialization with a particular imagination of how to fix the 'food desert problem'. In so many words, the HFFI crafted the food desert spatial imaginary as a geographic way of describing lack of access to food solely through the lens of retail environments. This is then twinned with the affirmation, invitation, and justification of grocery store development and private wealth investment.

Despite an abundance of studies and reports which showed no positive causal link between increased retail and food access, the HFFI rolled forward this approach, financing grants and loans for grocery store rehabilitation and development (Holzman, 2010). In the years that followed, additional research confirmed that expanding access to food retail has no significant effect on food consumption patterns or health (Cummins and Macintyre, 1999; Elbel et al, 2015; Rosenberg and Cohen, 2018), yet support for government-subsidized supermarket development financing initiatives has grown in recent years as the 'grocery store as development finance' model has steadily increased in popularity. As Wolf-Powers argues, this approach represents a distinctively neoliberal understanding of nutritional deprivation that reproduces assumptions that inequitable food access can be mediated and even solved through food retail development (Wolf-Powers, 2017). Notwithstanding constant criticism of the food desert concept *and* the lack of evidence that grocery store development impacts food inequities, this 'spatial targeting of tax relief' remains the dominant approach (Gotham and Greenberg, 2014; Wolf-Powers, 2017: 421). When understood under the rubric of the food desert spatial imaginary, it is apparent how this imaginary affirms, invites, and authorizes the practices of the HFFI which privilege private capital over systematic change (Jenkins, 2021).

Therefore, it is imperative to detail the material impacts of the food desert spatial imaginary through the HFFI. Since its implementation in 2011, the HFFI has awarded just shy of $300 million in federal grants while leveraging an estimated $1 billion in additional financing. Examining the different branches of the HFFI, we have found that the CDFI has funded $245 million of that to just 45 financial institutions from 2011 to 2019, while the CED funded $52 million to 65 development corporations in the 2011–16 period it operated. These awards are generally one-time investments of capital into food retail or food enterprise in places marked as food deserts or in census tracts adjacent to mapped food deserts.

Of the approximately 100 financial institutions and development corporations funded by the HFFI, the Reinvestment Fund alone has received the highest dollar amount with a total of $25 million over the course of eight awards. Through their financing alone, the Reinvestment Fund claims to have developed over 180,000 square feet of food retail space, created or retained 460 jobs, and supported nearly 1,000 grocery and food retail projects (Reinvestment Fund, 2021). Recipients of these grants ranged from community development corporations, food hubs, cooperatives, educational institutions, and state or local governments.

Long-term impacts of these awards are difficult to trace, as many of the financial institutions and development corporations do little reporting on HFFI deliverables. The few reports available indicate the priorities and projects prescribed by the food desert spatial imaginary hold fast within HFFI-funded projects. Every report and metric measuring the HFFI's success centres the opening or rehabilitation of grocery stores and jobs created, without any mention of how, if at all, these projects confront systemic inequitable food landscapes to create meaningful food access. While the HFFI boasts the provision of fresh produce and the support of healthy food access, it is more accurate to say that the HFFI provides funds to CDFIs for the explicit purpose of maintaining or increasing the number of food retail outlets that offer perishable foods. It is worth pointing out the numerous trajectories and formats the HFFI *could* have taken, given many community-driven food justice and redistribution models already in existence. The distribution of federal funds 'from above' means the programme misses out on the community experiences of food inequity and foregoes investing in landscapes and actions which would shape more equitable food policies.

Weaving together the USDA's food desert spatialization and the FFFI financing model shows how the food desert spatial imaginary begins to appear. Namely, in the context of a market-driven community development paradigm in the US (Wolf-Powers, 2017), the food desert spatial imaginary led policy makers to emphasize subsidies for grocery store chain development in low-income neighbourhoods as the singular response to food insecurity. The HFFI programme remains a stalwart component of US government's food access initiatives, made even more stark by recent investments in the programme. On 1 June 2022, the USDA announced a comprehensive and well-funded framework, aimed towards benefiting a wide umbrella of stakeholders in the food system (USDA Press, 2022). The new Food System Transformation framework focuses on four areas: food production, food processing, food distribution and aggregation, and markets and consumers. Regarding markets and consumers, the USDA has committed to increase HFFI funding by $155 million (USDA Press, 2022). The $155 million infusion in the HFFI demonstrates the USDA's commitment to and reliance on the food desert spatial imaginary. This gives further credence to how this imaginary continues to inform HFFI projects and other legislative proposals such as the proposed Healthy Food Access for All Americans Act.

The HFFI and its reliance on the food desert spatial imaginary are a glaring example of roll-back and roll-out neoliberalism (Peck and Tickell, 2002). Roll-back neoliberalism – the mobilization of governmental power and sources towards marketization and the subsequent disruption of opposition to these actions – is seen in the operation of the HFFI, with privatization of government investment and a reliance on market processes rather than policy to attempt redress of social inequality. In fact, federal, state, and local government contribution to non-profits operating social programmes has outstripped donations from foundations and individuals (Pratt and Aanestad, 2020). Roll-out neoliberalism within the HFFI constitutes the building of new institutional relationships between private and public organizations to create a new form of 'policymaking'. This is in addition to what Peck and Tickell note as the 'aggressive reregulation, disciplining, and *containment* of those marginalized or dispossessed by the neoliberalization of the 1980's' (2002: 389, emphasis added). The way the food desert spatial imaginary foregrounds market incentivization and tax breaks to address issues of food access – rather than policies which would address the systemic creation of these issues – not only precludes these solutions but also actively contains resources in the privileging of building grocery stores or inserting credit into certain spatialities.

Instead of these market-based solutions, the government should attend to social movements and community groups. These are best summed up by Karen Washington, who writes that 'whether you are a government official, philanthropist, or privileged individual seeking to invest in a local problem-solving capacity, don't ask what a community needs. The answer you receive will come from a place of deficit. Ask what a community wants. The answer you receive will come from a place of power' (Washington, 2022: para. 12). This quote demonstrates the power that the food apartheid spatial imaginary brings to the work of food justice and access. By foregrounding community experience, policy and funding schemes can be transformative and actually help rectify systemic inequalities and build more just futures.

Envisioning spatial imaginaries in RFG praxis

The dominance of the food desert spatial imaginary forecloses and excludes other imaginaries that would influence material interventions. At the same time, the food desert spatial imaginary has become so monolithic that it has also dominated food policy discussions and non-spatial interventions in the US such as the federal government's Supplemental Nutrition Assistance Program (SNAP).[3] The prioritization of fresh food financing represents the status quo as the 'path with least resistance' given institutionalized support systems around the New Market Tax Credit and other development tax credit programmes of which the HFFI piggybacks (Short et al, 2007; Wolf-Powers, 2014). Even so, building and rehabilitating grocery stores as a catch-all solution to address food inequity and lack of access remains inadequate. And still, the US government enacts these 'solutions' to combat inequitable food landscapes despite their inability to make lasting change.

By examining this monolithic response and tracing its creation and material outcomes, this chapter excavates what we call the food desert spatial imaginary. Following calls from activists, scholars, and food justice/community organizations, we argue that routing the food desert spatial imaginary from US legislation and policy would make space for more radical approaches and material interventions that more systematically attend to food inequities. This can include a negative income tax,[4] universal basic income, and raising the minimum wage, which would target one of the roots of food inequity – poverty. Additionally, expanding participant eligibility and permitted foodstuffs for SNAP would allow the programme to reach a larger proportion of the US population experiencing food inequity, rather than only those in the direst of circumstances. Moreover, there is the possibility to include legislation and interventions which can attend to other structural oppression influencing food inequity. These include the protection of current voting rights and reinstatement of voting rights to those who are incarcerated, outlawing the use of prison labour in general but specifically in relation to the current legal loophole in the Ashurst–Sumners Act of 1935, allowing prison-manufactured agricultural goods across state lines. Beyond grocery store and capital development, there are an abundance of more radical and community-demanded avenues for change; for example, as Washington suggests: 'land-based reparations, continuing conversations about the racialized nature of oppression in food systems and beyond, redistribution of wealth, discussions across lines of identity politics, and perhaps most importantly the direct access to capital for Black and brown communities in order to possess their own homes, businesses, and land' (Baker, 2020).

Bringing legal geographies and RFG together expands RFG to envision a struggle for food justice within the legal and policy realm. At the same time, this also brings attention to the role that spatial imaginaries can and do play in both the reproduction and entrenchment of food inequities *and* the potential for spatial imaginaries grounded in collective community experience to enact more just and radical futures. This analytic helps scrutinize the mobilization of state power through spatial imaginaries embedded in legislative programming while also gesturing towards the potency of spatial imaginaries as a site for justice-based struggle.

Acknowledgements

While we have many people to thank, we wanted to use this space to dedicate this work to Darcy Mullen, whose presence is missed greatly, within food studies and beyond, and whose all-too-brief presence among us offered much inspiration, joy, and fostered beautiful belonging.

Notes

[1] Scholarship on policy mobilities and 'traveling concepts' notes the potency of spatial concepts and metaphors in shaping and influencing policy thinking (Wolf-Powers, 2017). Wolf-Powers further notes that when paired with the increased reliance, popularity, and proliferation of spatial data, the food desert metaphor became even more potent in shaping policy.

[2] For an examination of community development planning and their relationship to justice and action, we suggest Laura Wolf-Powers' comprehensive analyses (Wolf-Powers, 2014, 2017).

[3] To be clear, the fiscal resources given to grocery store development are not overtaking SNAP, but rather there is a notable dominance of fresh finance initiatives in food policy discourses while there are increasing cuts to SNAP (Wolf-Powers, 2017).

[4] The employment of a negative income tax in relation to food access and legislation was discussed during the 1969 White House Conference on Food, Nutrition, and Health. Despite the idea being accepted by President Nixon, liberal members of Congress lobbied against it on the grounds of concerns over fiscal responsibility (Gershoff, 2001; Higgins, 2022).

References

Baker, S. (2020) 'Lessons from Karen Washington on Food Apartheid', *Penn State Presidential Leadership Academy*, [online] 8 November. Available from: https://sites.psu.edu/academy/2020/11/08/lessons-from-karen-was hington-on-food-apartheid/ [Accessed 2 December 2022].

Block, J.P., Scribner, R.A., and DeSalvo, K.B. (2004) 'Fast food, race/ethnicity, and income: a geographic analysis', *American Journal of Preventive Medicine*, 27(3): 211–17.

Block, J.P. and Subramanian, S.V. (2015) 'Moving beyond "food deserts": reorienting United States policies to reduce disparities in diet quality', *PLOS Medicine*, 12(12): e1001914.

Blomley, N.K. and Bakan, J.C. (1992) 'Spacing out: towards a critical geography of law', *Osgoode Hall Law Journal*, 30(3).

Brones, A. (2018) 'Karen Washington: It's Not a Food Desert, It's Food Apartheid', *Guernica*, [online] 7 May, Available from: www.guernica mag.com/karen-washington-its-not-a-food-desert-its-food-apartheid/ [Accessed 17 September 2019].

Capital Impact Partners (2018) 'Financing for Healthy Foods: Capital Impact Partners Policy Brief', *Capital Impact Partners*, [online], Available from: www.capitalimpact.org/wp-content/uploads/2018/09/Capital_ Impact_Healthy_Food_Financing_Initiative_Overview.pdf [Accessed 25 August 2022].

Cook, C. (n.d.) 'Covering Food Deserts', *Center for Health Journalism*, [online], Available from: https://centerforhealthjournalism.org/resources/ lessons/covering-food-deserts [Accessed 13 November 2022].

Cooper, D. (n.d.) 'Food Justice Blog & More', [online], Available from: www. daracooper.com/food-justice-blog--more.html [Accessed 11 July 2022].

Cummins, S. and Macintyre, S. (1999) 'The location of food stores in urban areas: a case study in Glasgow', *British Food Journal*, 101(7): 545–53.

Davis, D.K. (2011) 'Environmental imaginaries of the Middle East and North Africa', in D.K. Davis and E. Burke III (eds) *Environmental Imaginaries of the Middle East and North Africa*, Athens, OH: Ohio University Press, pp 1–22.

Delaney, D. (2001) 'Making nature/marking humans: law as a site of (cultural) production', *Annals of the Association of American Geographers*, 91(3): 487–503.

Delaney, D. (2015) 'Legal geography I: constitutivities, complexities, and contingencies', *Progress in Human Geography*, 39(1): 96–102.

Delaney, D. (2016) 'Legal geography II: discerning injustice', *Progress in Human Geography*, 40(2): 267–74.

De Master, K.T. and Daniels, J. (2019) 'Desert wonderings: reimagining food access mapping', *Agriculture and Human Values*, 36(2): 241–56.

Dimitri, C., Oberholtzer, L., Zive, M., and Sandolo, C. (2015) 'Enhancing food security of low-income consumers: an investigation of financial incentives for use at farmers markets', *Food Policy*, 52: 64–70.

Driver, F. (2005) 'Imaginative geographies', in P.J. Cloke, P. Crang, and M. Goodwin (eds) *Introducing Human Geographies* (2nd edn), New York: Routledge, pp 144–55.

Dutko, P., Ploeg, M.V., and Farrigan, T. (2012) 'Characteristics and influential factors of food deserts', *United States Department of Agriculture Economic Research Service*, [online], Available from: www.ers.usda.gov/ webdocs/publications/45014/30940_err140.pdf [Accessed 24 April 2023].

Elbel, B. et al (2015) 'Assessment of a government-subsidized supermarket in a high-need area on household food availability and children's dietary intakes', *Public Health Nutrition*, 18(15): 2881–90.

Gershoff, S.N. (2001) 'Jean Mayer 1920–1993', *Journal of Nutrition*, 131(6): 1651–4.

Gotham, K.F. and Greenberg, M. (2014) *Crisis Cities: Disaster and Redevelopment in New York and New Orleans, Crisis Cities*, New York: Oxford University Press.

Gregory, D. (1994) *Geographical Imaginations*, Cambridge, MA: Blackwell.

Guthman, J. (2008a) 'Bringing good food to others: investigating the subjects of alternative food practice', *Cultural Geographies*, 15(4): 431–47.

Guthman, J. (2008b) '"If they only knew": color blindness and universalism in California alternative food institutions', *The Professional Geographer*, 60(3): 387–97.

Guthman, J. (2013) 'Fatuous measures: the artifactual construction of the obesity epidemic', *Critical Public Health*, 23(3): 263–73.

Guthman, J. (2014) 'Doing justice to bodies? Reflections on food justice, race, and biology', *Antipode*, 46(5): 1153–71.

Hammelman, C., Reynolds, K., and Levkoe, C.Z. (2020) 'Guest editors' introduction: building a radical food geography praxis', *Human Geography*, 13(3): 207–10.

Harvey, D. (2006) 'The sociological and geographical imaginations', *International Journal of Politics, Culture, and Society*, 18(3–4): 211–55.

Higgins, A.K. (2022) *Critical Perspectives on Produce Prescription Programs & US Federal Nutrition Policy*, PhD Dissertation, West Virginia University, Available from: https://researchrepository.wvu.edu/etd/11317

Holzman, D.C. (2010) 'Diet and nutrition: White House proposes Healthy Food Financing Initiative', *Environmental Health Perspectives*, 118(4).

Howerton, G. and Trauger, A. (2017) '"Oh honey, don't you know?" The social construction of food access in a food desert', *ACME: An International Journal for Critical Geographies*, 16(4): 740–60.

Jenkins, D.A. (2021) 'Unspoken grammar of place: anti-Blackness as a spatial imaginary in education', *Journal of School Leadership*, 31(1–2): 107–26.

Martin, L. and Simon, S. (2008) 'A formula for disaster: the Department of Homeland Security's virtual ontology', *Space and Polity*, 12(3): 281–96.

Mercedes, M. (2020) 'Public health's power-neutral, fatphobic obsession with "food deserts"', *Medium*, [online] 13 November, Available from: https://marquisele.medium.com/public-healths-power-neutral-fatphobic-obsession-with-food-deserts-a8d740dea81 [Accessed 15 September 2021].

Mercedes, M. (2021) 'How to recenter equity and decenter thinness in the fight for food justice', *Medium*, [online] 28 February, Available from: https://marquisele.medium.com/how-to-recenter-equity-and-decenter-thinness-in-the-fight-for-food-justice-e364a895a6bf [Accessed 15 September 2021].

Mishan, L. (2021) 'The activists working to remake the food system', *The New York Times*, [online] 19 February, Available from: www.nytimes.com/2021/02/19/t-magazine/food-security-activists.html [Accessed 13 November 2022].

Nargi (2021) 'Critics say it's time to stop using the term "food deserts"', *The Counter*, [online] 16 September, Available from: https://thecounter.org/critics-say-its-time-to-stop-using-the-term-food-deserts-food-insecurity/ [Accessed 13 November 2022].

O'Neil-White, T. (2020) 'Food apartheid: coalition works to bring healthy foods to Buffalo's East Side', *WBFO NPR*, [online], Available from: https://news.wbfo.org/post/food-apartheid-coalition-works-bring-healthy-foods-buffalos-east-side [Accessed 16 April 2020].

Peck, J. and Tickell, A. (2002) 'Neoliberalizing space', *Antipode*, 34(3): 380–404.

Ploeg, M.V. et al (2009) 'Access to affordable and nutritious food: measuring and understanding food deserts and their consequences', *United States Department of Agriculture Economic Research Service*, [online], Available from: www.ers.usda.gov/webdocs/publications/42711/12716_ap036_1_.pdf [Accessed 24 April 2023].

Ploeg, M.V. et al (2010) 'Access to affordable and nutritious food: updated estimates of distance to supermarkets using 2010 data', *United States Department of Agriculture Economic Research Service*, [online], Available from: www.ers.usda.gov/webdocs/publications/45032/33845_err143.pdf?v=3691.9 [Accessed 24 April 2023].

Pratt, J. and Aanestad, K. (2020) 'NPQ's Illustrated Nonprofit Economy 3rd Edition', *The Nonprofit Quarterly*, [online] 24 February, Available from: https://nonprofitquarterly.org/infographics/npqs-illustrated-nonprofit-economy/ [Accessed 2 December 2022].

Reese, A.M. (2019) *Black Food Geographies: Race, Self-Reliance, and Food Access in Washington, D.C.*, Chapel Hill, NC: University of North Carolina Press.

Reinvestment Fund (n.d.) 'Pennsylvania Fresh Food Financing Initiative', *Reinvestment Fund*, [online], Available from: www.reinvestment.com/insights/pennsylvania-fresh-food-financing-initiative/ [Accessed 21 August 2022].

Reinvestment Fund (2021) 'Healthy Food Financing Initiative Award Book Targeted Small Grants 2021', *Investing in Food*, [online], Available from: www.investinginfood.com/wp-content/uploads/2022/06/2021-HFFI-TSG-Award-Book.pdf [Accessed 12 July 2022].

Reynolds, K. et al (2020) 'Envisioning radical food geographies: shared learning and praxis through the food justice scholar-activist/activist-scholar community of practice', *Human Geography*, 13(3).

Robeson, B. (2019) *Food Deserts Debunked and Decentered: From Deficit to Relational Mapping for Food Justice in Worcester, MA*, Master's Paper, Clark University. Available from: https://commons.clarku.edu/cgi/viewcontent.cgi?article=1249&context=idce_masters_papers

Rosenberg, N.A. and Cohen, N. (2018) 'Let them eat kale: the misplaced narrative of food access', *Fordham Urban Law Journal*, 45(4): 1091–120.

Said, E.W. (1979) *Orientalism*, New York: Penguin Random House.

Shannon, J. (2014) 'Food deserts: governing obesity in the neoliberal city', *Progress in Human Geography*, 38(2): 248–66.

Shannon, J. et al (2021) 'More than mapping: improving methods for studying the geographies of food access', *American Journal of Public Health*, 111(8): 1418–22.

Short, A., Guthman, J., and Raskin, S. (2007) 'Food deserts, oases, or mirages?: Small markets and community food security in the San Francisco Bay area', *Journal of Planning Education and Research*, 26(3): 352–64.

Silvey, R. and Rankin, K. (2011) 'Development geography: critical development studies and political geographic imaginaries', *Progress in Human Geography*, 35(5): 696–704.

Soja, E.W. (2010) *Seeking Spatial Justice*, Minneapolis, MN: University of Minnesota Press.

Taylor, D.E. and Ard, K.J. (2015) 'Research article: food availability and the food desert frame in Detroit: an overview of the city's food system', *Environmental Practice*, 17(2): 102–33.

USDA ERS (2011) 'Mapping Food Deserts in the United States', *Economic Research Service*, [online], Available from: www.ers.usda.gov/amber-waves/2011/december/data-feature-mapping-food-deserts-in-the-us/ [Accessed 17 September 2019].

USDA ERS (2020) 'Food Access Research Atlas', *Economic Research Service*, [online], Available from: www.ers.usda.gov/data-products/food-access-research-atlas/go-to-the-atlas.aspx [Accessed 17 September 2019].

USDA Press (2022) 'USDA Announces Framework for Shoring Up the Food Supply Chain and Transforming the Food System to Be Fairer, More Competitive, More Resilient', *The US Department of Agriculture*, [online], Available from: www.usda.gov/media/press-releases/2022/06/01/usda-announces-framework-shoring-food-supply-chain-and-transforming [Accessed 19 August 2022].

USDA Rural Development (2021) 'Healthy Food Financing Initiative', *USDA Rural Development*, [online], Available from: www.rd.usda.gov/about-rd/initiatives/healthy-food-financing-initiative [Accessed 14 November 2022].

Washington, K. (no date) 'FAQ', *Karen Washington*, [online], Available from: www.karenthefarmer.com/faq-index [Accessed 20 August 2022].

Watkins, J. (2015) 'Spatial imaginaries research in geography: synergies, tensions, and new directions', *Geography Compass*, 9(9): 508–22.

White, M.M. (2018) *Freedom Farmers: Agricultural Resistance and the Black Freedom Movement*, Chapel Hill, NC: University of North Carolina Press.

Widener, M.J. (2018) 'Spatial access to food: retiring the food desert metaphor', *Physiology & Behavior*, 193: 257–60.

Wolf-Powers, L. (2014) 'Understanding community development in a "theory of action" framework: norms, markets, justice', *Planning Theory & Practice*, 15(2): 202–19.

Wolf-Powers, L. (2017) 'Food deserts and real-estate-led social policy', *International Journal of Urban and Regional Research*, 41(3): 414–25.

8

Consuming Chinatown: Gentrifying through Taste and Design

Lynn Huynh

Bellaire Street, the primary road running through Houston's Asiatown,[1] is as familiar to me as the memory of the Corolla my grandfather drove to run our weekly errands. The ink of every Sunday's Chinese newspapers staining my fingertips, the weight of Hong Kong Food Market grocery bags, the taste of custard-filled Taiwanese pastries; such visceral memories of my childhood are starting places for me to map the aesthetics and food cultures of the racialized geography that makes up Asiatown. From the first strip mall built in the 1980s to the gentrification pioneered by international restaurant chains today, the transformation of Bellaire Street is reliant on the evolution of traditional Asian aesthetics and food/ie cultures to sustain commercial (re)development.

An ethnic enclave with a decades-long history and rapidly growing residential/retail opportunities, Asiatown exemplifies how Houston came to be one of the most diverse cities in the US (CultureMap, 2021). This narrative of multiculturalism has simultaneously justified the displacement of long-time Asian/Asian-American, Latinx, and Black working-class residents in the south-west corridor of Houston. Since 2004, Houston's Asian-American Business Council estimates that land values along the Bellaire strip have increased between 25 and 50 per cent (Gray, 2008) as developers invite over 2 million square feet of construction of high-end residential and retail opportunities under the guise of expanding Asiatown's diversity (Gray, 2008).

This chapter utilizes the lens of radical food geographies (RFG) praxis to examine how restaurants, particularly those within an ethnic enclave, are critical places in which gentrification unfolds while also challenging scholars and activists to consider the visual, cultural, and culinary indicators and consequences of displacement. I ask the research questions: what does gentrification look, taste, and feel like in the spatial imaginary of Houston's Asiatown? The evolution of Asian aesthetics, food trends, and consumer cultures that make up the social representations of Asiatown as a place and space are shaped by those impacted by gentrification and those who influence gentrification alike. Enactors of Asiatown's gentrification, mainly public-private partnerships, ethnic entrepreneurs/developers, global restaurant franchises, and upper-/middle-class consumers, economically and socially benefit from Asiatown's redevelopment, while Black, Latinx, and Asian/Asian-American long-time residents face rising poverty levels and expensive housing markets.

To examine this phenomenon, I rely on historical and discourse analysis of media such as archived press articles, restaurant websites, and restaurant reviews on public forums such as Yelp; my lived experiences observing Asiatown's geographic changes over time; and visual analysis of restaurants' exterior, interior, and visual branding. Press releases documenting Asiatown's growth from 1980 to 2021 by news outlets such as ABC13 and Houston Chronicle, as well as restaurant websites, provide me insight into how Asiatown, its restaurants, and its emerging food trends are branded under the public eye. Diners' reviews on Yelp and Google reveal how Asiatown visitors build lived experiences and emotional attachments towards both long-time and new restaurants alike. My own memory growing up in Houston's Asiatown was also integral to understanding the re/construction of Asiatown: the experience of driving past the newly constructed Bellaire Food Street shopping complex in 2019 elicited childhood memories of driving past a demolition site in the exact same spot, and before the demolition site, an apartment complex. I pursued the distance of this memory, perusing archives until I came across an article proving the existence of a living, breathing apartment complex that once sat where Asiatown's 'hottest' new foodie spot is located today.

My lived experiences as an Asian-American growing up in Houston's Asiatown shapes my positionality as both consumer and resident. I spent my early childhood living in Asiatown (approximately 1999–2006), and even after moving out of the neighbourhood, I frequently visited both newer and older Asiatown restaurants. I have personally dined at certain case-study sites – Bubble Egg and Two Hands. While I wrote and edited this chapter during my time in Austin and New York City (cities where I acknowledge my role as a transplant), I visited Houston's Asiatown often, noting which new restaurants/complexes had popped up and which long-time businesses shuttered in-between visits. My academic background in feminist studies and radical geography shapes my approach, introducing a lens of racial capitalism and visceral geographies (for further discussions on racial capitalism, see also Sbicca and Alkon, Chapter 4 and Klassen, Chapter 5 in this volume). My experience in the food and beverage industry, both as a service worker and as a marketing strategist (specifically in visual design), informs my discursive analysis of the role that aesthetics, visual brand identities, and restaurant operations play in shaping food cultures and consumer perspectives in relation to restaurants.

Using RFG to guide my research, this chapter identifies the role of racial capitalism in creating and reinforcing the uneven spatial, economic, and cultural power dynamics at play within Asiatown. Specifically, RFG provides a lens to critically analyse how restaurants, developers, and consumers use visual indicators to create taste hierarchies that delineate between which restaurants are allowed to not only survive, but also even play an implicit role in gentrification and which must succumb to these pressures. In turn, these hierarchies across restaurants influence who gets to reside and who gets to frequent an increasingly affluent and trendy Asiatown. Importantly, I conclude with an exploration of emerging organizations and strategies of community-led resistance against Chinatown retail and residential gentrification across the nation. In this way, this chapter introduces a radical re-imagination of how we protect our communities from the gentrification of taste, space, and culture through an emphasis on direct action as led by a praxis of RFG.

Theoretical frameworks

The term 'gentrification' was first coined by Marxist sociologist Ruth Glass (1964) to describe what is now known as classical gentrification: the invasion of working-class quarters by higher classes resulting in aesthetic upgrading, inflation of housing value, and increased social status of the neighbourhood (Lees et al, 2007). Knapp and Vojnovic's (2016) study of Asiatown reveals rising poverty amid declining housing value and income levels in the neighbourhood – all typical indicators of classical gentrification. In my attempt to expand our understanding of gentrification beyond the typical focus on residential housing, I explore the retail gentrification underway in Asiatown and its mutually constitutive relation to residential gentrification under racial capitalism: as gentrification displaces residents from their neighbourhoods, the process also displaces retail enterprises owned/operated by local residents, which consequently furthers continued residential exodus and so on. Displacement under racial capitalism widens the classed and racialized difference between those who own the means of production and those whose labour is exploited to further benefit the former (Card, 2021), pushing us to understand how race is commodified and marketed to empower gentrification.

Middle classes and creative producers – broadly identified as young, White, and educated – are often associated as the primary catalysts for displacement (Zukin, 2008). However, Asiatown's gentrification exposes the role of upper-class consumers, Asian entrepreneurs, and private developers as primary producers of gentrification forces. Whereas many of Asiatown's business owners in its early 1980s beginnings (and thus pioneering tastemakers) were working class, most of Asiatown's new wave of business owners are younger second-generation immigrants and/or usually well-educated working professionals (Zhou, 2016).

With greater socio-economic capital and mobility, this new wave of catalysts has the ability to recreate an aesthetic, experience, and environment that adapts elements of the country of origin to local trends and taste (Schmiz and Stock, 2019), creating a new visual landscape for Asiatown. This visual landscape, as reported by China Daily, represents both the Asian/Asian-American assimilation into contemporary aesthetics typically associated with Westernization and the divergence from stereotypical Oriental features:

> Move over dragons, red columns and green roofs, Houston's Chinatown is getting a sleek and modern makeover ... presented in a more elegant and undertone fashion – such as sparse use of the colors yellow or red, or a modern version of traditional latticed windows, usually in harmony with a modern setting. (Zhou, 2016)

Race 'as an aesthetic language and a visual logic within the neoliberal episteme' (Summers, 2019) informs consumer taste (the ability to decide what, who, or where is cool and trendy), as well as the decisions developers make in urban planning. Brandi Thompson Summers' work on the commodification, spatialization, and aestheticization of Blackness in DC's gentrifying urban core highlights how neoliberal capitalism, under the guise of multiculturalism, utilizes Black cultural elements as a city visual branding tactic. Consequently, this attracts the very consumerism that consequently displaces its long-time Black residents in a similar fashion that Houston's developers use the city's multicultural visual (re)branding to fuel Asiatown's gentrification.

The relationship between food and land in Asiatown's restaurant economy reveals how gentrification-induced changes in urban land use transform how people access, interact with, and relate to food. The city's foodscape – the type of food sold, the presentation, the values a food place seems to support, the aesthetics embraced and utilized – is a terrain in which consumer taste is developed in relation to the built environment (Alkon et al, 2020). Consumer taste is also informed by memory and nostalgia: elements of the spatial imaginary of Asiatown that heighten or erode a visitor's sense of belonging. Therefore, I view Asiatown's landscape and foodscape as visceral geographies in which the decision-making, experiences, and memories (of the Asiatown patron) is informed by the sensations, thoughts, and feelings that emerge from sensory interactions with the material world such as a restaurant (Hayes-Conroy and Hayes-Conroy, 2008: 465 as cited in Jones, 2018: 910).

Grounding gentrification analyses in feminist visceral geographies asks us to consider the consumption of food as not just a biological necessity, but also as an act informed by 'memory, perception, cognitive thinking, historical experience, and other material relations and immaterial forces' (Hayes-Conroy et al, 2008), which includes the aesthetic and culinary elements of restaurants. The visceral geographies of Asiatown's restaurant scene can be interpreted through Yelp, Google, and social media reviews that reveal how visual, culinary, and visceral elements of a dining experience can, for example, (re)connect to childhood memories of pre-gentrification Asiatown or challenge/expand one's conceptualization of an 'upscale' versus 'no frills' establishment. Ultimately, if gentrification impacts not only a neighbourhood's housing value and demographics but also the visceral, visual, and culinary conceptualizations of a neighbourhood (including its spatial imaginaries), then resisting gentrification also requires cultural, culinary, and visual means of building community in the face of displacement.

Bellaire Street is a site full of complexity. It is where the cycle of production and consumption fuel the making of an ethnic enclave. It is an economy that thrives under the realms of both multiculturalism and urban hipsterness. It is an assemblage of architectures physically formed via strip mall signage and parking lots but also digitally constructed by social media algorithms and platforms. These narratives exist across multiple and varying geographies, timelines, and memories, but studying them together and allowing them to exist within the same breath captures the essence of a collective memory that was once fragmented and splintered across now-shuttered buildings, archived press releases, and erected highways.

Case studies

In my visual and historical analyses of Asiatown restaurants, I compare Asiatown's oldest shopping complex, Diho Square now known as D-Square or D2 (Figures 8.1–8.2), to its newest, Bellaire Food Street (Figure 8.3), choosing two illustrative restaurants within each complex as my case studies: one locally owned restaurant and one chain restaurant. With four restaurants in total, I compare each restaurant's interior design (how kitchen and dining spaces are organized to curate a spatial experience and atmosphere for the consumer), presentation of food, and dining experience for typical clientele. An analysis of these visual, culinary, and experiential markers indicates how gentrification occurs not only through changes in land use and development but also through elements of the foodscape, such as the arrangement of furniture, restaurant and kitchen layout, lighting, logos, and customer reviews on social media.

Figures 8.1–8.2: A mainstay of Diho Square since the complex's construction, Welcome Food Center is an Asian grocery store that has undergone Diho Square's remodels.

Source: dihohouston.com [reproduced with permission]. (top): Welcome Food Center at Diho Square, 1989. Welcome Food Center at Diho Square/D2, 2021.

Changes across Diho Square and Bellaire Food Street

Built in the early 1980s, Diho Square was established as a strip mall bringing quality, affordable Asian goods to its residents. Its website boasts that Diho Square's founding was crucial to the development of the Bellaire St strip as it welcomed foreign direct investment from Asia to develop Asiatown and

Figure 8.3: Bellaire Food Street.

Source: Photographs from bellairefoodstreet.com.

even brought the first bubble tea to Houston. Its directory consists of an Asian supermarket (Welcome Food Center), hair salons, medical and law offices, a dance school, and many restaurants. The majority of businesses are locally owned, mom-and-pop shops. Despite mom-and-pop shops outnumbering chain restaurants, Diho Square's website only boasts the presence of trendy Asian restaurants such as Bubble Egg and Honey Pig BBQ, erasing the presence of the long-running locally owned restaurants marking its beginnings.

Diho Square has gone through two facade renovations – one in 2006 and another in 2020 (Figure 8.2). Its 2020 physical reconstruction implemented 'a lifestyle theme, with outdoor seating area, greens and plants, and a Samsung 8mm high resolution outdoor LED display' (Sandler, 2019), making it visually resemble Bellaire Food Street. Diho Square's new look was accompanied by a rename to 'D-Square' and a redesign of the complex's logo. According to Diho Square's website, 'the word "Diho" is hard to pronounce for many' and its new logo incorporates English as a 'common linkage that connects everyone'. The upgrading of Diho Plaza's marketing materials and its built environment mirrors the 'modernization' of Asian/Asian-American aesthetics mentioned earlier in the *China Daily* article, widening Asiatown's audience of nearby working-class, predominantly Black/Latinx/Asian residents to include upper-/middle-class, White consumers.

Bellaire Food Street (BFS) opened in 2019 (Figure 8.3) after its developer, Kevin Kan, tore down Diho Apartments (Sandler, 2019), an apartment complex my grandfather would always drive past on our weekly Asiatown pilgrimages for groceries. For Kan, BFS represents the modernization of the 'hole in the wall' image of Asian restaurants that are 'small, dimly-lit, [with] menus that are pitched to people who are already familiar with the cuisine' (CultureMap, 2019) by housing aesthetically modern Asian restaurants with 'trendy' food, a majority of which are global franchises. BFS' exclusive selection of globally trending restaurants reveals the role in which emerging consumer taste influences developers' decisions in shaping retail gentrification, consequently impacting a neighbourhood's livability. A shopping complex such as Diho Square that offers a multitude of services such as grocery shopping, doctor visits, and haircuts enriches the livability of a neighbourhood, and the reduction in these offerings in favour of trendy restaurants, such as BFS', is an important indicator of gentrification's impacts.

The evolution of restaurants under gentrification

A more detailed examination of locally owned and chain restaurants in Diho Square/D2 (Table 8.1) and BFS (Table 8.2) reflects how differences in a restaurant's founding year, pricing, scale of operations (mom-and-pop shop, local chain, international chain, national chain), ethnic cuisine, style of dining (casual dining, fast casual, upscale) reflect consumer taste and thus an image of Asiatown's retail gentrification.

Comparing Diho Square's oldest operating restaurant, the locally owned Hunan Plus, to one of its more recent stores, local chain Bubble Egg, demonstrates the shift towards embracing trendy food and aesthetics. Hunan Plus is a Chinese/Chinese-American restaurant serving dishes such as Kung Pao Chicken and Jing Du Pork Ribs, the majority of which are priced under $10. Inside, tables with lazy Susans and red decorative posters welcoming luck into the interior hang from the wall, creating a 'no frills' atmosphere consisting of unpretentious decorations, styling/plating of food lacking exorbitant garnishes, and a focus on the necessary essentials (rather than decorative) to operate a restaurant. The presence of lazy Susans, family-style plating of food, and table sizes (most of which seat four to eight people) encourage diners to sit down for extended periods of time, whether it be for lunch or dinner, thus fostering an environment in which memories around food/dining can be produced.

Hunan Plus' peer, Bubble Egg, is a locally owned spot offering Hong Kong egg waffles: thick waffles imprinted with a repeating ovular pattern, making it look like bubbles. Being the only dish featured on Bubble Egg's menu, the consumer is enticed into customizing their waffle concoction through a mixture of additional toppings, ice creams, and flavours. Unlike Hunan Plus' way of serving a pre-selected menu, Bubble Egg allows for the patron to customize not only their food but also their experience. The aesthetic composition, visual branding, and customizability of Bubble Egg's waffles compels the viewer to take a snapshot and memorialize what could

Table 8.1: All existing restaurants in Diho Square as of October 2020 (collected by author).

DIHO PLAZA / D SQUARE	1980s		Operational capacity	Ethnic cuisine	Style of dining
Restaurant	Year	Pricing (Yelp)			
Hunan Plus	1991	$	Mom–and–Pop	Chinese	Casual Dining/Family Style Dining
Hong Kong Cafe	1992	$	Mom–and–Pop	Hong Kong	Casual Dining/Cafe
Tapioca House	2000	$	Mom–and–Pop	Chinese	Dessert/Fast Food/Cafe
Hokkaido Japanese	2001	$	Mom–and–Pop	Japanese	Casual Dining/Family Style Dining
Shanghai Restaurant	2005	$$	Mom–and–Pop	Chinese	Casual Dining/Family Style Dining
Pine Forest Garden	2005	$$	Mom–and–Pop	Chinese	Casual Dining/Family Style Dining
Dim Sum King	2007	$	Mom–and–Pop	Chinese	Casual Dining/Family Style Dining
Go Go Ice	2011	$	Mom–and–Pop	Chinese	Dessert/Cafe
Twinkle	2011	$	Mom–and–Pop	Taiwanese	Dessert/Cafe
Kuen Noodle House	2015	$	Mom–and–Pop	Chinese	Casual Dining/Family Style Dining
Bubble Egg	2017	$	Local Chain	Hong Kong	Dessert/Cafe
Tasty Point	2018	$$	Mom–and–Pop	Taiwanese	Casual Dining/Family Style Dining
Ma Lu Bian Bian	2020	N/A	International Chain (from China)	China	Casual Dining/Family Style Dining
HONEY PIG	2020	$$	National Chain (from Virginia)	Korean	Casual Dining/Family Style Dining

Table 8.2: All existing restaurants in Bellaire Food Street as of October 2020 (collected by author).

BELLAIRE FOOD STREET	2019		Operational capacity	Ethnic cuisine	Dining style
Restaurant	Year	Pricing (Yelp)			
MeetFresh	2019	$$	International Chain (origin: Taiwan)	Taiwanese	Dessert
Beard Papa's	2019	N/A	International Chain (origin: Japan)	N/A	Dessert
Pepper Lunch	2019	$$	International Chain (origin: Japan)	Japanese	Fast Casual
Tom N Toms'	2019	$	International Chain (origin: South Korea)	South Korean	Cafe/Coffeehouse
Popfancy Pops	2019	$	Local Chain	N/A	Dessert
Ten Seconds Yunnan Rice Noodle	2019	$$	Mom-and-Pop	Chinese	Casual Dining/Family Style Dining
Migo Saigon Food Street	2019	N/A	Mom-and-Pop	Vietnamese	Casual Dining
Chongqing Chicken Pot	2019	$$	Mom-and-Pop	Chinese	Casual Dining/Family Style Dining
Soho Chicken	2019	$$	Mom-and-Pop	Asian Fusion/Korean	Casual Dining
Two Hands	2020	$	National Chain (origin: Los Angeles)	Korean	Fast Food
Tiger Sugar	2020	–	International Chain (origin: Taiwan)	Chinese	Dessert

be a unique experience, a practice that promotes the most relevant food trends as the most commercially appealing and/or successful restaurants for developers and consumers.

Bubble Egg's open kitchen allows patrons to watch their food be created and customized (a spectacle in and of itself). Its seating arrangement also widely differs from that of Hunan Plus. As a dessert place, it lacks the seating capacity to host extended visits and collective meals (an arrangement that also widely differs from that of Hunan Plus). Bubble Egg's bar stools and a singular rectangular table is instead built for short grab-and-go visits, providing an alternative dine-in experience that gives little room for affective sensations, prolonged conversations, and future sites of nostalgia to take place as opposed to Hunan Plus' dining room tables.

Yelp reviewers rave on Bubble Egg's profile with little mention or complaint of these extra prices – something that is not uniformly applied to the 'no frills' restaurants such as Hunan Plus, which are expected to have cheap prices as a reflection of their (lack of) intentional interior/exterior design and price level. This indicates that when consumers partake in a commercial culinary exchange, they are paying not only for the personalization of the food itself, but also for the experience and the environment of participating in a social and food trend.

In BFS, comparing the national franchise, fast-food Korean corn dog restaurant 'Two Hands' and locally owned, Vietnamese restaurant, Migo Saigon Street Food, provides insights into owner expectations of changing customer desires. Two Hands' interior is devoid of any signals to Korea or of any of the patterns, colour schemes, or aesthetics typically associated with Asian imaginary, culture, or geography. Its to-go packaging seems to have no connection to traditional Korean cultural motifs or colour schemes. Similar to Bubble Egg, the personalization of street food to fit the consumer's wants and imaginations is key to the Two Hands dining experience. Consumers choose their filling and have a range of sauces and flavour powders to enhance their choices – a process that can be witnessed from its open-kitchen layout.

Two Hands' neighbour, Migo Saigon Street Food, is inspired by Ho Chi Minh City in the 1960s. Migo Saigon Street Food advertises its 'contemporary Saigon street food with noodle bowls, small dishes, and the Viet coffee' on its Yelp description. Migo's dark cherry wood panelling, shutter-like window frames, and translucent lighting sconces give it 'the authentic feel of a late Vietnamese alley food' (Yelp reviewer Ngoc L) and creates an atmosphere that provides just enough illumination to watch the servers and cooks prepare food in the open kitchen. By plating food typically enjoyed with casual environments, Migo elevates Vietnamese street food to a level of elegance. However, consumers walking in expecting street food also expect that the dishes 'should be semi-inexpensive' as explained by a

Yelp reviewer. Affordability thus factors into a consumer's perception of the food in front of them.

Comparing the aesthetics, dining/food experiences, and patrons' usage of social media between Two Hands and Migo Saigon Street Food indicates a startling relationship between an eatery's ownership/scope and their culinary/aesthetic choices. The franchise imported from overseas, Two Hands, finds no need to recreate cultural decorations or dishes in order to extract social and monetary capital from consumers. On the contrary, the locally owned mom-and-pop shop, Migo Saigon Street Food, invests in design elements and foodscapes that intentionally encourage the patron to imagine Vietnam.

Each complex and case study possesses a distinct narrative. When we put these stories in conversation with one another, the narratives indicate how certain aesthetics and foods are utilized as signals to invite gentrification. Commodifying diversity in the neoliberal economy means that participating in traditional Asian aesthetics and the economy around Asian food become adventures for the citizen in their never-ending pursuit of finding what and where authenticity is. In Houston, Asiatown is the (changing) landscape for that journey in refining one's taste and defining it as superior to that of others.

Resisting gentrification

In resisting the violence of displacement under racial capitalism, we must undo our reliance on economic profit, on the commodification of taste and authenticity, and on the privatization of space. This process of undoing may seem infinite and even impossible, but it begins with our capacity to imagine alternative sources of power and other (not Othered) ways of living beyond capital.

Digital, creative, and relational ways of direct action such as community-based mapping, archiving projects, public art, and intergenerational relationship-building preserve both the architectural and the visceral memories of Chinatowns in the face of displacement. Groups such as Chinatown Art Brigade (CAB) use 'cultural, material, and aesthetic modes of production' to resist gentrification in Manhattan's Chinatown through interactive projects such as 'Here to Stay', a series of large-scale outdoor projections displaying anti-gentrification messages on the exteriors of luxury developments gentrifying Chinatown. CAB's 'Placekeeping in Chinatown' utilizes Augmented Reality to portray the stories of resistance and resilience that tenants associate with key Chinatown places (Chinatown Art Brigade, n.d.), thus relying on the visceral geography of residents' memories connecting them with the spatial imaginary of Chinatown. Through archival floor plans, oral histories, and archived photos, Cheryl Wing-Zi Wong's 'Reflective Urbanisms: Mapping NY Chinatown' utilizes interactive 3D mapping to document the architectural transformations and occupancy history of Chinatown buildings over time, thus connecting physical land transformations to the visceral geography provided by oral histories and photos provided by community members (Wing-Zi Wong, n.d.).

Boston's Chinatown Stabilization Campaign's tenant organizing and coalition building led to Boston Chinatown's first resident association successfully increasing affordable housing and the restoration of the Boston Chinatown Branch Library destroyed in 1956 as a result of interstate construction (Chinese Progressive Association, n.d.). While not directly related to Asiatown, one of Houston's primary anti-displacement organizations is Project Row Houses, an artist-founded non-profit preserving Houston's historically Black Third Ward by restoring historic sites such as Eldorado Ballroom, providing income-based housing and affordable creative studios, and organizing community enrichment programmes such as its Young Mothers Residential Program (Project Row Houses, n.d.). Manhattan Chinatown's oldest operating storefront (founded in the 1890s and run by the same family for five generations), Wing On Wo & Co houses the W.O.W. Project, 'a women, non-binary, queer, trans-led, community-based initiative that works to sustain ownership over Chinatown Manhattan's future by growing, protecting, and preserving Chinatown's culture through arts, culture, and activism' (Wing On Wo & Co, 2023). This is exemplified by their 'Bridging Futures' initiative in which Chinatown activist elders and younger creative/movement leaders are put in conversation with one another, collecting elder oral histories and art on movement building. Cultural memory built and sustained through coalition building, community programmes, interpersonal relationship building, and oral storytelling preserve the spatial imaginary of a neighbourhood in the face of gentrification.

Discussion

What allows for retail and residential gentrification in Asiatown to go largely unnoticed is Houston's narrative of multiculturalism, globalism, and progressiveness – a symbolic gesture that blankets the neoliberal privatization logics that demand the constant production and consumption of space, food, aesthetics, commerce, and people in the cycle of gentrification. BFS' construction, at the expense of pre-existing housing structures in a working-class neighbourhood, best exemplifies gentrification under the guise of 'multiculturalism'. In reality, the ongoing gentrification of Asiatown is bounded by an agenda that views every space and every identity as a commodity. The Asian/Asian-American identity is under constant production (by ethnic entrepreneurs, city agendas, and global investments) for consumption (through food, aesthetic, and market exchange). If our communities are being displaced and if our own identities have been transformed into marketplace commodities, what is left for ourselves?

This process of rendering food and space in Asiatown more palatable to upscale consumers seeking a trendy experience diminishes the historically cultural, affective, or social significance of Asiatown. Instead of the 'demand and increasing presence of local-organic-vintage-handmade-sustainable businesses' (Summers, 2019) often associated with gentrification, the presence of global fast-casual/fast-food franchises signals Asiatown's gentrification. The transnational global connections brought by Asiatown's foreign investments, culinary connections, immigrant populations, and traditional Asian aesthetics makes the 'cosmopolitan urban edge city' an international city as well. The food trends imported from overseas such as Two Hands' Korean hot dogs and Bubble Egg's Hong Kong desserts communicate the image of Houston as an international city, yet both business' names and interior design lack any signals to a country of origin or ethnic cuisine. Thus, the Asian/Asian-American identity is cleansed under aesthetic 'beautification', re/naming and re/designing. Franchises that package non-Western culture in aesthetically pleasing fashions (Summers, 2019), such as Two Hands or Bubble Egg's, welcome queues of foodie customers enchanted by the newness of the cuisine, who then become a part of the urban gentrification process as increased consumerism increases a neighbourhood's social capital and, thus, its land value as well, consequently displacing long-time residents. The rise of digital media such as Yelp and Instagram becomes the platform through which consumers develop the power to define what restaurants are or aren't worth going to, creating a direct monetary flow to certain aesthetically pleasing restaurants over others. Upper-class developers take note of these trends to build more complexes curated to these consumer tastes.

We must understand gentrification as not just the transformation of residential physical space from low to high value, but rather view it as the transformation of the ways people live their lives in relation to the city. Under new re/development, people's lives are radically altered as they adapt to the degrading of land, the relocation of communities, and the rebuilding of life. In Asiatown, this process takes shape through the evolution of how food and aesthetics are made, consumed, and negotiated. The emergence of street food trends and modernized aesthetics not only serve as signals of retail gentrification, but they also provide new parameters for consumers to measure their lived experiences across restaurants. In this process, the making of the Asian/Asian-American identity – something always already contested – is in constant flux as consumers, ethnic entrepreneurs, developers, and public officials (re)negotiate race according to their convenience.

A feminist geopolitical lens grounds the visceral emotions, memories, and cognitive associations attached to a consumer's experience of a restaurant: tasting food, engaging with service, experiencing the ambiance from interior/exterior decor, and interacting with how food is styled or packaged. Developing taste is in the 'lived context of social representation'

(Hayes-Conroy, 2008: 467) which, for many Yelp reviewers, meant relying on past memories shared with loved ones, comparisons to other experiences consuming similar cuisines, word-of-mouth testimonials from friends, or preconceived notions shaped by structural elements such as foreign events or mainstream media. Experiencing the modern interiors and open kitchen of a restaurant, like Bubble Egg's, internally prepares the consumer for a different set of expectations and experiences than in the 'no frills' environment of Hunan Plus.

In the wake of the COVID-19 pandemic, Chinatowns, including Houston's Asiatown, were left depleted as a result of the state's Sinophobic propaganda instigated by COVID and White supremacy. Responses to anti-Asian violence have included the demand to shop and support local Asian-owned businesses. The 'depoliticization of diversity' (Summers, 2019) coupled with the shop local movement allows the mainstream media and general public to believe that increased commercial exchange will save us, when in fact, increased commercial exchange in Asiatown (which has necessitated the commodification of the Asian/Asian-American identity into a palatable form of consumption) has heightened the impacts of gentrification. There must be a self-sustaining way of surviving, thriving, and living that exists beyond commercial participation, especially when such commercial participation perpetuates retail gentrification and residential displacement.

If gentrification is shaped by the contestation over land use and its potential for individual profit, then resisting gentrification requires that we engage with the built environment in ways that prioritize the relationships we have with ourselves, our neighbours, and the land through direct action under a praxis of RFG.

Places here and now: concluding reflections in the wake of violence

In this chapter, I confront the making of a city that praises its diversity in food, people, and place while simultaneously leveraging that praise to displace its most disenfranchised residents. By understanding how interrelated food, space, and race are within Asiatown, we come to more nuanced understandings of urban gentrification as a process that encompasses not just land use, but also ways of living. Under new (re)development, people's lives are radically altered as they adapt to the evolution of their neighbourhood's spatial imaginaries and the changes that come with it: the degrading of land, the relocation of community, and the rebuilding of life. In Houston's Asiatown, we see how this process takes shape through the evolution of how food and aesthetics are made, consumed, and negotiated in a space. The emergence of street food trends and modernized aesthetics not only serve as signals of retail gentrification, but they also provide new parameters for consumers to measure their lived experiences across restaurants. In this process, the making of the Asian/Asian-American identity – something already constantly contested – is in constant flux as consumers, ethnic entrepreneurs, developers, and public officials (re)negotiate race to their convenience.

Racial capitalism transforms urban landscapes, foodscapes, aesthetic languages, and neighbourhoods, but the one act of preservation that has been able to move across geographies and timelines is the permanence of memory attached to space, food, and community. Yelp reviewer K.N.'s 'memories of China Town as a child [and their father taking them] to Lai Lai's Dumpling House' in Metropole and user Lanha T.'s recollections of D-Square's Hunan Plus with 'a friend from college ... over a decade ago' creates a nostalgia that pervades into how we produce place out of space. In these calls to the past, I see my own self replicated, tying me to strangers bonded by remembrance if nothing else. The histories, personal narratives, and visceral geographies in this research demonstrate the profound power of memory as a collective way of understanding, creating, and relating to space, to food, and to each other. The individual and communal power of memorializing, whether it be through a digital reconstruction of past Chinatown urban plans or a Yelp review fondly recounting a memory of a shuttered restaurant, can extend RFG praxis to understand the multiple, and visceral, forms of action (including the preserving of memories through writing this chapter).

So much has changed since the last time the sun warmed the backseat of my grandfather's Corolla. Every memory I have since experienced within Asiatown has felt like I experienced another loss. The Golden Palace dim sum place my mother, brother, and I always frequented throughout my entire childhood was foreclosed. The 2000 Corolla is now scrapped in some junkyard. The passing of my grandmother two years ago leaves me with grief that is processed over and over again. My grandfather can no longer drive to grab the newspapers fresh from the print company. But we develop new ways of learning, of living, of building community and resilience. My mother, brother, and I find joy in choosing a new dim sum place. I pick up the newspaper for my grandfather every chance I get. I speak with my grandmother in every sacred space I enter.

Every drive down Bellaire Street has been a reflection and negotiation of my place in this world, in Asiatown, in every tension that exists within this space. They have brought me to this research, but they left me with more questions and fewer answers than I entered with. I wonder if I keep driving, will the answers become clearer, or am I driving in circles endlessly in search of a horizon that will never be in my reach as close as it seems? I let this writing process become the drive back home, an endless expansion of myself in relation to the changes of the world around me.

Acknowledgements

As a believer in the profound potential of collectivity, this work is not only the culmination of knowledge co-produced alongside researchers, but it is also a collection of the relationships I am perpetually nourishing: relationships to myself, the people I hold close to me, and the lives we have built for ourselves. To the universe, thank you for bringing these ways of being and becoming into my life. Consuming Chinatown is a work of memory and a memorial to the abundance of memory. For my younger brother, my parents, and my grandparents in particular, this chapter is an homage to the neighbourhood our family planted seeds in and watched the roots unfold and the leaves shake in joy. Home will always be wherever you are, and whatever journeys this body of work takes on, those journeys will always lead back to you.

Note

[1] Houston's current 'Chinatown' is known by a wide variety of names. It was first known as 'New Chinatown' to distinguish it from the original downtown location known as 'Old Chinatown'. As Old Chinatown was erased from the public memory due to Houston's urban renewal plans and contemporary gentrification ushered by predominantly White young urban professionals, 'New Chinatown' would increasingly be referred to as simply 'Chinatown' in most press articles. To acknowledge the ethnic diversity beyond Chinese/Chinese-Americans, New Chinatown/Chinatown is known by some Houstonians as Asiatown. In this work, I refer to Houston's Chinatown as Asiatown.

References

Alkon, A., Kato, Y., and Sbicca, J. (2020) *A Recipe for Gentrification: Food, Power, and Resistance in the City*, New York: New York University Press.

Card, K. (2021) 'Geographies of Racial Capitalism with Ruth Wilson Gilmore', *Antipode*, [online] n.d., Available from: https://antipodeonline.org/geographies-of-racial-capitalism/ [Accessed 28 February 2023].

Chinatown Art Brigade (n.d.) 'About', Chinatown Art Brigade, [online] n.d., www.chinatownartbrigade.org/about [Accessed 8 February 2023].

Chinese Progressives Association (n.d.) 'Chinatown Stabilization Campaign', *Chinese Progressives Association Boston*, [online] n.d., Available from: https://cpaboston.org/en/programs/chinatown-stabilization-campaign [Accessed 8 February 2023].

CultureMap (2021) 'Houston named the most diverse city in the US by new report', *ABC13 Houston*, [online] 20 April, Available from: https://abc13.com/houston-diversity-wallethub-most-diverse-cities-in-america/10531439/ [Accessed 20 November 2020].

Gray, L. (2008) 'Branding Chinatown: A boom for a Houston neighborhood', *Houston Chronicle*, [online] 9 January, Available from: www.chron.com/entertainment/article/Branding-Chinatown-A-boom-for-a-Houston-1768129.php [Accessed 20 November 2020].

Hayes-Conroy A. and Hayes-Conroy, J. (2008) 'Taking back taste: feminism, food and visceral politics', *Gender, Place and Culture*, 15(5): 461–73.

Knapp, A. and Vojnovic, I. (2016) 'Ethnicity in an immigrant gateway city: the Asian condition in Houston', *Journal of Urban Affairs*, 38(3): 344–69.

Lees, L., Slater, T., and Wyly, E. (2007) *Gentrification*, Oxfordshire: Routledge.

Project Row Houses (n.d.) 'About', *Project Row Houses*, [online] n.d., Available from: https://projectrowhouses.org/about/ [Accessed 1 February 2023].

Sandler, E. (2019) '13 new restaurants coming to ambitious Chinatown development', *CultureMap Houston*, [online] 6 February, Available from: https://houston.culturemap.com/news/restaurants-bars/02-06-19-bellaire-food-street-13-new-restaurants-chinatown-kevin-kan/ [Accessed 26 November 2020].

Schmiz, A. and Stock, M. (2019) 'Catering authenticities. Ethnic food entrepreneurs as agents in Berlin's gentrification', *City, Culture and Society*, 18.

Summers, B. (2019) *Black in Place*, Chapel Hill, NC: University of North Carolina Press.

Wing On Wo and Co (n.d.) 'The W.O.W. Project', *Wing On Wo and Co*, [online] n.d., Available from: https://wingonwoand.co/pages/the-wow-project [Accessed 1 February 2023].

Wing-Zi Wong, C. (n.d.) 'Reflective Urbanisms: Mapping NY Chinatown Community Engagement Events', *CW-ZW*, [online] n.d., Available from: www.cw-zw.com/current-news/reflective-urbanisms-mapping-ny-chinatown-community-engagement-events/ [Accessed 1 February 2023].

Zhou, M. (2016) 'A modern look for Houston's Chinatown', *China Daily*, [online] 22 April, Available from: https://usa.chinadaily.com.cn/2016-04/22/content_24775502.htm [Accessed 1 February 2021].

Zukin, S. (2008) 'Consuming authenticity: from outposts of difference to means of exclusion', *Cultural Studies*, 22(5): 724–48.

9

Developing Black Urban Agrarianism

Brittany D. Jones

As I sit in my chair, staring at the screen, listening to my research participant answer a question about his food justice work experience, he states a memorable metaphor: "Superman is not coming to save us because we have too much kryptonite." I asked him to elaborate. He goes on to say that we as Black Americans often find ourselves in one of two places: (1) spaces where we are tolerated or (2) spaces that uplift our culture to counteract said other spaces.

Black Americans have always had to create alternative spaces that reflect our identity, culture, history, and visions for the future. This also includes the systems we desire to institute in hopes to ensure self-sufficiency and autonomy. In this case, the space is the urban neighbourhood, and the vision is an equitable and accessible local food system tailored to their needs. What is preventing this progress are the acres of vacant land, which have performed as kryptonite to those with resources. The plots of green were not a bad omen to the interviewee, but rather a call to be creative and create a space that reflects both past influence and devotion to a better future through food. The residents of the neighbourhood in question, located in Toledo, Ohio, had to function as their own Superman/Woman. My dissertation,[1] 'Empowerment through Consumption: Land Ownership, Land Banks[2] and Black Food Geographies', sought to document and explore this type of perseverance as it relates to urban agriculture (UA) activities in Black neighbourhoods through the praxis of Black urban agrarianism (BUA).

Whether seen as nuisance or serene, vacant land establishes a perception of devaluation and indirectly communicates a message of 'nothingness' (Reese, 2019) for those who live within its boundaries or in its proximity. When speaking of *majority-melanated*[3] neighbourhoods, the terms 'vacant', 'disinvestment', and even 'urban core' all carry connotations tied to anti-Blackness and anti-poor motives to overtake space, which leads to displacement and erasure. As someone who was raised in this type of neighbourhood, I have witnessed the debilitating relationship between Black communities and numerous plots of green grass, which mirrors the weakening effect of kryptonite on Superman. Layering this with the historical trauma of forced agricultural labour during slavery in the US, it is no surprise that UA, via the reimagining of vacant urban lots, is not always embraced as a way towards self-sufficiency (Reese, 2019).

Hammelman et al (2020) describe what it means to integrate both theory and action in bringing about a more just and sustainable food system as components of radical food geographies (RFG) praxis. They state that RFG 'highlights the power relationships that produce and regulate them across scales' (2020: 220). Further, they argue that RFG critically engages 'geographic realities in deeply theoretical and action-oriented ways' (2020: 220; see also Levkoe et al, Chapter 1). This chapter explores the RFG framework in relation to the theorization and actualization of Black foodways through UA and BUA, the latter of which resists the universalistic, or sameness, mindset grounded in dominant White culture. My research uses two Ohio cities – Toledo and Dayton – as case-study examples of using BUA as a tool to dismantle food oppression within Black urban neighbourhoods of the Northern US. I argue that BUA is radical, as it is manifested with the intention of fostering an alternative food system that represents Black culture and strengthens legacy building. BUA is also presented as an example of Monica White's theory of Collective Agency and Community Resilience [CACR], as explained in her book *Freedom Farmers* (2018). From a geographic standpoint, BUA depicts the differences of internal and external food system obstacles experienced by northern US Black urban neighbourhoods versus those of the southern US. As a contribution to RFG, I argue that BUA can be used as a long-term strategy towards gaining and asserting spatial autonomy by way of land and food sovereignty.

BUA in the context of RFG

BUA focuses on the future of Black foodways and the need for a new contract of citizenship in urban spaces (Purcell and Tyman, 2014). Birthed out of survival strategies in the US, the concept of Black foodways describes the way food is consumed and produced within Black culture. It counteracts White dominance and oppression by preserving food systems unique to the African American experience. It also emphasizes a strong connection to the natural environment as a shared relationship (Smith, 2007). As an example of RFG, BUA can be considered a radical approach to alternative UA practice, while also acknowledging the violent history from which these foodways were conceived. RFG calls for support of a deeper discourse centring theory and action to eliminate oppressive systems, and uplifting those that advance self-sufficiency and self-determination. This would build upon how Black foodways have always incorporated action as a way to bring about equity. This has taken the form, for example, of community-owned grocery stores, neighbourhood farmers' markets, and school gardens. The impact of Black foodways have also been examined in the fields of sociology, anthropology, and environmental studies (Myers, 2015; Fiskio, Shammin, and Scott, 2016; White, 2018; Reese, 2019) and can be useful in expanding RFG. For the context of this chapter, I discuss Black-led UA from a social and political standpoint, where BUA operates within racialized spaces of cities with a manufacturing past, such as Toledo and Dayton, that became home to many Black people and communities during the Great Migration.

The theoretical basis of BUA stems mostly from White's concept of CACR.[4] CACR conceptualizes three strategies enacted by Black residents to organize and empower their communities in forming an ideal local food system that reflects their values and goals. It 'builds upon and amplifies the social movement concept of everyday strategies of resistance' (White, 2018: 6). The strategies within CACR are meant to capture 'the activities community members enact as a means to be self-reliant and self-sufficient' (White, 2018: 6). For example, a community may decide to establish a land trust organization to counteract land bank ownership in its neighbourhood or a group might organize a 'day at the market' where residents carpool to food outlets that are inaccessible by public transportation. The nature of these activities is shifting the focus and intention of the food justice movement as it is accentuating equity of access, in addition to cultural and ethnic stimuli (Alkon and Norgaard, 2009).

Commons as praxis, as the first CACR strategy, 'engages and contests dominant practices of ownership, consumerism, and individualism and replaces them with shared social status and shared identities of race and class' (White, 2018: 19). It calls for strategic organization that requires community agreement and execution for the betterment of all. The second strategy, *prefigurative politics*, involves the creation of a democratic system that reflects the ideology of all who have been excluded from the dominant political system and emphasizes the notion of free space, or 'everyday utopias' (Cooper, 2009 as cited in White, 2018: 19). Finally, *economic autonomy* is a third, crucial strategy of CACR. Economic exploitation of the Black community has left many vulnerable and dependent on the dominant system. This strategy of CACR calls for an alternative system of exchange of resources, such as bartering, which takes place within the community, thus adding to buying power, in addition to reinvestment opportunities led by the residents. The end goal is to gain independence from an oppressive structure and achieve spatial autogestion.

White's concept of CACR is powerful in uplifting the work of Black food activists, both past and present, showing the perseverance of Black people when it comes to feeding their community, and how collaboration is vital to preserving Black foodways. However, much of White's discussion of CACR engages primarily with rural spaces, or at least food produced in rural spaces and brought into cities – though White does focus on UA in a majority-Black neighbourhood through the works of the Detroit Black Community Food Security Network, considering the case of D-Town Farms in Detroit in the final chapters of her book (White, 2018: 117). BUA steps in by examining the foodways of urban Black communities, the obstacles with land management systems, and the movement towards reclamation of space. Bringing it all together, BUA provides an approach to building food system structures that preserve the legacy of Black food activists' memories and wisdom as an approach for self-sufficiency.

BUA combating food apartheid

'We were land-based agrarian people from Africa. We were uprooted from Africa, and we spent 200 years developing our culture as black Americans. And then we left the South. We uprooted ourselves and attempted to transplant this culture to the pavement of the industrialized North. And it was a transplant that did not take … ' (August Wilson, cited in Shannon, 1997)

Wilson's comments in the previous quote continue to hold true to the issues faced by Black Americans in the northern US. The Great Migration brought more than six million Black Americans to the northern cities – as well as to the West and Midwest – to escape racial terrorism, lynching, land theft, and segregation, while also seeking better employment, often in manufacturing or domestic work. Those who remained in the South continued to face these same adversities, while also dealing with oppressive sharecropping, crop liens, and tenant systems that reincarnated the plantation system (Myers, 2023). As a result, it was difficult to pass down farmland and agrarian knowledge to younger generations who did not find value in sustaining the family farm. Additionally, much land was lost to White-owned entities or individuals through a range of discriminatory lending and credit practices, and oppressive sharecropping, only to be transformed into commercial development or absorbed into family trusts (Gilbert et al, 2002; Figueroa and Penniman, 2020).

The idea of the agrarian lifestyle was also seen as beneath one by some Black Americans because it was tied to slavery. But today, many Black families equipped, with more resources and knowledge, are looking to reclaim their agrarian roots. In doing this, they strengthen autonomy through ownership of their physical surroundings. Through the efforts of Black placemaking, Black residents enact spatial agency by exerting control in or acting upon a desired part of the built environment (see Montgomery in Garth and Reese, 2020: 32). BUA is used as a tool to enhance constructive Black placemaking and combat food apartheid.

Food apartheid physically changed the urban landscape as it left Black communities vulnerable to exploitative solutions operated by economic and political authorities. Decades of out-migration, disinvestment, dispossession, and redlining have also made it difficult for Black residents to govern neighbourhood development (D'Rozario and Williams, 2005). These forces created an environment that is sometimes perceived as '*nothingness*', which assumes the area to be lifeless (Reese, 2019: 9). Similarly, the same association applies to the term food desert.[5] Describing the phenomenon of food inequity in this way – desert or nothingness – ignores the unique and imaginative ways in which Black food culture has survived and been (re)imagined in the urban North.

As a result, several activists and scholars use the term 'food apartheid' described by activist Karen Washington as a term that addresses disparities in the whole food system in relation to 'race, geography, faith, and economics' (as cited in Brones, 2018: 16). Food apartheid is deemed a more appropriate description than food desert because a desert is a natural occurrence that takes time, whereas what has happened and is happening in majority-Black communities do not reflect this definition and was done intentionally (see Joyner et al, 2022). Washington notes that responses to food apartheid can be seen as 'everyday strategies of resistance' where the everyday behaviours and ideologies of community members cultivate a social network that amplifies and normalize these shared values (as cited in Brones, 2018: 16; see also Bradley and Herrera, 2015; Joyner et al, 2022; see also Zurawski and Higgins, Chapter 7).

An example of food apartheid is the unnerving presence of dollar stores, or as I call them, *stoplight stores*,[6] in low-to-mid-income neighbourhoods that are majority-melanated. Shannon (2021) found that between 2008 and 2018, their locations increased by 60 per cent across 27 metropolitan areas targeted for the study. In turn, the stoplight stores serve as a replacement for adequate food outlets, despite offering sub-par, highly processed food items. I argue that BUA combats these symptoms of food apartheid as an 'everyday strategy of resistance' by encouraging community food production, improving the physical environment; creating a third space for community engagement (if land is converted for this activity); and executing the first pillar of CACR, *commons as praxis*. The pillar emphasizes shared ideology, social class, and identity of the residents performed through collective behaviours for the betterment of their food system. The weight of togetherness and collectivism are essential to the success of building sustainable, self-reliant communities.

As mentioned previously, Legacy Cities, or post-industrial era cities, such as Chicago, Baltimore, Cleveland, and Detroit, are beginning to see the benefits of using UA as an alternative for vacant land repurposing and strengthening land tenure in disinvested communities as a response to land loss, exodus from agriculture, and food apartheid. Some cities are hesitant to do this because the activity does not promise a long-term economic return, given that commercial uses usually yield higher profit, often through increased tax revenue. Therefore, the success of UA in these cities is affected by the differing resident demographics, the state of the land and community mentality about UA, and the network of municipal and community players. I now turn to a discussion of how BUA can be used to understand UA activities in Toledo and Dayton, particularly as a method of community development and neighbourhood revitalization.

Case studies: Dayton and Toledo

Dayton and Toledo, also Legacy Cities, were selected as research sites due to their manufacturing history, historical and sizable Black population, strong land bank presence, and burgeoning work towards improving their local/regional food system. Little research exists on UA in these two cities, especially Black-led UA. Research that does exist usually pertains to economic development via land or housing (Hackworth and Nowakowski, 2015) or the food system as a whole (Cuy Castellanos et al, 2017). Therefore, my research explored the manifestation of BUA within these geographically similar cities in the Midwest.

In Toledo, the fourth most populous city in Ohio, BUA is manifested through organizations such as Mighty Organics, a 3-acre farm enterprise; the Junction Coalition, a community group functioning through the Frederick Douglass Community Center, which intertwines food security and production with community development and economic solidity; Community Reinvestment Coalition Englewood SW (CRC-ESW), a non-profit neighbourhood corporation that used UA as a response to increasing food security during the COVID-19 pandemic; and, Urban Wholisitics, a newly formed non-profit aimed at greening initiatives and land-keeping within disinvested communities of colour, which includes food production and agricultural entrepreneurship. These four organizations are centrally located in majority-Black neighbourhoods, all of which have been classified as 'food deserts' by the United States Department of Agriculture and are subject to food apartheid. As someone who was born, raised, and currently resides in Toledo, I have witnessed these entities rise and fall as they try to change the mindsets of those who live within the boundaries they serve when it concerns agriculture. Findings from my research reinforced previous observations about agriculture's negative association in the Black community

(White, 2018; McCutcheon, 2019; Reese, 2019). This mostly came from middle-aged interviewees (aged 45–59), while the elderly (aged 60 and above) and younger generations (aged 30 and younger) were adamant about seeing UA become part of everyday life within their neighbourhoods. All understood that UA was 'more than just food' (Jones, 2021: 142), and that the culture needs to control this factor to become self-sufficient.

In 2014–2015, Dayton ranked as one of the cities with the highest food hardship in a 2016 report by the Food Research and Action Coalition (Driscoll, 2018; Bachman, 2019). These findings motivated the prioritization of food-related issues through several organizations. Gem City Market, which opened in 2021, is a testament to CACR as it was established to be a disruptor, with the intention of revitalizing Black empowerment and resilience in the neighbourhood. The full-scale coop grocery store provides reasonable prices and fresh produce from local growers. Additionally, there is a health clinic, a teaching kitchen, and a community meeting room/library that centres Black culture and literature. In terms of land, particularly land trusts, Dayton's Unified Power, an organizational arm under Co-Op Dayton, invests in retaining community members in West Dayton by controlling land and development via a trust. In doing this, they enact collective and cooperative governance where all will benefit, be owners of their space, and have their voices heard (Co-Op Dayton, 2023).

Interviewees in both cities agreed that their food justice work was a step towards reversing the damage of food apartheid. As such, they execute the initial step of CACR (*commons as praxis*) and inadvertently BUA. Black farmers and growers in both cities noted that their purpose for engaging in their activities is a response to there being *nothing* in the neighbourhood, such as grocers or fresh food. When it comes to BUA as a way to combat food apartheid, it is more than just having a meal on the table, creating 'soul food', or navigating the 'corner store jungle'. It is a culture that should be celebrated and considered as a template for its constant resistance against the status quo, while also engaging in new opportunities for progression.

BUA as an 'everyday utopia'

Even during times of turmoil, Black spaces have formed and thrived as a result of collective networks and the communal ideology of perseverance. These internal cultural economies and networks are what kept most families afloat and aided in their preservation in the face of discrimination and higher living costs. Examining race within the concept of food system development draws attention to how resistance from melanated communities has been met with force and violence. A prime example is that of the often-villainized Black Panther Party (BPP), formed in 1966. The BPP was integral to efforts for Black food security at the beginning of the group's formation, as its community service programmes, mainly the Breakfast for Children Program,[7] served as lifelines to these communities as a means of survival (Patel, 2012). Although the BPP was forced underground, its vision of community food security for Black American citizens continues forth in both practice and scholarship (Beckerman, 2021).

The second CACR strategy, *prefigurative politics*, is meant to solidify an alternative political system that is both democratic and requires residents to engage in self-reflection, thus creating an 'everyday utopia' (White, 2018: 10). The potential for a justice-oriented food politics is not fully acknowledged without this understanding. For Toledo and Dayton, the organizations engaging in BUA serve as safe spaces for alternative political systems to develop.

Interviewees in my study shared that their experiences, when gathering in these neighbourhood spaces, were that they felt heard and seen. Discussions that were viewed as politically incorrect or disruptive were met with understanding, and often led to a solution to combat the emotional discrepancy. The information exchange happening between the residents added to a political system created by them and for them, especially if a community development project was the main topic. For example, the Frederick Douglass Center in Toledo serves as the headquarters of the Junction neighbourhood and its activities. Until recently, this neighbourhood was often ignored and passed over by government-funded projects. Now, it is often the first to be offered any development project meant to improve the infrastructure, including using vacant land as a Community Supported Agriculture (CSA) project and hosting farmers' markets. Similarly, Dayton's Unified Power is the powerhouse for those in West Dayton as they seek to control land and create a system of reinvestment with the understanding that development is managed collectively by the people (Unified Power, 2022). The idea of the city as just a sterile, grey environment is dismissed because of the people intervening and making it their own, by their own rules. Urban spaces are more than just property rights and economic development, and the focus should be on how it is used, especially by the residents.

BUA as an alternative economy

The third CACR strategy is achieved once people create a system that reflects their economic strength. As White noted, this can be in the form of bartering for resources and produce from home gardens (2018: 8), along with the traditional capitalistic forms of grants, money exchange, and employment. Interviewees in my study agreed that economic control meant owning land within their neighbourhood. Owning physical space for food production allows residents to beautify the space and manage the type of food that is familiar to them. From personal experience, many neighbours had a home garden where the produce was used for meals, preserved, or given away. However, as people moved out of the neighbourhood, agricultural wisdom and the gardens diminished. For farmers in the two cities, a typical process offered for those interested in farming urban land is that of leasing from their respective city or county land bank. This agreement lasts at least two years with the understanding that the lessee maintains the property and does not install permanent fixtures like hoop houses or fences. Although a step in the right direction, these programmes are only temporary and include strict stipulations for one to obtain the desired land.

Referring back to the BPP, part of their Ten Point Program[8] was that of creating land trusts for the purposes of food production and education (Beckerman, 2021). In Black food spaces, the idea of preservation from an economic development standpoint inhibits the growth of deep food knowledge where 'sustainability views of nature through recollection and old ways' (Myers, 2015) never have the chance to develop into new skills. This is due to the view of land as a commercial commodity for city economic development instead of economic growth for the specific neighbourhood. With food access becoming part of many municipalities' top priorities (especially as a response to the COVID-19 pandemic), UA is being tested as a solution to temporary, or in some cases, permanent vacant land repurposing efforts. However, in the hands of municipal organizations, economic advancement continues to re-emerge as a barrier to neighbourhoods because of the lack of ownership.

Considering that large-scale UA, in general, is practised by more non-profit entities, most work is grant funded and constrained by strict deliverables. The common one- and two-year grants do not allow for full maturation of beds, which need three to five years to produce, as one interviewee explained. Non-profits dominate this field, particularly within Dayton, as many of them have a food production component attached to their mission. The top three (Homefull, Mission of Mary, and the Dayton City Food Bank) have reached financial sustainability to where market distribution or a mass of partnership funding aids their operation for long-term. Other non-profits (such as Edgemont Solar Garden or Dayton Urban Grown), rely on short-term grants (one to two years) and consumer/community support, which has suffered due to COVID-19 restrictions. In Toledo, UA is realized through more entrepreneurial enterprises often tied to a patchwork of church or novice neighbourhood-based non-profits. Although both cities are addressing the same issue, fragmented efforts towards land ownership, entrepreneurship, and equity continue.

The future of Black food via BUA

BUA has the potential to mend the strained relationship between the Black community and agriculture, along with providing alternative ways to navigate a food environment that was not built in their best interests. Through the three pillars of CACR – *commons as praxis, prefigurative politics,* and *economic autonomy* – BUA is supported for longevity and positions itself as a reference for how to create race-based food spaces as seen in both Toledo and Dayton. Significantly, being self-sustainable and sufficient is an end goal and there is no fear in thwarting domineering power structures.

In this chapter, I have argued that BUA counteracts the harm done to Black people in post-industrial urban spaces because it addresses the physical, mental, emotional, and spiritual needs of individuals, families, and their communities. The consequences of food apartheid in Legacy Cities, as discussed previously, continue to expose many gaps dealing with food security, race, and the built environment. The recent reawakening of Black agrarianism and associated actions towards addressing food apartheid have prompted more exploration integrating the spatial aspect with that of Black foodways (Grant et al, 2012; Taylor, 2018; White, 2018; Reese, 2019; Summers, 2019; Garth and Reese, 2020). However, much of this work engages more with rural spaces, which leaves a gap in examining foodways preserved by CACR. BUA begins to fill this gap.

This can also be said about RFG, where using research and data to elevate the work of residents can generate a platform to attract the necessary resources and inspire other projects. Additionally, this discussion of BUA adds to the concept of RFG by highlighting the resistance against power inequities reproduced in oppressive food systems in distinct areas. RFG attests that the praxis is rooted in 'active resistance to structures that (re)produce power inequity and oppression in food systems in specific places and across spaces' (Hammelman et al, 2020: 211). BUA stresses the repressive control of governmental bodies on their space and how to organize said space reflective of their aspirations. For example, BUA-based activity can begin to address land grabbing by municipal entities (such as county land banks) through both theory and action because it gives precedence to communities producing safe spaces to spend dollars or grow culturally appropriate foods that represent resiliency and honour the ancestors (Myers, 2015).

With municipalities investing in food system infrastructure, especially as a response to the COVID-19 pandemic, UA is a solution to temporary, or in some cases, permanent vacant land repurposing efforts with an economic return. However, in the hands of land banks or other municipal organizations, political and administrative processes continue to re-emerge as barriers, in addition to the imbalance of power over the parcel's use. BUA is a tool of resistance in such cases because it challenges the capitalist idea of land solely for commercial development versus a space for communal ownership. BUA also emphasizes communal self-management and organizational structure as a counteraction to state control over space and activities that take place within it, which is also noted as a function of RFG.

Through case studies in Dayton and Toledo, Ohio, I have considered the activity of urban Black communities as they manage obstacles from land management systems and move towards reclamation of space. Both cities need equitable governance over these activities as a means to transfer power from the hands of state control to those of existing and newly formed organizations focused on ethnic/racial alliances to reach economic and food resilience. RFG and its focus on identifying oppressive structures in order to dismantle them through collective activism and scholarship is witnessed through self-governance via BUA as a response to a system that classified them as incapable of self-care and built without them in mind. Black food spaces are structured to operate as sites for liberation and imagining the future of Black foodways.

Black agrarianism is a generational and cultural practice. As such, BUA honours these same concepts. It starts with a connection to the past, sustaining and recording wisdom whether orally or physically (with the five senses). Recalling the three strategies of CACR, BUA calls for "a civic responsibility to food", as one Dayton interviewee stated, that reverberates food sovereignty through a democratic matter rooted in a shared experience (Jones, 2021: 145). Many interviewees who are either practitioners or advocates were introduced to the concept of growing your own food through their grandparents or a close relationship, such as an uncle or a friend. This is the future of Black food – this is BUA. Kryptonite has not defeated Superman yet, and green lots do not stand a chance against a Black community with a plan.

Notes

[1] My dissertation was a mixed-methods project from 2019 to 2021, comprising data obtained from 53 semi-structured virtual interviews via WebEx (29 for Toledo, Ohio and 24 for Dayton, Ohio), analysis of eight years of the respective city and county land banks, vacant land transaction records via the county Auditors' databases (2010–18), and analysis of select socio-economic and demographic variables from both the 2014 and 2018 five-year American Community Survey (ACS).

[2] Land banks were 'designed and empowered specifically by state legislation to address the inventory of problem properties the private market has discarded and convert these neighbourhood liabilities into assets that advance community-based goals' (Alexander, 2011). They are highly regarded as the 'solution' for vacant land management, where eminent domain can be easily enacted (Alexander, 2011, 2005; Schwarz, 2009; Heins and Abdelazim, 2014: 11; Mansa, 2016). Ohio has 57 land banks out of 88 counties (Center for Community Progress, 2022). However, they are also regarded by some as 'land grabbing' due to their power to enact eminent domain in the name of 'community development', and deciding a 'proper' use and owner for the land without consulting taxpayers.

[3] I use this term in lieu of *minority* as an empowerment term. 'Majority-melanated' neighbourhoods are communities of predominately residents of colour.

[4] Although not discussed in White's book, CACR also challenges Henri Lefebvre's *Right to the City* (1991) theory by exploring how Black residents manifest this theory in urban spaces that both welcomed and exiled them since America's inception. BUA offers an alternative perspective on Black urban food production within the neoliberal city.

5   The United States Department of Agriculture defines 'food deserts' as areas where there is 20 per cent poverty rate and a third or more of the residents have to travel over a mile for a suitable grocer (for example, full-service grocery stores).

6   'Stop light stores' is a term I use to describe the association of neighbourhood characteristics in the colour of the stores' signage. The store, Family Dollar, has the colour red, and is usually found in impoverished, distressed neighbourhoods. Dollar General, identified by its black-and-yellow sign, is found in areas of middle income. Finally, Dollar Tree, indicated by green, is found in higher-income areas and, at times, next to Big Box stores such as Target or Wal-Mart.

7   Eventually, this programme was operating through 45 BPP branches nationwide, serving up meals to thousands of children. This was part of their Ten Point Plan for Black liberation within the US.

8   As Beckerman states, the BPP's Ten Point Program was a document that 'detailed their mission – both what they wanted, and what they believed'. It declared that all humans had the right to basic necessities and called for institutional change for the betterment of the Black culture.

References

Alexander, F.S. (2011) 'Land Banks and Land Banking', *Center for Community Progress*, [online], Available from: https://communityprogress.org/publications/land-banks-and-land-banking-2011/ [Accessed 8 March 2021].

Alkon, A.H. and Norgaard, K.M. (2009) 'Breaking the food chains: an investigation of food justice activism', *Sociological Inquiry*, 79(3): 289–305. DOI: https://doi.org/10.1111/j.1475-682x.2009.00291.x

Bachman, M. (2019) 'Food justice the focus of Dayton food and farming conference', *The Yellow Springs News*, [online], Available from: https://ysnews.com/news/2019/01/food-justice-the-focus-of-dayton-food-farming-conference [Accessed 16 July 2022].

Beckerman, M. (2021) 'What the Black Panther Party taught us about building a food movement', *Planet Forward*, [online], Available from: www.planetforward.org/idea/black-panther-food-community [Accessed 16 July 2022].

Bradley, K. and Herrera, H. (2015) 'Decolonizing food justice: naming, resisting, and researching colonizing forces in the movement', *Antipode*, 48(1): 97–114. DOI: https://doi.org/10.1111/anti.12165

Brones, A. (2018) 'Karen Washington: It's Not a Food Desert, It's Food Apartheid', *Guernica* , [online], Available from: www.guernicamag.com/karen-washington-its-not-a-food-desert-its-food-apartheid/ [Accessed 28 July 2022].

Center for Community Progress National Land Bank Map (2022) *National Land Bank Map*, [online], Available from: https://communityprogress.org/resources/land-banks/national-land-bank-map/ [Accessed 16 May 2022].

CO-OP Dayton (n.d.) *CO-OP Dayton*, [online], Available from: www.coopdayton.org/ [Accessed 25 August 2022].

Cooper, D. (2009) 'Intersectional travel through everyday utopias: The difference sexual and economic dynamics make', in E. Grabham, D. Cooper, J. Krishnadas, and D. Herman (eds) *Intersectionality and Beyond: Law, Power and the Politics of Location*, New York: Routledge-Cavendish, pp 299–325.

Cuy Castellanos, D., Jones, J.C., Christaldi, J., and Liutkus, K.A. (2017) 'Perspectives on the development of a local food system: the case of Dayton, Ohio', *Agroecology and Sustainable Food Systems*, 41(2): 186–203.

Driscoll, Kara (2018) 'As grocers build in suburbs, food deserts grow in Dayton', *Dayton Daily News*, 28 April 2018, www.daytondailynews.com/business/grocers-build-suburbs-food-deserts-grow-dayton/XXkuprR7ry2eJkcP4lv5xL/ [Accessed 9 January 2023].

D'Rozario, D. and Williams, J.D. (2005) 'Retail redlining: definition, theory, typology, and measurement', *Journal of Macromarketing*, 25(2): 175–86. DOI: https://doi.org/10.1177/0276146705280632

Figueroa, M., Penniman, L., Feldman, M., Treakle, J., Pahnke, A., Calo, A., Iles, A., and Bowman, J. (2020) 'Land access for beginning and disadvantaged farmers', *Green New Deal Policy Series*, pp 1–11.

Fiskio, J., Shammin, M.R., and Scott, V. (2016) 'Cultivating community: Black agrarianism in Cleveland, Ohio', *Gastronomica*, 16(2): 18–30.

Gilbert, J., Sharp, G., and Felin, M.S. (2002) 'The loss and persistence of Black-owned farms and farmland: a review of the research literature and its implications', *Journal of Rural Social Sciences*, 18(2): 1.

Grant, G.R., Wood, S.D., and Wright, W.J. (2012) 'Black farmers united: the struggle against power and principalities', *Journal of Pan African Studies*, 5(1): 3–22.

Hackworth, J. and Nowakowski, K. (2015) 'Using market-based policies to address market collapse in the American Rust Belt: the case of land abandonment in Toledo, Ohio', *Urban Geography*, 36(4): 528–49. DOI: https://doi.org/10.1080/02723638.2015.1011416

Hammelman, C., Reynolds, K., and Levkoe, C.Z. (2020) 'Toward a radical food geography praxis: integrating theory, action, and geographic analysis in pursuit of more equitable and sustainable food systems', *Human Geography*, 13(3): 211–27. DOI: https://doi.org/10.1177/1942778620962034

Heins, P. and Abdelazim, T. (2014) *Take it to the Bank: How Land Banks Are Strengthening America's Neighborhoods*, Washington, DC: Center for Community Progress.

Jones, B.D. (2021) *Empowerment Through Consumption: Land Ownership, Land Banks, and Black Food Geographies*, University of Toledo. [Doctoral dissertation, University of Toledo]. OhioLINK Electronic Theses and Dissertations Center. http://rave.ohiolink.edu/etdc/view?acc_num=toledo1628166946903064

Joyner, L., Yagüe, B., Cachelin, A. and Rose, J. (2022) 'Farms and gardens everywhere but not a bite to eat? A critical geographic approach to food apartheid in Salt Lake City', *Journal of Agriculture, Food Systems, and Community Development*, 11(2): 67–88.

Lefebvre, H. (1991) *The Production of Space*, Oxford: Blackwell.

Mansa, M. (2016) 'Tennessee Housing Development Agency Issue Brief: Land Banking To Eliminate Blight and Support Affordable Housing', *Tennessee Development Housing Agency*, [online], Available from: https://thda.org/pdf/Land-Bank-Issue-Brief.pdf [Accessed 16 February 2021].

McCutcheon, P. (2019) 'Fannie Lou Hamer's freedom farms and Black agrarian geographies', *Antipode*, 51(1): 207–24. DOI: https://doi.org/10.1111/anti.12500

Meyers, G.P. (2015) 'Decolonizing a food system: Freedom Farmers' Market as a place for resistance and analysis', *Journal of Agriculture, Food Systems, and Community Development*, 5(4): 149–52.

Myers, G.P. (2023), Farms To Grow, Inc Production. *Rhythms of the Land*. United States.

Patel, R. (2012) *Stuffed and Starved: The Hidden Battle for the World Food System*, Melville House.

Purcell, M. and Tyman, S.K. (2014) 'Cultivating food as a right to the city', *Local Environment*, 20(10): 1132–47. DOI: https://doi.org/10.1080/13549 839.2014.903236

Reese, A.M. (2019) *Black Food Geographies: Race, Self-Reliance, and Food Access Washington, D.C.*, Chapel Hill, NC: University of North Carolina Press.

Reese, A.M. and Garth, H. (2020) *Black Food Matters: Racial Justice in the Wake of Food Justice*, Minneapolis, MN: University Of Minnesota Press.

Schwarz, L. (2009) 'The neighborhood stabilization program: land banking and rental housing as opportunities for innovation', *Journal of Affordable Housing and Community Development Law*, 19: 51.

Shannon, S.G. (1997) 'A transplant that did not take: August Wilson's views on the Great Migration', *African American Review*, 31(4): 659. DOI: https://doi.org/10.2307/3042334

Shannon, J. (2021) 'Dollar stores, retailer redlining, and the metropolitan geographies of precarious consumption', *Annals of the American Association of Geographers*, 111(4): 1200–18.

Smith, K.K. (2007) *African American Environmental Thought: Foundations*, Lawrence, KS: University Press of Kansas.

Summers, B.T. (2019) *Black in Place: The Spatial Aesthetics of Race in a Post-Chocolate City*, UNC Press Books.

Taylor, Dorceta E. and Kerry J. Ard. (2015) 'Research article: food availability and the food desert frame in Detroit: an overview of the city's food system', *Environmental Practice*, 17(2): 102–133, doi: 10.1017/s1466046614000544.

Unifiedpower (n.d.) 'Home', *Unified Power*, [online], Available from: www.daytonunifiedpower.com/ [Accessed 16 August 2022].

White, M.M. (2018) *Freedom Farmers: Agricultural Resistance and the Black Freedom Movement*, Chapel Hill, NC: University of North Carolina Press.

PART III

Human and More-than-Human Relations

10

Beyond 'Good Intentions': Fostering Meaningful Indigenous–Settler Relationships to Support Indigenous Food Sovereignty

*Rosie Kerr, Charles Z. Levkoe, Larry McDermott,
Jessica McLaughlin, Julie Price, Glenn Checkley, Alex Boulet,
Erika Bockstael, Sarah Craig, and Amanda Froese*

An invitation into ethical space

We invite the reader to enter with us into ethical space. Originally coined by literary theorist Roger Poole (1972) and further developed by Cree Elder and legal scholar Willie Ermine (2000, 2007), ethical space aims to bring together Indigenous and settler knowledge systems to co-create relational space where different ways of knowing[1] can interact. According to Ermine (2007: 193), 'ethical space is formed when two societies, with disparate worldviews, are poised to engage each other. It is the thought about diverse societies and the space in between them that contributes to the development of a framework for dialogue between human communities'. He uses a metaphor of two people sitting on a bench and reflects on 'the electrifying nature of that area between entities that we thought was empty' (Ermine, 2007: 195). The space between people is where ideas and assumptions form the foundation for relationships. Acknowledging unjust power relations that undergird historical and current realities in (so-called)[2] Canada, encounters between Indigenous and settler Peoples,[3] require explicit rules for engagement to enable ethical relationships to be negotiated. Ethical space acts as an intermediary between knowledge systems where participants commit to processes that nurture relationships on all levels. Ethical space is a process for open communication and collaboration, wherein participants commit to respecting different ways of knowing. Larry McDermott, an Algonquin Elder and co-author of this chapter, explains that those engaging in ethical space are responsible for holding up the integrity of the circle and ensuring that everyone feels safe and heard. In writing this chapter collectively, the authors, both Indigenous and settler, hold each other in ethical space. We invite the reader to journey with us as we struggle collectively towards an understanding of how we can support, enable, and in some cases, get out of the way of those who are actualizing Indigenous food sovereignty (IFS).

Indigenous–settler partnerships

Throughout the ongoing colonization of Turtle Island, Indigenous Peoples[4] have faced extensive oppression and injustices. After centuries of land expropriation, imposed starvation, forced sterilization, and forced cultural assimilation under the Indian Act, including the removal of children from their families through residential schools (Manuel and Derrickson, 2021), in 2019, the Federal Government of Canada acknowledged their role in an ongoing genocide. Despite this acknowledgement, it is estimated that almost half of Indigenous Peoples in Canada face food insecurity, with even higher rates for those living in remote communities ([Library of Parliament], 2020). In addition, there are currently 99 First Nation communities facing drinking-water advisories (Luo, 2021). Indigenous Peoples experience high rates of poverty (NCCIH, 2020) and unequal access to health services (NCCIH, 2019), education (NCCIH, 2017a), and housing (NCCIH, 2017b). The concept of settler colonialism is used to refer to these ongoing processes as systems of oppression that aim to systematically eliminate Indigenous Peoples in place of a settler society (Wolf, 2006). In Canada, these actions are embedded within a series of geographic, political, economic, and social logics that work to assert legitimacy of the settler government's authority and hegemony (Baker, 2009). The impacts of settler colonialism have interrupted intergenerational knowledge around harvesting and preserving traditional foods, and resulted in limited Indigenous control over the use of traditional territories for food provisioning.

Despite these many challenges, Indigenous Peoples play an active role in struggles for self-determination and social and environmental justice (Alfred-Taiaiake, 2009; Simpson, 2017). Recognizing these realities and inspired by Indigenous thought and action, many settler people are seeking to establish partnership-based initiatives with the intention of working towards decolonization by decentring dominant Euro-Western structures and supporting IFS (Morrison, 2011; Settee and Shukla, 2020). Contemporary definitions of IFS as outlined by Coté (2016) recognize food as a 'sacred gift from the Creator' and include 'a responsibility to uphold and nurture healthy and interdependent relationships with the eco-system that provides the land, water, plants, and animals as food' (Coté, 2016: 9). It also provides a framework for cultural resurgence needed for enacting self-determination. To exercise food sovereignty, Indigenous Peoples must have access to land and resources to revitalize language and cultural practices that were stolen or banned. Thus, IFS must include addressing calls for land back, reparations, and support for cultural resurgence (see also Chapter 13 in this volume for further discussion of IFS).

There is increasing attention to settler colonialism and IFS in scholarly literature and food movements (Morrison, 2011; Cote, 2016; Bohunicky et al, 2021). However, despite 'good intentions', many initiatives fail to benefit Indigenous Peoples and have little impact on underlying structures that maintain systems of oppression and dispossession. Tuck and Yang (2012) assert that, too often, efforts aimed at decolonization tend to uphold settler colonialism and its underlying power structures. They observe that far too many efforts by settlers serve as a move to innocence that problematically relieves feelings of guilt and/or responsibility without having to give up power and/or privilege.

Meaningful Indigenous–settler partnerships must involve far more than just good intentions. While the intent to have a positive impact may be a valuable starting point, simply providing surface-level support without disrupting settler normality serves to reinforce power and privilege. Working through tensions and feelings of discomfort are part of the unlearning and relearning process, but efforts to engage and act must involve critical reflexivity and focus on meaningful shifts in power (Davis et al, 2017; Hiller, 2017). Barriers to authentic partnerships keep decision-making in the hands of settlers and downplay incommensurable values and priorities (Lowman and Barker, 2015; Elliot, 2018; Bohunicky et al, 2021). Further, tensions surrounding the ways that many Indigenous–settler partnerships operate can include misunderstandings and ignorance of cultural norms and practices, tensions around governance, and different ways of knowing that manifest in different approaches, goals, and assumptions about what is acceptable as evidence in decision-making (Austin et al, 2018; Shepherd and Graham, 2020). Thus, for settlers to confront their own complicity in settler colonialism, engagements must move beyond good intentions to build meaningful relationships that advance Indigenous self-determination. In this chapter we explore possibilities for settlers to move beyond good intentions when working in support of IFS. We draw on our collective experiences within four Indigenous-led and Indigenous-serving organizations that have been working in partnership with communities to support IFS for many years. Through these stories, we aim to share and glean insights from a series of personal and collective experiences, to learn from our own work individually and with each other. In addition, we invite readers engaging in similar work to join us as part of our learning journey.

We also offer our collective reflections and learnings as part of an ongoing discussion towards advancing a radical food geographies (RFG) praxis. RFG offers a promising framework to explore these issues because of its valuing of diverse ways of knowing, the recognition that injustice is produced in relationships, its emphasis on space and place as relational, and its multiscalar approach (see Levkoe et al, Chapter 1 and Hammelman et al, 2020). The theme of *human and more-than-human relations* is particularly relevant to our shared work as we focus on food systems relationships that extend among and beyond people to include all living things, land, and spirit. Throughout this chapter we aim to extend the concept of RFG by focusing on how *ways* of working in Indigenous–settler partnerships reveal and challenge our assumptions and our ways of knowing.

Placing ourselves

We are a collaborative of Indigenous and settler Peoples whose work is dedicated to supporting IFS through supporting Indigenous-led community-based projects. Our group includes people with personal and professional relationships; some that date back over a decade and others quite new. We work together as a consortium that includes five Indigenous-led and Indigenous-serving organizations. Larry McDermott is Algonquin from *Shabot Obaadjiwan* First Nation and is the executive director of Plenty Canada.[5] Jessica McLaughlin is a member of the Long Lake 58 First Nation and at the time of writing this chapter was the co-director of *Gaagige Zaagibigaa*[6] with settler Alex Boulet. Julie Price and Amanda Froese are settlers living in Winnipeg and working with the Northern Manitoba Food, Culture, and Community Collaborative.[7] Erika Bockstael is a settler and former director for Canadian programmes with Canadian Feed the Children.[8] Glenn Checkley is from *Biinjitiwaabik Zaaging Anishinaabek* (Rocky Bay First Nation) and at the time of writing was the director of Indigenous Partnerships & Programs with Canadian Feed the Children. Sarah Craig is a member of the Algonquins of *Pikwàkanagàn* and at the time of writing was a programme coordinator at Plenty Canada. Charles Levkoe and Roseann (Rosie) Kerr are settler scholar-activists with the Sustainable Food Systems Lab at Lakehead University.[9] In response to the COVID-19 pandemic in 2020, we came together to collaborate on the *Ginawaydaganuc* Project to work with Indigenous communities across Canada to identify shared concerns about systemic injustices that create barriers to food sovereignty.

Part of the collective work focuses on sharing our learnings and experiences around building meaningful relationships between Indigenous and settler communities. Our decision to write this chapter was one of the ways we chose to mobilize our collective experiences and reflect on our ongoing work together. To write this chapter we met multiple times to share and discuss stories and learnings. Rosie also held one-on-one conversations with each co-author to record specific stories and discuss their reflections.

Our approach in this chapter aims to honour Indigenous ways of sharing learnings through stories. As such, key expressions of personal experiences and teachings are presented in the voice of specific authors to maintain the integrity of their perspective and to avoid overgeneralizing or homogenizing their experiences. The stories and perspectives come from experiences over many years. Through our collective analysis we selected particular stories for this chapter that demonstrate our collective learnings. While we write with a common voice, at times we use 'we/they' to differentiate between our positionalities (including our social locations and identities). The stories and the reflections we share are our own and should not be taken as universally applicable. Our experiences are context-based and relational. They are unique to each author and the dynamic that is co-created in our collaborations.

Sharing our stories

In this section, we share a series of stories that illustrate the opportunities and tensions of working in Indigenous–settler partnerships. These stories highlight that the ways we interact with each other are complex and sometimes difficult. Through these stories we reflect on ways to move beyond good intentions. In each subsection, we offer a synthesis of our learnings as we reflect on the stories and our conversations surrounding them.

Respecting diverse knowledge systems and cultural protocols

Indigenous Nations have distinct cultures with different knowledge systems, yet there has been a common experience of settler colonialism, ongoing expropriation of land, and denial of self-determination. Recognizing these realities is a first step towards developing mutually respectful partnerships. Much learning is needed in each relationship we cultivate. Our group noticed a hesitancy among settlers when they/we encounter something we/they don't understand. Larry explained it in this way:

> 'I have seen people say "Wait, I don't understand, I need to understand." We need to have faith that we don't have to understand but we do have to know. Our heart knows in ways that our mind doesn't. People get stuck in thinking they must understand it all right away – like something you can write down on paper and intellectualize. You can write down on paper what you think it will be like when you jump into the water, but until you actually jump, you don't really know.'

Alex shared a story about how settler hesitancy can unconsciously deny the importance of Indigenous cultural resurgence and may stand in the way of its enactment:

'When our organization changed its name to *Gaagige Zaagebigaa*, I had a phone call from a funder who expressed concern that no-one would understand or be able to pronounce it. They thought it would scare funders away. It was a really shocking and frustrating conversation. They thought they were doing me a favour by telling me this. But there was no understanding of why and how we chose that name. We followed the protocol of our council and the knowledge holders to come to that name. It was intentionally chosen to be in *Anishinaabemowin* and not in English, as an assertion of sovereignty and connection to culture. In English we say, cultivating forever, but it doesn't translate exactly. There are a lot of concepts embedded in it that are not easily translated that have to do with our treaty responsibilities, the concept of creation, spirit, and how those things tie into *Anishinaabe* world view.'

In this story, the funder likely meant well, but the unexamined assumptions that Indigenous Peoples should operate within the norms of the dominant settler culture led to frustration. This story illustrates a lack of understanding of the importance of Indigenous cultural revitalization to the work of IFS, and an assumption that the settler world view takes precedence. Choosing an *Anishinaabemowin*[10] name was an intentional act to reflect the organization's commitment to Indigenous sovereignty and ways of working that align with cultural protocols. The work of partnering with Indigenous communities must support cultural reclamation and resurgence. Jessica explained that to support IFS at a grassroots level, "we need people to feel Indigenous. I need to feel who I am. I need to feel *Anishinaabe*. I need to be connected to place. I need to be given that opportunity."

Through our work, it has become clear that advancing IFS is about much more than food. Given the history of genocide and the ongoing implementation of policies that make it difficult for Indigenous communities to be sovereign, our projects create space for Indigenous Peoples to articulate and practice their own cultures and governance structures. Naming *Gaagige Zaagebigaa* was an assertion of culture and sovereignty. Rather than resisting this naming, settlers are invited to learn how to pronounce these words and understand their meaning. In our continued work we ask ourselves: Are there ways that our actions can support enacting Indigenous culture rather than standing in the way?

Shifting ways of working

As a group, we discussed how ways of working with Indigenous Peoples have continued to operate within terms dictated by settler logics. This serves to reproduce settler normality, devalues Indigenous culture and knowledge systems, and it constrains Indigenous sovereignty. Julie shared a story of how her ideas of success shifted because of an experience partnering with an Indigenous community. She was invited to Manto Sipi for their autumn harvest celebration after working on a garden project.

> 'I had been hearing all summer how great the garden was going. There had been 50 youth in the community that had built raised beds and did tons of planting. I was excited to see the garden because I had been getting some pushback from my colleagues to move the project to apply for a large multi-year grant. This was going to be the proof that Manto Sipi was ready. We pulled up to the garden and my stomach just fell into my feet. I thought, wow, it is so full of weeds. I can't see anything growing. I can't even see where the raised beds are. I turned to look at Miriam Okemow, who was my main contact there, and she was just beaming. While I had been freaking out, she had been harvesting. She had an armful of the things that were planted to show to Chief and Council. She was so happy and so excited by what had grown in this garden. When I turned to look at her with her arms full of harvest with a big smile on her face, I realized that we were seeing this garden with totally different eyes, and it was my eyes that needed to change. I was looking at it with my Southern Manitoba farmer eyes, my gardening background with the voices of my ancestors in my ears who defined crop success by how marketable they were. She was looking at it as a first-time gardener. This was a labour of love and all the kids had been there helping. This was a very strong learning moment for me. My version of success actually doesn't matter at all. It is not my community. What matters is that the community feels they are being successful and they are moving forward; that they are taking steps that feel achievable for them and that they can celebrate.'

This story illustrates important shifts in understanding that led to different ways of working. There was an important recognition that success can mean different things to different people. Values and beliefs are shaped by our cultures and experiences. Julie's recognition of the problems with standard measures of success plays a major role in her ongoing commitment to creating more equitable partnerships with communities. To move beyond good intentions, each partner needs to consider on whose terms decisions are being made.

This point *not only* applies to metrics for measuring the success of a project, but also to structures and protocols put in place by organizations who provide funding or support to Indigenous communities. Julie told a story of how her experiences in Manto Sipi led her to question the way she was approaching partnerships and what hoops she was making communities jump through to receive grants. She reflected on this learning from over ten years ago in this way:

> 'I felt like everything I was asking them to do was so far off from what they were doing and how they were operating. It was probably after

three years of working with Manto Sipi that I asked, what is going on here? Why does this feel so hard? It was clear to me that it wasn't about the energy the community was putting in. It was about the things I was requiring them to do. They needed to have by-laws in place that included a hierarchical governance structure and specific rules about how often they meet. But this was not the cultural protocols of how this group operated. It was so colonial. I wasn't asking them about the ways that they work together and share responsibility to ensure that things get done. This was the kind of community that we were wanting to serve, and they were doing the kind of work that we wanted to fund, but it was our own internal processes that were preventing us from supporting their work in a substantial way.'

These experiences highlight shifts in thinking and ways of working that are needed to decolonize the relationships that organizations have with Indigenous communities. If we are to move beyond good intentions, to create authentic relationships, the goals and decision-making processes need to be developed collaboratively in recognition of the ways of knowing of each partner. In these shifts, self-reflection on processes and practices in our ways of working are important. It has been essential for all of us to critically examine the institutional processes of our organizations and our different ways of working. When we come into partnership with each other, we bring biases and assumptions. We realize that, too often, settlers take for granted that our/their way of doing things is the only way or the best way.

Through experience, we have come to realize that our different ways of working were not always compatible. Thus, we were compelled to find ways to move forward which sometimes means letting others take the lead and putting our own ego and needs aside. In our partnership work, the settlers among our author group have learned to step back at times and follow the leadership of Indigenous communities. While this approach is sometimes in tension with our organizational mandates, it has led to insights and outcomes that were more relevant to communities.

As Julie shared through her story, failing to appreciate that each Indigenous community understands success differently revealed tensions. Her story shows that when we/they impose structures on Indigenous communities as conditions for supporting a project, we/they assume that those communities do not have legitimate structures of their own. Our/their imposition simultaneously becomes an exercise of power, and an erasure of Indigenous culture. As a group, we have made a collective commitment to decolonizing our work which includes asking questions such as: Who is expected to learn and change? Who is considered to have expertise? Who gets to decide what is important and how it is measured?

Practising relationships of trust, integrity, and reciprocity

Building meaningful partnerships begins with cultivating relationships based on mutual trust, integrity, and reciprocity. Our group spoke about the importance of cultivating authentic two-way relationships. Julie suggested that "two-way relationships mean that everyone has gifts to give and are also open to learning and changing". Relationships of reciprocity respect and value the knowledge that Indigenous Peoples bring to partnerships and work against the 'White saviour' mentality that assumes outsiders have the knowledge and expertise to solve issues affecting communities (see Willuweit, 2020). Shifting power to Indigenous Peoples as experts that bring a wealth of knowledge and experience is a valuable starting place.

In our discussions developing this chapter, Glenn asked us to think about gratitude and in which direction it is expected to flow. He shared a story about expectations of gratitude that revealed assumptions about power in partnerships:

> 'As a funder, we do interviews with communities and the last question asks: Do you have anything else you would like to say? Most people say, "Thank you." It just becomes awkward, like they are expected to say this. *We* should be the ones saying, "Thank you for the work that you are doing in pushing forward Indigenous wellbeing." When an organization like ours provides funding, we need to recognize that we build our reputation on the work of communities. We can continue what we do, expand our reach. We have jobs because of the good work communities do. We can seek greater funding opportunities because of it. We should be expressing *our* gratitude not asking for theirs. Many funding organizations need that gratification, and you see it in granting and reporting requirements. They need to be told how great they are and how appreciative people are for the funding. This must change.'

Glenn's story highlights how the expectation of gratitude from funders sets up an unbalanced power dynamic where the work and contributions of Indigenous communities are not adequately recognized or valued. Expectations of gratitude from funders also ignore how capitalist structures of wealth that make philanthropy possible are implicated in the inequality that creates issues relating to social and environmental injustices they are supposedly trying to ameliorate. To move beyond good intentions, we need to reflect on our processes, our language, and our expectations of communities. We propose that in partnering with Indigenous communities, gratitude should flow in both directions to reflect what each member of the partnership has gained from the experience.

Speaking about relationships of mutual respect and reciprocity, Larry pointed to the importance of operating with integrity:

'It is important that when Western cultures engage with Indigenous cultures and Nations, there is a mutual commitment to integrity. It is more than saying, I will provide $100 if you sign this contract. That is superficial. Ways of working are more than just mechanics. There is a deep emotional and spiritual integrity that is needed, and we need to make the time. Integrity is not about our title or our achievements, it is a deep place that we actually have to work on finding. Integrity is about knowing who we are as individuals. It is that universal place, of consciousness, of life, that is part of all creation. Integrity is a commitment to the mental, physical, emotional, and spiritual ways of knowing. The Algonquin Nation has our cultural practices that help get to that place of integrity. Other Indigenous Nations and Peoples have their own practices as well. I had Elders, William Commanda and others who feel that when integrity is practised, when truth is sought, when there is humility and love, both individually and collectively we can move to a place that I would call integrity. Integrity can mean speaking my truth as I know it, but it is also to be humble enough to know that I am always growing. What is important to understand is that integrity isn't static. As we grow, that integrity changes. Then we have accountability to what we have learned. And this is both internally as to who we are, and who we once thought we were. Who we are evolves. If it doesn't, we are in trouble. The more integrity we bring to the way we operate, the easier it will be to bring integrity to our communities and also for those communities to bring integrity, knowledge and guidance to us. It is a big circle.'

In cultivating relationships of mutual trust, time and gifting are essential. Jessica explained how important it is to offer gifts and spend time with Elders who are contributing knowledge and time. In a recent experience planning an event, she didn't know if she needed a sacred fire. She reached out to a fire keeper to ask for insight:

'I put together a gift: tobacco seeds, tobacco, our organization's strategic plan, coffee, jam, and I took him out for lunch. I learned so much about fire keeping; he is a great teacher and a great resource for me. That was four invaluable hours of my day. That doesn't really exist in other realms of building relationships or ways of working. You don't see government or funders being like, "Let's go for lunch and I will bring you a gift." I am going to take the time, listen, ask questions, answer questions. We are going to spend time together.'

Jessica's story is a demonstration of the time and care that is required to build meaningful relationships with Indigenous Peoples. It also shows that relationships are about reciprocity, listening, and showing respect for Elders and knowledge keepers. This approach is often missing in the work of settler organizations. Julie explained that she is sometimes questioned by people about the value of time dedicated to developing relationships with Elders. She explained:

> 'I had a meeting with an Elder who we are asking for help, to be an advisor. This is an Elder that I have been waiting to sit with for a few months. I put together a gift and a sage offering and we met at 4:30. I ended up sitting with them until 8:30 and buying them a meal. Some people I know said, "Doesn't your work have boundaries? A four-hour meeting on a Friday evening?" I tried to explain that this is part of what it takes to do this work well. That is part of the reason the job is not a typical job that you can put neatly in a box. If you really want to be in relationship, sometimes it will take you outside of work hours.'

This is an example of how the settler ways of working come into tension with Indigenous approaches. We have experienced how the time and energy needed for reciprocal relationship building that respects Indigenous cultural protocols and practices are not always accounted for in the ways that settler organizations are accustomed to operating. In this work, it is important to de-centre the needs of the organization and prioritize the needs of community members.

Larry asserts that "it is in the power of relationships where transformation happens". These stories illustrate how both justice and injustice are produced and reproduced through relationships. An essential part of creating more equitable relationships is shifting the balance of power. This shift comes with respecting the diverse knowledge systems and cultures of Indigenous Peoples. Recognizing, respecting, and expressing gratitude for the contributions and knowledge of Indigenous Peoples in partnerships creates more equitable relationships. When we/they recognize the value of the teachings we/they share and the knowledge systems we/they hold, we shift the balance towards valuing Indigenous ways of knowing and away from settler normality. The reactions of settler people in Julie's life show a tension between the way that different cultures conceptualize work, and how individual contributions of time are valued differently. As Larry explains, working with integrity means bringing one's whole self to relationships, not just the professional self.

During our group's reflections about our attempts to create relationships of trust, integrity, and reciprocity when collaborating with Indigenous communities, the settlers in our group expressed a desire for unlearning what we have been taught, and what we take for granted. Unlearning involves recognizing that our ways of knowing are specific to our cultural communities and contexts. The lived realities, opportunities, and challenges faced by others are often very different than our own. Learning (and unlearning) means becoming comfortable with discomfort and takes time, effort, and humility. Moving beyond good intentions takes time and care. It involves acknowledging unexamined assumptions and being open to unlearning the ways we are accustomed to working together. As we cultivate relationships, we settler authors have been challenged to recognize that our way of knowing is not the *only* way of knowing and that relationships must consider the people we are working with along with the more-than-human. Accepting this challenge has helped us get out of the way of Indigenous Peoples enacting their identities, ways of being, and sovereignties. Getting out of the way involves critical reflexivity to identify the ways we are working that may be creating barriers rather than supporting and making space for this enactment.

Contributions to RFG praxis

In this chapter, we have shared stories and reflections that consider ways to move beyond good intentions through co-constructing ethical space, building meaningful relations, and engaging in appropriate actions. These stories about the ways we work together reveal the assumptions and biases we hold. We reflect on difficult conversations and moments of discomfort and frustration that fostered important learnings in this work. We understand the changes that are needed as both personal and structural. Our reflections on how to move beyond good intentions connect closely to RFG ideas, but they also reveal gaps in the praxis.

RFG emphasizes collaboration. Recently, there has been more discussion of Indigenous perspectives and/or Indigenous–settler partnerships within food studies and radical geographies (see Cote, 2016; Davis et al, 2017; Bohunicky et al, 2021). We add to this discussion by asserting that, when we take time and put the effort into building relationships, collaboration becomes more meaningful and mutually beneficial. In cultivating these relationships, we have come to understand how our different ways of knowing shape the way we engage with each other and with the world around us. For example, from an Indigenous perspective, food systems include relationships with all living things, to the land and waters, and to the sacred. Collaborating in ethical space with Indigenous Peoples means valuing our/their knowledge, experiences, and contributions to more equitable, sustainable futures.

RFG emphasizes that place and context matter. Far too often Indigenous Peoples are treated as a monolithic group with a common culture. However, each Indigenous community has unique relationships with the land we/they live on that shapes their/our culture and language based on a shared history in particular places. Acknowledging these differences is an essential point in the process of moving beyond good intentions. Thus, ethical space needs to be cultivated collectively, with individuals, communities, and in particular places. RFG must recognize that social and environmental systems are inherently intertwined and interdependent.

RFG addresses power and underlying structures of oppression. We have shared stories that explore our learnings and insights through examining our ways of working and adapting approaches to enact more meaningful and equitable partnerships. Radical food geographers must ask what we mean when we speak about justice and sustainability and for whom. For Indigenous–settler partnerships addressing food systems, this work must include addressing settler colonialism and disrupting the dominant ways of knowing.

RFG emphasizes action. Using a process of co-constructing ethical space, we engage in relationships and develop shared visions for how to work together and work with others. The process of constructing ethical space begins with the recognition that we have different world views that shape the ways that we relate to the world and each other. In co-creating ethical space, it is important to put aside objectives or expected outcomes of the project and begin by discussing our own motivations for the partnership, protocols, and responsibilities for decision-making, and our visions for what we hope to build together. For settlers in our group, there are times that we need to follow Indigenous leadership and learn different processes and cultural protocols. The results may not be what we expect, but they may be better suited to the Indigenous communities we partner with. Building meaningful relationships and having an impact on the broader structures of settler colonialism takes time and effort. Advancing IFS is not a short-term project with a finite goal but will require ongoing critical reflexivity, negotiation, and engagement with each other.

Acknowledgements

We would like to express our gratitude to the Indigenous Elders, youth, leaders, and communities we work with who continue to guide our learning and unlearning. Thank you to all who have come before us and love to all who will come after us. This work was supported by Mitacs through the Mitacs Accelerate programme and a grant from the McConnell foundation.

Notes

[1]   Ways of knowing refers to the diverse epistemologies, knowledge systems, and ways of understanding the world.

[2]   The use of (so-called) Canada troubles the notion of the Canadian state and calls attention to Indigenous histories and identification of land and territories.

[3]   Although this chapter is specifically about settler–Indigenous partnerships, ethical space is also important to cultivate among Indigenous groups and between humans and our more-than-human relatives.

[4] In this chapter, we use the term 'Indigenous' to refer to the original inhabitants of what is now known as Canada. This includes First Nations, Inuit, and Metis Peoples. In our use of this term, we recognize that each Indigenous group in Canada has a unique culture, language, and history.

[5] Plenty Canada is a non-profit organization that facilitates access to and shares resources with Indigenous Peoples and other community groups around the world in support of their environmental protection and sustainable development goals (www.plentycanada. com/).

[6] *Gaagige Zaagibigaa* is an organization that supports Indigenous Peoples in northern Ontario to assert and maintain control over their food systems (www.facebook.com/GaagigeZA).

[7] The Northern Manitoba Food, Culture, and Community Collaborative is a collaborative of northern community people, northern advisors, funders, and organizations working together to foster healthier and stronger communities in northern Manitoba, through improved access to healthy foods and the development of resilient local economies (www. nmfccc.ca/).

[8] Canadian Feed the Children is a registered Canadian charity that has been supporting Indigenous-led food security projects in Canada since 1992 (https://canadianfeedthec hildren.ca/).

[9] The Sustainable Food Systems Lab at Lakehead University is a hub for academics and community-based practitioners that aims to build meaningful relationships that enable knowledge sharing between research, policy, and practice with the goal of healthy, just, and sustainable food systems for all (https://foodsystems.lakeheadu.ca).

[10] *Anishenaabemowin* is the name of the *Anishinaabe* language.

References

Alfred-Taiaiake, G.A. (2009) *Peace, Power, Righteousness: An Indigenous Manifesto*, Oxford University Press. Oxford, UK.

Austin, B.J., Robinson, C.J., Fitzsimons, J.A., Sandford, M., Ens, E.J., Macdonald, J.M., Hockings, M., Hinchley, D.G., McDonald, F.B., Corrigan, C., and Kennett, R. (2018) 'Integrated measures of Indigenous land and sea management effectiveness: challenges and opportunities for improved conservation partnerships in Australia', *Conservation and Society*, 16(3): 372–84.

Barker, A.J. (2009) 'The contemporary reality of Canadian imperialism: settler colonialism and the hybrid colonial state', *American Indian Quarterly*, 33(3): 325–51.

Bohunicky, M., Levkoe, C.Z., and Rose, N. (2021) 'Working for justice in food systems on stolen land? Interrogating food movements confronting settler colonialism', *Canadian Food Studies/La Revue canadienne des études sur l'alimentation*, 8(2): 135–65.

Coté, C. (2016) '"Indigenizing" food sovereignty. Revitalizing Indigenous food practices and ecological knowledges in Canada and the United States', *Humanities*, 5(3): 57.

Davis, L., Hiller, C., James, C., Lloyd, K., Nasca, T., and Taylor, S. (2017) 'Complicated pathways: settler Canadians learning to re/frame themselves and their relationships with Indigenous peoples', *Settler Colonial Studies*, 7(4): 398–414.

Elliott, M. (2018) 'Indigenous resurgence: the drive for renewed engagement and reciprocity in the turn away from the state', *Canadian Journal of Political Science/Revue canadienne de science politique*, 51(1): 61–81.

Ermine, W. (2000) 'A critical examination of the ethics in research involving Indigenous Peoples', PhD Dissertation, University of Saskatchewan.

Ermine, W. (2007) 'The ethical space of engagement', *Indigenous Law Journal*, 6(1): 193–203.

Hammelman, C., Reynolds, K., and Levkoe, C.Z. (2020) 'Toward a radical food geography praxis: integrating theory, action, and geographic analysis in pursuit of more equitable and sustainable food systems', *Human Geography*, 13(3): 211–27.

Hiller, C. (2017) 'Tracing the spirals of unsettlement: Euro-Canadian narratives of coming to grips with Indigenous sovereignty, title, and rights', *Settler Colonial Studies*, 7(4): 415–40.

Library of Parliament (2020) 'Food Insecurity in the North Canada, An Overview', Background Paper, Publication No. 2020–47-E.

Lowman, E.B. and Barker, A.J. (2015) *Settler: Identity and colonialism in 21st Century Canada*, Winnipeg, MB: Fernwood Publishing.

Luo, C.X. (2021) 'The Water Crisis in Canada's First Nations Communities', *University of Windsor*, [online], Available from: https://storymaps.arcgis.com/stories/52a5610cca604175b8fb35bccf165f96 [Accessed 28 July 2023].

Manuel, A. and Derrickson, G.C.R.M. (2021) *Unsettling Canada: A National Wake-up Call*, Toronto: Between the Lines.

Morrison, D. (2011) 'Indigenous food sovereignty: a model for social learning', in H. Wittman, A.A. Desmarais, and N. Wiebe (eds) *Food Sovereignty in Canada: Creating Just and Sustainable Food Systems*, Halifax, Nova Scotia: Fernwood Publishing, pp 97–113.

National Collaborating Centre for Indigenous Health (2017a) *Education as a Social Determinant of First Nations, Inuit and Métis Health*, Prince George, BC. Available from: www.ccnsa-nccah.ca [Accessed 28 July 2023].

National Collaborating Centre for [Indigenous] Health (2017b) *Housing as a Social Determinant of First Nations, Inuit and Métis Health*, Prince George, BC. Available from: www.ccnsa-nccah.ca [Accessed 28 July 2023].

National Collaborating Centre for Indigenous Health (2019) *Access to Health Services as a Social Determinant of First Nations, Inuit and Métis Health*, Prince George, BC. Available from: www.ccnsa-nccah.ca [Accessed 28 July 2023].

National Collaborating Centre for Indigenous Health (2020) *Poverty as a Social Determinant of First Nations, Inuit, and Métis Health*, Prince George, BC. Available from: www.ccnsa-nccah.ca [Accessed 28 July 2023].

Poole, R. (1972) *Towards Deep Subjectivity*, London: Allen Lane, The Penguin Press.

Settee, P. and Shukla, S. (eds) (2020) *Indigenous Food Systems: Concepts, Cases, and Conversations*, Canadian Scholars.

Shepherd, R.P. and Graham, K.A.H. (2020) 'Evaluation in Indigenous contexts: an introduction to practice', *Canadian Journal of Program Evaluation*, 34(3).

Simpson, L.B. (2017) *As We Have Always Done: Indigenous Freedom through Radical Resistance*, Minneapolis, MN: University of Minnesota Press.

Tuck, E. and Yang, K.W. (2012) 'Decolonization is not a metaphor', *Decolonization: Indigeneity, Education & Society*, 1(1): 22–40.

Willuweit, F. (2020) 'De-constructing the "White saviour syndrome": a manifestation of neo-imperialism', *E-International Relations*, [online], Available from: www.e-ir.info/2020/07/13/de-constructing-the-white-saviour-syndrome-a-manifestation-of-neo-imperialism/ [Accessed 3 July 2023].

Wolfe, P. (2006) 'Settler colonialism and the elimination of the native', *Journal of Genocide Research*, 8(4): 387–409. DOI: https://doi.org/10.1080/14623520601056240

11

Reshaping Collective Dreams for a Just Food Future through Research and Activism in Western Avadh, India

Sudha Nagavarapu, Surbala Vaish, Om Prakash,
Kamal Kishore, Richa Singh, Richa Kumar, and
Sangtin Kisan Mazdoor Sangathan (SKMS)

The food sovereignty movement offers a compelling vision for food systems, articulating the rights of communities to define and build ecologically sound and locally empowering foodways (Sélingué, 2007). It challenges the hegemony of global industrial agri-food systems, as well as state oppression, and has inspired numerous movements and even governments to reimagine how we produce, process, and consume our food. However, despite recognizing the unequal power relations between corporations, state actors, farming communities, and consumers, the food sovereignty articulation ignores deep inequities within communities themselves. Unequal gender relations are embedded within families and communities, and increased labour requirements of ecological farming may fall disproportionately on women's shoulders, without any increase in their autonomy (Agarwal, 2014). Further, devolution of power to the community level can easily lead to the capture of resources by powerful community members. Brown (2018) documents how ecological farming methods developed in the aftermath of the 2004 tsunami in deltaic Tamilnadu, India, were sought to be consolidated through community-based organizations (CBOs). These quickly devolved along caste lines, with dominant caste farmers taking control of village-level federations, and perpetuating untouchability practices, such as segregated seating and food served in disposable utensils for Dalits[1] (Brown, 2018). Thus, ecological structures can themselves become oppressive.

Figure 11.1: Map of India with the study region.

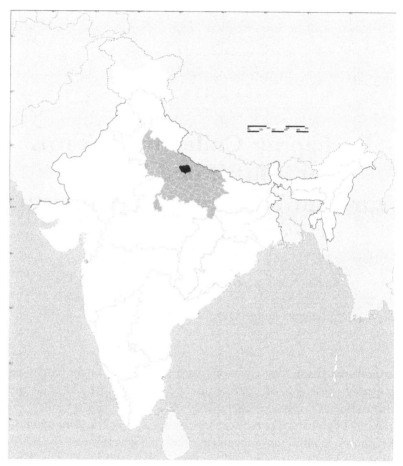

Source: CC-BY-SA Haros/Wikimedia based on PlaneMad/Wikimedia (https://commons.wikimedia.org/wiki/File:Uttar_Pradesh_district_location_map_Sitapur.svg).

At the same time, very little research on agriculture, diets, and food security in the Global South has been undertaken with communities as equal partners in the research process. Both quantitative studies (that outsource fieldwork to local partners, with design and analysis done only by academic researchers) and ethnographies (where the lone researcher documents various concerns in a self-reflexive manner) do not give co-authorship or consider communities as active co-researchers.[2] Thus, while the ills of monoculture farming or the malnutrition puzzle in India have been extensively researched (Gupta, 1989; Deaton and Drèze, 2009), there are few instances where marginalized communities themselves co-produce research, analyse findings, and use them to develop or refine action.

Figure 11.2: Study region with nearby cities.

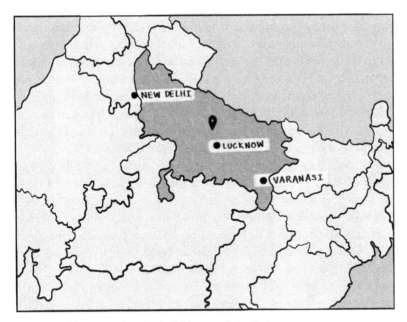

Source: Designed by Senjuti Sangia. Available at avadh.foodcultures.org.

In late 2016, a chance meeting between Richa Kumar (henceforth, Richa K[3]), a sociologist of agriculture, and Sudha, a researcher-activist, led to the development of a grounded, empirically rich, and action-oriented collaboration, whose trajectory we describe in this chapter (see Figures 11.1 and 11.2 for maps showing the study region). Over the next six years, we pioneered an approach where a group of activists, researcher-activists, and scholars associated with Sangtin Kisan Mazdoor Sangathan (SKMS), a grassroots collective in western Avadh (part of Uttar Pradesh state, North India) and the Indian Institute of Technology Delhi, came together to work towards a just food future grounded in, what we later realized, could be described as radical food geographies (RFG) praxis. The important ideas of challenging hegemonic structures, interrogating individual privileges, bringing to the table a diverse set of perspectives, and pluralizing pathways of knowledge creation and informing subsequent action, which form an integral part of RFG, are reflected in our work.

Recognizing that 'knowledge creation is not only the purview of academics and that the collection of data and production of knowledge is not inherently neutral or benevolent'(Hammelman et al, 2020b: 6; see also Levkoe et al, Chapter 1, this volume), this group began work with an explicit political recognition of unequal privileges, differing standpoints, and a desire for self-reflexivity during the research process. This understanding led to three important outcomes. First, it enabled a robust framing of the research questions, strengthened the process of data collection, and brought to the table a diversity of views that have contributed to a rich set of findings. Second, it facilitated action at multiple scales – from struggles to publish research first-authored by a southern researcher-activist in reputable academic journals, to group members incorporating changes in their own diets and diversifying the crop mix on their own farms. Third, it has enabled activists to understand at a deeper level the historical injustices that have shaped their present (Hammelman et al, 2020b: 2). This has brought renewed vigour towards building local capacity for institutional change, even in the face of great difficulties.

These 'reciprocal engagements' (Hammelman et al, 2020b: 6) are the hallmark of RFG praxis. Our work also pushes the boundaries of RFG praxis in two important ways. One, in a praxis which has yet to establish itself outside the Global North, we bring a set of diverse perspectives on food, health, and nutrition from the Global South. Two, in a domain where analysis and action has centred on gender and race, we bring in the dimension of caste, which has had a profound impact on South Asia and its worldwide diaspora.[4] This is especially important in agri-food systems in South Asia, where the majority of farmers come from marginalized castes, and the food sovereignty approach has often glorified farming communities without explicitly recognizing hierarchies within them, or making efforts to actively challenge them. The chapter is structured as follows: the first three sections explain the circumstances that led to a collaborative study between activists and researchers in western Avadh, section four provides a brief overview of the findings of the study, section five elaborates on how the varied nature of the team contributing to strengthening research questions and shaping the research agenda from below, section six describes how the study led to action at multiple scales, and the conclusion helps us critically review the challenges that RFG praxis has presented and possibilities that lie ahead.

A foundation in research and activism

SKMS' roots lie in a collective writing and reflection project undertaken between 2002 and 2004 by seven field workers in a large women's organization, supported by Richa Singh (henceforth, Richa S), a co-author of this piece, who was their district coordinator, and Richa Nagar, a scholar-activist and creative writer based at the University of Minnesota. From this collective journey emerged *Sangtin Yatra*, a book in Hindi that chronicled the writers' lives and struggles with hierarchies of caste, gender, and location. The authors further discussed how NGOization[5] manifested in their organization – interventions were planned elsewhere by dominant-caste women, and field staff were expected to follow orders, while issues faced by their communities were artificially compartmentalized into 'projects' (Sangtin

Writers and Nagar, 2006). Backlash from the book's publication resulted in Richa S resigning from her post, and, in a renewed commitment, she, along with Surbala (another co-author) and other activists, reconstituted Sangtin as a grassroots organization that would identify and work on local concerns in western Avadh. During Sangtin's campaign for irrigation waters in 2005, local farmer-labourers mobilized under the banner of SKMS. Since then, this predominantly Dalit collective with more than 5,000 *Saathis* has campaigned for the effective implementation of pro-poor government programmes, organized campaigns against oppressive and discriminatory policies, and resisted caste- and gender-based violence (see Nagar, in journeys with SKMS, 2021).

The founding principles of Sangtin and SKMS have driven research collaborations, with proposals rejected on this basis or if the field organizations were not considered equal partners. For example, an offer to support ecological farming, through which carbon credits would be generated and sold, was rejected, as SKMS had concerns that the funders were more focused on carbon emissions than farmer welfare. The two organizations have collaborated on action-research projects, such as national surveys on food insecurity, and have taken up projects based on local needs, such as a pioneering intervention on Lymphatic Filariasis (LF), a neglected tropical disease, which is endemic in the region (Gogia and Sangtin, 2016).

A faltering agricultural intervention

SKMS had learnt from people's movements that, along with *sangharsh* – struggles for realizing rights, *nirmaan* was also necessary – creative ways of living that would improve well-being and incomes.[6] Agriculture was a natural starting point. Erratic rains during 2011 and 2012 had adversely impacted the *kharif* (monsoon) crops of small and marginal farmers, with dry spells hurting paddy and groundnut while excess rain damaged the sesame and pulse crops. When exploring the addition of resilient crops to the mix, we heard about *saanwa* (barnyard millet), a treasured cereal grain from the past. Older people fondly remembered its taste, and described how *saanwa* panicles were worshipped during harvest festivals in September and October.

While it is commonly believed that irrigated crops such as wheat and paddy rice were the traditional staples in India, in fact, rain-fed farming of a wide range of millets, pulses, and oilseeds was the norm prior to the Green Revolution in the 1960s–70s (see Figure 11.3). The extensive state support for cultivating, processing, and marketing wheat and rice through the Green Revolution expanded the acreage under paddy and wheat at the expense of millets and pulses (Kumar, 2023). Further, while the Green Revolution supported the development of machinery for processing rice and wheat, no such support was provided for millets. Instead, they continued to be

Figure 11.3: A mixed crop field with barnyard and foxtail millet, pulses, and oilseeds.

Source: SKMS.

processed by hand, a tedious undertaking which further contributed to the decline of husked millets. In the last decade, however, millets have returned to the public consciousness due to their climate resilience and nutritional benefits (Devkota et al, 2014; Nagavarapu, 2023).

After further discussions and a visit to a millet-processing unit in South India, SKMS decided to promote the production of millets in the region and subsequently take on the challenges of processing. A pilot initiative was launched in 2013, wherein five farmers planted millet seeds and obtained a good harvest, and gradually expanded in the following years. In 2015, when a 42 per cent deficit in monsoon rainfall was recorded in Sitapur district (Kaur and Purohit, 2016), those farmers who had planted millets in their mixed-crop fields, and irrigated once, harvested a bumper crop. Further expansion followed, and the 2016 *kharif* season included training sessions for about 45 farmers and three demonstration plots. However, farmers did not implement the discussed interventions, such as composting and biosolutions to improve soil heath. They were not convinced that these were necessary for the hardy millets, a crop they were familiar with. The demonstration plots failed, and production was much below expected levels. These setbacks led to soul searching. Why didn't the positive example of 2015 motivate more farmers to plant millets? Should SKMS persevere in this initiative, or abandon the effort altogether?

Converging paths leading to a research agenda

Around the same time, Richa K had published her ethnographic research on the impact of soyabean monocultures on agriculture, ecology, and livelihoods in Central India, which had led her to question the positive role attributed to modern agricultural techniques in bringing food security (Kumar, 2016). She was seeking a field organization that would support grounded and comprehensive research on changes in farming and food, and this was discussed during a chance meeting with Sudha, who was coordinating Sangtin's interventions in agriculture. Sudha felt that such research could provide insights into the challenges faced by SKMS and facilitated discussions with the larger team. The desire for a true collaboration, where the field team would be involved in all steps of the research process (including analysis), was articulated. This was the first step towards embarking on RFG praxis with an earnest effort to 'disrupt inequitable relationships, including those that exist between academics and community-based activists'(Hammelman et al, 2020b: 8). Thus, a multidisciplinary study of food and farming transitions in western Avadh was conceptualized. 'Radical food geography praxis demands reflection on how our own histories with oppression, positions of privilege, and world views shape our work and pushes those with more privilege to actively move to dismantle these structures' (Hammelman et al, 2020b: 8) In our research team, Sudha and Richa K, who coordinated and documented the research, are the only team members proficient in English[7] and were conscious of how their privileged social position coming from dominant caste, well-off, urban families shaped their engagement with others. Om Prakash and Kamal Kishore, who hail from the study region, are Dalit men who have faced marginalization and deprivation.

Through long-term engagement with SKMS, they have developed an acute understanding of oppressive relations in the region. Their fieldwork and analysis provided a grounded vocabulary and perspective for understanding farming, health, and nutrition. Surbala and Richa S are both grassroots activists living in the study region who helped conceptualize, plan, and undertake the research. Although belonging to dominant castes, they have struggled against patriarchal and conservative societal mores, while consciously being self-reflexive about their social position vis-à-vis the further marginalized Dalit members of SKMS. We wish to recognize SKMS

Figure 11.4: Focus Group Discussion.

Source: SKMS.

as an institutional co-author, because its *Saathis* (co-travellers), beyond the individual authors, provided much of the primary material for the research, and also placed in context the research findings.

The research team selected two contiguous villages of Ballapur Panchayat,[8] which has an active SKMS base, for a multi-season consumption survey in 2017 to record current diets. To understand historical practices, we conducted 27 focus group discussions (FGDs) in 24 villages (including Ballapur) in 2017–18, focusing on elderly respondents from various communities (see Figure 11.4). Between 2017 and 2019, more than100 farmers, government officials, traders, and processors were interviewed to document oral histories and policies, and to track specific commodities. Historical agricultural data and secondary literature, including colonial-era documents, provided additional material and valuable insights. By triangulating these various sources, we attempted to understand the factors that shaped farming and food transitions, and their impacts on various communities in western Avadh.

Remaking land, reshaping diets

As we embarked on our research, we knew that malnutrition was high in the region – Sitapur was listed as one of the worst districts nationwide for childhood stunting in multiple national family health surveys (IIPS and ICR, 2022). We were also aware that the nationwide shift from millets and pulses to rice and wheat, facilitated by the Green Revolution, had led to a decline in intake of proteins and micronutrients (Kumar et al, 2007). Many proponents of ecological farming describe a glorious agricultural past that was destroyed by the Green Revolution (Brown, 2018; Meek, 2022).

While acknowledging that such narratives were simplistic, we also believed that the policies linked to the Green Revolution were most instrumental in transforming diets and landscapes. However, our research revealed that this was but one arc of transition that was imbricated with a history of discrimination and unequal access to resources (Nagavarapu and Kumar, 2022). These 'uneven power dynamics'(Hammelman et al, 2020b: 8) played out on a heterogeneous geographical landscape, privileging some groups while marginalizing others. Yet, it also intertwined with cultural and aspirational logics of Dalit communities, forcing us to understand food transitions at a multiscalar level and from multiple standpoints (Hammelman et al, 2020b: 9).

We discovered that some rich farmers in the region availed of irrigation (often monopolizing collective irrigation schemes) to plant Green Revolution crops in the 1960s, while most small and marginal farmers continued to cultivate a diverse range of millets, pulses, oilseeds, vegetables, and fibre (such as hemp) even into the 1990s. These farming families consumed not just cultivated foods, but also foraged for greens, wild fruits, fish, mushrooms, and small game. Dominant caste, rich families consumed wheat and paddy rice even before the 1960s, while intermediate castes and Dalits relied on millets and pulses. Dalit families, who were at the bottom of the social hierarchy, usually ran out of food grains in the lean seasons and subsisted on donated, collected, or hunted foods.

Other factors also determined diets and well-being. For instance, Chipariya village was settled in the late 1800s by the nearby *zamindar* (landlord), in whose fields the villagers (from various underprivileged castes) worked. Their marginal tracts were often submerged for months by the nearby river, leading to total loss of production. A few kilometres upstream, the lands of Dalits in Bareliya and Pitouli villages were submerged only for a short while, and left enriched. The Chipariya villagers were accustomed to foraging for wild foods like *jharua ka daana* (browntop millet), while Dalits upstream had rarely consumed it. Thus, we discovered that the marginalization of Dalit households was also shaped by a confluence of history and geography.

Secondary literature, including colonial records of the region, helped us understand that hunger and deprivation were the result of deeply exploitative sociocultural systems, where Dalits did not have access to land or other resources to prevent seasonal hunger. The colonial British state of the 19th century privileged some communities and dispossessed others, exacerbating existing hierarchies. Further, by curtailing practices of migration, fallowing, and foraging that were adapted to geographical and climatic variability, it pushed people into precarity and hunger (Nagavarapu and Kumar, 2022).

Postcolonial land reforms of the 1950s were implemented in this unequal landscape, and erstwhile *zamindar* (landlord) families managed to retain control over their fertile lands. Thus, eventually, the only lands available for distribution were 'wastelands', scrub forests, wetlands, pastures, and so on, which had served as commons providing fodder, timber, and wild foods to local communities. These were converted into agricultural land for the landless, who were encouraged to cultivate Green Revolution crops (Mearns, 1999). Government land improvement programmes and rising wages (aided by seasonal migration) helped marginal farmers move to rice and wheat cultivation, and attractive rates offered by new sugar factories incentivized sugarcane production. More recently, in Uttar Pradesh, the ascendancy of Hindutva[9] has led to the enforcement of cow slaughter bans, resulting in the menace of freely roaming stray cattle. These animals attack crops, especially millets and pulses, further discouraging farmers from cultivating them (Nagavarapu, 2019).

We also discovered how the commodification of certain foods further transformed diets. In a region where milk, butter, *ghee* (clarified butter), and buttermilk were consumed in huge quantities, today many poor families consume only a little milk in their tea, if any (Kumar et al, 2019). This has been observed throughout rural India, where the proliferation of dairy cooperatives, along with increased household expenses, have led to farming families selling their milk rather than consuming it (Nichols, 2017).

Finally, many foods that marginalized communities relied on, which were associated with scarcity, deprivation, and tedium, were considered *dehati*– 'uncultured'. Those who traditionally consumed these foods aspired to consume rice, wheat, tea, and packaged foods such as biscuits – the 'foods of the rich'. Thus, a multiscalar analysis showed that a range of factors from particular sociohistorical structures and geographies of unevenness in western Avadh, to commodification of certain foods and national and international systems that promoted the Green Revolution, converged to transform diverse landscapes into monocropped fields of rice, wheat, and sugarcane by the 2000s, and to produce the dietary transformations and poor health outcomes that are visible today.

The research journey: learnings, reflections, and course corrections

Kamal Kishore was in one of the teams that conducted the consumption survey in Ballapur. Six teams, comprising one woman and one man, visited families on three (non-consecutive) days during each of four seasons in 2017, and recorded all the foods they had consumed the previous day. "Initially, people were unwilling to share details about what they ate", Kamal Kishore recounted.

> 'But as we met them regularly and kept explaining why we were collecting this data, they became more forthcoming. And then we

realized how limited their diets were – only *rotis* made of wheat flour, *alu ki sabji* [a savoury potato dish] and rice, with tea and rusk [a crispy snack made of flour] for breakfast. We assumed that they would consume at least a little milk or pulses every day, but that was not the case. We then began looking at our own diets, and realized how lacking in nutrients they were.'

The survey team had been constituted of SKMS *Saathis* who lived within a few kilometres of Ballapur, and they were not materially different from the families they surveyed. Their personal involvement allowed them to speak convincingly with other *Saathis* who had also believed that their diets were not that deficient, and spurred changes in diets.

A sobering moment occurred when members of the survey families were being weighed and their heights measured. Om Prakash, who was helping with the weighing, exclaimed, "Show me one woman here who weighs above 40 kg!" To put this in context, an adult woman with a height of 5 feet should weigh at least 40.8 kg to place within normal body mass index (BMI)levels, and most of the women being weighed hadn't crossed 35 kg. We also found that 40 per cent of women were severely anaemic (Kumar et al, 2019). The discussions about Sitapur's malnutrition statistics have gained authenticity and urgency from these personal experiences.

Meanwhile, a visit by Richa K and Richa S to a wheat flour factory revealed that even 'whole wheat flour' had undergone bran removal, with the bran sold separately as animal fodder. This and other visits to food–processing units opened the eyes of the group to the ubiquity of processed foods and their associated health problems. It led to important shifts in the purchasing habits of team members, especially Richa K, as they became more conscious of avoiding highly processed wheat flour, white rice, and white sugar.

The first round of FGDs brought the topic of uncultivated foods and foraging to the forefront. Richa K and Sudha were particularly excited to discover the diversity of foraged foods mentioned by the respondents, and their contribution to the nutritional intake of poorer households. However, Richa S warned against uncritically glorifying foraging, and reminded the team of the socio–ecological context in which it was undertaken – as an activity to tide over months of low cereal availability and carbohydrate deprivation faced by poor communities. The browntop millet that poor families relied on is now being lauded as a superfood. However, its association with a history of scarcity and tedium cannot be ignored. The pleasure and pain associated with the memories of Dalit foods, and their invisibility among recognized Indian cuisines, has received some attention in recent decades (Rege et al, 2009; Deepak, 2018).

Keeping this in mind, subsequent FGDs addressed hunger, and stories describing people's hardships emerged. Many described getting by with just buttermilk and jaggery on some days. Women faced the double burden of caste and gender, sometimes subsisting on fruits and greens. Hunger was closely linked to indebtedness – respondents described *devda* – short-term loans with crippling interest rates – which even led to themgiving up their entire winter crop as payment. Interestingly, Surbala shared personal experiences from the other side, of how her relatives lent money at these usurious rates and she sometimes interceded for the borrowers, suffering verbal abuse for her efforts (cf. Mishra, 2010). What became clear was that hunger was not the result of low food availability but of inequity, as had been established by Amartya Sen's (1982) seminal work on the Great Bengal famine of 1943.

The foraging stories hadan impact on the team. Surbala, who is vegetarian, now speaks eloquently about the importance of fish in local diets. Almost every discussion about foraging brings out new stories, providing insights into the relationships and negotiations between agrarian communities.

From research to articulation, action, and impact

Our research findings were shared periodically with the SKMS core team and advisory group of about 100 *Saathis*, and this helped shape how we analysed and communicated our findings. We realized that we needed a new lexicon to describe nutrition, as diets dominated by processed carbohydrates and low in other nutrients have resulted in the double burden of malnutrition, manifesting as both undernutrition and overweight/obesity (Popkin et al, 2020). In the past, plumpness was associated with prosperity, and even today thin people are called *kamzor*, which also means weak. Our research team decided, instead, to use height and strength as markers of nutrition.

Not only is childhood stunting high in India, research shows that Indians, especially those in the poorest quintiles, are getting shorter (Choudhary et al, 2021). This is visible in the region, and we found height a useful measure to communicate falling nutrition levels. On strength, Om Prakash eloquently shares: "My grandfather could lift a 100 kg sack easily. I can manage 30–50 kg, and my sons can't even lift that much." Strength, we have found, is an effective narrative, and our cooking workshops are now labelled *takati khana shivir* –strength-embodying food workshops.The research findings have also been used to seed discussions among local youth. During an event organized for the youth forum associated with SKMS, participants were asked to name fruits. They listed apples, bananas, pomegranates, even kiwi fruit (which gained popularity during the COVID-19 pandemic). But none mentioned the local, freely available fruits such as *ber* (jujube, a sweet or sour berry) or *jamun* (a plum-like purple fruit). When asked why, many mentioned that these were considered inferior. Subsequent discussions sparked interest, with some youth designing posters (see Figure 11.5), collecting local fruits and posting photos on WhatsApp groups.

Our discussions have had some unexpected impacts. During the COVID-19-induced lockdown of 2020, when markets were inaccessible and employment opportunities few, some *Saathis* drew upon the research stories and foraged for wild fruits and greens. Others have opted to plant fruit trees rather than fast-growing eucalyptus or poplar (which are harvested for timber). Recipes for consuming millet *rotis* with buttermilk or fish, both good protein sources, are shared and the need for dietary fibre is communicated in easily relatable ways.

Team members have also engaged with urban audiences through a TED talk, academic lectures, articles, and online platforms. A presentation of our research process and its outcomes at the International Institute for Information Technology (IIIT), Bangalore, in 2019 led to another collaboration to disseminate our findings, and the 'Recovering Food Narratives' portal was designed and set up at www.foodcultures.org. This bilingual portal documents food narratives from the region in text and video formats, bringing the voices of SKMS *Saathis* and other informants directly to viewers, along with providing links to secondary literature.

A core motivation for our research was to ascertain whether we were on the right path with our millet intervention, described earlier in this chapter. What we realized was that ecological farming interventions typically involved farmers with some resources to tide over periods of transition and financial uncertainty. In the absence of massive funding and/or in the desire for quick results, most interventions remain restricted to relatively privileged farming households (Brown, 2018). However, as our research revealed, SKMS *Saathis* had faced generations of oppression, which had been exacerbated by the colonial encounter. Thus, they had little capacity to withstand poor results on the farm, and were too marginalized in their communities to be able to drive systemic change. Our counter-hegemonic work to promote millets among these farmers required a different approach. Rather than continue with model farms and initial adopters drawn from SKMS *Saathis*, we instead reached out to a much larger group of marginal farmers across the region from 2018 onwards.

Through a newly energized *kheti khana* (farming and food) team, which developed fresh narratives and expanded their outreach, millet farming has now been seeded across several villages in western Avadh, even among farmers who are not connected to SKMS. Our team also discovered indigenous varieties of millets in the region, which helped with adoption. Meanwhile, some *Saathis* innovatively used paddy 'polishers' available in local *chakkis* (processing units)[10] to make millet rice. This idea quickly spread, and the reduction in tedium made millet rices more easily available.

Wholegrain millet rices of good quality, however, required machines designed for this purpose. Thus, with the help of Dwiji Guru (a

Figure 11.5: Poster comparing local fruits with expensive 'city' fruits.

Source: Sangtin (sangtin.org).

millet-processing consultant), SKMS' community-oriented processing unit was inaugurated in August 2022. This unit contains four machines for cleaning and hulling grains and can be used for millets as well as other grains (see Figure 11.6). We hope that this unit, the first of its kind in the state, will further promote mixed cropping, and provide nutritious food to local communities.

2023 was declared the International Year of Millets (IYM) by the UN. In India, millets have been rechristened as *Sri Anna*(divine foods), implying that

Figure 11.6: Saathis at the processing unit.

Source: SKMS.

they are desirable foods for dominant caste consumers. With their growing popularity, millets are now priced beyond the reach of their traditional consumers (Meek, 2022; Nagavarapu, 2023). They are being promoted as monocultures and incorporated in long supply chains. Thus, proposed alternatives to exploitative food systems may instead reproduce sociocultural hierarchies (Hammelman et al, 2020a).

These developments have strengthened our resolve to build counter-hegemonic food systems in western Avadh. It might be institutionally easier to buy millets from intermediaries rather than directly from farmers, or to sell millet rices to urban retailers instead of developing a local market. However, that would defeat the goal of achieving food sovereignty for farmers and consumers within the region. Further, SKMS' ethos of building capacity from within its member base, rather than bringing in professionals who invariably belong to dominant castes and classes, has carried over to the millet enterprise, where SKMS *Saathis* are being trained to operate the machines, maintain accounts, and manage marketing. Some basic skills, such as operating a digital scale, needed to be taught and a few unit operators were found to be careless with maintaining grain quality. However, hitherto unacknowledged skills were also discovered, and the joy and sense of ownership among the unit team is palpable. Thus, the process has been both challenging and rewarding.

Conclusion

As a collective of marginalized communities, founded on the principle of *apna mudda, apni aguvayi* – 'our issue, our advocacy' – SKMS was experienced in interrogating oppressive structures and policies. This collaboration with scholars and scholar-activists helped to further untangle the historical legacy of unequal resource endowment and discrimination that has shaped food systems in the region. It provided a platform for marginalized groups to contribute towards shaping the larger discourse on the relationship between food, farming, and health, while also shaping action to bring about a just food future for local communities. The vocabulary of RFG, which 'centers diverse ways of knowing, while also being actively involved in socially relevant efforts for change' (Hammelman et al, 2020a: 208) has provided a structure to help explain our efforts to a wider audience.

And yet, despite these efforts, the deep-rooted oppressive relationship between caste and commensality continues to torment us. In February 2019, we organized a town hall for local farmers, intellectuals, and government officials to disseminate our findings. Along with the speeches and presentations, we meticulously planned the food and its packaging, for which we used small earthen pots that were specially ordered. The food was well received, and several attendees praised us for the environmentally conscious packaging. However, in the debrief after the event, senior *Saathis* shared that some *Savarna* (caste Hindu) attendees had politely refused the food we offered. SKMS *Saathis*, overwhelmingly Dalit, are considered untouchable, and there are strict rules for accepting food across the caste hierarchy. Amid jubilation over our success, we had to grapple yet again with deep-rooted and persistent discrimination. Despite challenging caste in the realm of the economic or the social, much work remains to be done in engaging caste in its most visceral, material form – in its relationship with food.

This chapter has sought to push the boundaries of RFG praxis by bringing in a unique perspective from an academic-activist collaboration based in the Global South as well as interrogating privilege and oppression in food systems from the historical lens of caste. The idea of expanding the scope of what counts as knowledge, especially legitimized academic knowledge, by bringing the voices of a diverse set of actors from the world of activism into it is an important contribution of RFG praxis. It goes to the heart of the question of representation. At the same time, we have sought to challenge hierarchies that exist within both these worlds. Given that even academic authors from the Global South have faced difficulties publishing in journals from the Global North (which claim to be 'global'), our experiments at RFG have succeeded only when our research has been selected by authors from the Global North to be included in a book or journal special issue (Nagavarapu and Kumar, 2022; this volume).

Within the space of activism, *savarna* and Dalit *Saathis* have laboured to create shared leadership across caste and gender in SKMS, and to ensure that discriminatory practices are identified and addressed. Throughout this research, too, there were several discussions about whether the research team, which is dominated by *savarna* members, can or should be documenting and curating the oral histories of predominantly Dalit communities (cf. Spivak, 1988). Our efforts at self-reflexive research and praxis are a small step in the direction of challenging these fundamental inequities in our society and at pushing the boundaries of RFG praxis.

Notes

[1] Dalit refers collectively to certain oppressed social groups in India who are considered to be 'untouchable' and outside the caste hierarchy.

[2] See Gold and Gujar as a rare exception (Gujar and Gold, 1992) and Gupta(2014) for a critique.

[3] As some authors do not have a last name, first names will be used henceforth, with initials of the last name provided for authors who share a first name. When multiple names are used, they are both first names.

[4] Caste was recognized as part of anti-discrimination laws in Seattle, Washington, in the US in 2023 (see Krishnamurthi and Krishnaswami, 2021).

[5] NGOization refers to the depoliticization of social movements that occurs when they adopt the bureaucratic structures of nongovernmental organizations (NGOs) (Kamat, 2004).

[6] The idea of *sangharsh* and *nirmaan* dates back to Gandhian philosophy, and has been adopted by numerous movements. A pioneering example was Chhattisgarh Mukti Morcha (CMM), which fought for workers' rights and also built a hospital for their health needs (Khare and Varman, 2018).

[7] All the authors are proficient in Hindi and the local authors also speak Avadhi, a regional dialect.

[8] A *Panchayat* is the smallest unit of governance in rural India, comprising a group of villages.

[9] This term, coined by V.D. Savarkar to describe Hindu nationalism, is the ideology of the political party currently governing India and Uttar Pradesh (Jaffrelot, 2017).

[10] *Chakkis* are ubiquitous in the region, and local families get paddy dehusked or grains milled in quantities as little as 5 kg.

References

Agarwal, B. (2014)'Food sovereignty, food security and democratic choice: critical contradictions, difficult conciliations', *Journal of Peasant Studies*, 41(6): 1247–68.

Brown, T. (2018)*Farmers, Subalterns, and Activists: Social Politics of Sustainable Agriculture in India*, Cambridge: Cambridge University Press.

Choudhary, K.K., Das, S., and Ghodajkar, P. (2021)'Trends of adult height in India from 1998 to 2015: evidence from the National Family and Health Survey', *PLOS ONE*, 16(9): e0255676.

Deaton, A. andDrèze, J. (2009) 'Food and nutrition in India: facts and interpretations', *Economic and Political Weekly*: 42–65.

Deepak, S. (2018) 'There is no Dalit cuisine – To Counter a History That is Far from Sweet', *Popula*, [online] 20 November, Available from: popula.com/2018/11/20/there-is-no-dalit-cuisine/ [Accessed 10 February 2023].

Devkota, R., Karthikeyan, M., Samaratunga, H., Gartaula, H., Kiran, S., Nayak, B.K., and Nadhiya, M. (2014)'Increasing gender equality among small millet farmers in South Asia', *Stories of Change*, Canada: International Development Research Centre.

Gogia, S.B. and Sangtin (2016)'Elimination of lymphatic filariasis', *National Medical Journal of India*, 29(1): 37.

Gujar, B.R. andGold, A.G. (1992) 'From the research assistant's point of view', *Anthropology and Humanism Quarterly*, 17(3–4): 72–84.

Gupta, A. (1989) *Postcolonial Developments: Agriculture in the Making of Modern India*, Durham, NC: Duke University Press.

Gupta, A. (2014)'Authorship, research assistants and the ethnographic field', *Ethnography*, 15(3): 394–400.

Hammelman, C., Reynolds, K., and Levkoe, C.Z. (2020a) 'Guest editors' introduction: building a radical food geography praxis', *Human Geography*, 13(3): 207–10.

Hammelman, C., Reynolds, K., and Levkoe, C.Z. (2020b) 'Toward a radical food geography praxis: integrating theory, action, and geographic analysis in pursuit of more equitable and sustainable food systems', *Human Geography*, 13(3): 211–27.

IIPS and ICF (2022) 'National Family Health Survey (NFHS-5), India, 2019–21: Uttar Pradesh', Mumbai: IIPS.

Jaffrelot, C. (2017)'India's democracy at 70: Toward a Hindu state?', *Journal of Democracy*, 28(3): 52–63.

Kamat, S. (2004)'The privatization of public interest: theorizing NGO discourse in a neoliberal era', *Review of International Political Economy*, 11(1): 155–76.

Kaur, S. and Purohit, M.K. (2016) *Rainfall Statistics of India – 2015*, New Delhi: Indian Meteorological Department, Ministry of Earth Sciences.

Khare, A. and Varman, R. (2018)'Shaheed Hospital: alternative institution, ideology, and social movement', *Alternative Organisations in India: Undoing Boundaries*: 152–82.

Krishnamurthi, G. and Krishnaswami, C. (2021) 'Title VII and caste discrimination', *Harvard Law Review*, 134: 456–82.

Kumar, P., Mruthyunjaya, and Dey, M.M. (2007)'Long-term changes in Indian food basket and nutrition', *Economic and Political Weekly*, 42(35): 3567–72.

Kumar, R. (2016)*Rethinking Revolutions: Soyabean, Choupals, and the Changing Countryside in Central India*, New Delhi: Oxford University Press.

Kumar, R. (2023)'Standardised foods and compromised consumers: can the repeal of the three farm laws turn the clock back?', *Sociological Bulletin*, 72(1): 38–55.

Kumar, R., Agrawal, A., Prakash, A., Nagavarapu, S., Singh, R., and Vaish, S. (2019) 'Remaking farms and reshaping diets: implications for untangling under-nutrition in rural India', *Final Technical Report for Faculty Interdisciplinary Research Project* (FIRP) No. MI01429, Indian Institute of Technology Delhi (2017–18).

Mearns, R. (1999)*Access to Land in Rural India*, The World Bank.

Mishra, A. (2010) *Hunger and Famine in Kalahandi: An Anthropological Study*, Pearson Education India.

Meek, D. (2022)'From marginalized to miracle: critical bioregionalism, jungle farming and the move to millets in Karnataka, India', *Agriculture and Human Values*, 39(3): 871–83.

Nagar, R. in journeys with SKMS (2021)'Gender, caste and movement: lessons from Sangtin Yatra', *Gender, Place, and Culture*, 28(2): 161–75.

Nagavarapu, S. (2019) Gau Raksha Is Disrupting the Bovine Economy and Threatening Farmers' Fields', *The Wire*,[online]5 May, Available from: thewire.in/agriculture/gau-raksha-bovine-economy-agricultural-produce [Accessed 20 November 2022].

Nagavarapu, S. (2023) 'The Reincarnation of Millets: From Derided to Divine', *The India Forum*, [online] 24 April, Available from:www.theind iaforum.in/environment/reincarnation-millets-derided-divine [Accessed 5 May 2023].

Nagavarapu, S. and Kumar, R. (2022)'Constituting the norm: interrogating the Anthropocene through food geographies in the more than human worlds of western Avadh, India', *Geographical Journal*, 188(3): 370–82.

Nichols, C. (2017)'Millets, milk and maggi: contested processes of the nutrition transition in rural India', *Agriculture and Human Values*, 34: 871–85.

Popkin, B.M., Corvalan, C., andGrummer-Strawn, L.M. (2020) 'Dynamics of the double burden of malnutrition and the changing nutrition reality', *The Lancet*, 395(10217): 65–74.

Rege, S., Tak, D., Thosar, S., and Aranha, T. (2009)*Isn't this Plate Indian? Dalit Histories and Memories of Food*, Pune: Krantijyoti Savitribai Phule Women's Studies Centre, University of Pune.

Sangtin Writers and Nagar, R. (2006)*Playing with Fire: Feminist Thought and Activism Through Seven Lives in India*, Minneapolis, MN: University of Minnesota.

Sélingué, M. (2007) *Declaration of Nyéléni*, Available from:www2.world-governance.org/IMG/pdf_0072_Declaration_of_Nyeleni_-_ENG-2.pdf [Accessed 10 November 2022].

Sen, Amartya, K. (1982)*Poverty and Famines: An Essay on Entitlement and Deprivation*, Oxford University Press.

Spivak, G.C. (1988) 'Can the Subaltern Speak?', in C. Nelson and L. Grossberg (eds) *Marxism and the Interpretation of Culture*, London: Macmillan, pp 271–313.

12

Food–Making in the Sisterhoods of Bourj Albarajenah Refugee Camp: Towards Radical Food Geographies of Displacement

Yafa El Masri

Palestinian refugees were forcefully displaced from their native cities and villages in British-mandated Palestine to neighbouring areas in 1948, seeking protection from violence that accompanied the establishment of the state of Israel (Morris, 2004; Pappé, 2007; Masalha, 2012). It is estimated that around 100,000 of the 700,000 displaced Palestinians sought refuge in Lebanon, just across the borders from many northern villages of Palestine (Khalidi and Khalidi, 2006; Minority Rights Group International, 2008). Palestinians displaced from the villages of Ghabsiyeh, Kabri, Kwikat, Sheikh Daoud, and Tarshiha eventually settled together in a refugee camp in the Lebanese capital (Beirut) which became known as Bourj Albarajenah. My mother's family was displaced from Kabri to Lebanon in 1948, so I was born and raised as a stateless Palestinian refugee in Bourj Albarajenah.

In Lebanon, Palestinian refugees cannot be naturalized, despite living there for generations. This deprives us from equal access to services provided by the local public system, most notably health and education (Abdulrahim and Khawaja, 2011; Hanafi et al, 2012). We are also excluded from owning property and entering the job market, which often maintains us locked within the refugee camp premises. This exclusion causes 93 per cent of Palestinian refugees in Lebanon to live below the poverty line and over 62 per cent to suffer from food insecurity (UNRWA, 2022). In summary, Palestinian refugees are subject to a double-layered land injustice: exclusion from their native lands in Palestine and exclusion in the host community. In this chapter, I explore how collective cooking within camp sisterhoods

Figure 12.1: Women preparing food together in Bourj Albarajneh Palestinian refugee camp during the Art on the Wall and Culture for All festival.

Source: Photo is courtesy of ARCPA/AL-JANA Center, 2021 (reproduced with permission).

(Figure 12.1) is a means of resistance in the face of this double injustice restricting Palestinian refugees from land, both in homeland and in exile (see also Nadar and Casolo, Chapter 14, for a discussion about histories of Palestinian land dispossession). Using ethnographic and auto-ethnographic recordings of growing up in Bourj Albarajenah, I analyse how food-making within my mother's sisterhood has enabled us to attain food self-sufficiency and food sovereignty for decades.

bell hooks (1986) defines a sisterhood as a sustainable form of commitment, solidarity, and support among women, built upon a community of interests, shared beliefs, and goals around which to unite. hooks argues that sisters do not bond over victimization but rather over shared strengths and resources with the aim of reaching co-created political goals. Reflecting on the lives of women in Bourj Albarajenah refugee camp, it is essential to look beyond refugee women's double victimization as both women and refugees, and rather explore their bonding and agencies that enable them to shape their daily lives.

In their work on radical food geographies (RFG), Hammelman et al (2020) and Levkoe et al (Chapter 1, this volume) explain that understanding relationships, exchanges, and mobilities between people and places, and the underlying power dynamics, can highlight the oppressive systems in which food injustice is produced, but can also make visible and foster partnerships which resist these systems. In this chapter, I discuss how sisterhoods – as a system that incorporates relationalities with humans and the land – offer effective forms of informal food networks in settings of exclusion and forced displacement. I discuss how these networks contribute to creating more justice in local food systems, address food self-sufficiency by sharing culturally relevant food, and foster food sovereignty by safeguarding the relationship with the colonized land.

RFG examines how relationships with the land and people are made in ways that produce inequality but also how these relationships can be transformed to create more equitable food systems (Hammelman et al, 2020; Levkoe et al, Chapter 1). In sharing my research findings, I begin by focusing on the exchange of knowledge that concerns our native Palestinian villages and occurs between women during the several stages of meal preparation. Settler colonialism in Palestine has been focused on controlling the maximum amount of space by eliminating, marginalizing, displacing, and separating Palestinians from their native lands (Salamanca et al, 2012; Dana and Jarbawi, 2017). This system of oppression deprives millions of Palestinians from access to their homes but also from other cultural elements derived from the land and constitutes their identity, such as food and folklore. I demonstrate how Palestinian refugee sisterhoods are resisting this land injustice. Further, I suggest that women are creating a pedagogy of Palestinian history and more-than-human geography, thus contributing to the protection of group identity by sharing information about native food ingredients and herbs throughout the food-making process.

Despite these efforts, the Lebanese legal system excludes Palestinian refugees from socio-economic rights. The research findings also show how women respond to this injustice through sharing the ingredients and meals with one another at times of great struggle when food is limited. These food networks created by women allow Palestinian refugees to achieve self-sufficiency in refugee camps, but also to access food of cultural value which in turn allows the community to establish food sovereignty and resist socio-economic exclusion.

The discussion then reflects on both the exchange of knowledge and resistance through sharing meals by grounding it in the literature. I conclude with a reflection on these findings and argue for the need to address the peculiarity of RFG in settings of displacement. Through the case study from Bourj Albarajenah, I argue for conceiving informal food networks, in this case established by sisterhoods, as a radical tool that could be used by forcefully displaced communities to rearrange food geographies, and establish channels of access to the homeland and its culinary traditions.

Informal food networks: sisterhoods and RFG

RFG builds on foundations in radical geographies and critical food systems scholarship by identifying uneven power dynamics in local and global food networks and systems (Hammelman et al, 2020; Levkoe et al, Chapter 1).

This theoretical engagement with systems of power and structures of oppression is significant to highlight and endorse active resistances to these systems and structures that (re)produce power inequity and oppression in food systems.

Among practices of resistance to the exploitation of global food industries is an increased focus on informal food networks (Colombino, 2014; Dansero et al, 2019). These networks aim to weave a more localized socio-economic fabric that creates new relationships between food security outcomes and community interests, thus contributing to the sustainability of food self-sufficiency and food sovereignty in marginalized spaces (Kurtz et al, 2019). Research on local food systems demonstrates that the ability to access food from informal sources plays a critical role in making food accessible to poor urban households and that without them, households would be significantly worse off (Raimundo, Crush, and Pendleton, 2016).

Informal food networks are closely intertwined with communities. Food relationships establish networks that create 'small worlds' that are able to hold strong independently of geographic distance and location (Parasecoli, 2014). Food situates people into networks, of people and of places that might be located far away from their kitchens and dining rooms (Colombino, 2014). Food is to be seen as a connection between people and their homelands and ethnic identities. Parasecoli (2014: 431) describes food as a hub of belonging for immigrants. He theorizes that both environmentally/socially aware alternative food activists and migrant communities 'share the desire to defend an often imagined past that is perceived as threatened with extinction, and to claim roots that are constantly antagonised or negated by the surrounding environment'. In the Palestinian refugee case, this negation is part of the settler-colonial project that oppresses Palestinians and denies them access to land and its cultural aspects such as food and herbs.

If colonialism is about separating humans from their lands, then decolonizing demands constituting practices of reconnection (Simpson, 2014). I argue that protracted refugee communities, who are forcefully separated from their homes, due to power struggles over their land, rely on informal food networks and food-making practices to resist this land and food injustices, rearrange the power dynamics, and reconnect to their land. It is because meals represent a *ritualized geography* where food links the people who are eating it to the places where recipes were created or food was grown, that displaced communities value the food of home (Dunn, 2011). And the reclamation of land sovereignty is heavily entangled with reclamation of social, cultural, agricultural, and culinary practices because the human is always more-than-human, meaning that one is always connected to other beings in their environment (Isaacs, 2020).

To move from the mere identification of uneven power structures towards empirically fostering resistances, Bodirsky and Johnson (2008) identified the potential of food knowledge in healing the ongoing trauma emerging from colonialism. By reflecting on food and displacement in Canada, they found that many contemporary Indigenous Peoples have expanded upon oral traditions with written stories of food gathering and recipes as a means to revitalize both food knowledge and community. Therefore, this research will further shed light on the plurality of ways in which food can contribute to confronting land and food injustice in settings of colonized and uprooted communities.

The agency of women in informal food networks

When speaking of women and food, research often highlights the subjugating position of women as cooking locks them into traditional gender roles. Research on women's domesticity and housework emphasizes the need to include an analysis of how a patriarchal paradigm subjugates women's choices and experiences (Foucault and Gordon, 1980; Code, 2007). Therefore, it remains essential to critically think about the ways that women's lives continue to be influenced by a structural dualism that creates an opposition between male/female, public/private, work/home (Code, 2007; Gillis and Hollows, 2008) and how practices such as cooking can potentially reinforce those structures.

On the other hand, women's resistance should not be separated from its environment, and resistors often utilize elements of their oppression to fight it (Mahmood, 2005). Rather than viewing agency as obvious practices leading to subverting norms and dismantling systems, agency is often secured through the very same conditions that have made the subject subordinate (Mahmood, 2005). This allows theorizing RFG as a multitude of forms of actions that redistribute power and access to food. In this case, women can utilize elements, such as the camp space or the kitchen space to access culturally relevant food, make political choices, and build food sovereignty. Latour (2014) provides a description of agency that is rooted in networks and collective forms of being in the Anthropocene, by explaining that being an agent cannot be limited to acting autonomously but must be centred on sharing agency with those who have lost their autonomy. This definition allows us to conceive the grassroots radical food movement of women in the refugee camp as a collective action mobilizing for the interest of themselves, other women, and the camp community.

Food-making can be understood as a practice of agency when the kitchen is reframed as a place for politics. The kitchen is indeed coded as a safe place for women to review their lives, reflecting on their experiences in ways that are not possible within mixed-gender spaces (Scicluna, 2017). Spaces shared with other women are also important opportunities to resist conventional feminine identities (Green, 1998). Diverse analysis of private conversations between women designates these talks as a main tool to explore their identities outside of societal expectations (Meah and Jackson, 2013; McKeown, 2015; Smith, 2019). The impact of kitchen talks can be expanded and explored at the level of community and its role in social cohesion and the formation of collective memory. This leads to an advancement in theorization on the role of sisterhood food-making in shaping the lives of the displaced Indigenous Palestinian community and thus contributing to a RFG of displacement.

Approach, methodology, and positionality

This chapter adopts a decolonial approach which centres ethnographic and auto-ethnography methods. A decolonial approach is one that fosters Indigenous knowledge and cosmologies (Tuhiwai Smith, 1999; El Masri, 2022). In relation to food, a decolonial approach provides resurgence of Indigenous practices and knowledges that relate to food, cuisines, and cooking methods, and explores hidden histories of relationships between humans and their ecosystems (Peña et al, 2017). This chapter prioritizes the knowledge of refugee women in Bourj Albarajenah as agents of food and knowledge of the land. This also involves prioritizing my voice as a refugee who has direct experience within the field of study.

Food-making and sisterhoods within refugee camps is an understudied topic due to the privacy and intimacy of the field. Often seen as 'secret lives', the lives of refugee women are less accessible to foreign researchers, require long-term personal relationships, knowledge of local language and dialect, and specific cultural and gender sensitivities. More importantly, it is often a site of a scholarship/activism divide, where place-based knowledges of refugee women are isolated and valued differently from the knowledge produced in academia. However, RFG praxis calls for identifying and addressing uneven power–knowledge dynamics through shared learning and a diminishing academic/activism divide (Reynolds et al, 2020). Action towards food justice requires an intersection but also a collaboration between knowledges produced at various scales and in various geographic and cultural settings (Reynolds et al, 2020). Therefore, in this chapter, I am both a scholar and an active participant.

As a Palestinian refugee woman from Bourj Albarajenah, I am able to explore these practices with extensive knowledge and existing relationships. This includes reflecting on my memories, diaries, and photo recordings collected throughout my life in Bourj Albarajenah refugee camp between 1990 and 2016. The period between 2017 and 2022 was spent abroad, but included periodic and long visits home, during which I spent time cooking with my mother's sisters. I collected photos and quotes, and more importantly, recorded the sisters' own interpretations of their food practices.

Writing at the intersection of refugee and scholar required an extensive amount of emotional labour, mainly because, as Domínguez (2000: 356) suggests, 'scholars who write about people they really care about face some serious editorial dilemmas'. I constantly reminded myself that 'Love does not mean [...] feeling so guilty about our own geopolitically defined position that we treat those with consult with kid gloves, both in "the field" [...] and in our published writing' (Domínguez, 2000: 357). So, I discussed my research findings with my mother's sisters, who helped me identify moments of survivor's guilt and to employ this emotionality in the politics of research.

The travels of stories, memories, and food from Palestine to Bourj Albarajenah

My mother began every day in Bourj Albarajenah with morning coffee with her sisters Amal, Aliya, Souad, and Zeinab. Drinking coffee was a social ritual of feminine gathering, which took place in the morning after the men left to work. My mother and her sisters made their coffee by manually grinding equal portions of cardamom and coffee grains. This combination is a tradition which has travelled with our families from Palestine to Lebanon.

My mother has never seen Palestine, but she was taught by her own mother how coffee and food were made back home. This is the same way she taught me, through including me in her sisterhood gatherings. She and her sisters narrated to me, with much nostalgia, stories they had learned about a home they never had. My mother told me how her mother spent mornings baking bread for the family, then grinding coffee and cardamom under an old fig tree in front of their house in Kabri, their village, where an Israeli kibbutz community now resides. Amal told me that Palestinians have been using their relationship to cardamom as a political tool of resistance:

> 'Most of our cardamom comes from Guatemala. But when the former Guatemalan President [Ramiro de Leon Carpio] decided to move the Israeli embassy to Jerusalem back in 1994, our entire community decided to boycott their cardamom. It went to a regional level and threatened the entire trade, it put the diplomacy between the Arabic region and Guatemala on the line.'

Interestingly, the Guatemalan government did backtrack on its decision to open an embassy in Jerusalem back then due to trade pressures from the Arab world and did not open one until 2018, following Donald Trump's decision to move the US embassy to Jerusalem. Hearing these daily stories educated me about the history of our families in Palestine, but also about the modes of grassroots and international resistance of my community. The sisters also shared their cooking plans for the day, and often discussed where

FOOD-MAKING IN THE SISTERHOODS

each dish comes from, and why it is prepared the way it was. For example, Souad, a sister from Gaza, who was living in Bourj Albarajenah because she is married to a man from Ghabsiyeh, was often criticized by the sisters for the overuse of spices in her dishes. She responded by telling us stories about Gaza's history as the principal port on the Mediterranean in antiquity, and the impact of that on Gaza's exposure to spice trade. She explained the location of the Gaza port at the end of the Nabataean spice road, through which herbs, spices, incense, and food were dispatched from southern Arabia to the European markets, which explains the variety in exposure to spices.

These conversations often continued to other food-related activities such as buying or collecting food ingredients (see Figure 12.2). We would buy herbs and vegetables from the Bedouin Palestinian women who forge ingredients from the mountains and spread them on fabric cloths at their usual spot at the entrance of the camp. These women would tell us stories about their face tattoos or give us advice about cooking certain plants. They introduced us to the black calla plant, which is often feared even by animals due to its high levels of toxicity and potential to cause irritation. The Bedouin vendors explained that this plant is dubbed as the "Palestinian plant", for its long history as a significant meal in the Palestinian cuisine, in addition to being used as a herbal remedy for stomach disorders. They explained that the secret to safely use the black calla is removing the stem all the way (even from the leaf), rubbing it with lemon then boiling it with salt until the toxins are neutralized. I later learned that the black calla's scientific name is *Arum Palaestinum*, in reference to Palestine.

We would also go to the mountain areas to pick our own herbs – mainly sage, thyme, and mallow. My mother and her sisters told us – the children – the story of sage and why it is so important for our kitchens. Sage is named *Maryameyye* in Palestinian dialect, meaning 'that of Mary'. The herb was named after the Virgin Mary who used to collect it and boil it for baby Jesus whenever he felt sick. The story claims that the sage tea healed Jesus' pains every time and therefore has become the most sacred plant in the Palestinian community. This was one of many stories that we heard about herbs and plants that grow in Palestine and provided a memory of our historical presence on that land.

Even when buying certain ingredients, the relationship to Palestinian land was made explicit. One example was the way our mothers purchased olive oil, whose main ingredient – olives – was a symbol for Palestinian lands. Normally, the sisterhoods would pool their resources and connections to find a way to ship bottles of olive oil from Palestine to Lebanon through Jordan. Every time we received a new bottle of oil, my mother would make us taste the difference between that and the local oil. Then they would dedicate this moment to the hundreds of olive fields that are being bulldozed and lands being confiscated in Palestine every day. In one of these

Figure 12.2: A photo I took of my mother's sisters, walking in Bourj Albarajenah alleyways, 2021.

moments, Aliya told us about a 5,000-year-old olive tree still standing strong in Bethlehem, that is said to be among the oldest olive trees in the world. She explained that olives grow best in Palestine because of its dry summers and slightly cool and rainy winters, elaborating that both the occasional summer rain and cold winters severely damage the olive trees and the quality of the harvest. When we had to purchase olive oil from Lebanon, they would say, "The closer the village of production is to Palestine, the better the oil". The more we would go south, we would find the finest quality of oil, because it was geographically closer to Palestine, there is full sun exposure all summer long, and the temperatures do not drop below 15°C in the winter, which are the ideal conditions for olive cultivation according to my mother and her sisters.

These stories of food, herbs, preparation methods, and ingredients were shared by my mother's sisterhood from generation to generation, but also throughout networks of women within the refugee camp. They reflect deep, inherited native knowledge of the Palestinian ecosystem and the pedagogy of Palestinian history and geography passed down through kitchen spaces.

Sharing food along the networks of sisterhoods

The sisterhoods of Bourj Albarajenah are also agents of mutual support at times of economic instability and food insecurity, mainly through food-sharing. According to UNRWA (2016), 62.2 per cent of Palestinian refugees in Lebanon suffer from food insufficiency. The levels of food insufficiency are directly proportional to diet diversity (UNRWA, 2016), which means that this condition forces families to shift from culturally relevant foods to more economical ingredients.

There are several ways in which these families coped with this lack of food. Less than half of the families who are struggling with food-sufficiency are eligible to receive UNRWA assistance. However, this small assistance remains short of covering family needs, especially within the recent economic crisis and ongoing inflation in Lebanon. UNRWA (2016) reports that Palestinian refugees develop their own mechanisms to battle food insecurity, calculating that around 41 per cent of severely food-insufficient families depend on food-sharing dynamics – ones similar to food-sharing within my mother's sisterhood.

My mother's sisters often discussed their personal worries, family concerns, and financial obligations while cooking. Within these small settings, women who have known each other for several decades felt safe to talk about often embarrassing economic problems, whether it's a husband who lost his job or a child in need of expensive medical care. This transparency and friendship enabled sisterhoods to detect and identify families dealing with food insufficiency within their group and initiate assistance accordingly.

At many times, it was my own family going through times of financial struggle. We were not eligible for UNRWA's assistance, but Zeinab received it quarterly. She shared her portions with my mother, thus enabling her to cook meals for our family. But life in the camp was often unpredictable and the roles do often turn, due to war, siege, or economic crises. At other times, my mother cooked for our family and Zeinab's, especially after Zeinab's divorce left her without income. The food-sharing among sisterhoods also included buying ingredients on behalf of a sister in need so that she could cook meals of her choice for the family, therefore protecting their privacy and agency.

In other times, food-sharing took the form of invitations, where our family would host each other for lunch for a few days before it becomes someone else's turn to host meals. The sisters would also send their children to eat with the family who is able to afford the food of that day, while adults held back and managed with smaller portions of food. According to Zeinab, this mechanism works so well because they were able to identify each other's vulnerability in an intimate and safe setting through strong personal relations:

> 'I hate having to go through the humiliating procedures of humanitarian aid: standing in food queues, presenting evidence to convince these employees that I am poor, putting my dignity on the line and making my poverty situation public. My sisters, on the other hand, understand what I need from my eyes. I barely need to ask.'

My mother's sisters have thus strategized food-making and food-sharing as more than a mechanism of friendship where women provide mutual care at times of struggle, but they also deployed food as a mechanism of support that extends to families throughout the refugee camp. My mother's sisterhood (but also various sisterhoods across Bourj Albarajenah) acts as a network for the identification and transport of knowledges as well as material and immaterial food support, therefore safeguarding their access to food and culture. These sharing practices also act as resistance to the socio-economic exclusion produced by Palestinian land dispossession.

Revisiting women's politics of cooking in Bourj Albarajenah

These auto-ethnographic reflections are a visualization of how refugee camp women use the camp and kitchen spaces (the same elements that are often created to lock them away) to fight colonial exclusion and refugee marginalization. Building on both definitions of agency as using the source of oppression to deconstruct it (Mahmood, 2005) and as sharing autonomy with others who have lost it (Latour, 2014), the acts of waiting and cooking in a refugee camp are interpreted as intentionally political. The political objectives of the sisterhoods demonstrate that kitchens are a place where collective strategies for identity and resistance are cooked up. The women have thus used the spaces of waiting, their experience of forced displacement, the gender roles assigned to them, the material help given to them by humanitarian aid, and their inherited memories to sustain a radical movement towards justice and decolonization.

Echoing hooks' (1986) theory, the bonding of refugees is based on more than common sufferings, but on the strength of their networks. The sisters in Bourj Albarajenah have been constructing a pedagogy based on food, stories, ancestral knowledge, and friendship, to transfer and preserve knowledge about their homelands. For Palestinians, being a native inherently requires knowing our unique ecosystems and nurturing a relationship of respect with its components – the herbs, plants, animals, trees, and climate. So, they extend their collective generational environmental memory of the coffee, cardamom, olives, spices, the black calla, and sage to the newer generations. Practices such as storytelling on the climate and soil conditions necessary for the best harvest of olives, for example, are all attempts at preservation and dissemination of ancestral knowledge about the more-than-human geography of our Palestinian villages.

The use of memory and stories in cooking can potentially play a critical part in defying the deliberate exclusion from the land and its cultural and material products because decolonizing requires the oppressed group to critique the story of the powerful and teach their community's way of life (Freire, 1970; Escobar, 2015). The sisters have chosen to present their inherited stories of their family villages, such as Kabri and Gaza, to reiterate their belonging to that land despite colonial forces. They demonstrated that the Palestinian can remain connected to ancestral land despite forced separation, because the Palestinian is spiritually an extension of the land and its components – the plants, herbs, trees, recipes, animals, spices, climate, and other beings. These practices and relations are forms of RFG praxis where local communities are organizing to confront the colonial narrative of their land and prioritizing and protecting their native knowledges of these places. Building this knowledge of Palestinian more-than-human geography (through collective cooking and stories) and constructing informal food networks (which provide food of cultural value), enables people to remain connected to the land from which they are forcefully displaced. Through a lens of RFG, these practices can be interpreted as acts of resistance to land and food injustice, and claiming of space in colonized lands despite the apparatus of oppression.

Examining how sisterhoods identify the inequality in access to land and food among families in the camp, and then how they are intentionally and strategically disrupting the maps of colonization by placing themselves and their families in Palestine and in relation to their native villages and cities enables an understanding of the role of informal food networks in advancing RFG. In disrupting these maps, they use the plants, spices, and stories to create *boomerang foods* that give them some form of return (Dunn, 2011). And when constructing informal food networks to resist food insufficiency as a threat to their culinary culture, they are creating what Parasecoli (2014) calls 'small worlds', which reconnect them to each other, and therefore to their land. Such informal food networks indeed weave a localized socio-economic safety network that keeps marginalized communities from falling through the cracks of poverty and forced disconnection (Kurtz, 2019).

Informal food networks can be a direct tool used by Palestinian refugees in exile, in the face of forced displacement, land injustice, and food injustice, to pursue political objectives in light of the absence of adequate political solutions. As a result, food becomes an essential component of the radical movement for Palestinian refugees towards the Right of Return.[1] And because food has such deep cultural significance regarding connection to the land, defending access to Palestinian food means protecting group identities and supporting the continuing struggle towards return. This is because food insufficiency is not only a matter of hunger but also lack of access to our identity. Although food sufficiency is often discussed in relation to poverty and underdevelopment, food-making in the sisterhoods of Bourj Albarajenah refugee camp presents the importance of informal food networks for its potential to protect collective cultural identity.

Towards an RFG of displacement

This chapter has presented evidence on collective cooking as a direct link to the land as it provides access to knowledge and memory of the colonized home, in addition to access to adequate food in exile. Therefore, protecting food sufficiency in displaced communities is a protection of the right to return. This highlights the importance of recognizing the peculiarity of RFG in refugee communities who are facing double systems of exclusion, from the homeland and in the host community.

The sisterhoods of Bourj Albarajenah are fighting inequality in both occupied Palestine and settings of refugee exclusion in Lebanon. Cooking is then an effort to claim space in the homelands they are displaced from, and to build home in the space that they are waiting in. The women of Bourj Albarajenah use their friendship networks to share food throughout the camp, using this food as a tool of decoloniality, proving refugee women as agents of resistance and mutual aid for redefining geographies of colonialism and food. Memories, relationships, and stories are therefore direct ingredients of food and critical components of resistance that should be recognized as factors in RFG in settings of forced displacement.

Since food is a link to the land, food insufficiency hinders connecting with home through food stories and recipes. Women recognize that less food diversity means interrupted access to food of cultural value and meaningful stories, and therefore is a disconnection from the land. This motivates their mobilization towards restoring food sufficiency and food sovereignty. This resonates with Escobar's (2015: 20) sentiment that 'within relational worlds, the defence of territory, life, and the commons are one and the same'. The attachment of refugees to specific territories through its culinary products and cultural symbols is only a reminder that the human is always entangled with other beings and elements in these dynamic assemblages (Isaacs, 2020).

In conclusion, geographies of access to food for refugees are mapped by host community policies and settler colonialism in settings of forced displacement, but these geographies of unequal access to food can be reshaped in radical forms, by refugee sisterhoods, to attain food justice, and maintain cultural identity through food. Ultimately, it is significant to underline the ways in which sisterhoods are providing dignified solidarity to families who are not protected by humanitarian aid or their host communities, or who are humiliated by them. This makes visible the importance of understanding the possibility, and even the necessity, of other forms of cooperation that aim to achieve food justice. The sisterhood experience presents a possibility of food-justice systems that differ greatly from the various top-down aid-based food programmes, but rather are weaved by social ties and memory to foster food sovereignty. This opens up an invitation to examine food sovereignty and even RFG praxis in displaced communities by acknowledging refugee-to-refugee, grassroots cooperation and refugee women's agencies as viable mechanisms towards achieving food justice during humanitarian crises.

Note

[1] In the Palestinian context, the Right of Return refers to the refugees' right to return to their pre-1948 and/or pre-1967 homes and lands. This right is affirmed by the United Nations General Assembly Resolution 194, article 11.

References

Abdulrahim, S. and Khawaja, M. (2011) 'The cost of being Palestinian in Lebanon', *Journal of Ethnic and Migration Studies*, 37(1): 151–166. DOI: https://doi.org/10.1080/1369183X.2011.521363

Bodirsky, M. and Johnson, J. (2008) 'Decolonizing diet: healing by reclaiming traditional indigenous foodways', *Cuizine: the Journal of Canadian Food Cultures/Cuizine: revue des cultures culinaires au Canada*, 1(1): 0–0. DOI: https://doi.org/10.7202/019373ar

Code, L. (2007) 'Feminist epistemologies and women's lives', in Linda Martín Alcoff and Eva Feder Kittay (eds) *The Blackwell Guide to Feminist Philosophy*, Hoboken, NJ: John Wiley & Sons, pp 211–34. DOI: https://doi.org/10.1002/9780470696132.ch12.

Colombino, A. (2014) 'The geography of food', *Bollettino della Società Geografica Italiana*, 7(4): 647–56. DOI: https://doi.org/10.13128/bsgi.v7i4.382

Dana, T. and Jarbawi, A. (2017) 'A century of settler colonialism in Palestine: Zionism's entangled project', *Brown Journal of World Affairs*, 24(1): 197–220.

Dansero, E. et al (2019) *Lo spazio delle politiche locali del cibo: temi, esperienze e prospettive*, Turin: Celid (Atlante del cibo).

Domínguez, V.R. (2000) 'For a politics of love and rescue', *Cultural Anthropology*, 15(3): 361–93.

Dunn, E. (2011) 'The food of sorrow: humanitarian aid to displaced people', in L. Coleman (ed) *Food: Ethnographic Encounters* (English edn), Berg, pp 139–50.

El Masri, Y. (2022) 'Decolonizing education in Bourj Albarajenah: cosmologies of a Palestinian refugee camp', *Globalizations*, 0(0): 1–18. DOI: https://doi.org/10.1080/14747731.2022.2038832

Escobar, A. (2015) 'Thinking-feeling with the Earth: Territorial Struggles and the Ontological Dimension of the Epistemologies of the South'.

Foucault, M. and Gordon, C. (1980) *Power/Knowledge: Selected Interviews and Other Writings, 1972–1977* (1st American edn), New York: Pantheon Books.

Freire, P. (1970) *Pedagogy of the Oppressed* (30th anniversary edn), New York: Continuum.

Gillis, S. and Hollows, J. (2008) *Feminism, Domesticity and Popular Culture*, New York: Routledge. DOI: https://doi.org/10.4324/9780203889633

Green, E. (1998) '"Women doing friendship": an analysis of women's leisure as a site of identity construction, empowerment and resistance', *Leisure Studies*, 17(3): 171–85. DOI: https://doi.org/10.1080/026143698375114

Habib, E. (2011). 'Borj Barajneh: reinterpretation of a Palestine refugee camp in Beirut', Master's, Politecnico Di Milano.

Hammelman, C., Reynolds, K., and Levkoe, C.Z. (2020) 'Toward a radical food geography praxis: integrating theory, action, and geographic analysis in pursuit of more equitable and sustainable food systems', *Human Geography*, 13(3): 211–27. DOI: https://doi.org/10.1177/1942778620962034

Hanafi, S., Chaaban, J., and Seyfert, K. (2012) 'Social exclusion of Palestinian refugees in Lebanon: reflections on the mechanisms that cement their persistent poverty', *Refugee Survey Quarterly*, 31(1): 34–53. DOI: https://doi.org/10.1093/rsq/hdr018

hooks, b. (1986) 'Sisterhood: political solidarity between women', *Feminist Review*, 23(1): 125–38. DOI: https://doi.org/10.1057/fr.1986.25

Isaacs, J.R. (2020) 'More-than-human geographies', in *International Encyclopedia of Geography*, John Wiley & Sons, pp 1–5. DOI: https://doi.org/10.1002/9781118786352.wbieg2041

Khalidi, W. and Khalidi, M.A. (2006) *All that Remains: The Palestinian Villages Occupied and Depopulated by Israel in 1948*, [Nachdr. der Ausg.] 1992, Washington: Institute for Palestine Studies.

Kurtz, H., Borron, A., Shannon, J., and Weaver, A. (2019) 'Community food assistance, informal social networks, and the labor of care', *Agriculture and Human Values*, 36(3): 495–505. DOI: https://doi.org/10.1007/s10460-019-09943-0

Latour, B. (2014) 'Agency at the time of the Anthropocene', *New Literary History*, 45(1): 1–18. DOI: https://doi.org/10.1353/nlh.2014.0003

Mahmood, S. (2005) *Politics of Piety: The Islamic Revival and the Feminist Subject* (revised edn), Princeton University Press. DOI: https://doi.org/10.2307/j.ctvct00cf

Masalha, N. (2012) *The Palestine Nakba: Decolonising History, Narrating the Subaltern, Reclaiming Memory*, Zed Books.

McKeown, J.K.L. (2015) 'The hens are clucking: women performing gossip in their leisure lives', *Leisure Sciences*, 37(5): 447–57. DOI: https://doi.org/10.1080/01490400.2015.1037472.

Meah, A. and Jackson, P. (2013) 'Crowded kitchens: the "democratisation" of domesticity?', *Gender, Place & Culture*, 20(5): 578–96. DOI: https://doi.org/10.1080/0966369X.2012.701202

Minority Rights Group International (2008) *World Directory of Minorities and Indigenous Peoples – Lebanon: Palestinians, Refworld*, Available from: www.refworld.org/docid/49749cf0c.html [Accessed 5 January 2023].

Morris, B. (2004) *The Birth of the Palestinian Refugee Problem Revisited* (2nd edn), Cambridge; New York: Cambridge University Press (Cambridge Middle East studies, 18).

Pappé, I. (2007) *The Ethnic Cleansing of Palestine* (reprint), Oxford: Oneworld.

Parasecoli, F. (2014) 'Food, identity, and cultural reproduction in immigrant communities', *Social Research*, 81(2): 415–39.

Peña, D. et al (2017) *Mexican-Origin Foods, Foodways, and Social Movements: Decolonial Perspectives*, University of Arkansas Press.

Raimundo, I., Crush, J., and Pendleton, W. (2016) 'Food insecurity, poverty and informality', in J. Crush and J. Battersby (eds) *Rapid Urbanisation, Urban Food Deserts and Food Security in Africa*, Cham: Springer, pp 71–83. DOI: https://doi.org/10.1007/978-3-319-43567-1_6

Reynolds, K. et al (2020) 'Envisioning radical food geographies: shared learning and praxis through the Food Justice Scholar-Activist/Activist-Scholar Community of Practice', *Human Geography*, 13(3): 277–92. DOI: https://doi.org/10.1177/1942778620951934

Salamanca, O.J. et al (2012) 'Past is present: settler colonialism in Palestine', *Settler Colonial Studies*, 2(1): 1–8. DOI: https://doi.org/10.1080/2201473X.2012.10648823

Scicluna, R.M. (2017) 'The kitchen as a place for politics: a contested and subversive place', in R.M. Scicluna (ed) *Home and Sexuality: The 'Other' Side of the Kitchen*, London: Palgrave Macmillan, pp 149–82. DOI: https://doi.org/10.1057/978-1-137-46038-7_6

Simpson, L.B. (2014) 'Land as pedagogy: Nishnaabeg intelligence and rebellious transformation', *Decolonization: Indigeneity, Education & Society*, 3(3). Available from: https://jps.library.utoronto.ca/index.php/des/article/view/22170

Smith, C.J. (2019) '"Writer. Eater. Cook.": deconstructing the feminist/housewife debate in the works of Ruth Reichl', *Women's Studies*, 48(7): 661–79. DOI: https://doi.org/10.1080/00497878.2019.1667805

Tuhiwai Smith, L. (1999) 'Decolonizing methodologies: research and Indigenous Peoples', *Social Policy Journal of New Zealand* [Preprint], (17). Available from: www.msd.govt.nz/about-msd-and-our-work/publicati ons-resources/journals-and-magazines/social-policy-journal/spj17/decol onizing-methodologies-research-and-indigenous-peoples.html

UNRWA (2016) *Survey on the Socioeconomic Status of Palestine Refugees in Lebanon 2015.* Available from: www.unrwa.org/sites/default/files/cont ent/resources/survey_on_the_economic_status_of_palestine_refugees_in_ lebanon_2015.pdf

UNRWA (2022) *Socio-Economic Situation of Palestine Refugees in Lebanon Crisis Monitoring Report*, High-Frequency Survey Results, Beirut. Available from: www.unrwa.org/sites/default/files/content/resources/lebanon_ crisis_monitoring_report_september_2022.pdf

13

The Possibilities of Geopoetics for Growing Radical Food Geographies and Rooting Responsibilities on Indigenous Lands

Christine Añonuevo, Sarah de Leeuw, Katya Korol-O'Dwyer, and Monika Krzywania

We are four researchers with past and present ties to the Health Arts Research Centre located within the territory of the Lheidli T'enneh First Nation,[1] in the city now known as Prince George in the region of northern British Columbia (BC), Canada. As a collective, our research delves into the health inequities between Indigenous Peoples and settlers in so-called[2] Canada, inequities that are rooted in systemic racism and upheld by colonial governance systems through policies, laws, and everyday practices (Allan and Smylie, 2015). Tracing the implications of these inequities for sovereign Indigenous foodways, and with our hearts and minds seeking redress, we take up Morrison's (2011: 98) call to '[respect] the sovereign rights and power of each distinct nation' to practise Indigenous food sovereignty. In this chapter, we reflect on the complex enactment of settler solidarity with Indigenous Peoples and nations that stems from honouring ancestral land rights and title, and respecting the jurisdiction of Indigenous legal systems, systems that are foundationally life-affirming (McGregor, 2009), and which protect and sustain sovereign foodways (Daigle, 2016, 2019b). We discuss the opportunities that such solidarity, forged through an ethics of settler responsibility (Phung, 2019), might contribute to growing radical food geographies (RFG) praxis (Hammelman et al, 2020; see also Levkoe et al, Chapter 1, this volume).

Seeking to build solidarity through an ethics of settler responsibility is well aligned with the three interconnected elements of RFG praxis advanced by the editors of this book. First, our 'theoretical engagement with power and structures of oppression' focuses on the ongoing coloniality perpetuated by the Canadian state in sanctioning contested industrial resource extraction projects on Indigenous lands and criminalizing Indigenous land defenders who assert their sovereign rights in opposition. We call on settler scholars and activists to educate ourselves about Indigenous rights and title, and to respect and uphold the governance of Indigenous legal systems. Second, by discussing the example of settler–Indigenous solidarity at the Senden Sustainable Agriculture Resource Centre detailed throughout this chapter, we reiterate the role of civil society – and especially grassroots – actors in grounding academic work on food systems and driving social change. Finally, we deploy a geographic lens that is rooted in geohumanities, and geopoetics specifically, a praxis that may not be well known to food system scholars, and which seeks to motivate action by prompting us to reckon with the messy, fleshy, dirty materialities of growing food.

As three non-Indigenous White settlers and one settler of colour, we do not write on behalf of Indigenous Peoples. We live and work in so-called northern BC, where, for multiple generations, Indigenous Peoples have been refusing settler state resource extraction projects that impede their access to sovereign foodways. Christine is a Filipina researcher who is married to a Gitxsan–Wet'suwet'en partner. The Gitxsan and Wet'suwet'en nations are neighbouring First Nations in so-called northern BC with long-standing political ties. Christine's personal and professional lives are intertwined with responsibilities to her partner, family, and the Gitxsan Nation, where she presently works, resides, and raises her children, and where much of the work of this chapter is situated. The other three researchers work in Lheidli T'enneh First Nation Territory, guided by professional relationships with Dakelh[3] knowledge keepers. Inspired by Phung's (2019) writing on an ethics of settler responsibility, we write collaboratively as witnesses to settler incursions on Indigenous lands, in an attempt to disrupt extractive knowledge production practices and to honour the Indigenous scholars, community Elders, and cultural knowledge keepers who we are privileged to be in ongoing relationship with.

Efforts to sustain Indigenous lands and foodways are continually threatened by the ongoing trespass of resource extraction projects that do not have the free, prior, and informed consent of Indigenous rights and title holders. In the 1980s and 1990s, the Gitxsan and Wet'suwet'en nations challenged the settler state of Canada in the case of *Delgamuukw/Gisday'wa v. The Queen*[4] to assert that their lands and their relationships to land and water had never been extinguished by treaty and never ceded to war. We highlight this watershed legal case of Indigenous rights and title because it demonstrates the historical and contemporary resistance of Indigenous nations, led by Hereditary House Chiefs,[5] to protect and sustain food systems for future generations. It is the responsibility of settler researchers such as us to educate ourselves about land claims and their interconnection with broader struggles for Indigenous environmental justice.

We anchor this chapter in two key provocations. First, drawing from a growing geopoetics tradition in geography, we share a poetic intervention, woven throughout this chapter, to grapple with the on-the-ground materialities of ongoing land theft and degradation. Defined in the barest sense as 'Earth-making' (Magrane et al, 2020), geopoetics uses poetry to engage and problematize space, place, ecology, power, difference, landscape, and the human and more-than-human relationships that are necessarily implicated herein (de Leeuw and Magrane, 2019; Magrane et al, 2020). In the words of de Leeuw and Magrane (2019: 146), geopoetics invites:

> an opportunity to reorder or refresh the world. This is a radical proposition, an ethical one. What world, what earth, is to be made? What world, what earth, is to be reproduced? What relationships are to be privileged and honoured? Who is making the made world, and according to whose form and representation? For whom is the world being (re)imagined?

It is thus a method that is especially well suited to the section theme of (re)imagining and (re)making relationships among people and our more-than-human relations to transform food systems. In this vein, we demonstrate how geopoetics can be used to disrupt and unsettle taken-for-granted (by settlers) systems of land tenure and, of course, relationships with Land herself. Second, as diverse settlers in so-called Canada, we use this geopoetics praxis to enact an ethics of settler responsibility, laying a foundation for (re)generating relations of solidarity that support the flourishing and thriving of Indigenous communities and lands, and the reclamation of sovereign foodways. As an example of such Indigenous–settler solidarity and (re)generative relationship-building, we highlight the work being done at the Senden Sustainable Agriculture Resource Centre, a non-Indigenous organization in Gitxsan Territory, where Christine has been involved for over a decade. The Centre facilitates land-based learning for community members that is rooted in intergenerational relationships with local Indigenous leadership.[6]

This chapter nudges readers to critically reflect on their memories and dreams of growing, harvesting, preserving, and sharing food on stolen land. Our collaborative poem is one example of how geopoetics, and arts-based methods more broadly, can disrupt (and move beyond) academic norms of Eurocentric and anglophone knowledge production.[7] Through reorganizing our world(s) in radical and inventive ways, geopoetics can hold to account our diverse scholarship, questioning whether our efforts are truly furthering food justice in ways that gesture towards Indigenous resurgence and Land Back[8] movements. We contend that solidarity with Indigenous Peoples and Indigenous food sovereignty movements cannot be decoupled from solidarity with broader struggles for Indigenous legal land governance and environmental justice.

Rooting (our) responsibility in so-called Canada

I am Christine Añonuevo.
I am a daughter of the Filipino diaspora.

I am a partner, mother & auntie, accountable to the communities that I belong to.

My research interests
are rooted in my lived experiences, relationships

and desire to rematriate lands and water
through right relations and kinship ties.

I am Sarah, and by my last name (de Leeuw)
you can read lion and my Dutchness,

My father leaving Holland after WWII
years later with my mother moving

further and further and further north
onto Haida, Ts'msyen, Nisga territories.

I am Katya Korol.
I am a non-Indigenous woman, raised by Ukrainian grandparents who healed through food.

I am mixed-settler ancestry
Seeking to do research with and for Indigenous communities.

I am a newcomer to the diverse territories
on which I live, play and seek to do this research

I am questioning my own legitimacy in doing this work.
Engaging with spoken and written Indigenous voices has been,

and will continue to be, crucial in helping me navigate
these complicated and necessary questions.

I am Monika Krzywania.
I am a settler in so-called Canada.

I am born to Polish immigrants.
I have benefitted

From unearned privilege in my life:
I am a White, heterosexual, and able-bodied settler

in a society founded on settler colonialism,
patriarchy, and White supremacy.

I am grounded in embodied experiences
of pregnancy, birth, and parenting.

Rooting (research method) responsibility

As settler researchers, we strive to use our roles as witnesses of the legacy
of genocide and ongoing structural violence to support the creation of
alternate life-affirming and life-sustaining futures (Maynard and Simpson,
2022). To build an RFG movement *from the ground up*, we turn to the need
to rematriate lands and waters as directed by Indigenous communities and
Hereditary leadership (Kahealani Pacheco and Konsmo, 2016). We use
geopoetics to interrogate relationships with words and world views, and to
make visible the power of place-based knowledge. Michi Saagiig Nishnaabeg
scholar-activist-artist Leanne Simpson (2014: 16) comes to mind:

> We cannot just think, write or imagine our way to a decolonized future.
> Answers on how to re-build and how to resurge are therefore derived
> from a web of consensual relationships that is infused with movement
> [...] through lived experience and embodiment.

Simpson's words beckon us to consider how we move in, through, and take
up space, and how we want to live in relationship with one another and
with the lands and waters we commune with. Geopoetics, when informed
by critical theory, can resist normative structures of power and engage with
diverse and grounded knowledges in the pursuit of (re)turning to new worlds
and ways of being (de Leeuw and Hawkins, 2017; de Leeuw and Magrane,
2019; Magrane et al, 2020). As a research method in geography's creative
're/turn' (de Leeuw and Hawkins, 2017), we envision that geopoetics might

be able to enhance RFG in generative and nuanced ways. Aligned with RFG's 'theoretical engagements with power and structures of oppression', desire to cultivate action-oriented collaboration with academic, social movement, and civil society activists, and emphasis on geographic enquiry, our use of geopoetics in this chapter also urges readers to do RFG *with feeling*, to falter, fret, and to be spurred forth by pain, guilt, anger, sadness, joy. In discussing geopoetic practice as 'route-finding', Magrane and colleagues (2020) galvanize geopoetics as a field of action which forces us to reckon with space and to make sense of our place in this world, and to work towards (re)imagining and (re)making alternate futures.

As an 'embodied endeavour' (de Leeuw and Magrane, 2019: 148), geopoetics is directly informed by the lived experience of being in communion with the stuff of geography – the soils and the waters, but also the material spaces of our intimate, daily lives. Geopoetics refutes the scaffolding of knowledge in a linear and ordered process (as is also the case with the format of this chapter). Our poem incites the reader's affect and invites them to use their intuitive register to interpret its meaning. We hope to encourage readers to think but also to feel, and for that emotive sense to motivate and inform action for redress.

Our poem makes an effort to actively and productively engage in messiness. We do so in dialogue with scholar-activist and activist-scholar calls for more complex, integrative, holistic, and radical engagements with food geographies (Reynolds and Cohen, 2016; Reynolds et al, 2018, 2020). We have taken up geopoetic practice as a prompt to use language to try to write/right wrongs of the past and present (de Leeuw, 2017). As an example of this, the colonial spelling of Tsimshian negates the proper spelling of Ts'msyen.[9] By using Ts'msyen, our poem makes an effort to respect the original people of the Ts'msyen Territory. Furthermore, to resist colonial logics regarding land as private property, Land has been capitalized when referred to as an animate being, as she has been positioned ontologically by many Indigenous scholar-activists (see, for example, Whyte, 2015; Coté, 2016; Daigle, 2019). Inspired by these scholar-activists, we use geopoetics to ask: how can we render the possibilities of understanding Land and orienting and relating to her?

Rooting (radical food) responsibility

We are questioning
the role of radical food geographies

The role of radical food
The role of geography.

The role of role of think about
Kyle Powys Whyte 'selective memorialization'.[10]

Settler projects justify their existence
through an absence of memory.

The role of radical food geographies
We press fast forward one moment

We rewind the next.
We position ourselves

as either reconciling for the wrongs of ancestors
in a *distant* past or we fetishize

pre-contact communities
as emblems of environmental stewardship.

This space the role of
Who are we in this space?

Senden is rooted on Gitxsan traditional territory.
Three acres of land with a large garden, greenhouse,

root cellar, bee-keeping centre
and historic farmhouse.

Youth complete our programme to have the skills,
knowledge, and confidence to be resilient
and engaged

members of healthy communities and their families
living on Gitxsan territories

based on connection to self
others, and the land.

The role of
Land back.

The role of
Land back.

The land is holding, holding the backs
Of children's graves.[11] Canadian. Settlers.

On the graves, land back, settlers and food.
Ground. UNDRIP.[12] Reconciliation.

There is no food sovereignty, Indigenous
food sovereignty
without political sovereignty.

There can be no conversations
about working toward food sovereignty

when the structural arrangements of power[13]
that uphold settler colonialism, racial capitalism,

and patriarchy remain unproblematized,
and, in fact, upheld by the academy[14]

The ground reaches back.
This is not your good intentions.[15]

Radical is not a garden.
Radical is not truthless.

Where are the Elders?
Where are the Elders?

Pressing fast forward.
Pressing rewind.

House groups/Cultural systems are care.
Extended families, aunties, uncles

and grandmothers support youth in the Skeena watershed.
The power and strength of grandmothers who are
raising children

Aunties are oftentimes more like mothers
less of a distinction in Gitxsan culture

and oftentimes aunties are more
The understanding that youth do better

and have more pride when they are tapped
into their cultural systems of care.

Primacy of relationships.
We centre Indigenous womxn at the Senden site

Support language learning,
Respect relationships with the Elders, our knowledge keepers

Whose stories hold the sustenance to the land.
These factors contributed to

high levels of engagement from
the Gitxsan community to participate meaningfully.

Rooting (Senden) responsibilities

Our poem uses the example of the Senden Sustainable Agriculture Resource Centre, of which co-author Christine is an integral member, to illustrate embodied and lived realities of growing, nourishing, gifting, and sharing food, which we believe are at the root of enacting an ethics of settler responsibility (Phung, 2019). Located on the Gitxsan Nation on Hereditary Chief Wilp Nikateen's territory at the reclaimed site of a historical settler homestead and dairy farm, Senden is a hub of community knowledge exchange and relationship-building. Here, settlers and Indigenous community members come together to share their knowledge about food sovereignty. The Centre has land and culture advisors and food managers who are Gitxsan, with a dedicated mandate of offering youth programmes that centre Gitxsan language, territory management, seasonal food preservation, and intergenerational land-based learning.

The work at Senden implements an ethics of responsibility through genealogical remembering and a critical reorientation of the roles we and our ancestors play in disrupting the structural dynamics of ongoing coloniality. The Centre is Gitxsan-led and its staff build relationships with Gitxsan Elders, house groups, and members upon whose territory the Centre is located, moving beyond tokenistic land acknowledgements. Through reciprocal relationships, the Centre engages youth and community members in food sustenance, preservation, and storage aligned with the seasons. In doing so, the Centre serves as an action-oriented space that embodies place-based solidarity with rights and title holders, and attempts to decolonize and improve relations by respecting local legal knowledges and practices associated with sustenance, including exchanging food as sacred gifts in non-exploitative ways. According to Gitxsan protocols that are witnessed in the feast hall, the Centre recognizes that food cannot be divorced from the oral stories, language, cultural lineage, and traditional governance where it is grown and harvested. When food is shared with others, it is a gift of medicine, health, community, and kinship.

The Centre engages youth in Land-based learning programmes, where Hereditary Chief Nikateen welcomes Indigenous youth and gifts them with oral stories about the territory. Youth engage in language learning, harvesting tea, growing vegetables, and learning about whose territories they are on. Territorial lessons are anchored in maps produced from legal cases in which the Gitxsan and Wet'suwet'en proved Indigenous title existed. Indigenous youth learn how to request permission to enter the territory and how not to trespass. Many of these lessons are representative of the legal system that has governed Indigenous northern geographies since time immemorial. Witnessing and honouring the laws of the rights and title holders, as well as building relationships and sharing the food that we grow and harvest is a critical duty for RFG scholar-activists. Showing up in community – by which we mean in mind, body, and spirit and respecting the Indigenous laws and governance embedded in a particular territory – directly challenges and resists capitalistic and patriarchal power structures that continue to oppress sovereign foodways. We suggest that showing up in community in this way might constitute an embodied RFG praxis rooted in an ethics of responsibility. Sharing food and creating spaces where sacred food knowledge is passed down and preserved is a generative act of resistance and refusal.

Rooting (land back, land back) responsibilities

Where is the land, the ground, the muck, and the soil?
Whyte calls out: are you "perform[ing] heroics"?[16]

Where is the Indigenous food sovereignty?[17]
Land back. Back. Land. Land back.

The deliberate distribution of environmental benefits and burdens stratified by race and class, driven by institutional

and corporate power asymmetries.[18]
Universities. Conferences. Empire. Industry. Geography. Power asymmetries.[19]

Food sovereignty *is* environmental justice for Indigenous Peoples.[20]
Indigenous People are working everyday

THE POSSIBILITIES OF GEOPOETICS

to enact their cultural responsibilities
to the land and other kin.

Food sovereignty is as much about *accessing* healthy food
as it is about recognizing and revitalizing Indigenous
food knowledge.

The role of radical.
Land back.

The role of radical.
Landback. Elders. Aunties and grannies.

Food sovereignty movements
always reflect the tremendous diversity

across Indigenous Nations and peoples.
But resistance to coloniality is foundational.[21]

A disproportionate burden of food-related inequities
are borne by Indigenous communities.

This resultant from intergenerational effects
of environmental racism embedded in (neo)colonial
institutions.[22]

Look down to the ground you feed upon.
Land back. Land back.

Fights for environmental justice and food sovereignty
are about resisting calculated attempts

by colonial-capitalist forces
to interfere with Indigenous self-determination[23]

Indigenous self-determination
is embodied in place-based acts of resurgence.

Indigenous self-determination is renewing sacred
kinship ties with human and more-than-human kin.[24]

Challenge dominant, globalized,
neoliberal food production models.

Rooting (reflective) responsibilities

As White settler and settler-of-colour academics in the emerging space of RFG, we are guided by the intergenerational knowledge of Indigenous scholars, activists, Elders, and title holders through shared learning experiences deeply rooted in diverse food geographies and embodied through land-based experiences. We consider the nature of our participation in RFG movements, asking ourselves: can we trace how writing in these academic spaces contributes to meaningful change for those on the ground, fighting for their lands and waters? Our honest answer is that academic spaces may not be the most productive spaces to make meaningful change. Instead, we need to show up in mind, body, and spirit at the grassroots community level.

(How) does this chapter help those with their hands in the dirt? Our poem attempts to combine the head work and heart work of the lifelong and long-term commitment of decolonization as we learn and unlearn colonial ways of knowing and being. As the children and grandchildren of intergenerational forced migrants and immigrants who landed on Turtle Island, we honour the memory of the land and soil and communities that have been here since time immemorial. We do so through the radical act of remembering and refusing the historical amnesia of the settler state. Through highlighting Senden's youth programme, we offer an example of one place-based radical food practice. Do these words ease the burden on those protesting pipelines and old-growth logging that directly threatens food sovereignty practices? We hope our words can provide those studying, working, and aspiring in RFG academic and community spaces to be brave and find the courage to be in solidarity with Indigenous communities when they call on settlers to stand up against these and other threats to Indigenous lands and foodways.

Relatedly, we reflect on our own embodied experiences of growing, nurturing, and learning through food in the context of engaging in the (im)possibilities of an ethics of responsibility, acknowledging that we are, in many ways, still complicit in the continued occupation of stolen lands. We do not necessarily have the answers to these questions. Yet, we continue to grapple with them: how do we use our knowledge (academic and community-based) to stand as witnesses to uplift, support, and re-centre Indigenous ways of knowing and being – of growing, harvesting, sharing, and preserving food? As settlers, how do we share our time, skills, and food stories to align with Indigenous title holders and knowledge keepers in ways that are reciprocal, relational, and amplify (without speaking over or for) Indigenous ways of knowing, doing, and being in the world?

Rooting (more radical) responsibilities

Where is the sacred?
Land back, sacred land. Land back.

Enacting ethical reciprocity toward land
and water is enshrined in Indigenous governance systems

Indigenous political and legal orders codify protocols
of engagement across multiple scales.[25]

Within community and 'inter-Nation(al)[ly]'.
With human kin from other Nations.[26]

With more-than-human kin
from Plant and Animal Nations.

Lands back. Waters back. Nations back.
Plants and animals back.

Engaging Indigenous scholarship
about environmental justice and food sovereignty

is a crucial lesson for settler geographers.
A radical food geographies praxis

does not need to be built anew.
It is embodied in thousands of years of Indigenous survivance.

Land back. How to enact land back.
The role of radical food geographies. Enact land back.

Indigenous Peoples are being violently displaced from
their lands
Today. Right. Now. Violently displaced from lands.
Unrelenting violence.

Displaced from academic participation.
White privilege ensures self-interested curation.

Land back. Land back.
Land on alternative consumption narratives.

Land back on radical.
Land on bodies. On power.

Land back.
Land back.

Land back
On the radical.

Rematriating land

As researchers living and working in northern BC geographies, especially in places where Indigenous rights and title holders have defended their inherent land claims by affirming their oral histories and governance systems, we bear witness to ongoing settler colonial violence perpetrated against Indigenous Peoples, lands, and waters. This violence frequently takes the form of economic development projects that do not have the free, prior, and informed consent of Indigenous rights and title holders, and from which benefits and burdens are not distributed equitably. This is an abhorrent violation of Indigenous legal systems, which speak to the health of the land and all its relationships as sacred and interconnected (T'es and Añonuevo, 2022).

The ongoing incursions of government and industry on Wet'suwet'en territories to build gas pipelines undermine Indigenous self-determination and directly threaten sacred foods, medicines, and waterways (Spice, 2018). Land defenders continue to be subjected to egregious acts of violence – sustained by government-sanctioned militarized police raids – as they protest the invasion of pipelines on their territories (Hosgood, 2022; 'Militarized RCMP Enforcement, Violent Arrests Continue on Gidimt'en Land Defenders', 2021). Standing with the Wet'suwet'en people in their struggle to access their sovereign foodways necessitates solidarity with their opposition to the continued incursion of resource extraction projects on their territories.

For this reason, we are increasingly concerned by a trend of academic co-optation by settler scholars which risks circumventing struggles for Indigenous environmental justice and staking a claim to sacred Indigenous food knowledges and practices rooted in kinship ties. Foundational work by Indigenous scholars, working at the intersections of food studies, environmental humanities, law and social justice, and critical theory, has articulated the sacred Indigenous legal systems which honour Plants, Animals, Lands, and Waters as kin (Morrison, 2011; Whyte, 2015; Coté, 2016; Daigle, 2016, 2018; McGregor, 2018b; Todd, 2018; Whyte, 2021). As this web of kinship ties governs relations among humans and their kin, it embodies food sovereignty by ensuring reciprocity and a sacred respect for life. Indigenous food sovereignty scholars and groups have been generous with their wisdom and with the foresight that these kin-based governance systems offer hope for redress in the face of colonial-capitalist industrial and agricultural regimes.[27]

But what right do settler researchers like us have to Indigenous kin-based knowledge and practices of food? None. Instead, through our poem, especially as is exemplified by the work at Senden, we demonstrate our responsibility to *witness* Indigenous kin-based knowledge and share our own settler cultural practices of food to forge new alliances of Indigenous–settler solidarity. We cannot assert solidarity without first listening and being guided by rights and title holders. Knowing that we are fed by bloodied soil, we must continue to disrupt and unsettle, including through the use of geopoetic means. Doing less risks settler 'moves to innocence' (Tuck and Yang, 2012), wherein failure to undo and redress violence is disguised as an inherited pre-modern settler burden, as opposed to an ongoing state of coloniality that we (settlers) are actively complicit in reproducing.

We have used geopoetics to trace the connections between food sovereignty and Indigenous legal governance and environmental justice movements. Importantly, for many Indigenous scholars and organizers, these threads are already woven together, and have never been abstracted. Our chapter is deeply informed by this work to remind those of us settler scholars who work in an RFG framework that the fight to reclaim and rebuild sustainable foodways is also necessarily a political struggle for land rematriation. In so-called Canada, much of this activism has been amplified by the Land Back Movement. We emphasize that we are not speaking for Indigenous Peoples, but rather from our own lived experiences of witnessing Indigenous governance in action, and related struggles for asserting sovereign jurisdiction in Indigenous lands, waters, and foodways. From these acts of witnessing spring our ethics of responsibility to further act in ways that support Indigenous food sovereignty, aligned with the guidance of Indigenous legal governance. Furthermore, we are called upon to expose and oppose the false pretences and platitudes of reconciliation wrapped up in industrial activities promising prosperity and progress.

Throughout this chapter, we have turned to geopoetics as a tool to map the connections and relationships, at multiple scales, between food, geography, identity, and memory, at once looking inward, considering, how we are located socially and physically as individuals, and outward, reflecting on our roles as both scholars and community members seeking to stand in solidarity with Indigenous Peoples. Acknowledging a built-in tension, we ask: how can settler scholars stand in solidarity with Indigenous communities engaged in food sovereignty movements while we continue to occupy stolen lands? Senden provides a concrete and hands-on example of a community-based effort to honour local foodways, knowledge, and relationships that have always existed. Senden recognizes the deep-rooted knowledge embedded in the relationships Gitxsan communities have with their lands. As a non-Indigenous organization collaborating at the grassroots level with local Indigenous leadership to engage Indigenous youth, Senden puts into action the type of settler–Indigenous solidarity made possible by an ethics of settler responsibility. In doing this work, Senden and its staff continue to be in relationship with knowledge keepers and commit to unlearning colonial behaviours and attitudes. The work at Senden shows that celebrating and sharing food can constitute a radical and generative act of refusal to capitalistic and colonial world views.

As researchers, we use our voices, both in academic and community settings, as witnesses with responsibilities to our families and Indigenous communities to act in good relation, to be humble, and to use our time and skills to pass on a full basket of life and land to future generations, honouring teachings from Gitxsan leadership. For example, at Senden, the first harvest is always gifted to the matriarch upon whose land Senden is situated, creating a reciprocal, active, gift-giving relationship; here, traditional protocol is (re)activated and aligned with ongoing relationships rooted in a specific place, connecting the past with a sustainable present and future.

Such protocols help us to radically reconnect with land, water, and food practices in ways that value place-based relationship-building. This is doing RFG with feeling, with joy, and out of love for our relations and future generations. While the ongoing trespass of extractive industries on Gitxsan and Wet'suwet'en nations can never diminish or extinguish such protocols, this regime of settler state violence fundamentally undermines the possibility of settler–Indigenous solidarity. We believe that for scholars and activists seeking to grow an RFG praxis, an ethics of settler responsibility instructs us (settlers) to stand with Indigenous land defenders. Taking up the work of respecting, supporting, and sustaining Indigenous foodways, of (re)turning just food systems, cannot be separated from movements to achieve Indigenous environmental justice and political sovereignty. For whom is the world being (re)sown, (re)grown?

Notes

[1] The Canadian state recognizes three distinct groups of Indigenous Peoples: First Nations, Métis, and Inuit. The authors regret that we are unable to speak to the tremendous diversity and incredibly nuanced and complex politics of identity and recognition of Indigenous Peoples in Canada in this short chapter. Please see *First Peoples, Second Class Treatment* (Allan and Smylie, 2015) for an introductory discussion on this topic by two Indigenous scholars.

[2] We use 'so-called' in front of colonial place names to draw attention to naming as a geographic practice that has often sought to undermine historical and contemporary kin-based relationships between Indigenous Peoples and lands, and which also offers up possibilities for reclaiming these relationships.

[3] Dakelh (also Carrier) refers to a cultural and linguistic grouping of several First Nations in north central BC, including Lheidli T'enneh First Nation.

[4] *Delgamuukw/Gisday'wa v. The Queen* addressed the failures of the Canadian government to respect sovereign Indigenous land rights. The *Delgamuukw* court case involved Gitxsan and Wet'suwet'en Hereditary House Chiefs who claimed their traditional territories using extensive oral histories in their languages, as evidence of having never made a treaty with the government or otherwise relinquished their territorial rights. See *Eagle Down Is Our Law* (Mills, 1994) for further reading.

[5] See Unist'ot'en Camp (n.d.) 'Governance Structure', [online], Available from: http://unistoten.camp/about/governance-structure/ [Accessed 28 January 2024].

[6] See, for example, Senden Sustainable Agriculture Resource Centre (2018) 'Senden: Reconnecting youth to Gitxsan territory', [online] 13 March, Available from: www.youtube.com/watch?v=y-pIpxONTwE&ab_channel=ChristineA%C3%B1onuevo [Accessed 13 January 2024].

[7] Readers may also reference arts-based work at the Senden Sustainable Agriculture Resource Centre, Senden Sustainable Agriculture Resource Centre (2019) 'Senden: Deex Goot', [online] 24 March, Available from: www.youtube.com/watch?v=OSqJdTAl-xk [Accessed 13 January 2024].

[8] Land Back is an Indigenous sovereignty movement seeking to reclaim and rematriate Indigenous lands and waters that continue to be stolen by settler governments and institutions. See *Land Back: A Yellowhead Institute Red Paper* (Yellowhead Institute, 2019) for further reading.

[9] www.smalgyax.ca/

[10] Kyle Whyte in dialogue with Dana E. Powell following her keynote during the Indigenous Political Ecology Slow Symposium (Powell, 2021).

[11] Registers of confirmed deaths of named and unnamed residential school students were established by the Truth and Reconciliation Commission of Canada, with 3,200 deaths identified in 2015 (Truth and Reconciliation Commission of Canada, 2015). This number continues to be called into question as numerous Indigenous Nations have shouldered the burden of uncovering additional unmarked burial sites. On 27 May 2021, the Tk'emlúps te Secwépemc First Nation announced that preliminary findings from a survey of the former Kamloops Indian Residential School uncovered the remains of 215 children in unmarked graves.

[12] United Nations Declaration on the Rights of Indigenous People.

[13] Whyte (2015).

[14] Grande (2018); Daigle (2019a).

[15] Tuck and Yang (2012); de Leeuw, Greenwood, and Lindsay (2013); de Leeuw and Hunt (2018); Daigle (2019a).

[16] Powell (2021).

[17] Indigenous Food Sovereignty (IFS) as a set of embodied practices and lived realities vastly predates and survives settler colonial violence and the rise of industrial agriculture, as well as (neo)colonial–capitalist attempts at food system 'reform'. See the guiding principles developed by the Working Group on Indigenous Food Sovereignty (n.d.); see also Morrison (2011); Cidro et al (2015); Coté (2016); Daigle (2019b); Robin (2022).

[18] See the work of Bullard (2000) for a comprehensive summary of the environmental justice (EJ) movement; see also Reynolds (2021) explaining the connections between EJ and food sovereignty and food justice.

[19] Enduring power asymmetries typify contemporary government–industry relations in the province of BC, such as in the example of BC's 'free entry' system for claiming mineral rights (Clogg, 2013).

[20] McGregor (2009); Whyte (2015); McGregor (2018b).

[21] Morrison (2011); Whyte (2015); Coté (2016); Daigle (2019b).

[22] McGregor (2009); Whyte (2015); McGregor (2018b).

[23] Whyte (2015); Daigle (2018, 2019b).

[24] Coté (2015, 2016); Whyte (2015, 2021); Daigle (2016, 2019b); Simpson (2017).

[25] Mills (1994); Daigle (2016); McGregor (2018a); Todd (2018).

[26] Daigle (2016).

[27] See, for example, the guiding principles developed by the Working Group on Indigenous Food Sovereignty (n.d.).

References

Allan, B. and Smylie, J. (2015) *First Peoples, Second Class Treatment: The Role of Racism in the Health and Well-Being of Indigenous Peoples in Canada*, Toronto, ON: The Wellesley Institute.

Bullard, R.D. (2000) *Dumping in Dixie: Race, Class, and Environmental Quality* (3rd edn), Boulder, CO: Westview Press.

Cidro, J., Adekunle, B., Peters, E., and Martens, T. (2015) 'Beyond food security: understanding access to cultural food for urban Indigenous people in Winnipeg as Indigenous food sovereignty', *Canadian Journal of Urban Research*, 24(1): 24–43.

Clogg, J. (2013) 'Modernizing BC's Free Entry Mining Laws for a Vibrant, Sustainable Mining Sector', West Coast Environmental Law & Fair Mining Collaborative. Available from: www.wcel.org/publication/modernizing-bcs-free-entry-mining-laws-vibrant-sustainable-mining-sector [Accessed 30 August 2022].

Coté, C. (2015) 'Food sovereignty, food hegemony, and the revitalization of Indigenous whaling practices', in R. Warrior (ed) *The World of Indigenous North America*, New York: Routledge, pp 239–62.

Coté, C. (2016) '"Indigenizing" food sovereignty. Revitalizing Indigenous food practices and ecological knowledges in Canada and the United States', *Humanities*, 5(57). DOI: https://doi.org/10.3390/h5030057

Daigle, M. (2016) 'Awawanenitakik: the spatial politics of recognition and relational geographies of Indigenous self-determination', *Canadian Geographer/Le Géographe canadien*, 60(2): 259–69.

Daigle, M. (2018) 'Resurging through Kishiichiwan: the spatial politics of Indigenous water relations', *Decolonization: Indigeneity, Education & Society*, 7(1): 159–72.

Daigle, M. (2019a) 'The spectacle of reconciliation: on (the) unsettling responsibilities to Indigenous Peoples in the academy', *Environment and Planning D: Society and Space*, 37(4): 703–21.

Daigle, M. (2019b) 'Tracing the terrain of Indigenous food *sovereignties*', *Journal of Peasant Studies*, 46(2): 297–315.

de Leeuw, S. and Hawkins, H. (2017) 'Critical geographies and geography's creative re/turn: poetics and practices for new disciplinary spaces', *Gender, Place & Culture*, 24(3): 303–24.

de Leeuw, S. and Hunt, S. (2018) 'Unsettling decolonizing geographies', *Geography Compass*, 12(e12376).

de Leeuw, S. and Magrane, E. (2019) 'Geopoetics', in Antipode Editorial Collective et al (eds) *Keywords in Radical Geography:* Antipode *at 50*, Antipode Foundation (Antipode Book Series), pp 146–50.

de Leeuw, S., Greenwood, M., and Lindsay, N.M. (2013) 'Troubling good intentions', *Settler Colonial Studies*, 3(3–4): 381–94.

Grande, S. (2018) 'Refusing the university', in E. Tuck and K.W. Yang (eds) *Toward What Justice? Describing Diverse Dreams of Justice in Education*, New York: Routledge, pp 47–65.

Hammelman, C., Reynolds, K., and Levkoe, C.Z. (2020) 'Toward a radical food geography praxis: integrating theory, action, and geographic analysis in pursuit of more equitable and sustainable food systems', *Human Geography*, 13(3): 211–27.

Hosgood, A.F. (2022) ' "Disaster land grabs" worldwide and in British Columbia', *The Tyee*, [online] 20 June, Available from: https://thetyee.ca/News/2022/06/20/Disaster-Land-Grabs-Worldwide-BC/ [Accessed 30 August 2022].

Kahealani Pacheco, A.M. and Konsmo, E.M. (2016) 'Violence on the land, violence on our bodies: building an Indigenous response to environmental violence', Women's Earth Alliance & Native Youth Sexual Health Network, Available from: http://landbodydefense.org/home

Magrane, E., Russo, L., de Leeuw, S., and Santos Perez, C. (eds) (2020) *Geopoetics in Practice*, Routledge.

Maynard, R. and Simpson, L.B. (2022) *Rehearsals for Living*, Toronto, ON: Alfred A. Knopf Canada.

McGregor, D. (2009) 'Honouring our relations: an Anishnaabe perspective on environmental justice', in J. Agyeman, P. Cole, R. Haluza-Delay, and P. O'Riley (eds) *Speaking for Ourselves: Environmental Justice in Canada*, Vancouver, BC: UBC Press, pp 27–41.

McGregor, D. (2018a) 'Indigenous environmental justice, knowledge, and law', *Kalfou*, 5(2). DOI: https://doi.org/10.15367/kf.v5i2.213

McGregor, D. (2018b) 'Mino-Mnaamodzawin: achieving Indigenous environmental justice in Canada', *Environment and Society*, 9(1): 7–24.

'Militarized RCMP Enforcement, Violent Arrests Continue on Gidimt'en Land Defenders' (2021) *Gidimt'en Yintah Access*, [online], Available from: www.yintahaccess.com/news/2021raids [Accessed 30 August 2022].

Mills, A. (1994) *Eagle Down Is Our Law: Witsuwit'en Law, Feasts, and Land Claims*, Vancouver, BC: UBC Press.

Morrison, D. (2011) 'Indigenous food sovereignty: a model for social learning', in H. Wittman, A.A. Desmarais, and N. Wiebe (eds) *Food Sovereignty in Canada: Creating Just and Sustainable Food Systems*, Halifax: Fernwood Publishing, pp 97–113.

Phung, M. (2019) 'Indigenous and Asian relation making', *Verge: Studies in Global Asias*, 5(1).

Powell, D.E. (2021) 'Unsettling stories of ruin: native presence in the Anthropocene', in *Indigenous Political Ecology Slow Symposium*, Online/ University of Victoria.

Reynolds, K. (2021) 'Food, agriculture, and environmental justice: perspectives on scholarship and activism in the field', in B. Coolsaet (ed) *Environmental Justice: Key Issues*, Oxford & New York: Routledge, pp 176–92.

Reynolds, K. and Cohen, N. (2016) *Beyond the Kale: Urban agriculture and Social Justice Activism in New York City*, Athens, GA: University of Georgia Press.

Reynolds, K., Block, D., and Bradley, K. (2018) 'Food justice scholar-activism and activist- scholarship: working beyond dichotomies to deepen social justice praxis', *ACME: An International Journal for Critical Geographies*, 17(4): 988–98.

Reynolds, K., Block, D., Hammelman, C., Jones, B., Gilbert, J., and Herrera, H. (2020) 'Envisioning radical food geographies: shared learning and praxis through the Food Justice Scholar-Activist/Activist-Scholar Community of Practice', *Special Issue on Radical Food Geographies in Human Geography*, 13(3): 277–92.

Robin, T. (2022) 'Food as relationship: Indigenous food systems and well-being', in M. Greenwood, S. de Leeuw, R. Stout, R. Larstone, and J. Sutherland (eds) *Introduction to Determinants of First Nations, Inuit, and Métis Peoples' Health in Canada*, Toronto, ON: Canadian Scholars, pp 25–36.

Simpson, L.B. (2014) 'Land as pedagogy: Nishnaabeg intelligence and rebellious transformation', *Decolonization: Indigeneity, Education & Society*, 3(3): 1–25.

Simpson, L.B. (2017) *As We Have Always Done: Indigenous Freedom through Radical Resistance*, Minneapolis, MN: University of Minnesota Press.

Spice, A. (2018) 'Fighting invasive infrastructures: Indigenous relations against pipelines', *Environment and Society*, 9(1): 40–56.

Tes, W. and Añonuevo, C. (2022) 'Reflections on love and learning with the *Yintah*', in M. Greenwood, S. de Leeuw, R. Stout, R. Larstone, and J. Sutherland (eds) *Introduction to Determinants of First Nations, Inuit, and Métis Peoples' Health in Canada*, Toronto, ON: Canadian Scholars, pp 1–14.

Todd, Z. (2018) 'Refracting the state through human–fish relations: fishing, Indigenous legal orders and colonialism in North/Western Canada', *Decolonization: Indigeneity, Education & Society*, 7(1): 60–75.

Truth and Reconciliation Commission of Canada (2015) *Canada's Residential Schools: Missing Children and Unmarked Burials: The Final Report of the Truth and Reconciliation Commission of Canada, Volume 4*, McGill-Queen's University Press. DOI: https://doi.org/10.2307/j.ctt19rmbnh

Tuck, E. and Yang, K.W. (2012) 'Decolonization is not a metaphor', *Decolonization: Indigeneity, Education & Society*, 1(1): 1–40.

Whyte, K.P. (2015) 'Indigenous food systems, environmental justice, and settler-industrial states', in M.C. Rawlinson and C. Ward (eds) *Global Food, Global Justice: Essays on Eating under Globalization*, Newcastle upon Tyne, UK: Cambridge Scholars Publishing, pp 143–66.

Whyte, K. (2021) 'Indigenous environmental justice: anti-colonial action through kinship', in B. Coolsaet (ed) *Environmental Justice: Key Issues*, Oxford & New York: Routledge, pp 266–78.

Working Group on Indigenous Food Sovereignty (n.d.) *Indigenous Food Sovereignty, Indigenous Food Systems Network*. Available from: www.indigenousfoodsystems.org/food-sovereignty [Accessed 21 August 2022].

Yellowhead Institute (2019) 'Land Back: A Yellowhead Institute Red Paper', Available from: https://redpaper.yellowheadinstitute.org/wp-content/uploads/2019/10/red-paper-report-final.pdf.

14

Radical Food Geographies Un/Settlings: The Weaponization of Food and its Discontents in Occupied Palestine and the Ch'orti' Maya East

Danya Nadar and Jennifer J. Casolo

When acknowledged at all, dominant depictions of the Ch'orti' Maya highlands along the Guatemalan–Honduran border portray an Indigenous pocket of famine and 'premature death' (Gilmore, 2007):[1] barren ecosystems, tattered corn stalks on rock-stubbled hillsides, glaring sun, and Ch'orti' Maya (heretofore Ch'orti') families struggling to feed themselves. Hidden from view and blurred in memories are the centuries of colonization, forced labour, militarized repression, and the shifting racialized laws of citizenship these processes entailed that progressively pushed the Ch'orti' onto less and less land in the farthest reaches of Guatemala's eastern highlands. These processes, and the ways that Ch'orti' alternately fled land or donned *mestizo* (mixed blood) identities to survive, slowly severed Ch'orti' lands, knowledges, and relations from the more diacritically visible and populous Maya peoples in the west.

In response, multilateral, bilateral, state-led, and NGO development programmes have focussed on providing food aid, agricultural training, and direct intervention – most recently to stem 'climate migrants'. These programmes deny any kinship or spiritual relation between the Ch'orti' and their lands, and leave untouched the *ladino*[2] 'settler' appetite for river basin greenhouse vegetables, mountain coffee farms, and extractivist capital designs on subsoil minerals and hydropower. Further, they ignore the past and ongoing ways that Ch'orti' people manoeuvre through and/or contest the processes that erect barriers, assimilate, or erase Indigenous food knowledges, and facilitate the ongoing usurpation of Ch'orti' ancestral lands by *ladinos*.

As part of their efforts to reclaim, rebuild, and renovate Ch'orti' governance, knowledge, and practice, in October 2022 Ch'orti' ancestral authorities met with a strong ally in international aid who was visiting the Ch'orti' territory for the first time. Jenn attended the meeting, as co-founder of the Maya Ch'orti' Pluriversity, a nascent Ch'orti' initiative of higher education for rural Ch'orti' based upon a horizontal relationship between Ch'orti' and Western knowledges and epistemologies rooted in community research and practice. As the discussion turned to how the visiting institution might contribute to improving rural diets, Doña Juana,[3] an elected Ch'orti' authority, spiritual guide, native speaker, and expert on the nutritional and healing properties of flora, quipped: "We don't need somebody telling us what to plant or how; we know how to do that. What I want to know is on what land am I going to plant?"

Doña Juana's reaction reflects a broader discontent with state-led and international policies and practices around food. Right before the aid officer had arrived, the group had been discussing events from two days before. Over 30 Ch'orti' villagers, mainly women and children, had fallen to their deaths when the pick-up truck they had crammed into to collect their World Food Programme cash transfers in town rolled off the cliff. Those gathered denounced not only the driver's neglect but also the conditions that led the people to be travelling on the treacherous mountain road in the first place. Food or cash hand-outs benefitted *ladino* merchants, they decried, while building upon the historical destruction of their relationships, knowledges, and practices to nourishing and sowing the soil, or having soil to sow.

Across the Atlantic in the Bethlehem region of occupied Palestine, Danya spent time speaking with older Palestinian peasant women documenting how they spent their livelihoods safeguarding what they called ancestral crops and land practices to feed their families and communities. These practices were integral to their steadfast efforts to oppose the Israeli military occupation's attempts at usurping the land from under them.

Um Nadeem, a peasant from a nearby village, knew how to circumvent the physical and psychological barriers that threatened her relationship to ancestral crops. Turning 65 permitted her to pass through the Israeli checkpoint and wall dividing Bethlehem from Jerusalem while sneaking her ancestral crops across for sale on Jerusalem's high streets. It was different a decade ago, she recounted. She and other middle-aged peasant women would furtively lug half their weight in crops to the wall in the middle of the night. Dodging Israeli soldiers, they hurled their sacks and boosted each other over the barrier. She'd sleep at the al-Aqsa Mosque all week and return home to tend to the lands her children were upkeeping in between their shifts on Israeli settlements. Though she continued purchasing and cultivating the limited number of fertile lands remaining in and around her village, she knew her persistence in using ancestral seeds nevertheless risked annexation by the Israeli military who could deem the land as 'uncultivated'.

For knowledge keepers such as Doña Juana and Um Nadeem, separations of land and food relations negates human and more-than-human relations linked to their lived experiences and world views. Together, these stories prismatically illuminate the racialized violences through which food is weaponized, and how that weaponization is lived and refused. Our framing of the weaponization of food looks closely at the connected ways that land and related knowledge-practices are severed from the peoples that hold them through structures of (settler) colonialism and capitalism. These dynamics draw attention to the work of radical food geographies (RFG) praxis. RFG aims to deepen critical theory-practice on the structures of power, inequity, and oppressions produced through food systems operating across multiple arenas (see Levkoe et al, Chapter 1). Through RFG, we consider present-day food geographies that construct and have been constructed through the weaponization of food as advancing (settler)[4] colonial projects on, about, or because of land (Said, 1994). Further, we place these stories in conversation to, 'make use of the interconnectivity between places and movements; relationality between land and people (including questions of positionality)' (Hammelman et al, 2020: 219). In so doing, we focus on land–food relations and their intimate connection to human life, specifically in and between two autochthonous peoples.

Drawing on Gillian Hart's (2018) method of Marxist postcolonial geographies and relational comparison, we pry open the radical possibilities of interconnectivity for collaborations in social justice actions that go beyond thematic commonalities. Relational comparison and critical ethnography draw on dynamic understandings of place and space to posit that different regions of the world are 'always already interconnected' (Hart, 2018: 389). As such, the Bethlehem region of occupied Palestine and the Ch'orti' highlands on the Guatemalan–Honduran borderlands are not 'pre-given bounded national units or separate "cases"' of one global process (Hart, 2020: 241), but historically specific nodes in globally interconnected historical geographies. The racialized dispossession of Palestinian and Ch'orti' food knowledges and practices intimately tied to their world views are linked to the constraints produced by (settler) colonial projects' conceptualization of terra nullius, capitalist agrarian transformations, and US imperialism. Yet how and when they develop and are lived differ.

Understanding interconnections and divergences in the dynamics of the weaponization of food requires attention to dialogical everyday practices and the material and symbolic ways in which people and collectives manoeuvre through the conditions in which they find themselves. Yet, we cannot fully understand the 'genesis of the present' that Um Nadeem and Doña Juana

THE WEAPONIZATION OF FOOD AND ITS DISCONTENTS

live without 'starting in the present, working our way back to the past, and then retracing our steps' (Lefebvre, 1991 [1974]: 66). Using relational comparison helps us uncover the '*longue durée* processes of racial capitalism, settler colonialism and imperialism' (Hart, 2020: 242), marked by specific spatio-historical conjunctures.[5] Further, it points to the continuities and limits of the weaponization of food as a tool of (settler) colonial and extractivist projects, informing the praxis of struggle.

Below, we briefly introduce the contours of our theorization linking the weaponization of food with RFG through interconnected places and processes. Then we draw on vignettes and our personal reflections (presented in italics) as an alternative way to think relationally about how the weaponization of food furthers racialized processes of colonization and capitalist accumulation. Borders, barriers, 'uncultivated land', intergenerational cleavages of ancestral food knowledges, and ongoing racialized land dispossession shift and change through divergent but interconnected processes in time–space as the weaponization of food operates and is resisted. Using vignettes differs from sharing findings or themes: as short stories they condense the complex dynamics through which food and food knowledges are weaponized, and often protected, reclaimed, and revived. A final section places the vignettes in conversation with one another: first its political corollary – existence is resistance; and second, the analytical stakes of linking (yet distinguishing) between land/food and human relations, in terms of RFG.

Weaponization of food and RFG

Critical political economy and global food systems literature have signalled the ways in which hegemonic powers utilize food as a weapon to further imperial and capitalist designs. Various scholars highlight the multiple ways in which barriers to and destruction of food and food knowledges are employed in the development of agrarian capitalism – enclosures (E.P. Thompson, 2013), food embargoes, and food dumping as geopolitical tools that respectively sever or cement developing economies ties to a US-dominated world food system (Friedmann, 1982: 280), criminalization of women's agricultural knowledges (Federici, 2014), undermining peasant forms of market and trade (Patel and Moore, 2017) – as well as signal resistances to those effects. An RFG approach can help reveal the interconnected spaces and places of contestation and everyday practices that challenge these systems.

Complementing RFG through relational comparison, we view occupied Bethlehem and the Ch'orti' borderlands as 'dense nodes' of social relations produced in space–time (Massey, 1994). This conceptualization foregrounds not the place, but the processes by which its 'internal reality' is constituted and sustained (Hart, 2018). We then conceive of the weaponization of food as a key force actively at work in the production of places, helping expand

247

and reproduce the global capitalist food system and colonial dispossessions. Yet the divergent but interconnected ways that weaponization is utilized, experienced, and reworked in Palestine and Guatemala, signal the way weaponization works is neither predetermined nor sealed, nor are its effects simple variations of a general process. Rather they are produced in relation to and productive of the historical geographies at play.

We signal the differentiated extra-national processes in both the Ch'orti' eastern highlands and the Bethlehem region of occupied Palestine through which the weaponization of food works. Weaponization operates through the colonial state, racial capitalist accumulation, and/or related counterinsurgency silences. For example, the creation of laws, treaties, and extra-legal instruments[6] have erected borders, walls, and land enclosures, cutting through ancestral territories. These measures then criminalize plant foraging and livelihood practices, and restrict citizenship and mobility. They attempt to systematically sever the relationships between humans and land/food, eradicating ancestral knowledges associated with seeds and wild plants, creating economic dependencies, and producing hunger and malnutrition. Relatedly, weaponization produces and is reproduced in relation to the slow violences (Nixon, 2011), giving rise to socio-psychological barriers that cleave generations and communities from each other and their deep connection to seeds and soils. In the following vignettes we delve into the divergent ways these severings occur and are continually contested, suggesting in Gramscian terms that the concrete effects of weaponization are never complete and intimate present terrains of struggle.

Weaponization and its discontents

Starting in occupied Palestine, Danya gestures to Palestinians navigating physical and psychological barriers in the Bethlehem region, circumventing land enclosures and grappling with legal structures placing land relations against a backdrop of what Israel frames as 'uncultivated land'. What follows derives from conversations between Danya and Palestinian peasant farmers, youth leaders dedicated to (re)connecting with the land and supporting farmers, and members of older generations concerned with the disappearance of their ancestral foods in the Bethlehem region. Danya is of Egyptian heritage and a settler of colour in (so-called)[7] Canada. She has spent a total of six months in the West Bank in the summers of 2018 and 2019 researching a re-emerging youth movement dedicated to Palestinian ancestral seeds and foods as a way of subverting the military occupation's attempts to erase Palestinian ancestral knowledges. The area of focus was the Bethlehem region where most ancestral fruits and vegetables were historically grown to feed the Jerusalem metropolis (Clarno, 2017).

Ancestral crops in occupied Palestine belonged to a collective consciousness situated in place, both continuous and interrupted in time and space, offering the familiarity of flavours connecting Palestinians to territorial belonging (see El Masri, Chapter 12). Crop names often told stories of where they were traditionally grown, such as *Beit Jalese* apricots and *Sahouri* white cucumber from Beit Sahour. Some of the more popularly seasonal crops essential in Palestinian cuisine were sold in informal networks like *Battiri* aubergine, bottle gourd, Armenian cucumber, figs, and heirloom courgette. 'Forgotten crops', such as heirloom tomatoes and white cucumber, were found in select home plots, or when lucky enough, gifted through family, friends, and neighbours.

The apartheid wall severing across generations

8 July 2019
Occupied Bethlehem
  I sent with my friend Sara a bag of Battiri eggplants for her mother living in Jerusalem. Her mum was very excited to receive (what she considered) rare vegetables. Some of the Jerusalemites I spoke to with historic or ongoing family ties to Bethlehem still visited farmers' plots in neighbouring villages, buying directly from farmers. Speaking to young Jerusalemites on ancestral foods often provoked a puzzled look, 'what are ancestral crops?' The wall affected the knowledge and desirability of ancestral crops, a phenomenon cutting across generational lines.

Bethlehem and Jerusalem were historically considered twin cities: bounded across religious, cultural, and sustenance relationships. Movement between them was born out of annual Easter pilgrimages. Jerusalem was a Palestinian urban and cultural epicentre nourished by Bethlehem's villages surrounding it, abundant in vegetables thanks to centuries-old Roman artisanal wells. Jerusalemite author Hala Sakakini (1987: 106) recounts memories dating before the 1948 occupation of peasant women from neighbouring Bethlehemite villages coming to her doorstep selling, 'those purple, longish eggplants of Battir ... al-Walajeh and al-Khader bring back to mind the sweet "Jandaly" grapes ... from Beit Safafa ... elderly women used to bring us young marrows'. The distance between Jerusalem and its surrounding villages is less than a dozen kilometres yet the spatial and socio-psychological divisions caused by the apartheid wall built by Israel in 2003 have created deep rifts: the difficulties faced by older Palestinians living within the 1948 borders to access their favourite ancestral crops while the younger generations don't recognize them.[8] Many of the peasants Danya spoke to in Bethlehem historically sold their ancestral crops in Jerusalem's markets, but once the wall was built, became confined to selling in the West Bank markets or directly from their lands.

Colonial constructs of cultivation, colonial barrier constructions

3 August 2019
Occupied Husan

Overlooked by Betar Illit, an Israeli gated settlement built on hilltops, Abu George, Abu Mustafa and I walked past the various plots families cultivated while awaiting permits to harvest their olive groves encircled by the nearby settlement. Abu Mustafa pointed to the plots left by villagers working 12–18 hour days on settlements as construction workers or on Israeli agricultural plantations.

Abu Mustafa knew the Israeli military surveying the plots for annexation were guided by the double meaning of what was considered 'uncultivated': land left idle for up to ten years and the type of crop grown (Tesdell, 2013). Seeds worthy of sowing needed to be modern, productive, higher yielding; whereas lands growing ancestral crops outside of the capitalist mode of production were condemned to colonial usurpation. Constructed narratives of 'uncultivated' evoked European Jewish settlers' colonial anxiety to 'modernize' Palestine over 100 years ago, saving it from the Arab fellah's communal dryland farming techniques keeping land barren and desolate – soils too poor to yield beyond subsistence (Elazari-Volcani, 1932). 'Uncultivated' was recreated during Israel's 1967 military occupation of the West Bank, interrupting the area's food webs, seeds, and cultivation practices, speaking to their weaponization of food through the constructions of borders and (un)cultivated lands. Israel's settler colonial project works to displace Palestinians from their lands, territories, and forms of life facilitating the continuous expansion of settler economies and their populations (Bhandar, 2018).

The 1993 Oslo Accords, an interim peace agreement between the Palestine Liberation Organization and the state of Israel, spatially fragmented Palestinians in the West Bank from the rest of Palestine. The Bethlehem region is internally divided. Dotted with Palestinian-only urban and peri-urban centres called Areas A and Areas B constituting almost 13 per cent of the territory under nominal Palestinian control, scattered in a sea under complete Israeli military control called Area C, usurping more than 87 per cent of the area (PCBS, 2017). Area C is home to the region's most fertile lands where most Palestinian peasants sow their seeds with an abundance of natural springs (Clarno, 2017). Israel's military occupation encloses West Bank landscapes that Palestinians used to freely forage their favourite wild edible crops such as *akkoub* and *za'atar* as 'environmental protectorates'. Palestinians' restricted access to land and resources was instituted by creating 'systemic segregation, forcibly evicting and displacing Palestinian residents, demolishing civilian property [while] expanding Israeli settlements' (Ishaq and Hakala, 2013: 1). Built on hilltops, Israeli settlement constructions slowly descended onto Palestinian peasant lands. Palestinians cultivating in Area C wanting to dig, build, expand, or renovate their lands must place requests with Israel's military commander of which only a small number are permitted.

The Accords reaffirmed the West Bank's 'structural dependency' on the colonizer: Israel's military as the sole manager of the West Bank's borders, land management, water infrastructures and resources, movement of people, trade between itself and the West Bank, and the West Bank with the rest of the world (Dana and Jarbawi, 2017). Israel treated the border between itself and the West Bank as an international border and captive market: 'exporting' subsidized Israeli-produced B- and C-grade crops into the West Bank, flooding the market, and knocking out any Palestinian-produced competition (Marzin et al, 2019: 40).

Militarization and agricultural transformation

3 August 2018
Bus to Jenin
    Heading to visit Abu Sadek in Jenin, some passengers on the minibus chatted me up about what brings me to Palestine. Speaking about ancestral seeds and crops always instigates excitement and conversation: people expressing respect for the farmers remaining steadfast on the land against the occupation's best efforts to remove them, witnessing fertile lands transform into tobacco fields next to cement factories across Palestinian-owned monocrop fields grown to service Israel's economy. We spoke of farmers growing for Israel's market recently leaving their crops in the ground in protest of Israel dumping their own farmers' subsidized crops into the West Bank market – wiping out any Palestinian competition, at times forcing them out of agriculture altogether.
    Our conversation was interrupted by an Israeli military checkpoint asking for IDs. Some Palestinian men were asked to disembark for questioning. The driver was forced to leave without them. A silence overtook the minibus.

On the grounds of silence: weaponization and buried se(ed)crets

Below, Jenn sketches the production and breaking of silences through which the weaponization of food operates in the Ch'orti' East. As ongoing racialized violence made the protection of much of their lands untenable, Ch'orti' families alternatively shielded and shed their ancestral seeds, foods, and associated practices. Jenn is a US-born settler of Canadian/Northern European and Italian diasporas. Between 2005 and 2008, she spent 26 months with the nascent Ch'orti' organization, the Union of Ch'orti' Indigenous Peasant Organizations, *Nuevo Día*, as an engaged PhD candidate in the eastern highlands of Guatemala. Since then, Jenn has lived primarily in Guatemala and/or near the Ch'orti' Guatemalan–Honduran borderlands accompanying *Nuevo Día*. Choosing to walk with the organization's changing priorities and long-term strategy rather than an academic research agenda, she has accompanied its evolution from an ad-hoc group of indebted peasants seeking to forestall foreclosures to a formidable force of Ch'orti' men and women reconstituting themselves as Ch'orti' Nation (Casolo, 2020). Her co-praxis includes working with Ch'orti' women to craft and propose a gender policy in 2015, written expert testimony supporting the legal restitution of Ch'orti' ancestral lands provided in 2016, co-facilitation of community-based documentation of ancestral knowledges in 2017, and now co-founding the Ch'orti' Pluriversity.

Silence of the lands: Ch'orti' severings and seeds of famine

When Jenn first started walking with *Nuevo Día* in 2005, Jacob Omar Jerónimo (Ch'orti'), coordinator of *Nuevo* Día, told her: "Anyone who speaks of land gets killed." Ch'orti' mobilization at the time focused on agricultural debt forgiveness; not the restitution of ancestral lands, crops, or knowledges. For more than four centuries colonial-capitalist processes had expelled from or forced Ch'orti' to abandon more and more of their lands and forests. The 20th-century efforts by Indigenous and peasants to reclaim lands, albeit in productivist ways, were quelled by the US-sponsored coup d'état (1954) and pilot genocidal counterinsurgency campaigns (1960s), which in the Ch'orti' East translated to 50 years of militarized development and perpetual terror (González-Izás, 2014; Casolo et al, 2020).

In the face of the Cold War convulsions, those Ch'orti' families that stayed buried signs of their existence. Language was abandoned, with ancestral knowledges of seeds, wild plants, and crops 'forgotten' for fear of reprisals. And when town *ladino* dwellers laid claim to Ch'orti' lands, no one spoke. Both after the first scorched-earth campaigns (1970s) and post-1996 Peace Agreements, pacification processes took advantage of these grounds of silence to usher in Green Revolution technologies and later boutique crops for export (Copeland, 2012). Land-poor families and smallholders were pushed into taking small loans so that they could purchase hybrid seeds and fertilizer to overwork the little land they had left or turn forests and orchards into coffee plantations. They, then, would need to sell the grains they produced when prices were low to pay their debts thus leaving stores empty before the next harvest season. These projects further severed Ch'orti' families from their lands and knowledges, and tied them to neoliberal market dynamics, sowing the seeds of ever-intensifying cycles of hunger.

Yet, Jenn has witnessed how the slow and rocky process of Ch'orti' struggle has given voice to a less visible but equally present story of ancestral seeds and plants carefully guarded and tendered throughout the centuries, carried in escape, and mourned when a crop is lost. As Ch'orti' alternatively fought, faded, faked, and opted for flight to save bodies, lands, and/or knowledges, they no longer recall many of the ancestral names. But seeds are sown and practices remembered. Jenn heard time and again: "When you don't use chemical fertilizers or pesticides, you can plant the old way, using three seeds: maize, bean, and squash." Their meaning is linked to the cosmos: three seeds like the three stones of the hearths people used with the round *comal* before stoves were built. These stones, the lower portion of Orion's Belt, for Maya cosmology are the hearthstones of creation. Without the threat of chemical pesticides required by hybrid seeds, the tiny wild tomatillos and iron-rich black nightshade can also thrive. But with little land of your own, it is hard to produce enough to eat and sell.

Refusing to forget: seeds, crops, rituals, lands, lives (Guatemalan–Honduran borderlands, 2016–17)

As part of a broader strategy for the restitution of Ch'orti' lands and governance, *Nuevo Día* joined with two Honduran Ch'orti' organizations to document traditional ecological knowledge (TEK) in hamlets on both sides of the border. The organizations jointly drafted a research protocol stipulating what constituted Ch'orti' TEK, what could be documented (no spiritual or medicinal practices), who the knowledge belonged to, and under what conditions it could be shared. *Nuevo Día* asked Jenn to co-facilitate the Guatemalan Ch'orti' systematization. Meeting with 12 ancestral authorities, she asked how they might say "document traditional ecological knowledge" in Ch'orti'? "What does it mean?" A long discussion ensued. Were they remembering? Restoring? Not all authorities present spoke Ch'orti'; but they worked together to find the words that would explain their understanding of the systematization. They finally approved: *ka morojse xe najpi'x kamener –* meaning "we gather together what has already been forgotten, what is ours".

> *8 June 2017, rural Jocotán – last village*
> *Over 50 people – children, youth, women, and men – awaited us on the large patio outside the schoolhouse ready to gather what had already been forgotten … what was theirs. Lively discussions, poetry and marimba filled the morning session. With a mixture of enthusiasm and timidity, participants responded to my questions proffering names of and stories about plants, seeds, practices that flourished or had flourished in the community. Some mentioned that they guarded their native seeds only sharing with those they could trust; everyone lamented how the plant their village was named after, agave, had practically disappeared. Many families still planted arrequite that made sweeter tortillas, and all sowed 40-day maize that could be harvested before 'the hungers came'.*

253

Then, I asked what proved to be the most sensitive question: 'Do you still practise the traditional ceremonies, [e tojma'r]?'

Their replies echoed what I had learned elsewhere of the fate of the ritual offerings to the earth and sky so that the rains might come, and the harvest be bountiful. 'No, it was dangerous. They accuse you of witchcraft.'

'Some people practise secretly in their own fields.'

'The youth are not interested in the old seeds, nor in the old ways.'

'Now with the Indigenous councils, we have started practising again.'

One ancestral authority spoke up, retelling his uncle's story, the story of the assassination and silencing of the last raincallers in the village. He wove a complicated tale with unspoken ties to the years of militarization following the 1954 US-sponsored coups. We knew the coup and ensuing civil war had caused thousands of Ch'orti' to abandon their lands; so why kill the raincallers who establish right relations if not to create the psychological conditions under which Ch'orti' could no longer produce on the land?

In most communities where 'gatherings' took place, people unearthed only part of their story – a first step in what would five years later become core curriculum for the first degree major of the Pluriversity. Other secrets and seeds, their meanings, and uses would need to remain buried, or known by only a few, for the time being.

Secure borders? Severings and sutures

The geopolitical border cutting through Ch'orti' territory, a product of national political rivalries and negotiations, severs and safeguards. Cultivating ancestral crops to feed families has required both making and crossing borders. Fleeing persecution and massacres from the years 1954 to 1972 and the related loss of their commons for planting, Guatemalan Ch'orti' and their descendants founded and/or inhabit dozens of hamlets within ten miles of the Honduran border (Metz, 2022). Agustin,[9] a Honduran Pluriversity student, shared how decades earlier, when leaving Olopa, Guatemala, his relatives and their neighbours had carefully carried their seeds with them in the trek across the border. Accessing land through tenant farmer relations for a local Honduran tobacco farmer, they could gather the same wild *chikarar, chaya, bledo,* and *loroco*; they could sow their native maize, bean, and squash varieties.

Knowledge mobilization and pluri-praxis

Days after arriving in Guatemala in 2022, Danya joined Jenn at a meeting of newly founded *Nuevo Día* offshoots: the Ch'orti' Institute for Science and Technology – *Upejkna'r e Ja'* and the Ch'orti' Pluriversity. *Nuevo Día's* decades of struggle permeated the meeting. The conversation placed the restitution and innovation of Ch'orti' ecological and political science at the centre. Ancestral authorities and their allies presented their commitment to fostering Indigenous-driven research-action to thwart ongoing academic knowledge extraction: research in the territory must help shape Pluriversity materials and courses. These steps were necessary actions for students and community members to revitalize and strengthen ways of life, to govern and thrive on their lands.

After the meeting ended, the ancestral authorities moved into the main room. Huddled in smaller groups, they spoke in whispers of the latest false accusations and threats that they and other Indigenous authorities were facing. A web of sinister extra-legal and state-sanctioned interests (Solano, 2021) – mining, timber, megaprojects, and related money-laundering – was destroying what remained of their forests, watersheds, lands, and community relations. What the Ch'orti' called 'gathering' and restoring hidden knowledges of food and land practices constituted part of their broader struggle for restitution of ancestral lands, the regeneration of ecosystems, and the defence of an idea and place – Ch'orti' territory.

Danya recognized these feelings. The seeming contrast between the official meeting and the clusters of concerns that followed were two sides of the same struggle: autonomous governance of their ancestral territory as critical to Ch'orti' reproduction of life. She was reminded of conversations she had with Palestinian peasants in occupied Palestine. The Palestinian proverb, *to exist is to resist* (الوجود مقاومة) pushes back against Israel's settler colonial narratives and violent occupation denying Palestinians of their past, present, and future connections to land and territories. The various ways Palestinians resisted Israel's decades-long occupation, their ongoing relationships to their ancestral practices of intergenerational sharing and gathering of seeds, crops, and stories operated as a testimony to their very existence rooted in the land and in relationships with one another.

RFG, weaponization of food, and the land question

This chapter explored the weaponization of food as a key force at play in two sites of ongoing colonial dispossession: occupied Bethlehem and the Ch'orti' East. Our vignettes and accompanying analyses engage with RFG to sketch the contours of a relational comparison. What haunted us from our first conversations became evermore glaring. The multi-arena expressions linking the weaponization of food to racialized dispossession in these two places begged the question: are we conflating social relations of land with social relations of food? We argue, instead, that the weaponization of food exposes the specificities of land–food dialectics without totalizing the forces behind Indigenous dispossessions. Grappling with changes in these land–food articulations is crucial. Our vignettes and perspectives speak to each other by highlighting how the conceptual contradictions that emerge from shifting land–food dynamics through racial capitalism and processes of ongoing (settler) colonialism move the conversation to the possibilities of praxis.

First, returning to Doña Juana and Um Nadeem, in very different circumstances, speak from the certainty that seeking, reclaiming, and regenerating land, and planting their ancestral seeds are intricately connected to one another and to them. Passing on these knowledges/practices and feeding their families and communities are the threads through which they weave connections between their intimate relationship with land, defence of territory, and self-determination. Second, no singular global narrative about the weaponization of food and its relationship to ongoing racialized dispossession holds explanatory power over land–food relations. Borders and barriers both oppress and protect. In the Bethlehem region, the weaponization of food works through physical and socio-psychological barriers: walls that sever intergenerational food knowledges, 'environmental protectorates' that limit foraging of wild edible plants, or pockets of Palestinian families squeezed onto reservations like isolated dots in swaths of Israeli-controlled land. Yet, these barriers and their attempts to limit and stifle Palestinian land relations constitute a terrain of struggle: the legal justifications for annexing land as 'uncultivated' haven't stopped Palestinians from growing ancestral crops, while those growing hybrids for the local or Israeli markets get wiped away by imagined borders and market dynamics. Safeguarding seeds means keeping them alive through story and memory, sowing and sharing.

Similarly, the scattered Ch'orti' communities isolated from one another and Guatemala's Indigenous western region shifted their relationship to boundaries, barriers, and seeds in relation to how they resisted racialized military repression and now reclaim meaning and governance over their territory. When land-territory could not be defended, Ch'orti' families abandoned their lands to save their lives, fleeing to Honduras with ancestral seeds and plants in hand. Many who remained in Guatemala erected a different kind of barrier: forgetting, hiding seeds and ritual practices, and establishing intergenerational trust to ensure their world view would never be lost. Now, they and their children are those organizing Indigenous councils, reclaiming their commons, and spearheading a vibrant struggle.

Third, this approach highlights the need to wrestle with the interconnected and divergent ways in which land–food dynamics vis-à-vis the weaponization of food are navigated. RFG stays with the tensions, neither solely about food nor eliding land–food relations. Discerning connections between processes and places unsettle dominant discourses. When and how do food politics diverge from anti-colonial land struggles? How might ancestral crops and knowledges suture intergenerational understandings of territory? Under what conditions might food politics open pathways to autonomy and the restitution of lands and vice versa? The differentiated politics that emerge through engaging with land–food dialectics underlines the limits of global agrarian transformations and settler colonial nation-building working through the weaponization of food. RFG cannot talk about food without talking about land relations, both of which the Ch'orti' and Palestinians consider critical for their continued existence as peoples. Further, experiences in both places problematize human/more-than-human binaries. Grappling with the meanings and materiality of land–food constellations is about 'strategy', but also about ontology. Whether Ch'orti' planting rituals and governance are revived and/or the flavour of an heirloom crop keeps alive Palestinian pasts and futures; there are a myriad of conversations to be had.

The questions around these highlighted land–food struggles cannot be resolved without engagement. We spoke to Jacob Omar Jerónimo, also Provost of the Pluriversity, about our RFG reflections as an entry to building a course through which students studying Ch'orti' land and forest practices could reflect on their studies and their communities' struggles in relation to Palestinian youth. Omar reminded us: 'What we need is for the students to be able to critically grasp the politics of food and territory; not just learn ancestral practices, but their relation to ongoing struggles." Our praxis in support of these struggles takes place in the research-reflection 'classroom' grounded in intra- and intergenerational sharing.

Final reflections

As co-authors coming from distinct life histories and engaged research experiences, we located our insights in the broader web of food, cultivation, and knowledges structured by distinct geographies of colonialism and capitalism. We asked questions about who produces and controls food, to what extent, for what purposes, and with what material and meaningful effects. By using relational comparison, we showed through vignettes the interconnected and divergent ways in which the weaponization of food has operated, grasping key forces at play that converge and interact with place-based processes and memories in other spheres (Hart, 2018). Our conversation brings into sharper relief the contradictory roles of barriers, risky mobilities, and the links between refusing the ongoing weaponization of food, remembering ancestral practices, and resisting ongoing racialized dispossession. When placed in a single frame and seen as a whole, dynamics and possibilities for existence and beyond become perceptible. This process has clarified the necessity for ourselves and for RFG to grapple with the different ways that colonial and racial capitalist dynamics come together, are expressed, and reinforce death-dealing binaries. Our RFG approach to how Palestinians and Ch'orti' navigate the weaponization of food catalyses a broader analysis of the death-dealing articulations of hunger and dispossessions, and the concrete ways that ancestral seeds and knowledges root struggles for autonomy and self-determination.

Acknowledgements

This chapter is dedicated to the Ch'orti' and Palestinians whose words and stories we have tried to honour, and we hope that it can contribute to emerging conversations across ongoing struggles to freely thrive. We especially recognise Jacob Omar Jerónimo, and members of Upejkna'r e Ja', the Grand Council, and the Pluriversity for their part in provoking, unpacking, and/or refining the relational comparison and political reflection. All errors are our own. To Gert Van Hecken and Peter Marchetti, thank you for your tireless efforts throughout our writing process. This chapter draws on research supported by the Social Sciences and Humanities Research Council (SSHRC) Ref.: 752-2021-0301 and the financial support of the FWO junior research project grant G0D8620N.

Notes

[1] Gilmore (2007: 28) defines racism as 'state-sanctioned or extra-legal production and exploitation of group-differentiated vulnerability to premature death'.

[2] A Guatemalan term meaning assimilated people of mixed heritage who identify as non-Indigenous.

[3] Juana Ramírez Ramos, elected authority to the Grand Council of Indigenous and Ancestral 'Authorities of the Ch'orti' Nation.

[4] (Settler) refers to ongoing conversations between the authors and with Latinx geographer Megan Ybarra about how and when settler colonialism may be a useful concept for processes in different Guatemalan territories.

[5] Our conversations focused on two key conjunctures: (1) Cold War-era projects that ushered in Green Revolution technologies as a linchpin for accumulation though agrarian modernization and the expansion of (settler) colonial regimes; and (2) the consolidation of neoliberal hegemony with the fall of the Soviet Union. The former worked hand in hand with counterinsurgency goals in the two occupied spaces, re-ordering territory *and* diffusing any potential uprising from the Ch'orti' (Casolo and Doshi, 2013) and West Bank Palestinians (Tesdell, 2013). The second conjuncture we read through the 'neoliberal' 'peace processes' of the early 1990s.

[6] For a more elaborate conversation of the impact of legal entities perpetuating spatial divide and oppressions, see Zurawski and Higgin's (Chapter 7) discussion of radical legal geographies.

[7] Using 'so-called' interrupts the violent structures and narratives of which the settler-colonial state we now call 'Canada' was founded upon, foregrounding Indigenous geographies and histories instead.

[8] Also see El Masri (Chapter 12) for a deeper understanding of what these barriers could entail – feelings of (be)longing, interruption, connection, sisterhood, and (re)imagination.

[9] Agustin Perez Suchite.

References

Bhandar, B. (2018) *Colonial Lives of Property: Law, Land, and Racial Regimes of Ownership*, Durham, NC: Duke University Press.

Casolo, J. and Doshi, S. (2013) 'Domesticated dispossessions? Towards a transnational feminist geopolitics of development', *Geopolitics*, 18(4): 800–34.

Casolo, J., Jerónimo, J. O., and Sendra, J. (2020) 'La (re)construcción de la autonomía de un pueblo: identidad Maya Ch'orti' y defensa del territorio', *EcoPol*, 60: 122–26.

Clarno, A. (2017) *Neoliberal Apartheid: Palestine/Israel and South Africa after 1994*, Chicago; London: University of Chicago Press.

Copeland, N. (2012) 'Greening the counterinsurgency: the deceptive effects of Guatemala's rural development plan of 1970', *Development and Change*, 43(4): 975–98.

Dana, T. and Jarbawi, A. (2017) 'A century of settler colonialism in Palestine: Zionism's entangled project', *Brown Journal of World Affairs*, xxiv(1): 1–24.

Elazari-Volcani, J. (1932) 'Jewish colonization in Palestine', *Annals of the American Academy of Political and Social Science*, 164(1): 84–94.

Federici, S. (2014) *Caliban and the Witch* (2nd revised edn), Brooklyn, NY: Autonomedia.

Friedmann, H. (1982) 'The political economy of food: the rise and fall of the postwar international food order', *American Journal of Sociology*, 88(Supplement): S248–86.

Gilmore, R.W. (2007) *Golden Gulag: Prisons, Surplus, Crisis, and Opposition in Globalizing California, American Crossroads*, Berkeley, CA; London: University of California Press.

González-Izas, M. (2014) *Territorio, actores armados y formación del Estado*, Guatemala: Cara Parens-Universidad Rafael Landívar.

Hammelman, C., Reynolds, K., and Levkoe, C.Z. (2020) 'Toward a radical food geography praxis: integrating theory, action, and geographic analysis in pursuit of more equitable and sustainable food systems', *Human Geography*, 13(3): 211–27.

Hart, G. (2018) 'Relational comparison revisited: Marxist postcolonial geographies in practice', *Progress in Human Geography*, 42(3): 371–94.

Hart, G. (2020) 'Why did it take so long? Trump–Bannonism in a global conjunctural frame', *Geografiska Annaler: Series B, Human Geography*, 102(3): 239–66.

Ishaq, N. and Hakala, P. (2013) 'Area C: more than 60% of the occupied West Bank threatened by Israeli annexation', Directorate-General for External Policies, Brussels: European Parliament.

Lefebvre, H. (1991 [1974]) *The Production of Space*, (reprinted edn), Oxford: Blackwell.

Marzin, J., Uwaidat, A., and Sourrisseau, J.M. (2019) 'Study on small-scale agriculture in the Palestinian territories', CIRAD – Agricultural Research for Development. Submitted to the Food and Agriculture Organization of the United Nations (FAO). https://agritrop.cirad.fr/592999/1/Marzin%20 Uwaidat%20Sourisseau%202019%20Study%20on%20SSA%20in%20Palest ine%20with%20FAO%20WBGS%20final.pdf [Accessed 19 April 2024].

Massey, D.B. (1994) *Space, Place, and Gender*, Minneapolis, MN: University of Minnesota Press.

Metz, B.E. (2022) *Where Did the Eastern Mayas Go? Decolonizing Ethnography and the Historical, Relational, and Contingent Interplay of Ch'orti' Indigeneity*, Albany, NY: University Press of Colorado; Institute for Mesoamerican Studies, Louisville.

Nixon, R. (2011) *Slow Violence and the Environmentalism of the Poor*, Cambridge, MA: Harvard University Press.

Patel, R. and Moore, J.W. (2017) *A History of the World in Seven Cheap Things: A Guide to Capitalism, Nature, and the Future of the Planet*, Berkeley, CA: University of California Press.

PCBS (2017) 'Project Mid-Year Population for Bethlehem Governorate by Locality (2017–2021)', The Palestinian Central Bureau of Statistics, West Bank.

Said, E.W. (1994) *Culture and Imperialism* (1st edn), New York, Vintage Books.

Sakakini, H. (1987) *Jerusalem and I: A Personal Record*, Habesh: The Commercial Press.

Solano, L. (2021) 'La criminalización a comunidades y liderazgos Ch'orti' que luchan por la defensa del territorio y las riquezas naturales: una constante en el departamento de Chiquimula y el oriente de Guatemala (No. 77), Enfoque', *El Observador*, Guatemala.

Tesdell, O.L. (2013) *Shadow Spaces: Territory, Sovereignty, and the Question of Palestinian Cultivation*, Minneapolis, MN: University of Minnesota Press.

Thompson, E.P. (2013) *Whigs and Hunters: The Origin of the Black Act*, 2nd ed. London: Breviary Stuff Publications, Allen Lane.

15

Epilogue

Colleen Hammelman, Kristin Reynolds, and Charles Z. Levkoe[1]

You see the tree, you see the mountain, you see the buildings, and so this is what you study. But the explanation of these things, these geographies, has its roots in economic questions, social structure, political relations.

Graciela Uribe Ortega, 2000
(as cited in Smith and Desbiens, 2000: 550)

We envision radical food geographies (RFG) as more than a theoretical contribution. RFG is characterized by three interconnected elements: (1) theoretical engagement with power and structures of oppression both inside and outside the academy; (2) action through academic, social movement, and civil society collaborations; and (3) analysis through a broadly defined geographic lens. We see a political imperative to create more just and sustainable food systems, and we propose that by bringing together radical geographies, critical food systems scholarship, and action beyond and within academic settings, we may contribute to meaningful social change. RFG is a praxis, and we therefore embarked on this book as a process and a project.

The quote from Graciela Uribe Ortega that begins this concluding chapter reminds us that geographic thinking is not only about grand theories and codified description, but also about creativity and the situatedness of sociospatial relationships in political contexts. In this vein, RFG can help us collectively think about and act against the grain of inequitable power and knowledge dynamics in food systems that are pervasive at historical, contemporary, and global scales.

As we described in Reynolds et al (Introduction, this volume), and the RFG concept, have evolved out of several intersecting moments (including meetings, workshops, conferences, publication projects), ongoing conversations, and actions among the co-editors, contributors, colleagues, and community partners. Preparing this book, in particular, included opportunities for engagement between the authors and encouraged co-development of this evolving RFG praxis. Through the project-based approach, we sought to practise RFG in an engaged co-creation process and by navigating through (and unlearning) dominant perceptions of scholars/scholarship (including in writing styles and differential access to academic resources) as not only a writing exercise, but also a practice in finding our voices and confronting hegemonic ways of working, knowing, and communicating.

Importantly, the RFG project goes beyond writing about (or describing, as suggested by the Uribe Ortega quote above) an analytical framework. As we reflected, as editors, about the process of curating the book, we wanted to invite feedback from authors about their participation in this project. Some contributors to the book reflected that this approach was rewarding, at times challenging, and helped expand their conceptualization of RFG praxis. For several contributors, participating in the RFG book project provided an opportunity to reflect on their own work and experiences (including working through difficult memories and loss), to highlight actions underway in their hometowns and communities, and to deepen their analysis of food systems through engagement with theories of power and oppression. That we actively supported the inclusion of knowledges not situated or originating in university settings was also appreciated by some of the author groups. One group of authors noted: "Like with grassroots collectives across the world [our grassroots co-authors] have provided the primary material and analysis for numerous researchers, and only rarely is this acknowledged."

We began this book with the story of Josué de Castro, the Brazilian geographer, physician, diplomat, and activist whose influential writing on the geopolitics of hunger was radical at the time for its attention to power structures in the food system in the mid-20th century, and whose courageous efforts continued following his exile from Brazil in 1964 and through the remainder of his life and career. We conclude the book with the quote from Chilean geographer Graciela Uribe Ortega, whose legacy we also touched upon in Reynolds et al (Introduction, this volume), and whose story of exile from Chile following the 1973 coup, and subsequent stature as a foundational thinker in the critical and radical geography traditions, continues to inspire. de Castro and Uribe Ortega exemplify two among many scholars and activists, both historical and contemporary, who were and are exiled and/or face violence and a loss of their livelihoods because of their ongoing pursuit of social justice and confrontation of inequitable power dynamics.

We recognize that for many scholar-activists/activist-scholars (including several contributors to this book), critical expression can face the risk of harsh punishment. With respect for Castree's (2000) stance on the limitations of 'radicalism' from critical geographers within the Ivory Tower (see Levkoe et al, Chapter 1, this volume), our measured hope is that the juxtaposition of geographically and sociopolitically diverse authors within the pages of this book contributes not only to the enrichment of RFG praxis, but also to a broadened reflection on radicality and solidarity in food systems, and of knowledges and ways of communicating that exist beyond Eurocentric and anglophone epistemological dominance.

To conclude the volume, we suggest four ways to grow RFG within and beyond the bounds of this book.

First, RFG *values diverse and subaltern knowledge sources produced and communicated through a multiplicity of mechanisms, sources, and locations* as a part of disrupting dominant power–knowledge dynamics. This includes elevating, for example, the expertise of elders, activists, practitioners, and those with origins in the majority world. Recognizing diverse approaches to understanding and creating more just and sustainable food systems can serve to break down false binaries (such as scholar/activist, local/global, human/non-human) by valuing the many ways of producing knowledge and engaging in action; by expanding sources of knowledge represented in academic publications; and by forging relationships in sites of learning and unlearning.

Second, by engaging with scale, spatial imaginaries, and relationships, RFG seeks to *uncover invisibilities and realities rendered less visible/audible by dominant paradigms*. Telling, witnessing, sharing, and unpacking multiscalar experiences with food systems can make visible differing subjectivities and social and spatial power relations (Askins, 2018). This also includes breaking down normalized structures of writing by prioritizing the (at times, extra) work needed to ensure the inclusion of voices from places and positionalities often excluded from dominant (Eurocentric and anglophone) academic publishing. Further, calling attention to the production and utility of different spatial imaginaries, as we have attempted to do in this volume, can reveal oppressive histories, multiple sources of knowledge, and the material impacts of power relationships (Ramírez, 2015).

Third, RFG *elevates ethical space* by demanding reflection, particularly on the part of those of us who walk in this world with various social and/or geopolitical privileges, how our own histories with oppression, privilege, and world views shape our work. Our hope is that this book has been one contribution to impelling those with more (race, class, religious, caste, economic, geopolitical citizenship) privilege to actively move to dismantle these structures as part of an ethical imperative. In line with RFG praxis and action research processes, this volume has emphasized embedding reflection into research, where relevant, to make space for understanding and contending with oppressive histories and ongoing power imbalances. Such reflections also require active listening in relational ways.

Finally, *RFG emphasizes praxis* by valuing the multiple forms that theory and action can take. RFG demands theoretical engagements that contest the production and reproduction of oppressive political, economic, and social structures both inside and outside the academy. RFG praxis also demands collaborative action to create more just and sustainable food systems. The work presented in this volume demonstrates that radical action can take multiple forms, including actively building new futures, cooking and sharing food, building active and meaningful relationships, street protest, pedagogy, advocacy and legal process, forming convivial spaces of reflection and mutual support, and continuing to exist – and that all of this is relative to spatial, historical, social, demographic, and political context.

Onward

As a world-making project, RFG praxis has the potential to confront power, engage multiple forms of knowledge and epistemologies, imagine radical transitions, and mobilize resistance. Furthermore, RFG compels a strong political stance that contributes to food systems that are more just and sustainable, along with recognition of the interdisciplinary, intersectional, and interrelational ways that humans interact with food environments that may support or hinder such work. In doing so, RFG makes clear that while food (in)justice is produced and reproduced in particular places by particular structures, such places and structures are inextricably linked with others across multiple scales.

This book thus contributes to growing RFG praxis by attending to power structures, diverse forms of knowledge, and resistance to food systems inequities in various geographic, spatial, and social locations. The book ends here, but the project to grow RFG praxis is far from over. At this point in the process, we invite readers – activists, scholars, students, practitioners, and all who flow through each of those identities – to continue the journey with us in the RFG project.

Onward together.

Note
[1] Equal authorship.

References

Askins, K. (2018) 'Feminist geographies and participatory action research: co-producing narratives with people and place', *Gender, Place & Culture*, 25(9): 1277–94.

Castree, N. (2000) 'Professionalisation, activism, and the university: whither "critical geography"?', *Environment and Planning A: Economy and Space*, 32(6): 955–70. DOI: 10.1068/a3263

Ramírez, M.M. (2015) 'The elusive inclusive: Black food geographies and racialized food spaces', *Antipode*, 47(3): 748–69. DOI: 10.1111/anti.12131

Smith, N. and Desbiens, C. (2000) 'An interview with Graciela Uribe Ortega', *Environment and Planning D: Society and Space*, 18(5): 545–56.

Index

References to figures appear in *italic* type; those in **bold** type refer to tables. References to endnotes show both the page number and the note number (165n8).

A

agave 253
agency 216
  of women in informal food
    networks 210–11
agrarianism
  Black 163, 164
  critical 24
  see also Black Urban Agrarianism (BUA);
    Senden Sustainable Agriculture
    Resource Centre
agriculture 22, 24, 159, 191, 193
  Black community and 162
  Community Supported Agriculture (CSA)
    project 161
  ecological farming 187, 191, 194, 199
  exploitation of migrant workers
    in Canada 9
  in the Global South 188
  industrial 22, 23
  organic *see* organic agriculture
  racial capitalism and 88–9
  relationship between Black communities
    and 159, 162
  Senden Sustainable Agriculture Resource
    Centre 225, 231
  sustainable 73
  urban agriculture (UA) 154, 155, 156, 157,
    159, 160, 162, 163
alternative food networks (AFNs), in North
    America 24–5
ancestral crops
  in Ch'orti' territory 254
  in Palestine 245, 249, 250, 256
anglophone
  epistemological dominance 4, 263
  food systems and
    geography epistemologies 5
  knowledge production 225
Anthropocene 10, 210

arrequite (crop grown by Ch'orti') 253
Ashurst–Sumners Act (1935) (US) 129
Asian/Asian-American identity 148,
    149, 151
Asiatown *see* Chinatown, Houston, US
auto-ethnography 11, 211

B

Ballapur, India, food consumption survey
    in 194, 196–7
Bellaire Food Street, Houston, US 140,
    141–3, *142*
  Migo Saigon Street Food (Vietnamese
    restaurant) 146–7
  'Two Hands' restaurant 146–7
Bethlehem 245, 246, 255
  as 'dense node' of social relations produced
    in space–time 247
  as historic twin city with Jerusalem 249
  weaponization of food in 248, 255, 256
Biinjitiwaabik Zaaging Anishinaabek (Rocky
    Bay First Nation) 174
Black Africa, geography of marginality in 20
Black Americans
  creation of alternative spaces 154
  issues faced in northern US by 157
Black communities
  Detroit Black Community Food Security
    Network 157
  economic exploitation of 156
  effects of food apartheid on 158
  land management systems and reclamation
    of space 164
  relationship between agriculture
    and 159, 162
  see also Dayton, OH; Toledo, OH
Black farming 24
Black foodways 155–6, 157, 163, 164
Black geographies scholars, in the US and
    Canada 21

INDEX

Black Panther Party (BPP) 160–1
  Breakfast for Children Program 161
  Ten Point Program 162, 165n8
Black placemaking 158
Black Urban Agrarianism (BUA) 10, 154–67
  in the context of RFG 155–7
  theoretical basis of 156
Bourj Albarajenah (refugee camp in
    Beirut) 206–7
  coffee drinking as a social ritual of feminine
    gathering 212
  travels of stories, memories, and food from
    Palestine to 212–15
  women preparing food together in *207*
  women's politics of cooking in 216–18
boutique crops 252
Buffalo, NY, murder at Tops store in 37–8,
    48–9

C

CACR *see* Collective Agency and
    Community Resilience (CACR)
Canada
  Black geographies scholars in 21
  exploitation of migrant workers in organic
    agriculture in 9
  food and displacement in 210
  health inequities between Indigenous
    Peoples and settlers in 223
  Indigenous food sovereignty in 11
  labour standards in organic agriculture in 94
  number and proportion of migrant
    agricultural workers in 90
  ongoing coloniality in 224
  racialized migrant labour in organic
    agriculture in 86–101
  residential schools for Indian children
    in 172, 239n11
  Rooting our responsibility in so-called
    Canada (poem) 226–7
  temporary foreign worker programmes
    (TFWP) in 89–91, 95
Canadian organic standards, definition of
    fairness 87
Cape Town, South Africa 54, 55, 56–7, 65
capitalism 8, 11, 23, 88, 246, 257
  agrarian 247
  alternatives to 110
  neoliberal 105, 114, 139
  patriarchal 54
  racial *see* racial capitalism
  racialization of 88–9
Capitalocene 10
cardamom, as a political tool of resistance by
    Palestinians 212
caste 190, 203n4
  relationship between commensality and 202
Chhattisgarh Mukti Morcha (CMM)
    movement 203n6

Chicago coalition 44, 47
Chinatown, Houston, US 136–53
  after COVID-19 pandemic 150
  Chinatown Art Brigade (CAB) 147
  resistance of gentrification in 147–8
  spatial imaginaries of 10, 136–53
Chinatown, Manhattan 147, 148
Chipariya village, India 195
Ch'orti' Institute for Science and
    Technology 254
Ch'orti' Maya East 244–5, 246, 255
  as 'dense nodes' of social relations produced
    in space–time 247
  depictions of 244
  efforts to reclaim governance, knowledge
    and practice of 245
  geopolitical border cutting through 254
  knowledge mobilization and
    pluri-praxis 254–5
  land–food relations in and between people
    in 11
  Maya Ch'orti' Pluriversity 245, 252,
    254, 255
  weaponization of food in 248, 251, 255
Ch'orti' Maya people 244–5, 256
  documentation of traditional ecological
    knowledge of 253
  efforts to reclaim lands in the 20th
    century 252–3
  higher education for 245
  planting rituals and governance 257
  racialized dispossession of food knowledges
    by 246
  relation between the land and 244, 257
  scattered communities of 256
  traditional ceremonies 254
  weaponization of food in 257
cities
  division of labour in 108
  Legacy Cities 159, 163
  post-industrial era 159
Collective Agency and Community
    Resilience (CACR) 155–64
  strategies 156–7, 164
  theory as developed by Monica White 155
colonial barrier constructions 250
colonial place names, use of 'so-called' in
    front of 238n2
colonialism 1, 19, 22, 48, 209, 210, 218,
    246, 256
  geographies of 257
  healing of trauma emerging from 210
  in Palestine 208
  settler 11, 24, 172, 173, 175, 183, 208,
    218, 247
community gardens 73, 111, 112,
    114, 115n6
community kitchens
  Callas Foundation *56*

267

in Cape Town, South Africa 55–7
in Chile 105–19
decision-making of 112
experience and vision of 66
food distribution mechanisms 109–11
gender perspective of 108
insights into post-apartheid South Africa 67
methods for exploration of 59–61
recognition and identity dimensions
111–12, 114
research and action 113–15
retreat for volunteers 59, *60*
role of women in 108, 112–13
in South Africa during the COVID-19
pandemic 8, 54
violence and police persecution against 112
cooking, use of memory and stories in 217
COVID-19 pandemic 106
affect on provision and distribution of food
within cities 109
Chinatowns in cities after 150
ethic of care during 77
food and gentrification after 74–6
food and gentrification before 73–4
foraged foods in India during 199
impact of 76
institutional targeted political
organizing 78–80
links between food, labour and housing
before and in the wake of 72
in South Africa 53
in the US 71
critical ethnography 246
critical feminism 57–9, 66
critical food systems 4, 6, 21–4, 58
scholarship 7, 8, 17, 21–5, 208, 261
cultivation, colonial constructs of 250

D

Dalits 187, 191, 202, 203n1
lands in in Bareliya and Pitouli villages 195
marginalization of 193, 195
memories of foods of 197
reliance on millets and pulses 195
Saathis 191, 203
Dayton, OH 155, 159–60, 164
Black Urban Agrarianism (BUA)
in 159–60
food hardship in 160
food production by non-profits in 162
Gem City Market 160
Unified Power 160, 161
De Castro, Josué 1–2, 3, 19–20, 262
debt forgiveness, agricultural 252
decolonial geographies 21
decolonization 172, 173, 209, 211, 216,
217, 234
*Delgamuukw/Gisday'wa v. The
Queen* 224, 239n4

Detroit Black Community Food Security
Network 157
digital media 149
displaced communities, food sufficiency
in 218
displacement 76
in Canada 210
of communities by gentrification 74
of Palestinians 216
under racial capitalism 138, 147
radical food geographies of 206–22
of working-class residents in Houston 136
dispossession(s) 76
of communities by gentrification 74
of land 12
of Palestinian and Ch'orti' food
knowledges 246
of Palestinian land 216
racialized 255, 256, 257
distribution
dimension of justice 107, 109–11, 114
food preparation and 67
infrastructure 46
dollar stores 158, 165n6

E

ethical space 171–2, 182–3, 263
ethics, of settler responsibility 225
Eurocentric 12n3
conceptualizations of geographies 21
epistemological dominance 263
knowledge production 225

F

fairness, in organic agriculture in
Canada 87, 95
Farm to School programmes 38
farming *see* agriculture
feminism, 'the personal is political'
perspective 54, *55*
feminist geographers 8, 19, 20
Food, Conservation, and Energy Act (2008)
(US) 124
food activism 19, 25, 49, 61, 62, 65
food apartheid 37, 123–4, 125, 128, 159
BUA as a way to combat 157–60
concept as coined by Karen
Washington 158
examples of 158
in Legacy Cities 163
food chain workers 71, 78, 79
food consumption survey, in Ballapur,
India 194, 196–7
food deserts 158, 159
construction of 124–5
as a spatial imaginary 120, 121, 122, 129
USDA definition of 165n5
food distribution networks 114
food inequity 158

INDEX

food injustice 9, 42, 43, 54, 122, 125, 207, 210, 264
  in Buffalo, NY 38
  resistance to 209, 217
food insecurity 2, 54, 62, 67, 75, 106, 107, 127, 191, 215
  in Cape Town, South Africa 55, 56–7
  faced by Indigenous Peoples in Canada 172
  suffered by Palestinian refugees in Lebanon 206
food insufficiency
  in displaced communities 218
  suffered by Palestinian refugees in Lebanon 215
food justice 4, 22, 25, 37–8, 47, 49, 55, 73, 105, 107, 120, 122, 127, 128, 129, 154, 160, 211, 218, 219, 226
  activism 61
  forms of cooperation to achieve 219
  movement 23, 39, 76, 156
  struggle for 124
food knowledge, potential for healing the trauma emerging from colonialism 210
food movements 73, 74, 78, 94, 125, 173, 210
food networks *see* informal food networks
Food Research and Action Coalition 160
food security 53, 54, 56, 59, 61, 62, 107, 113, 159, 160, 161, 163, 188, 193, 209
food sovereignty 4, 10, 22, 42, 107, 108, 113, 155, 164, 190, 201, 207, 208, 209, 210, 218, 219, 231, 234, 236–7
  Indigenous *see* Indigenous food sovereignty
  movement 23, 25, 187
Food System Transformation framework 128
food-making
  in Bourj Albarajenah Refugee Camp 206–22
  as a practice of agency 210
foodways
  Black foodways 155–6, 157, 163
  links between African and US 21
  migrant 21
  sovereign 223, 224, 232
  sustainable 237
foraged foods, in Western Avadh, India 197, 198
France, roots of critical and radical geography in 20

G

Gandhian philosophy 203n6
Gaza 213
gender relations, unequal 187
gender roles, productive and reproductive 108
gender-based violence, in South Africa 64–6
gentrification
  of Chinatowns 136–53

classical 138
  Diho Square and Bellaire Food Street 140–51
  and displacement 72
  and food after the COVID-19 pandemic 74–6
  and food before the COVID-19 pandemic 73–4
  green (eco-gentrification) 73
  theoretical frameworks 138–40
geopoetics 225–6, 227–8
Gitxsan Nation 224, 231, 238
Gitxsan Territory 225
Global South, research on agriculture, diets, and food security 188
global urban processes, colonial thinking in studying 20
Good Food Buffalo Coalition (GFBC), New York State, US 8, 38, 39, 43–4, 47, 48
Good Food Purchasing Program (GFPP) 38, 41–3
  access to resources as barrier to racial justice 46–7
  barriers to fostering racial justice 44–7
  infrastructure as barrier to racial justice 46
  lessons learned from identification of barriers to racial justice 47–8
  limitations of 42–3
  MWBE policies as barriers to racial justice 45–6
  reliance on market mechanisms 42
Great Migration 156, 157
Green Revolution 191, 194–5, 196, 252
green urbanism 73, 74
grocery stores
  building and rehabilitating to address food inequity 129
  'grocery store as development finance' model 126
Guatemala
  boycott of cardamom from Guatemala by Palestinian refugees 212
  Ch'orti' in 244
  Indigenous western region 256
  opening of an embassy in Jerusalem by Guatemalan government 212
  see also Ch'orti' Maya East

H

Healthy Food Financing Initiative (HFFI)
  construction and implementation 121–2
  food desert spatial imaginary in 125–8
homelessness, in the US 75
Honduras, fleeing of Ch'orti' families to 256
housing market
  ethnoracial disparities in 75
  gentrification driving of 76
  threats of financialization of real estate to 9, 72

269

Houston, US
  Bellaire Food Street 140, 141–3, **145**
  Bellaire Street 140
  Bubble Egg restaurant 143–6
  Chinatown/Asiatown 10, 136–7
  Diho Square (D-Square/D2) 140,
    141–3, **144**
  evolution of restaurants under
    gentrification 143–7
  Hunan Plus restaurant 143
  relationship between food and land in
    restaurant economy in 139
  resistance of gentrification 147–8
  restaurants in Bellaire Food Street **145**
  restaurants in Diho Square **144**
human and more-than-human relations
  10–12, 174, 225, 246
hunger
  causes of 1
  during the COVID-19 pandemic 61
  geopolitics of 262
  in South Africa 53
  universal 1
  in Western Avadh, India 198
  see also food (in)security

I

India
  childhood stunting in 198
  famine in 23
  kheti khana (farming and food) team 199
  map of *188, 189*
  mixed crop field with millet, pulses, and
    oilseeds *192*
  Panchayat (group of villages) 203n8
Indian Act (Canada) 172
Indigenous food sovereignty 11, 223, 226,
  237, 239n17
  definitions of 172
  Indigenous–settler relationships to
    support 171–86
Indigenous lands 89
  defenders of 238
  extraction projects on 224
  geopolitics for growing RFG and rooting
    responsibilities on 223–43
  Rooting (land back, land back)
    responsibilities (poem) 232–3
  Rooting (more radical) responsibilities
    (poem) 235–6
  Rooting (radical food) responsibility
    (poem) 228–31
  rooting (reflective) responsibilities 234
  sovereign jurisdiction in 237
  threats to 234
Indigenous Nations 225, 239n11
  food gathering stories and recipes 210
  groups recognized by the Canadian
    state 238n1

  respect for diverse knowledge systems and
    cultural protocols of 175–6
  settler colonial violence against 236
Indigenous Peoples *see* Indigenous Nations
Indigenous–settler partnerships 172–4
  addressing of food systems by 183
  offering gifts and spending time with
    Elders 180–1
  operating with integrity in 180
  opportunities and tensions of working in 175
  practising relationships of trust, integrity,
    and reciprocity 179–82
  respect for diverse knowledge systems and
    cultural protocols of 176
  shifting ways of working and
    thinking 176–8
informal food networks 207, 218
  agency of women in 210–11
  close intertwining with communities 209
  to resist food insufficiency 217
  role in advancing RFG 217
  sisterhoods and RFG 208–10
infrastructure, processing and distribution 46
Israel
  land deemed as 'uncultivated' in 246, 248,
    250, 256
  Palestinian refugees from establishment
    of 206

J

Jerusalem 249
  Guatemalan embassy in 212
  peasants selling ancestral crops in 245, 249
  as twin city with Bethlehem 249
Juana, Doña (Ch'orti') 245, 246, 256
justice *see* food justice; racial justice; socio-
  environmental justice

K

knowledge
  Eurocentric and anglophone production
    of 225
  Indigenous kin-based 237
  mobilization and pluri-praxis of 254–5
  place-based 227
  sources 263
  traditional ecological knowledge
    (TEK) 253

L

labour standards, in organic agriculture in
  Canada 94
Land Back Movement 226, 237, 239n8
land banks 163, 164n2
  counteracting ownership of 156
land practices, safeguarding by Palestinian
  peasant women 245
land/Land
  –food dynamics 256–7

INDEX

Land-based learning programmes 232
rematriation of 236–8
role in human and more-than-human
 relationships 11
Rooting (land back, land back)
 responsibilities (poem) 232–3
understanding of 228
Latin America 2, 19
feminist geographers in 20
impacts of industrial development in 19
intertwining of radical geography and
 politics in 20
ollas comunes (community kitchens) in 105
soup kitchens in 57
Lebanon, Palestinian refugees in 11, 206
Legacy Cities 159, 163
legal geographies 122–4
Long Lake 58 First Nation 174
Los Angeles Food Policy Council 41

M

maize 253
majority world 1, 12n2, 20, 21, 89, 263
malnutrition, in Western Avadh, India 194
Manto Sipi Cree Nation 177–8
Marxism 18, 23, 88, 246
Marxist postcolonial geographies 246
Michi Saagiig Nishnaabeg Nation 227
migrant labour, in organic agriculture in
 Canada 91–3
militarization, and agricultural
 transformation 251
millet(s) 191–3
browntop 197
in Western Avadh, India 199–201
minority- and women-owned businesses and
 enterprises (MWBE) 45–6, 47
minority world 3, 4, 12n2, 18, 20
Movement for Black Lives 79
multiculturalism 148
mutual aid, place-based 77–8
mutual respect 180
MWBE (minority- and women-owned
 businesses and enterprises)
certification 45, 47
policies as barriers to racial justice 45–6

N

negative income tax, in relation to food access
 and legislation 130n4
neoliberalism, roll-back and roll-out 128
NGOization 190, 203n5
nirmaan (creative ways of living) 191, 203n6
North America
alternative food networks (AFNs) in 24–5
radical geographies scholarship in 24–5
radical geography in 17–18
'nothingness' environments 158
Nuevo Día 251–2, 253, 254

nutrition, height and strength as markers
 of 198

O

Ohio, US
Black Urban Agrarianism in 10, 154–67
land banks 164n2
olive oil 213–14
olives 213–14, 217
ollas comunes (community kitchens) *see*
 community kitchens
organic agriculture
efforts to address unfairness in 93–5
estimation of the number of migrant
 workers employed on farms 91
International Federation of Organic
 Agriculture Movements (IFOAM) 87
labour standards in Canada 94
racial capitalism in 95
racialized migrant labour in Canada 86–101

P

Palestine
Bethlehem *see* Bethlehem
land–food relations in and between people in 11
peasant women selling crops in 245–6
settler colonialism in 208
Palestinians 255
land relations 257
navigation of the weaponization of food
 by 257
racialized dispossession of food knowledges
 by 246
patriarchy
within geography 19
in South Africa 65
photovoice data 59, 60, 66
political ecologists 23
power, in partnerships 179
power relations 10, 187, 263
in Canada 171
in the production and reproduction of
 space 20
praxis, emphasis of RFG on 264
public institutions, procurement of food
 by 40–1, 48

R

racial capitalism 9, 71, 72, 74, 87, 88–9, 94,
 95, 121, 138, 151, 247
and agriculture 88–9
analyses of 81
definition of 88
displacement under 138, 147
exploitations of 78
impacts on food systems 123
land–food dynamics through 256
and the organic movement 95
violence of displacement under 147

racial justice 24, 37–52
  advancement through values-based procurement 48–50
  as core Good Food Buffalo Coalition value 44
  GFPP barriers to fostering 44–7
  infrastructure as barrier to 46
  MWBE policies as barriers to 45–6
racism, definition of 258n1
radical geographies
  foundations 17–21
  use of plural form of 12n4, 26n3
radical geography 18
  histories of 19
  and politics 20
  use of singular form of 12n4, 26n3
reciprocity, relationships of 179, 180
recognition, dimension of justice 114
refugee camps
  Bourj Albarajenah Refugee Camp 206–22
  food-making and sisterhoods within 211
  waiting and cooking in 216
refugees
  access to food 218
  bonding of 216
Right of Return, for Palestinian refugees 217, 219n1
Rocky Bay First Nation 174

S

sage 213
Sangtin Kisan Mazdoor Sangathan (SKMS), Uttar Pradesh, India 11, 189, 202
  agricultural intervention 191–3
  community-oriented millet and grain processing unit 200
  focus group discussion *194*
  foundation in research and activism 190–1
  marginalization of Dalit members of 193
  Saathis (co-travellers) 197, 198, 199, 201, 202
Sangtin Yatra (Hindi book) 190
Santiago, Chile 106, 109, 115n2
scale 8–9
  and sociospatial imaginaries 114–15
Seasonal Agricultural Worker Program (SAWP), in Canada 89
Senden Sustainable Agriculture Resource Centre 225, 231, 237–8
  settler–Indigenous solidarity at 224
  youth programme 234
Shabot Obaadjiwan First Nation 174
shame, experienced by South African women in the wake of violence 62–4
sisterhoods
  of Bourj Albarajenah refugee camp 206–22
  definition of 207
  in settings of exclusion and force displacement 207–8

small farms and businesses, barriers to integrating into institutional food supply chains 47
social capital, of networks during crises 55–7
social media 140
social movements 4, 9, 19, 20, 24, 61, 72, 73, 79, 106, 115, 128
  corollary 24
  depoliticization of 203n5
  food-related 21
  global 25
  linking to values-based public institutional food procurement (VBP) programmes 41, 49
  in urban centres 112
socio-ecological injustices 23
socio-environmental justice 107, 114
solidarity, through ethics of settler responsibility 224
South Africa
  community kitchens in 8
  DALLA campaign in 65
  gender-based violence in 64–6
  kitchens established by women during the COVID-19 lockdown in 53–4
  responses to crises in 53–70
South Asia, importance of caste in agri-food systems in 190
spatial imaginaries 9–10, 120, 122–3, 263
  definition of 122
  in RFG praxis 129–30
street food 146
  trends 149, 150
Supplemental Nutrition Assistance Program (SNAP) (US) 129, 130n3

T

tax credit programmes 129
Temporary Foreign Workers (TFWs), in Canada 89, **92**
Toledo, OH 159–60, 164
  Black Urban Agrarianism (BUA) in 159–60
  Frederick Douglass Community Center 159, 161
  Junction Coalition 159
  Mighty Organics 159
  urban agriculture in 162
traditional ecological knowledge (TEK) 253
Truth and Reconciliation Commission of Canada 239n11
Ts'msyen Territory 228
Turtle Island 172, 234

U

United States Department of Agriculture (USDA) 121, 122, 124, 126, 127, 128
universal hunger 1
UNRWA 215

INDEX

urban agriculture (UA) 160
  benefits of using 159
  Black foodways through 155
  in Black neighbourhoods 154, 157
  Black-led 156, 159
  in Dayton, OH 159
  large-scale 162
  as a solution to vacant land repurposing 163
  in Toledo, OH 159, 162
urban food systems 41, 55, 73, 154, 155,
  156, 157, 159, 160, 163
urban greening initiatives 73
Uribe Ortega, Graciela 2, 19, 20, 261, 262

V

values-based public institutional food
  procurement (VBP) 40–1, 49
  examples of 38
  Farm to School programmes 38
  Good Food Purchasing Program
    (GFPP) 38, 42–3
  impact of 39
  limitations of 38, 40
veganism 23
violence 22, 160, 237
  anti-Asian 150
  anti-violence campaigns 55
  caste-based 191
  of displacement under racial capitalism 147
  domestic 61
  gender-based 53, 61, 62, 64–6, 191
  against Indigenous Nations 236
  against marginalized peoples 3
  and police persecution against community
    kitchens 112
  racialized 37, 49, 246, 251
  settler colonial 236
  settler state 238
  structural 53, 227

W

Washington, DC
  Black residents in 24
  coalition 41
ways of knowing 3, 11, 172, 174, 183n1
  colonial 234

Indigenous 181, 234
  interaction of 171
weaponization of food 246–8, 255, 257
  and buried se(ed)crets 251–4
  and its discontents 248–51
  link to racialized dispossession 255, 256
West Bank 248, 249, 250, 251
Western Avadh, India 187–205
  Dalits in 195
  factors determining diets and well-being
    in 195–6
  oppressive relations in 193
  wheat flour factory in 197
Western Europe
  early radical geography in 19
  radical geographies scholarship in 24–5
Wet'suwet'en Nation 224, 238
Wet'suwet'en territories 236
women
  agency in informal food networks 210–11
  care work throughout the pandemic 77
  DALLA campaign 65
  early 20th-century women writers on food
    and cooking 21
  ecological farming 187
  exposure to the COVID-19 virus 112
  food distribution networks 114
  kitchens established by women during
    the COVID-19 lockdown, in South
    Africa 53–4, 55, 57, 58, 59, 60, 61, 64
  land practices safeguarded by 245
  minority- and women-owned businesses
    and enterprises (MWBE) 45–6, 47
  mutual aid network 78
  Ollas communes (communal kitchens) 105–6,
    108, 111
  politics of cooking in Bourj Albarajenah
    (refugee camp in Beirut) 216–18
  preparing food together in Bourj
    Albarajenah (refugee camp in Beirut) 207
  role in community kitchens 108, 112–13
  roles in transformation of urban spaces 108
  selling crops in Palestine 245–6
  shame experienced by South African
    women in the wake of violence 62–4
  violence against 62, 64–6

Printed in the USA
CPSIA information can be obtained
at www.ICGtesting.com
LVHW011834041124
795688LV00004B/524